April 23–26, 2018
Lyon, France

Association for Computing Machinery

Advancing Computing as a Science & Profession

DH '18

Proceedings of the 2018 International Conference on
Digital Health

Sponsored and supported by:

**ACM SIGKDD, ICPS, Digital Biomarkers,
Frost & Sullivan, The WEB Conference,
International Journal of Environmental Research
and Public Health, Invest Lyon, UCL - IRDR,
UCL European Institute, Maddyness, Bayer, Only Lyon,
and UCL Global Engagement**

**Association for
Computing Machinery**

Advancing Computing as a Science & Profession

The Association for Computing Machinery
2 Penn Plaza, Suite 701
New York, New York 10121-0701

Notice to Past Authors of ACM-Published Articles

ACM intends to create a complete electronic archive of all articles and/or other material previously published by ACM. If you have written a work that has been previously published by ACM in any journal or conference proceedings prior to 1978, or any SIG Newsletter at any time, and you do NOT want this work to appear in the ACM Digital Library, please inform permissions@acm.org, stating the title of the work, the author(s), and where and when published.

ISBN: 978-1-4503-6493-5 (Digital)

ISBN: 978-1-4503-6145-3 (Print)

Additional copies may be ordered prepaid from:

ACM Order Department
PO Box 30777
New York, NY 10087-0777, USA

Phone: 1-800-342-6626 (USA and Canada)
+1-212-626-0500 (Global)
Fax: +1-212-944-1318
E-mail: acmhelp@acm.org
Hours of Operation: 8:30 am – 4:30 pm ET

Welcome to Digital Health 2018

Warm welcome to the 8th International Conference on Digital Health (www.acm-digitalhealth.org), supported by UCL Institute for Risk and Disaster Reduction and The Web Conference 2018, held in-cooperation with ACM Special Interest Group on Knowledge Discovery and Data Mining (SIGKDD) in Lyon, France on 23rd-26th April 2018.

Leveraging a growing success of previous editions (2008 London, 2009 Istanbul, 2010 Casablanca, 2011 Malaga, 2013 Rio de Janeiro, 2014 Soul, 2015 Florence, 2016 in Montreal, 2017 London), the International Digital Health succeeded in becoming a unique prime interdisciplinary venue with world class networking opportunities highly praised by participants every year. A DH 2017 participant highlighted: "*This has been an amazing conference. So many interesting people and presentations. More importantly, it's been like meeting a group of friends*".

From a small interdisciplinary scientific conference bringing together IT researchers and health professionals, DH embraced the third angle of triangle: the start-ups and innovators in digital health. DH 2018, again co-located with the Web conference 2018, will bring together the three core audiences essential for cutting edge innovation transforming the future of health: IT / big data, public health and industry / start-ups in digital health. With focus public health informatics, global health, social media and big data analytics, pandemics preparedness, precision medicine and emergency medicine, in 2018 we achieved the widest topical outreach. Through a strategic stakeholder collaboration with digital incubators in Lyon DH will again offer an exciting programme including SME clinic and the Digital Health Innovator Prize. We were also proud to achieve a diversity - a gender balanced panels, women serving as Programme Chairs but also growing diversity of geographical representation including speakers from low and middle-income settings (Brazil, Nepal, etc.).

Following the successful publication strategy, DH 2018 proceedings again are included in the ACM Digital Library and extended papers published in the Frontiers Digital Health.

We are excited about the great keynotes in store this year, including Elad Yom-Tov (Microsoft), Wouter Van Solinge (University Medical Centre Utrecht), Per Aarvik (Standby Task Force) and strategic panels chaired by leading international experts in the domain including Prof Virginia Murray (PHE) and Dr Martin Seychell (EC).

We have a great academic programme including 7 full papers, 16 short papers, 2 extended medical abstracts, 25 posters and 3 demonstrators, and 1 abstracts from PhD students – plus a line-up of industry and healthcare speakers confirmed. Look forward to the top quality scientific programme, innovation and excellent networking opportunities - DH 2018 is where the digital health minds meet again!

For more up-to-date information, follow and like DH 2018 on social media:
Twitter account: @digihealthconf hashtag: #DH2018
Facebook: http://www.facebook.com/ACMDigitalHealth

Finally, we would like to thank to everyone who contributed to the 8th International Conference in Digital Health 2018 ensuring the event will be an overwhelming success: WebConf 2018 team, authors of the submitted papers, posters and demos, speakers, the Senior Programme Committee members and Programme Committee members, Organizing committee chairs, session chairs and above all the DH 2018 coordinator: Dr Caroline Wood and the back-office team at UCL IRDR.

Patty Kostkova, Floriana Grasso, Carlos Castillo, Yelena Mejova, Arnold Bosman and **Michael Edelstein**
March 2018

Table of Contents

Session: Machine Learning for Health

Session: Smart Devices & Serious Games

Session: Mapping & Modelling Diseases

Session: Data Summarisation

Session: Prediction & Screening

PhD Reports

Author Index

DH 2018 Conference Organization

General, Business and Scientific Chair: Patty Kostkova *(University College London, UK)*

Programme Co-Chairs: Floriana Grasso *(University of Liverpool, UK)*
Carlos Castillo *(Eurecat, Spain)*
Yelena Mejova *(QCRI, Qatar)*
Arnold Bosman *(Transmissible, Netherlands)*
Michael Edelstein *(Chatham House, UK)*

Conference Coordinator: Caroline Wood *(University College London, UK)*

Proceedings Coordinator: Juan Beltrán *(University College London, UK)*

Poster and Demo Chair: Andreea Molnar *(Lancaster University, UK)*

Web Chair: Andy Boscor *(University College London, UK)*

PhD Track Chair: Yelena Mejova *(QCRI, Qatar)*

Senior Programme Committee: Bruria Adini *(Tel Aviv University / Ministry of Health, Israel)*
Alain April *(ETS, Montreal, Canada)*
Eyhab Al-Masri *(University of Waterloo, Canada)*
Isaac Bogoch *(University of Toronto, Canada)*
Pamela Briggs *(Northumbria University, UK)*
Nigel Collier *(University of Cambridge, UK)*
Dustin DiTommaso *(Mad Pow, USA)*
Claudio Eccher *(FBK-IRST, Italy)*
Baltasar Fernández Manjón *(Complutense University of Madrid, Spain)*
Pietro Ghezzi *(Brighton and Sussex Medical School, UK)*
Hamed Haddadi *(Queen Mary University of London, UK)*
Ilan Kelman *(UCL IRDR, UK)*
Larry Madoff *(ProMED/International Society for Infectious Diseases, USA)*
Nuria Oliver *(Telefonica, Spain)*
Hans Ossebaard *(National Health Care Institute, Netherlands)*
Sudha Ram *(University of Arizona, USA)*
Alberto Sanna *(Scientific Institute San Raffaele, Italy)*
Michele Tizzoni *(ISI Foundation, Italy)*
Erik Van Der Goot *(European Commision's Joint Research Centre, Italy)*

Programme Committee: Iheb Abdellatif *(Harrisburg University of Science and Technology)*
Saeed Abdullah *(The Pennsylvania State University)*
Harshavardhan Achrekar *(University of Massachusetts Lowell)*
Akram Alomainy *(Queen Mary University of London)*
Alexandra Balahur *(European Commission Joint Research Centre)*
Luis Eduardo Bautista Villalpando *(ETS)*
Olivier Bodenreider *(US National Library of Medicine)*
Dawn Branley *(Northumbria University)*
Elena Cardillo *(Institute for Informatics and Telematics Italian
    National Council of Research)*
Jordi Conesa *(UOC)*
Mike Conway *(University of Utah)*
Olivier Corby *(INRIA)*
Ulises Cortés *(Universitat Politècnica de Catalunya)*
Jean Costa *(Cornell University)*
Aaron Crandall *(Washington State University)*
Aron Culotta *(Illinois Institute of Technology)*
Krittika D'silva *(University of Cambridge)*
Karen Day *(The University of Auckland)*
Berardina Nadja De Carolis *(Dipartimento di Informatica
    Universita' di Bari)*
Tarik Derrough *(ECDC)*
Gayo Diallo *(ISPED & LABRI University of Bordeaux)*
Jim Duggan *(National University of Ireland Galway)*
Luis Fernandez Luque *(Qatar Computing Research Institute)*
Aidan Findlater *(University of Toronto)*
Reva Freedman *(Northern Illinois University)*
Amira Ghenai *(University of Waterloo)*
Christophe Giraud-Carrier *(Brigham Young University)*
Natalia Grabar *(STL CNRS Université Lille 3)*
Felix Greaves *(Phe)*
Cathal Gurrin *(Dublin City University)*
Jaap Ham *(Eindhoven University of Technology)*
Asha Herten-Crabb *(Chatham House)*
Helmut Horacek *(Saarland University)*
Muhammad Imran *(Qatar Computing Research Institute)*
Jeonggil Ko *(Ajou University)*
Spyros Kotoulas *(IBM)*
Marilyn Lennon *(University of Glasgow)*
Lenka Lhotska *(Czech Technical University in Prague)*
Peter Lucas *(Radboud University)*
Kerry Mckellar *(Northumbria University)*
Jochen Meyer *(OFFIS Institute for Information Technology)*

DH 2018 Sponsors & Supporters

Confirmed at the time of these proceedings were published in
March 2018. Additional sponsors may have joined after that date.

Supported by

ADAM Genomics Schema - Extension for Precision Medicine Research*

Fodil Belghait
École de Technologie Supérieure
1100 Notre-Dame West
Montreal, Canada
fodil.belghait.1@ens.etsmtl.ca

Beatriz Kanzki
École de Technologie Supérieure
1100 Notre-Dame West
Montreal, Canada
beatriz.kanzki@ens.etsmtl.ca

Alain April
École de Technologie Supérieure
1100 Notre-Dame West
Montreal, Canada
alain.april@etsmtl.ca

ABSTRACT

High-throughput sequencing technologies have made research on precision medicine possible. Precision medicine treatments will be effective for individual patients based on their genomic, environmental, and lifestyle factors. This requires integrating this data to find one, or a combination of, single nucleotide polymorphisms (SNPs) linked to a disease or treatment [1]. In 2013, the University of California Berkeley's AmpLab created the ADAM genomic format that allows the transformation, analysis and querying of large amounts of genomics data by using a columnar file format. However, while ADAM addresses the issue of processing large genomics data; it lacks the ability to link the patients' clinical and demographical data, which is crucial in precision medicine research. This paper presents an ADAM genomic schema extension to support clinical and demographical data by automating the addition of data items to the currently available ADAM schema. This extension allows for clinical, demographical and epidemiological analysis at large scale as initially intended by the AmpLab.

CCS CONCEPTS

• **Database Theory** → **Database structures and algorithms**; *Data integration*

KEYWORDS

Database; Genomics; Precision Medicine; Bioinformatics

ACM Reference format:
Fodil Belghait, Beatriz Kanzki, and Alain April. 2018. ADAM Genomics Schema - Extension for Precision Medicine Research. In *DH'18: 2018 International Digital Health Conference, April 23-26, 2018, Lyon, France*. ACM, NY, NY, USA, 4 pages.
DOI: https://doi.org/10.1145/3194658.3194669

1 INTRODUCTION

Next generation sequencing (NGS), has dominated the space in genomics research and has progressively entered the clinical practice [4]. One of the many efforts to leverage this type of technology is ADAM, a set of formats, APIs, and processing stage implementations for genomic data [3]. ADAM proposes a scalable pipeline for processing genomic data on top of high performance distributed computing frameworks. It uses Spark [6] as a compute engine and Parquet for fast data access [3].The way these two technologies accomplish very high performance and efficiency are as follow:

1. Spark is an open-source fast compute engine for large-scale data processing, which provides an interface for programming entire clusters with implicit data parallelism and fault tolerance [5]

2. Parquet is also an open-source columnar data storage format available to Hadoop and Spark. When accessing a large amount of data, Parquet has offers interoperability, space and query efficiency.

While the ADAM format scales well when processing genomics data, its current schema (shown as the left part of figure 1) does not currently include the patient clinical and demographical data fields. We know that the availability of these data fields are crucial for research in the field of precision medicine [6] . To allow ADAM's processing pipeline for NGS technologies in this field, it is essential that these data entities be included. Precision medicine [7], aims at tailoring healthcare treatments for patients by using clinically actionable genomic mutations in guiding treatment and prevention of diseases. As shown in the current ADAM schema, ADAM includes genomic data [8]. To maximize discovery, NGS technologies coupled with the ADAM processing pipeline will have to be adapted to include the clinical needs as well. This paper describes the extension proposed to the current ADAM genomic schema to leverage its current framework and toolset to perform large-scale clinical analysis for precision medicine researchers. One design characteristic of our proposal is that individual data items can be dynamically added. This easily allows the extended schema to be used for different research topics aiming at different goals in the field of precision medicine.

2 METHOD

2.1 Model Description

In most genomic sequencing pipelines, the endpoint is an interpretation phase, which is typically done by the analysis and visualization of the results. The objective of this extended schema is to allow researchers, especially in precision medicine, to collocate all their study data for more efficient analysis. This includes patient data, such as genomics, clinical and demographical data, as well as the research analysis meta data provided by the ADAM framework. The intention is to have all this data placed into the same database schema. We intend to release this extended schema as well as the source code for efficient loading using Apache Spark and Parquet file format in ADAM. This will help promote BigData analysis in precision medicine as it removes the current issue of dealing with heterogeneous data types and sources for the patient clinical data outside of ADAM.

2.2 Extended Schema

The extended ADAM genomics schema is currently composed of three sub-schemas in Fig. 1. : Genomics, Clinical and Analysis. Each of those is subdivided into categories and classes, which will be further explained.

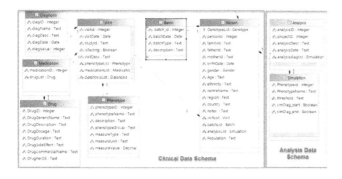

Figure 1 : ADAM genomics extension schema

2.3 Genomics Data Schema

The genomics schema is the core schema of the ADAM framework [3]. Currently, the schema cannot be altered by extensions in order to ensure its compatibility with existing ADAM frameworks' APIs.

2.4 Clinical Data Schema

The clinical data schema, presented in the left part of figure 1, provides precision medicine researchers with the data entities that can contain the clinical and demographical data of the patient. This is especially useful to allow cross analysis and data mining along with the genomics data of the patient. It contains the following five data classes: personal, visit and diagnostic history as well as phenotype and medical treatment.

2.4.1 *Personal history.* The personal history plays the role of a main index to all patient information. Medical history is directly stored in this class. However, complex data such as genomic and simulation data will be stored in a separate class, and the person class will store a reference to the latter. Here are examples of data categories stored in this class:

1. Demographic data such as age, ethnicity, population group, and information regarding patients' location: his country and the region from where he originated;
2. Reference to patients' clinical and genomic data, along with the reference to all analysis performed with the data can be found.

2.4.2 *Visit history.* The visit history class stores all the information required to keep track of each medical visit during the clinical experiment period along with all the major clinical information gathered during these visits such as: identified phenotypes, diagnostics' list, prescribed therapy and the list of medications.

2.4.3 *Diagnostic history.* The diagnostic history class contains the most relevant information from each diagnostic evaluated for the patient such as the diagnosis' name, description, and a binary value to specify if the patient has been diagnosed positive or negative for a specific health problem.

2.4.4 *Phenotype.* This class contains test results such as blood, urine test and other tests to diagnose health problems. The physician often uses set thresholds to locate specific issues. Having access to this information will allow for different diagnostic research based on varying threshold values and allow for more precise analysis of this data linked to a patients' genomic data.

2.4.5 *Medical Treatment.* This class is used to store information about the medication prescribed to the patients. It includes: medication generic and commercial names, treatment duration, dosage and secondary effect and can be combined with patients demographical and genomics data to enable precision medicine.

Overall, the clinical data schema proposed is intended to provide precision medicine researchers with the basic data items required to conduct a large-scale analysis using one single data store that can take advantage of recent BigData computing power and resources.

2.5 Analysis Data Schema

We have seen that our goal is to enable large-scale, complex and detailed analysis patient data analysis using BigData and machine learning algorithms, across these three collocated data schemas. This colocation will allow precision medicine researchers to use the power of open source BigData technology easily to identify potential correlations such as candidate genes responsible for specific diseases and impact of therapies and medications on a patients' health. This impact is typically evaluated using patients' category such as: age, gender, ethnicity, weight, etc. The objective of this schema extension, located at the right of Fig. 1., is to allow researchers to better organize, track and reproduce their analysis results. It is composed of the following two main data classes:

2.5.1 Analysis. This contains general information that identifies the project with which the analysis is associated, along with a reference to all the simulations that have been done for each analysis.

2.5.2 Simulation. For each analysis, researchers can make several simulations for every phenotype with different thresholds and compare the results. This class stores all the information that identifies each simulation. The phenotype analyzed along with the threshold measurement used. This information will allow for the adjustment of the threshold values and the re-execution of the same simulation using different sets of data.

3 SCHEMA EXTENSION PROCESS

3.1 Extended schema creation process flow

We also designed an automated process to extend the current ADAM schema using the following workflow, shown in Fig. 2:

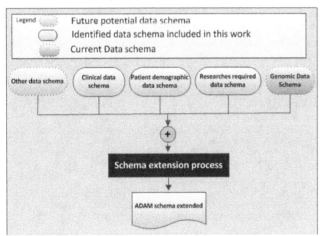

Figure 2: ADAM schema extension workflow

The schema extension workflow executes five sequential steps as follows:

1. Identify all the data fields required for your specific precision medicine analysis;
2. Verify if the current ADAM schema or one that has already been extended recently in the community has all the required data items you are looking for;
3. If some data fields are missing, write the needed fields definition, using the Avro format shown in Fig. 3, so that they can be added in an extended schema;
4. Modify the schema extension script, to add the Avro definition of these new data fields;
5. Execute the script that will generate the new ADAM extended schema composed of the existing ADAM data fields structure, in Avro format with the Parquet files.

Figure 3: Example of AVRO record definition

```
record diagnosis {

/** id diagnosis  */
 union { null, integer } diagID = null;

/** nameDiagnosis */
 union { null, string } diagName = null ;

/** descDiagnosis */
 union { null, date } diagDesc = null ;

 /** date Diagnosis */
 union { null, date } diagDate = null ;

 /** value Diagnosis, binary value to indicate if
    the patient has been diagnosed positive or
    negative for the current phenotype          */
 union { null, integer } diagValue = null ;
 }
```

Following these simple steps will allow you to use this personalized extended schema without creating any impact on the existing ADAM APIs that are currently available to load data using many different genomics file formats. However, now you will need to create your own APIs in order to populate your added data fields.

4 SCHEMA EXTENSION PROCESS DESCRIPTION

To use our automated extension script, you will require the following software tools:

1. Apache Maven: an popular open source tool used to build and manage Java-based projects [9];
2. Apache Hadoop: the well known BigData open source framework used to support processing and storage of very large datasets across distributed clusters of computers designed to scale up from single servers to thousands of machines easily [10];
3. Apache Avro: a recent open source framework offering remote procedure call communication protocol and data serialization. Avro uses the JSON format for data types and protocols definition and serializes the data in a compact binary file. Our automated extension script uses the following two components of Avro [11] as well as the ADAM schema:
   a. avrotools.jar: can be obtained from avro.apache.org ;
   b. avro2parquet.jar: can be obtained from github at /tispartick/avro2parquet ;
   c. bdg.avdl: which is the current ADAM schema that can be obtained from github at bigdatagenomics.

Once you have installed the needed toolset you are now ready to run our automated script: /ExtendAdamSchema.sh and it will generate an extended ADAM schema. The script executes the following 3 steps sequentially:

1. First, it prepares the execution environment: It downloads and installs Apache Maven;
2. Second, it executes the schema conversion steps to generate the new ADAM Avro schema;
3. Third, it converts the new ADAM schema into Parquet files ready to receive your data.

After a successful execution, the script will generate, for each schema, a number of files: Analysis.avsc, Diagnosis.avsc, Medication.avsc, Phenotype.avsc, Simulation.avsc, Variant.avsc, Batch.avsc, Drug.avsc,Visit.avsc, Person.avsc and Genotype.avsc.

4 FUTURE RESEARCH

It is planned that in addition to this automated process and tool that easily extend the ADAM schema without impacting its current APIs, we will de designing other open source tools like:

4.1.1 *Large scale data loader.* The new schemas need to be loaded efficiently with large amounts of data. In this research project, we are currently designing an automated and scalable process to efficiently merge and load data efficiently into an extended ADAM genomics schema using Spark clusters. The challenge here is to merge and load very large quantities of heterogeneous data quickly and easily as clinical data is typically located in some existing relational database and the genomic data come from a number of very large gen/sample files.

4.1.2 *Machine learning APIs.* Once the data is quickly loaded into the extended ADAM genomics format, precision medecine researchers will want to consider different types of analysis in order to identify different patterns. In this research project, we are building APIs to allow easy integration of the extended ADAM genomics schema to open source BigData machine learning frameworks like H2O.ai and TensorFlow.

4.1.3 *Case study using Advance data.* The ADAM schema extension script, the large scale data loader as well as a machine learning API for H2O.ai will be experimented in a next phase of our research project. We will be using large amount of data originating from the Advance diabetes clinical data, their demographical data as well as the patients' genetic data. This data was provided to us by the Centre Hospitaier de l'Université de Montréal. This test of a large scale precision medicine study using Spark clusters and H2O will be performed hopefully during the fall of 2018.

4 LIMITATIONS

Our script was designed and tested on AWS using original versions of all open source software libraries. This is a choice we made and this is by no means an out-of-the-box solution and will require you to master a number of open source BigData frameworks. Your results may vary if you use our script Cloudera, Hortonworks or MapR.

4 CONCLUSIONS

This paper has presented an open source process and toolset to extend the data elements of the current ADAM schema in order to add the patients' clinical and demographical data required for precision medicine research involving very large amount of data. A firs advantage of the approach is not to disturb ADAM current APIs by not modifying the ADAM schema. A second advantage is that as the ADAM schema evolves, there is minimal impact to your extended schema, as you only have to rerun it against the new version of ADAM schema. The final advantage of collocating this data is that it now allows for large-scale precision medicine investigations that involve machine learning on the whole genome.

ACKNOWLEDGMENTS

This research is done without any funding. Researchers and students in software engineering at École de Technologie Supérieure (ÉTS) conduct this work freely during their master degree capstone project and accept to release the results as part of the University Berkeley ADAM project. Diabetes researchers and bioinformatics staff at Dr. Pavel Hamet research unit located at the Centre Hospitalier de l'Université de Montréal (CHUM) support us in understanding the data with the hope of finding an early predictor for early diagnosis and treatment of diabetes type 2.

REFERENCES

[1] T. C. Carter and M. M. He, "Challenges of Identifying Clinically Actionable Genetic Variants for Precision Medicine," Journal of Healthcare Engineering, vol. 2016, pp:1–14, 2016.
[2] F. A. Nothaft, M. Massie, T Danford et al., "Rethinking Data-Intensive Science Using Scalable Analytics Systems", Proceedings of the 2015 ACM SIGMOD International Conference on Management of Data, May31-June 4, Melbourne, Australia, pp:631–646, 2015.
[3] M. Massie, F. Nothaft, C. Hartl et al., "ADAM: Genomics Formats and Processing Patterns for Cloud Scale Computing", Technical Report No. UCB/EECS-2013-207, University California Berkeley, 2013, 22p. [Online] available at:
https://pdfs.semanticscholar.org/2228/b4208c5ea6754df6edcae805038f3e4785 7c.pdf (Accessed: March/10/2018).
[4] R. Gullapalli, M. Lyons-Weiler et al., "Clinical integration of next-generation sequencing technology", Clinics in laboratory medicine, vol. 32, no. 4, pp:585–599, 2012.
[5] E. A. Ashley, "Towards precision medicine", Nature Reviews Genetics, vol. 17, no. 9, pp:507–522, 2016.
[6] M. Zaharia, M. J. Franklin, A. Ghodsi, et al., "Apache Spark: a unified engine for big data processing", Communications of the ACM, vol. 59, no. 11, pp:56–65, 2016.
[7] AD.M. Roden and R.F Tyndale, "Genomic Medicine, Precision Medicine, Personalized Medicine: What's in a Name? Clinical Pharmacology & Therapeutics, vol. 94, no. 2, pp:169–172, 2013.
[8] B. Louie, P. Mork, F. Martin-Sanchez, et al., "Data integration and genomic medicine", Journal of Biomedical Informatics, vol. 40, no. 1, pp:5–16, 2007.
[9] The Apache Software Foundation, "Apache Maven Project", [Online]. Available: https://maven.apache.org (Accessed: March/10/2018).
[10] The Apache Software Foundation, "Apache Hadoop", 2014. [Online] available at: http://hadoop.apache.org/ (Accessed: March/10/2018).
[11] The Apache Software Foundation, "Apache AvroTM 1.8.1 Documentation", 2018. [Online] available at: http://avro.apache.org/ (Accessed: March/10/2018).

Towards Consistent Data Representation in the IoT Healthcare Landscape

Roberto Reda
University of Bologna
Master's Degree in Computer Science
and Engineering
Bologna, Italy
roberto.reda@unibo.it

Filippo Piccinini
Istituto Scientifico Romagnolo per lo
Studio e la Cura dei Tumori (IRST)
S.r.l. IRCCS, Oncology Research
Hospital
Meldola (FC), Italy
filippo.piccinini@irst.emr.it

Antonella Carbonaro*
University of Bologna
Department of Computer Science and
Engineering
Bologna, Italy
antonella.carbonaro@unibo.it

ABSTRACT

Nowadays, the enormous volume of health and fitness data gathered from IoT wearable devices offers favourable opportunities to the research community. For instance, it can be exploited using sophisticated data analysis techniques, such as automatic reasoning, to find patterns and, extract information and new knowledge in order to enhance decision-making and deliver better healthcare. However, due to the high heterogeneity of data representation formats, the IoT healthcare landscape is characterised by an ubiquitous presence of data silos which prevents users and clinicians from obtaining a consistent representation of the whole knowledge. Semantic web technologies, such as ontologies and inference rules, have been shown as a promising way for the integration and exploitation of data from heterogeneous sources. In this paper, we present a semantic data model useful to: (1) consistently represent health and fitness data from heterogeneous IoT sources; (2) integrate and exchange them; and (3) enable automatic reasoning by inference engines.

CCS CONCEPTS

• **Information systems → Resource Description Framework (RDF); Web Ontology Language (OWL);** • **Applied computing → Health informatics;**

KEYWORDS

health informatics, semantic web technologies, Internet of Things, ontology-based data representation

ACM Reference Format:
Roberto Reda, Filippo Piccinini, and Antonella Carbonaro. 2018. Towards Consistent Data Representation in the IoT Healthcare Landscape. In *DH'18: 2018 International Digital Health Conference, April 23–26, 2018, Lyon, France.* ACM, New York, NY, USA, 6 pages. https://doi.org/10.1145/3194658.3194668

*Corresponding Author

1 INTRODUCTION

Traditionally, health-related data such as heart rate or blood pressure, were recorded in a doctor's office or a hospital only. Nowadays, fitness trackers such as Fitbit or Jawbone Up beside keeping track of users' physical activities (e.g., steps taken, stairs climbed and distance travelled), provide also a convenient way for continuously collecting through embedded sensors several physiological data of the wearer such as heart rate, body temperature, caloric expenditure, sleep and stress level. Internet of Things (IoT) technologies have become a milestone advancement in the digital healthcare domain [18, 21] and researchers have shown an increased interest in the sheer enormity of volumes of health and fitness data gathered from wearable devices and mobile health applications.

The intrinsic potential of IoT health datasets can be exploited using sophisticated data analysis techniques, such as automatic reasoning, to find patterns and extract information and new knowledge in order to enhance decision-making and deliver better healthcare to the population. Moreover, personal health information sharing and analysis in conjunction with non-traditional health data sources (e.g., social media, web contents, and smart environmental devices) can provide an important component to facilitate the development of the next generation of health services, in particular, services for research purposes [25] and public health surveillance [22]. However, due to the high heterogeneity of data representation and serialisation formats, and a lack of common accepted standards, the IoT healthcare landscape is characterised by an ubiquitous presence of data silos which prevents obtaining a consistent representation of the whole knowledge. Without a shared data model for such integration concepts, it is also impossible to actuate automatic data analysis processes such as inference reasoning, especially within inter-domain data contexts.

Semantic Web (SW) technologies are a promising solution for the integration and exploitation of health data. SW describes a new way to make resource content more meaningful to machines, whereas the meaning of data is provided by the use of ontologies. Ontologies, as a source of formally defined terms, play an important role within knowledge-intensive contexts overcoming the problem of interpreting homonyms and synonyms in different sources. Ontologies can also be reused, shared, and integrated across applications. They provide a common agreed understanding of a domain by specifying a formal representation of the entities and relationships involved in concepts and the associated background knowledge. Therefore, the use of SW technologies as data representation formalism enables the creation of a common model thus interconnecting a variety of heterogeneous raw data sources.

In the context of healthcare, such a data model could be employed to analyse information from semi-structured data sources, like IoT devices along with generic or domain specific datasets, and unify them in an interlinked data processing area. This scenario could promote interoperable communication among various information technology systems and can be used for automatic reasoning processes.

When automated reasoning is required, the Web Ontology Language (OWL) is the adopted language [16]; in fact, it is oriented to knowledge representation and its description logic level permits to use reasoning over the knowledge base. Indeed, on the basis of the asserted knowledge, it is possible to automatically derive new knowledge about the current context and detect possible inconsistencies in the context information.

In this paper, we propose a ontology-based eHealth system useful to: (1) consistently represent health and fitness data from heterogeneous IoT sources; (2) integrate and exchange them; and (3) enable automatic reasoning by inference engines. The novelty of the proposed approach lies in exploiting SW technologies to explicitly describe the meaning of sensors data and facilitate the integration and interoperability of data collected by different sources.

The remainder of this paper is organised as follows. Section 2 introduces the main previous works highlighting the main open-issues in the field. Section 3 describes the technological aspects of the context. Section 4 shows the overall architecture of the proposed framework and illustrates the entire workflow by which data are semantically annotated according to our ontology. Section 5 discusses the semantic reasoning and computation process over semantically annotated data by using SW technologies. Finally, some considerations close the paper.

2 RELATED WORKS

From a data-centric perspective, one of the main issues which characterises the IoT fitness and wellness systems, is that devices are not interoperable with each other. Their data are based on proprietary formats of representation and do not use common terms and vocabularies. Moreover, reusability and information sharing among different IoT contexts is complicated by the fact that often devices are not designed for inter-domain applications.

SW technologies can be employed in IoT systems (SWoT) to overcome these challenges. Rarely, existing fitness and wellness data aggregators make use of SW technologies. Therefore, they just partially solve the data integration, sharing, and analysis problems.

For example, *Apple Health* [3] is an information hub for integrating in a single location point data from eHealth apps for *iOS* devices. *Apple HealthKit* [2] provides APIs that allow third-part developers and medical sensor manufacturers to directly store their data within the *Apple Health* app. Apple allows users to store and aggregate health content which can optionally be exported in XML format, or encrypted and uploaded on *Apple's iCloud* servers. On the other hand, apps and devices which rely on *HealthKit* are restricted to run on *iOS* platforms only.

Google Fit [1] is the *Apple Health* equivalent for *Android* operating systems. *Google Fit* is currently limited to fitness data only,

whilst *Apple Health* supports a wider variety of medical data. *Google Fit* aggregated content is accessible via the Web portal or through a REpresentational State Transfer (REST) APIs. *Google Fit* defines fixed set of data types which can be stored and third-part developers need to inform Google to add and share new ones.

Google Fit and *Apple Health* are intended to be data aggregators for their respective ecosystems and let health and fitness applications, as well as wearable devices, gathering health information in one single location point. However, they are not interoperable among each other or with other systems; therefore data remain confined to their respective platforms.

MyFitnessCompanion [13] is a health and fitness app which aims to enable users to aggregate their data in one place in a similar way to *Apple Health* and *Google Fit*. *MyFitnessCompanion* integrates off-the-shelf a significant number of commercially available devices; it can interact with a wide range of wireless devices and wearable health trackers, and also aggregates data from third-part apps. However, *MyFitnessCompanion* can be used just on an *Android* platform.

MELLO [20] is an ontology for representing health-related and life-logging data including definitions, synonyms, and semantic relationships. The unified representation of lifelog terms facilitated by *MELLO* can help to describe an individual's lifestyle and environmental factors, which can be included with user-generated data for clinical research and thereby enhance data integration and sharing. However, *MELLO* does not make use of SW technologies.

Recently, Patel et al. created SWoTSuite [23], which is an infrastructure that enables SWoT applications. It takes high-level specifications as input, parses them and generates code that can be deployed on IoT sensors at the physical layer and IoT actuators, and user interface devices at the application layer. *SWoTSuite* hides the use of SW technologies as much as possible to avoid the need of designing ontologies, annotating sensors data, and using reasoning mechanisms to enrich data.

From the above proposed solutions, it is possible to underline the main issue affecting eHealth approaches: the semantic interoperability of eHealth smart things and their data is crucial but still poorly resolved in representing disjointed contexts. Moreover, transforming semantic data model into a specialised domain model and therefore enabling logical reasoning about collected information should be strengthened to support more general knowledge management and provide semantic reasoning.

3 SEMANTIC WEB FOR DATA MODEL REPRESENTATION

The goal of SW is to extend the current Web by publishing open datasets described by Resource Description Framework (RDF) triples and by setting RDF links between data items across multiple sources. The idea behind SW approaches is using the Web in order to expose, connect, and share data through dereferenceable Uniform Resource Identifiers (URIs). Using URIs, everything can be referred to and looked up both by people and software agents. SW technologies easily allow users to connect together separate datasets, share information and knowledge on the Web.

The SW architecture, as shown in Figure 1, is based on a layered approach, and each layer provides a set of specific functionalities.

Semantic layers, on the top of the stack, include ontology languages, rule languages, query languages, logic, reasoning mechanisms, and trust. Ontologies constitute the backbone of the SW expressing concepts and relationships of a given domain, and specify complex constraints on the types of resources and their properties.

Rule languages allow writing inference rules in a standardised way which can be used for reasoning in a particular domain. Among various rule languages, there are RuleML and SWRL (Semantic Web Rule Language) [15]. The latter combines RuleML and OWL, and includes a high-level abstract syntax for Horn-like rules.

On the highest layers there are logic and reasoning, logic provides the theoretical underpinning required for reasoning and deduction. First order logic and description logic are frequently used to support the reasoning system which can make inferences and extract new insights based on the resource content relying on one or more ontologies. In [12] Noy presents an introduction to the major themes in SW research.

Despite the growing number of IoT devices and applications, IoT technology is still in its infant stage and has a big room for research in variety of issues such as standards, heterogeneity of different devices, and common service description languages.

Interoperability, defined as the ability to interconnect different devices and sources along with data integration, is one vital issue still unsettled [5]. Barnaghi et al. in [5] highlighted four growing levels of interoperability in IoT: (1) technical interoperability (involves the heterogeneity of hardware and software components and the related communication protocols); (2) syntactical interoperability (involves data formats and data representation to agree on common vocabularies to describe data; (3) semantic interoperability (involves the interpretation of meaning of data exchanged); and (4) organisational interoperability (involves the heterogeneity of the different infrastructures). Each level depends on the successful realisation of the previous one.

Interoperability is particular relevant in the healthcare and fitness domain where a multitude of diverse vendors collect the same type of data, storing and exchanging them in many different ways. Semantics gives a structure to data and captures the meaning. In recent years, there has been a great deal of interest in the development of semantic-based systems to facilitate data integration and knowledge representation of heterogeneous data [6–8, 10].

Within the SW context, ontologies play a central role in resource representation, since they explicitly define concepts and relationships related to a particular domain, in a structured and formal way (i.e., ontologies are machine-processable) [9, 27]. They specify complex constraints on the types of resources and allow expressiveness and powerful logical inferences.

eHealth domain is characterised by the presence of a huge amount of information resources, and the knowledge formation process is often associated with multiple data sources. Moreover, systems, grammars, structures and semantics of resources within eHealth domain are heterogeneous and often a multitude of diverse devices collect the same type of data (same concepts) but store and exchange them in many different ways so generating semantic and syntactic conflicts. In this regard, interoperability and heterogeneous data integration are two vital issues still unsettled. SWoT aims to combine SW technologies to IoT by providing interoperability and data integration among ontologies and data [19, 24].

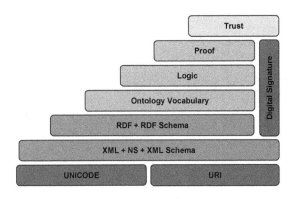

Figure 1: The Semantic Web stack: The stack of RDF-based languages and technologies recommended by the World Wide Web Consortium.

4 FROM LOW-LEVEL DATA TO SPECIALISED DOMAIN CONTENT

In Figure 2 is shown the overall architecture of the framework we developed to transform the heterogeneous IoT health and fitness datasets into an enriched semantic model serialisation, that is, an RDF graph. The two main components of our semantic data annotation framework are the *IoT Fitness Ontology* (IFO) and the *Mapping Process*. After the data are semantically annotated, the reasoning process can provide proper insights about them by making inferences using rule engines (or other advanced techniques) that are allowed by SW technologies.

The next subsections describe in details the characteristics of the most common IoT health datasets (Section 4.1), the IFO ontology (Section 4.2) and the mapping process (Section 4.3). Reasoning is discussed separately in Section 5, and an example of automatic classification is provided.

4.1 IoT Health Datasets

From a low-level data perspective, the context of IoT is characterised by a high heterogeneity of data representation and serialisation formats.

IoT raw data collected by smart fitness devices can be manually retrieve when devices or mobile apps are provided with data export functionalities. IoT data is normally stored within smart systems in Comma Separated Value (CSV) or eXtensible Markup Language (XML) serialisation formats. Alternatively, datasets can be downloaded from the Cloud through RESTful APIs provided by the device vendor, in JavaScript Object Notation (JSON) format.

Listing 1 and Listing 2 show how the same concept of body weight is represented using different formats by different IoT vendors, respectively JSON format for Fitbit and CVS format for Nokia Health.

```
{"weight":[{ "bmi":23.57,"date":"2015-03-05",
 "logId":1330991999000, "time":"23:59:59",
"weight":73, "source": "API"}]}
```

Listing 1: Excerpt of Fitbit body weight data in JSON format.

```
Date,Weight,"Fat mass","Muscle Mass",Comments
"2017-08-10 20:31:00",82.00,10.00,,,
"2017-08-07 11:10:50",81.00,,,
```

Listing 2: Excerpt of Nokia Health body weight data in CSV format.

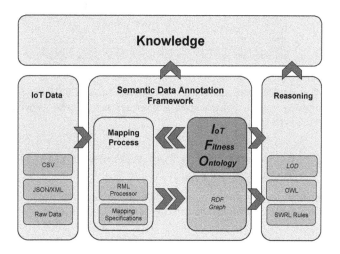

Figure 2: Architecture of the proposed system. Data from IoT heterogeneous sources are semantically annotated according to the IFO ontology through the Mapping Process, the output is an RDF graph (data are turned into information). Reasoning performed over the ontologies and information generates Knowledge.

4.2 The IFO Ontology

The IFO ontology along with the Mapping Process is one of the two main core components of our semantic data annotation framework.

The ontology we developed aims to formally represent the most common and important concepts within the domain of the IoT fitness systems and wellness appliances. The IFO ontology describes the IoT data not just by its measurement value, but also by its relationships with other data sources and with descriptive properties like where and when data were produced. IFO ontology is organised in a hierarchical structure and built around the concept of *Episode*. The class Episode is the root of the entire hierarchy of the all episodes modelled. An Episode represents any possible event that can be measured by an IoT fitness device, for example an episode could be a systolic blood pressure measurement or the number of total steps taken during a day.

To each episode is associated a time reference and a numeric measurement value with the related unit of measurement. The time reference can be a single point in time or a time interval, that is, the start time and the end time of the event. These information are essential because they allow to numerical quantify the object of the event and give it a temporal collocation and duration useful for the reasoning process. More importantly, the ontology also relates the

described concepts to health data standards domain ontologies like SNOMED-CT.

The ontology was written using the OWL language and modelled with Protege as ontology-editing environment. The characteristics and functionality provided by several IoT wearable devices and wellness appliances, as well as health mobile applications available in the market, were considered and carefully analysed in order to identify the concepts described in the IFO ontology. The first version of the IFO ontology consists of 93 classes, 16 object properties, 7 data properties, and 47 individuals.

To assess the correctness of the content and the accuracy of the model, the IFO ontology has been evaluated and revised by a field expert.

4.3 Mapping Process

Mapping is essentially the process by which data are translated into RDF format. Thus, data become semantically annotated according to an ontology [4]. In our system, the mapping process is a fundamental component along with the IFO ontology. Basically the mapping process is done as follows: (1) raw data are retrieved manually from devices or from the Cloud; (2) mapping rules are defined and stored within a repository; (3) the mapping processor takes as input the raw data collected by the IoT devices and the mapping specifications to generate the corresponding RDF graph.

The main challenge for the mapping process is to support the large number of different data structures and serialisation formats by which IoT health and fitness datasets are stored. We chose to implement the mapping stage using the RML language for the mapping specifications and the RML mapper as mapping processor [11].

RML is a declarative mapping specification language and it is based on the RDF syntax. RML extends the R2RML language which is the W3C standard for mapping relational databases into RDF. RML aims to be a source-independent mapping language which means that it is specifically designed for dealing with heterogeneous data sources. RML relies on a target expressions language relevant to the source format in order to refer to specific values within the input file. For example, given a data source serialised in XML format, an XPath expression can be used as a specific query language to extract the specified values and in a similar way values stored in a JSON file can be referenced using JSONPath. RML Mapper is a Java RML mapping processor implementation and the latest version we used in our system, natively supports CSV, XML and JSON data formats, therefore there was no need to extend or modify the existing software code.

RML makes use of triple maps as mapping specifications input in order to generate the resulting RDF graph according to the IFO ontology. Essentially a triple map contains a rule to generate zero or more RDF triples which share the same subject for each extract of data from the input source.

We manually defined mapping specifications for three IoT health systems: *Fitbit*, *Apple Health* and *Nokia Health*. Even though just a limited number of devices were selected, RML language allows mapping definitions that can be reused across different implementations for different source formats, thus reducing implementation costs to support semantic representation on a large variety of IoT data. It is worth to note that when mapping rules are created manually, they are prone to errors, especially when dealing with large and complex data sources. However, RML has been successfully employed in semi-automatic example-driven mapping approach which significantly facilitate the creation of mapping rules exploiting the knowledge contained in existing RDF graphs as described in [14].

Listing 3 shows an example of RML triple map, in this case, the mapping rule is used to semantically data about body weight gathered from a Fitbit device (see Listing 1).

```
<#FitbitBodyMass>
rml:logicalSource [
    rml:source "fitbitWeight.json";
    rml:referenceFormulation ql:JSONPath;
    rml:iterator "$.weight";
];
rr:subjectMap [
    rr:termType rr:BlankNode;
    rr:class fo:Measure;
];
rr:predicateObjectMap [
    rr:predicate fo:hasNumericalValue;
    rr:objectMap [
        rml:reference "@.weight";
        rr:datatype xsd:float;
    ];
];
```

Listing 3: RML triples map FitbitBodyMass to generate portion of RDF graph according to the IFO ontology. In this case JSONPath has been used as target expression language.

5 REASONING

The next real challenge in the IoT landscape will be to make the collected data meaningful and useful.

According to Sheth, the next step in evolution of IoT data will involve more advanced data analytics, that is, integrated and knowledge-enhanced analytics of IoT data, which implies a shift from raw data processing to more intelligent data processing [29]. Moreover, IoT health and fitness data are often complemented by non-traditional health data sources such as social and Web data, collective intelligence, and curated knowledge (i.e., ontologies) [22] which should be taken into account as well.

Reasoning is the process of generating new knowledge from an ontology and its instance base and it represents one of the most powerful features of SW technologies especially for dynamic and heterogeneous environments. A semantic reasoner is a software system whose primary goal is to infer knowledge which is implicitly stated by reasoning upon the knowledge explicitly stated, according to the rules that have been defined. Reasoners are also used to validate the ontology, that is, they check its consistency, satisfiability and classification of its concepts to make sure that the ontology does not contain any inconsistencies among its term definitions.

```
SystolicBloodPressure(?sbpe) ^
hasMeasure(?sbpe, ?sbpm) ^
hasNumericalValue(?sbpm, ?sbpv) ^

DiastolicBloodPressure(?dbpe) ^
hasMeasure(?dbpe, ?dbpm) ^
hasNumericalValue(?dbpm, ?dbpv) ^

hasTimeFrame(?sbpe, ?sbpt) ^
startTime(?sbpt, ?sbptv) ^
hasTimeFrame(?dbpe, ?dbpt) ^
startTime(?dbpt, ?dbptv) ^

swrlb:equal(?dbptv, ?sbptv)

swrlb:lessThan(?dbpv, 80) ^
swrlb:lessThan(?sbpv, 120) ^

-> NormalBloodPressure(?dbpe) ^
   NormalBloodPressure(?sbpe)
```

Listing 4: An IFO episode of Systolic Blood Pressure and an IFO episode Diastolic Blood Pressure are classified as *Normal Blood Pressure* according to two reference values using an SWRL rule. The timestamp is checked to assure that the two episodes are related to the same measurement.

After the low-level IoT data have been semantically annotated, eHealth services can provide proper insights about them by using the inference and role engines that are offered by SW technologies in order to achieve useful actionable knowledge, exploiting the intrinsic data potential to its maximum.

Among several rule languages designed for the SW, the most popular is the Semantic Web Rule Language (SWRL) [26]. SWRL language can enhance the ontology language by allowing knowledge engineers to describe relations that cannot be described using Description Logic (DL). An SWRL rule is defined in form of *if-then* clauses and contains logical operations. Additionally, SWRL provides many sets of built-in functionality, such as mathematical functions and string operations.

With the SW standards defined, more applications demand inference engines in providing support for intelligent processing of the health data. Rule-based inference engines and rule-based reasoners have been already successfully used in many domains such as clinical decision support systems [17] and for generating custom-designed exercise plans based on a user's profile and health status incorporating data on physical fitness [30].

In such cases, it is important to collect a number of different factors in a whole vision and perform reasoning tasks gathering different reasoning sub-tasks, such as temporal and spatial reasoning. Our system is able to support classification of episode findings using ontology-represented measurements about temporal relationships, vital signs and statistical information about IoT data (Listing 4 shows an example of SWRL rule used to classify blood pressure measurements within the knowledge base).

These situations provide conditions for the establishment of a more complex but also a more realistic scenario, where for example heart rate, pressure and body weight are to be considered in conjunction with medical diabetes treatments [28]. However, most of the current IoT applications and services utilising SW reasoning technologies are still in their early stages. Therefore, further research need to be done in order to overcome the resource-constraints, mobility, and real-time requirements challenges for applying these advanced methods in IoT environments.

The workflow we illustrate in this paper can be used to create knowledge from information and information from existing health and fitness dataset using semantic representation, reasoning technologies, and to incorporate domain knowledge into the computation which is a key step for every future innovative healthcare system.

6 CONCLUSION

Current IoT systems are mostly tailored for vertical applications and utilise knowledge from some specific domains only. To fully exploit the potential of IoT health and fitness devices, these disparate silos need to be replaced with horizontal integrated systems, and harnessed by knowledge acquisition and sharing capabilities.

Our research addresses the issues of the source/format heterogeneity of data captured by IoT healthcare devices by formally representing the semantics of the connected objects, the domain and their relationships. In particular, in this paper we proposed an ontology-based eHealth system which transforms low-level health and fitness data obtained from heterogeneous IoT devices into an enriched information model encoded using RDF. The proposed system is also able to map the information into a specialised domain model by providing support for logical reasoning.

The novelty of our work lies on the application of Semantic Web technologies to provide knowledge representation of semi-structured data sources and external domain datasets in order to construct a unified interlinked data model and enable semantic reasoning capabilities over it. The presented approach can significantly facilitate the sharing, exploitation and creative reuse of existing IoT health and fitness data sources thus fully exploiting their intrinsic potential.

Our innovative semantic system can be used wherever there is the need to create knowledge from information and information from data using semantic representation, reasoning technologies and incorporating domain knowledge into the computation.

REFERENCES

[1] [n. d.]. Google Fit. https://www.google.com/fit/. ([n. d.]). Accessed: 2017-12-21.
[2] [n. d.]. HealthKit - Apple Developer. https://developer.apple.com/healthkit/. ([n. d.]). Accessed: 2017-12-21.
[3] [n. d.]. iOS - Health - Apple. https://www.apple.com/lae/ios/health/. ([n. d.]). Accessed: 2017-12-21.
[4] Florence Amardeilh. 2008. Semantic annotation and ontology population. *Semantic Web Engineering in the Knowledge Society* (2008), 424.
[5] Payam Barnaghi, Philippe Cousin, Pedro Maló, Martin Serrano, and Cesar Viho. 2013. Simpler iot word (s) of tomorrow, more interoperability challenges to cope today. *RIVER PUBLISHERS SERIES IN COMMUNICATIONS* (2013), 277.
[6] Antonella Carbonaro. 2009. Collaborative and semantic information retrieval for technology-enhanced learning. In *Proceedings of the 3rd International Workshop on Social Information Retrieval for Technology-Enhanced Learning (SIRTEL 2009), Aachen, Germany.*
[7] Antonella Carbonaro. 2010. Improving web search and navigation using summarization process. In *World Summit on Knowledge Society*. Springer, 131–138.
[8] Antonella Carbonaro. 2010. WordNet-based Summarization to Enhance Learning Interaction Tutoring. *Journal of e-Learning and Knowledge Society* 6, 2 (2010),

67–74.
[9] Antonella Carbonaro and Rodolfo Ferrini. 2007. Ontology-based video annotation in multimedia entertainment. In *Consumer Communications and Networking Conference, 2007. CCNC 2007. 4th IEEE*. Citeseer, 1087–1091.
[10] Antonella Carbonaro and Rodolfo Ferrini. 2007. Personalized information retrieval in a semantic-based learning environment. *Social Information Retrieval Systems* (2007), 270–288.
[11] Anastasia Dimou, Miel Vander Sande, Pieter Colpaert, Erik Mannens, and Rik Van de Walle. 2013. Extending R2RML to a Source-independent Mapping Language for RDF.. In *International Semantic Web Conference (Posters & Demos)*, Vol. 1035. 237–240.
[12] Noy Natalya F. 2004. Semantic integration: a survey of ontology-based approaches. *ACM Sigmod Record* 33, 4 (2004), 65–70.
[13] Valerie Gay and Peter Leijdekkers. 2015. Bringing health and fitness data together for connected health care: mobile apps as enablers of interoperability. *Journal of medical Internet research* 17, 11 (2015).
[14] Pieter Heyvaert, Anastasia Dimou, Ruben Verborgh, and Erik Mannens. 2017. Semi-automatic example-driven linked data mapping creation. In *5th International Workshop on Linked Data for Information Extraction co-located with the 16th International Semantic Web Conference (ISWC 2017)*. 1–12.
[15] Ian Horrocks, Peter F Patel-Schneider, Harold Boley, Said Tabet, Benjamin Grosof, Mike Dean, et al. 2004. SWRL: A semantic web rule language combining OWL and RuleML. *W3C Member submission* 21 (2004), 79.
[16] Ian Horrocks, Peter F Patel-Schneider, and Frank Van Harmelen. 2003. From SHIQ and RDF to OWL: The making of a web ontology language. *Web semantics: science, services and agents on the World Wide Web* 1, 1 (2003), 7–26.
[17] Sajjad Hussain, Samina Raza Abidi, and Syed Sibte Raza Abidi. 2007. Semantic web framework for knowledge-centric clinical decision support systems. In *Conference on artificial intelligence in medicine in europe*. Springer, 451–455.
[18] SM Riazul Islam, Daehan Kwak, MD Humaun Kabir, Mahmud Hossain, and Kyung-Sup Kwak. 2015. The internet of things for health care: a comprehensive survey. *IEEE Access* 3 (2015), 678–708.
[19] Antonio J Jara, Alex C Olivieri, Yann Bocchi, Markus Jung, Wolfgang Kastner, and Antonio F Skarmeta. 2014. Semantic web of things: an analysis of the application semantics for the iot moving towards the iot convergence. *International Journal of Web and Grid Services* 10, 2-3 (2014), 244–272.
[20] Hye Hyeon Kim, Soo Youn Lee, Su Youn Baik, and Ju Han Kim. 2015. MELLO: Medical lifelog ontology for data terms from self-tracking and lifelog devices. *International journal of medical informatics* 84, 12 (2015), 1099–1110. https://doi.org/10.1016/j.ijmedinf.2015.08.005
[21] Jaeho Kim and Jang-Won Lee. 2014. OpenIoT: An open service framework for the Internet of Things. In *Internet of Things (WF-IoT), 2014 IEEE World Forum on*. IEEE, 89–93.
[22] Michelina Mancuso, Xiaoquan Yao, Dan Otchere, Drona Rasali, Erica Clark, Lawrence W Svenson, Julie Reyjal, and Bernard CK Choi. 2016. Proof of Concept Paper: Non-Traditional Data Sources for Public Health Surveillance. In *Proceedings of the 6th International Conference on Digital Health Conference*. ACM, 91–92.
[23] Pankesh Patel, Amelie Gyrard, Soumya Kanti Datta, and Muhammad Intizar Ali. 2017. SWoTSuite: A Toolkit for Prototyping End-to-End Semantic Web of Things Applications. In *Proceedings of the 26th International Conference on World Wide Web Companion*. International World Wide Web Conferences Steering Committee, 263–267.
[24] Dennis Pfisterer, Kay Romer, Daniel Bimschas, Oliver Kleine, Richard Mietz, Cuong Truong, Henning Hasemann, Alexander Kröller, Max Pagel, Manfred Hauswirth, et al. 2011. SPITFIRE: toward a semantic web of things. *IEEE Communications Magazine* 49, 11 (2011), 40–48.
[25] K Thomas Pickard and Melanie Swan. 2014. Big desire to share big health data: A shift in consumer attitudes toward personal health information. In *2014 AAAI Spring Symposium Series*. 2168–7161.
[26] Thanyalak Rattanasawad, Kanda Runapongsa Saikaew, Marut Buranarach, and Thepchai Supnithi. 2013. A review and comparison of rule languages and rule-based inference engines for the Semantic Web. In *Computer Science and Engineering Conference (ICSEC), 2013 International*. IEEE, 1–6.
[27] Simone Riccucci, Antonella Carbonaro, and Giorgio Casadei. 2007. Knowledge acquisition in intelligent tutoring system: A data mining approach. In *Mexican International Conference on Artificial Intelligence*. Springer, 1195–1205.
[28] Louise E Robinson, Tim A Holt, Karen Rees, Harpal S Randeva, and Joseph P O'Hare. 2013. Effects of exenatide and liraglutide on heart rate, blood pressure and body weight: systematic review and meta-analysis. *BMJ open* 3, 1 (2013), e001986.
[29] Amit Sheth. 2016. Internet of things to smart iot through semantic, cognitive, and perceptual computing. *IEEE Intelligent Systems* 31, 2 (2016), 108–112.
[30] Chuan-Jun Su, Chang-Yu Chiang, and Meng-Chun Chih. 2014. Ontological knowledge engine and health screening data enabled ubiquitous personalized physical fitness (ufit). *Sensors* 14, 3 (2014), 4560–4584.

An Ontology of Psychological Barriers to Support Behaviour Change

Yousef Alfaifi
Computer Science department,
Liverpool University, UK
Y.Alfaifi@liverpool.ac.uk

Floriana Grasso
Computer Science department,
Liverpool University, UK
Floriana@liverpool.ac.uk

Valentina Tamma
Computer Science department,
Liverpool University, UK
V.Tamma@liverpool.ac.uk

ABSTRACT

Helping people to adopt and maintain healthier lifestyles is a primary goal of behaviour change interventions. Successful interventions need to account for different barriers (informational, environmental, or psychological) that prevent people from engaging in healthy behaviours. Computational approaches to modelling these interventions focus primarily on informational needs, or on persuasive techniques. The study presented in this paper is specifically aimed at creating a formal conceptual model of the *psychological* notion of *barriers* to healthy behaviour, by means of an *ontology*, i.e. an explicit and machine readable specification of a conceptualisation shared by all the stakeholders [34]. The model accounts for other related patient concepts to understand patient behaviour better. This machine-readable knowledge can function as a background to finding the right interventions for behaviour change. Whilst the model is generic and expandable to include other diseases and behaviours, our study uses *type 2 diabetes* to contextualise the problem of behaviour change.

KEYWORDS

Behaviour Ontology, Behaviour change Ontology, Physical Activity Behaviour, Type 2 Diabetes

ACM Reference Format:
Yousef Alfaifi, Floriana Grasso, and Valentina Tamma. 2018. An Ontology of Psychological Barriers to Support Behaviour Change. In *DH'18: 2018 International Digital Health Conference, April 23–26, 2018, Lyon, France.* ACM, New York, NY, USA, 5 pages. https://doi.org/10.1145/3194658.3194680

1 INTRODUCTION AND MOTIVATION

Comprehensive e-health interventions provide mechanisms that deal not only with the symptoms of a condition but also with the psychological health of the patient [24]. Behavioural medicine aims to provide interventions to address *unhealthy behaviour* through *behaviour change* [18, 19]. Watching TV instead of engaging in physical activity and eating unhealthy food on a daily basis are examples of unhealthy behaviour [19]. Interaction between individuals and contextual factors influence this behaviour [18], making interventions a complex psychological problem [19]. Matching these two

levels (behaviour and behaviour change) requires organising the knowledge scientifically to enable data aggregation and result comparison across behavioural studies [9, 35]. In addition, the lack of shared terms and labels (including uncertain and mixed ones) is common across related studies, therefore making it difficult to devise a comprehensive framework to compare different approaches. In behavioural studies, the lack of shared labels and the uncertainty about the meaning of labels, and behavioural factors hinder the aggregation of knowledge based on these studies. Clearly, knowledge aggregation is an essential step in understanding and studying human behaviour [19].

Ontology is an explicit and machine readable specification of a conceptualization [34] that effectively supports knowledge sharing and aggregation. For example, the Gene Ontology[1] [10] derives from over 100,000 peer-reviewed scientific studies, which allows for integration of different data sources [19].

In the behavioural medicine field, early efforts sought to create ontologies (hierarchical taxonomies) for behaviour and behaviour change interventions, however not many have attempted to translate these conceptual models and shared vocabularies into machine readable ontologies. Where these ontologies are defined in terms of the entities used to label behavioural medicine phenomena, but more importantly the relationships existing between these entities. For example, a behaviour ontology taxonomy from the World Health Organization (WHO) classified some human behaviour (e.g. self-care) based on the International Classification of Functioning, Disability and Health (ICF) [27]. Modelling behaviour (e.g. via domain determining, controlled vocabularies) supports deciding the proper strategies for behaviour change [19, 21–23]. Thus, a preliminary version of a hierarchical taxonomy of *behaviour change techniques (BCTs)* was proposed by Michie and colleagues. BCTs include 93 techniques with clear and distinct labels, definitions and examples [21].

To contextualise the problem of behaviour change, we want to focus on a specific scenario and have thus selected physical activity behaviour for type 2 diabetes (T2D). Diabetes is one of the most prevalent diseases worldwide [4, 28]. More than 422 million patients suffer from diabetes [28], with T2D affecting at least 90% of diabetic patients [4]. T2D, also known as 'non-insulin-dependent' diabetes, happens when the body cannot use insulin effectively [4, 28]. This means the pancreas works properly to produce insulin, but the body's cells do not absorb it. Medications and healthy behaviour (e.g. regular physical activity) can help manage the disease [28]. Thus, promoting healthy behaviour to diabetic patients will help the body control blood sugar levels by stimulating muscles

---

[1]http://geneontology.org/

to use glucose without using insulin. Unfortunately, different *barriers* prevent patients from performing healthy physical activity. These barriers usually pertain to both diabetic patients and the general population. There are few attempts to classify barriers, which is an initial step to model the knowledge formally. These barriers include *psychological* [26] and *physical* barriers such as *environmental, health, social and personal* ones [31]. Psychological barriers can include, for example, a lack of knowledge and low self-efficacy [26]. In addition, physical barriers affect psychological barriers either partially or wholly [7, 32]. For instance, a health barrier, such as diabetes, can prevent a patient from performing some physical activities or priorities constituting a psychological barrier [7]. In another example, a lack of motivation or enjoyment (*psychological barriers*) can result from a lack of support or a partner (social barriers). This study focuses on *psychological barriers,* taking into consideration other related barriers in order to provide a comprehensive picture of the interactions existing between them. Our assumption is that psychological barriers prevent patients from progressing or transitioning from one stage to another (Section 3.3) in changing their physical activity behaviour. In other words, promoting healthy physical activity through behaviour change requires accounting for the barriers [3]. A review of the existing ontologies (e.g. BioPorta Ontologies[2]) and studies indicates there is no barrier ontology, or taxonomy, to import or reuse. Nevertheless, studies for more than a decade have highlighted the term *'barrier identification'* as crucial in interventions, especially for T2D [30].

This study is an extension of previous studies on barriers and their impact on behaviour and behaviour change, especially physical activity [2, 3]. This paper focuses more on modelling the psychosocial barriers yet also considers other related patient concepts to better understand the patient's physical activity behaviour. This conceptual modelling (ontology's machine-readable format) of behaviour supports the ability to computationally determine the most appropriate type of intervention to overcome these barriers.

The rest of this paper is organised as follows: Section 2 presents related studies and how this study differs from them. Section 3 discusses the conceptual model components of the patient's physical activity behaviour, including barrier modelling. Finally, Section 4 provides a brief conclusion and suggested future works.

2 RELATED STUDIES

Behavioural medicine and health professionals manage diseases through behaviour change interventions. Behaviour change includes regular physical activity, taking medications, healthy eating, etc. A better understanding of the patient's behaviour (e.g. physical activity) helps determine the proper behaviour change interventions [19, 21–23]. Different behavioural studies focus on interventions to stimulate healthy behaviours. Some of these studies are summarized below.

The argument approach, proposed by Hunter [17], is a framework to support a specific type of intervention (an argument) for behaviour change. This approach derives from computational persuasion or persuasion technology, which [14] defines as 'learning to automate behaviour change'. Some examples of these persuasion

technologies are reminder messages and recording the user's ongoing behaviour. Persuasion technology not only positively influences argument intervention for behaviour change, but also allows users to explore their behaviour themselves. This argument-based persuasion technology supports a progression throughout the stage of change (Section 3.3).

Another study [19] is a cooperative work between behaviour medicine and information science experts. This study reviews the current efforts to create ontologies of behaviour and behaviour change. Our discussion of the ontology presents some of these efforts, such as BCTs [21] and the taxonomy of disability behaviour [27]. The study describes the efforts in this area that are in the early stages and still need much work.

Many different studies strive to model behaviour and behaviour change. The contribution of our study comes as we combine a new machine-readable format for physiological barriers that will enhance behaviour modelling (to understand the behaviour better) and help decide the best interventions for behaviour change.

3 CONCEPTUAL MODEL COMPONENTS

The integrated conceptual model of the patient's physical activity behaviour not only supports a better understanding of the behaviour but also helps a software application select the best intervention (e.g. feedback) to influence this behaviour. Thus, the behaviour model, which includes barrier modelling, links to the behaviour change intervention (e.g. BCTs [21]), based on a related study [22], via the barrier concept in two different directions (Figure 1). The behaviour model describes all informational needs, namely all concepts used to describe the patient's physical activity behaviour. Furthermore, the model specifies the relationships associating these concepts with their respective individuals. Therefore, we decided to subdivide the conceptual model into self-contained modules or theories that detail specific aspects of this context model (e.g. Section 3.3). This means we can further detail each concept represented as an individual module. For example, the patient concept extends to all attributes and features such as the patient's condition and diseases. Using the ontology development process [16, 25] helps create each of these modules. These processes or steps require the following tasks:

(i) determine the domain and scope of the ontology

(ii) enumerate important terms in the ontology

(iii) develop relations or hierarchical taxonomies among these concepts or terms, respectively

(iv) reuse existing ontologies as much as possible

(v) translate the conceptual model into the web ontology language (OWL), which could be a future work

This work aims to create the barrier concept (conceptual model) from scratch (Section 1). During this process, we will discuss all of these steps except the last step (codifying the model into OWL format), which is beyond the scope of this paper. Reusing existing flexible ontologies, instead of creating one from scratch, is a good practice and a powerful process in ontology development [16, 25]. General User Model Ontology (GUMO) is an one of the existing ontology that supports the modeling of the conceptual model [15]. GUMO derives from situational statements divided into three parts:

---

[2]BioPortal

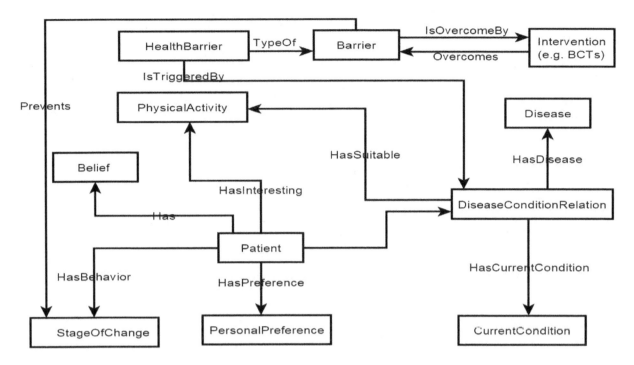

Figure 1: High-level model of the physical activity behaviour

auxiliary, predicate and range [12, 15]. For example, if a patient shows an interest in cycling, in GUMO, *'HasInteresting'* is the auxiliary, *'cycling'* is the predicate and *'low, medium, high'* is the range (probability). GUMO includes about 1000 groups of these components, such as *HasPreferences* and *HasBelief*, to support especially the modeling of the patient components (e.g *PersonalPreferences*). Figure 1 shows a high-level model of the physical activity behaviour. We will now describe the most important components of the behaviour model.

3.1 Barrier Component

One of the main goals of this study is to formalise the model of barriers and the underlying assumptions in a machine-readable format. As mentioned earlier (Section 1), there is no existing barrier ontology or hierarchical taxonomy to reuse or to extend. Therefore, and based on ontology development methodology [16, 25], we decided to create a barrier ontology from scratch as follows:

Steps 1 and 2 determine the scope and enumerate the vocabularies or terms, respectively, of the barriers domain. These two steps constitute 'acquired knowledge'. Our previous work discussed these in further detail [3]. Moreover, our hypothesis to capture the specified barriers based on their signs derives from research in [2].

Step 3 develops the hierarchical relationships among the barrier concepts. The type of hierarchical taxonomy among the concepts is *(SubClassOf)*. This step aims to classify the barriers into five categories: health, environmental, psychological, personal and social barriers (Figure 2). For example, we could represent an environmental barrier (e.g. a weather condition such as rain) in a hierarchical taxonomy as follows:

- *Barrier*
  - *Health*
  - *Psychological*
  - *Personal*
  - *Social*
  - *Environmental*
    * *HeavyTraffic*
    * *ClimaticCondition*
    * *DifficultParking*
    * *PoorAccess*
    * *LackOfSafety*
    * *LackOFacility*
    * *EquipmentCost*
    * *WeatherCondition*
      · ***Raining***
      · *Cold*
      · *Hot*

Step 4 involves extending the domain to include related existing ontologies. Disease Ontology (DO)[3] is the only ontology reused in the barrier domain, but not in behaviour ontology. It includes 8,043 hierarchical relationships (*Is_A*) to identify the health barriers [33]. Figure 2 shows how the DO identifies T2D as a disease (health barrier), under the health barrier concept.

3.2 Patient Component

The patient profile is the central of the physical activity behaviour and relates to most concepts in the behaviour ontology (Figure 1). The patient concept identifies necessary information or properties

[3]http://disease-ontology.org

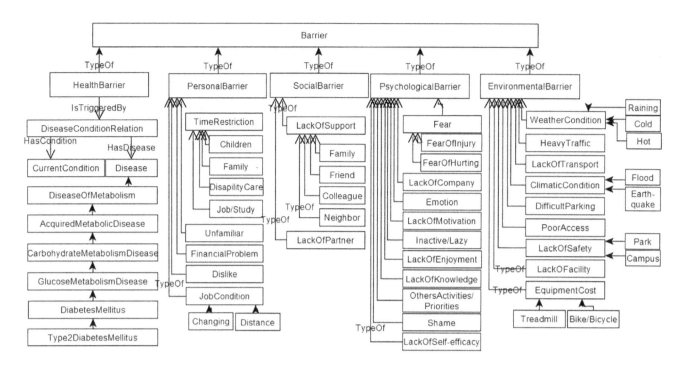

Figure 2: Barriers ontology's taxonomy (partial view)

about the patient such as patient ID, name and date of birth. In addition, this concept supports applying of GUMO (Section 3)

3.3 Stage of Change Component

The stage of change is an attitude of change in a specific behaviour or action [29]. This concept aims to determine the current patient's behaviour of physical activity [8]. Identifying the current patient behaviour helps to decide the best intervention techniques [21] to overcome this behaviour (e.g. walking activity). The stage of change [29] extends to include four properties: the *short-term activity level*, the *long-term activity level*, knowledge about intending to perform a physical activity *(Knowledge)* and the behaviour requiring change *(Goal)*. Therefore, the patient will have one of the stage of change values: pre-contemplation, contemplation, preparation, action or maintenance [5, 11]. In addition, the stage of change is responsible for assessing the patient transition through these stages of change. Influencing patient behaviour (intervention) will take place stage by stage to avoid any negative reflections or risks. For example, patients with no intention of physical activity behaviour (the pre-contemplation stage) can take action towards intending to alter their behaviour within the next six months (the contemplation stage). So, the intervention does not mean to motivate a person who initially does not think about physical activity to go and run a marathon, for example.

3.4 Belief Component

This concept relates to the patient's beliefs, which have a high priority in the patient's life. The patient belief concept is useful in

identifying the type of influence or emphasis that can affect intervention, especially in the argument technique [17]. Possible values of the belief concept include: health, work, social relations and self-efficacy [20]. The probabilities of these values are high, medium or low. Thus, the behaviour change strategies (e.g. argument) will focus primarily on beliefs with high probabilities.

3.5 Physical Activity Component

The physical activity concept includes different types of physical activities (e.g. athletic sports). The model reuses existing physical activity ontology[4] from Open BioPorta Ontologies.[5] The activity ontology extends to include some required properties such as the level of physical activity *(intensity)*, *frequency* and *place* (activity place) [1]. The intensity property helps link the barriers (e.g. the health barriers) to the type of activity. Therefore, the restricted values will be in the disease definition rather than the physical activity properties *(intensity)*. Similarly, an 'indoor' value of the 'place' property *(place=indoor)* can overcome environmental barriers (e.g. bad weather, an unsafe area or a lack of transportation). Thus, the value restriction is on the environmental barrier instead of the activity property *(place)*.

4 CONCLUSION AND FUTURE WORK

Managing and preventing disease complications via behaviour changes are the central goals of e-health and behavioural medicine.

---

[4]Physical activity ontology
[5]https://bioportal.bioontology.org

Engaging in regular physical activity is an important lifestyle modification. Psychological barriers can prevent patients from performing regular physical activity. A comprehensive conceptual model of patient physical activity behaviour, including barriers, supports selection of proper motivational interventions to promote behavioural changes in patients.

Some of the proposed works are as follows: i) convert barriers and behaviour models to the OWL, ii) build a computer-readable format of behaviour change to determine the right interventions (e.g. suggestion and argument) to overcome the physiological barriers and iii) extend the behaviour model to include other general medical user models, such as electronic health records (EHR) [13], or the Unified Medical Language System (UMLS) [6].

The model of behaviour and behaviour change focuses on physical activity behaviour for T2D. However, we can generalise or extend the general approach (and hence the basic structure of the ontology of barriers) to a number of conditions (e.g. asthma). In general, it also extends to all situations in which one seeks to model motivation and motivational advice, and therefore constitutes a contribution.

REFERENCES

[1] Barbara E Ainsworth, William L Haskell, Stephen D Herrmann, Nathanael Meckes, David R Bassett Jr, Catrine Tudor-Locke, Jennifer L Greer, Jesse Vezina, Melicia C Whitt-Glover, and Arthur S Leon. 2011. 2011 Compendium of Physical Activities: a second update of codes and MET values. *Medicine and science in sports and exercise* 43, 8 (2011), 1575–1581.

[2] Yousef Alfaifi, Floriana Grasso, and Valentina Tamma. 2016. Developing a Motivational System to Manage Physical Activity for Type 2 Diabetes. *Artificial Intelligence for Diabetes* (2016), 22.

[3] Yousef Alfaifi, Floriana Grasso, and Valentina Tamma. 2017. Towards an Ontology to Overcome Barriers to Physical Activity for Type 2 Diabetes. *Digital Health Conference, London* (2017).

[4] American Diabetes Association et al. 2016. Standards of medical care in diabetes-2016. *Diabetes care* 39, Supplement 1 (2016), S1–S112.

[5] Robert J Bensley, Nelda Mercer, Judith Anderson, Deanne Kelleher, John J Brusk, Ric Underhile, Jason Rivas, Melissa Lupella, and André C De Jager. 2004. The eHealth Behavior Management Model: a stage-based approach to behavior change and management. *Preventing chronic disease* 1, 4 (2004).

[6] Olivier Bodenreider. 2004. The unified medical language system (UMLS): integrating biomedical terminology. *Nucleic acids research* 32, suppl 1 (2004), D267–D270.

[7] Laurien M Buffart, Tessa Westendorp, Rita J Van Den Berg-Emons, Henk J Stam, and Marij E Roebroeck. 2009. Perceived barriers to and facilitators of physical activity in young adults with childhood-onset physical disabilities. *Journal of Rehabilitation Medicine* 41, 11 (2009), 881–885.

[8] Kim Buxton, Jon Wyse, and Tom Mercer. 1996. How applicable is the stages of change model to exercise behaviour? A review. *Health Education Journal* 55, 2 (1996), 239–257.

[9] Bruce F Chorpita, Mary Jane Rotheram-Borus, Eric L Daleiden, Adam Bernstein, Taya Cromley, Dallas Swendeman, and Jennifer Regan. 2011. The old solutions are the new problem: How do we better use what we already know about reducing the Burden of mental illness? *Perspectives on Psychological Science* 6, 5 (2011), 493–497.

[10] Gene Ontology Consortium et al. 2015. Gene ontology consortium: going forward. *Nucleic acids research* 43, D1 (2015), D1049–D1056.

[11] Eva del Hoyo-Barbolla, Rita Kukafka, María Teresa Arredondo, and Marta Ortega. 2006. A new perspective in the promotion of e-health. *Studies in health technology and informatics* 124 (2006), 404.

[12] Elisabetta Erriquez and Floriana Grasso. 2008. Generation of personalised advisory messages: an ontology based approach. In *Computer-Based Medical Systems, 2008. CBMS'08. 21st IEEE International Symposium on*. IEEE, 437–442.

[13] Paul A Estabrooks, Maureen Boyle, Karen M Emmons, Russell E Glasgow, Bradford W Hesse, Robert M Kaplan, Alexander H Krist, Richard P Moser, and Martina V Taylor. 2012. Harmonized patient-reported data elements in the electronic health record: supporting meaningful use by primary care action on health behaviors and key psychosocial factors. *Journal of the American Medical Informatics Association* 19, 4 (2012), 575–582.

[14] Brian J Fogg. 2009. A behavior model for persuasive design. In *Proceedings of the 4th international Conference on Persuasive Technology*. ACM, 40.

[15] Dominik Heckmann, Tim Schwartz, Boris Brandherm, Michael Schmitz, and Margeritta von Wilamowitz-Moellendorff. 2005. GUMO-the general user model ontology. *Lecture notes in computer science* 3538 (2005), 428.

[16] Matthew Horridge, Simon Jupp, Georgina Moulton, Alan Rector, Robert Stevens, and Chris Wroe. 2009. A practical guide to building owl ontologies using protégé 4 and co-ode tools edition1. 2. *The University of Manchester* 107 (2009).

[17] Anthony Hunter. [n. d.]. Towards a framework for computational persuasion with applications in behaviour change. *Argument & Computation* Preprint ([n. d.]), 1–26.

[18] Steven H Kelder, Deanna Hoelscher, and Cheryl L Perry. 2015. How individuals, environments, and health behaviors interact. *Health behavior: Theory, research, and practice* 159 (2015).

[19] Kai R Larsen, Susan Michie, Eric B Hekler, Bryan Gibson, Donna Spruijt-Metz, David Ahern, Heather Cole-Lewis, Rebecca J Bartlett Ellis, Bradford Hesse, Richard P Moser, et al. 2017. Behavior change interventions: the potential of ontologies for advancing science and practice. *Journal of behavioral medicine* 40, 1 (2017), 6–22.

[20] Ling-Ling Lee, Antony Arthur, and Mark Avis. 2008. Using self-efficacy theory to develop interventions that help older people overcome psychological barriers to physical activity: a discussion paper. *International journal of nursing studies* 45, 11 (2008), 1690–1699.

[21] Susan Michie, Stefanie Ashford, Falko F Sniehotta, Stephan U Dombrowski, Alex Bishop, and David P French. 2011. A refined taxonomy of behaviour change techniques to help people change their physical activity and healthy eating behaviours: the CALO-RE taxonomy. *Psychology & health* 26, 11 (2011), 1479–1498.

[22] S Michie and R West. 2016. A guide to development and evaluation of digital behaviour change interventions in healthcare. *London: UCL Centre for Behaviour Change* (2016).

[23] Susan Michie, Caroline E Wood, Marie Johnston, Charles Abraham, Jill Francis, and Wendy Hardeman. 2015. Behaviour change techniques: the development and evaluation of a taxonomic method for reporting and describing behaviour change interventions (a suite of five studies involving consensus methods, randomised controlled trials and analysis of qualitative data). *Health Technology Assessment* 19, 99 (2015).

[24] David C Mohr, Stephen M Schueller, Enid Montague, Michelle Nicole Burns, and Parisa Rashidi. 2014. The behavioral intervention technology model: an integrated conceptual and technological framework for eHealth and mHealth interventions. *Journal of medical Internet research* 16, 6 (2014).

[25] Natalya F Noy, Deborah L McGuinness, et al. 2001. Ontology development 101: A guide to creating your first ontology. (2001).

[26] James M Olson. 1992. Psychological Barriers to Behavior Change: How to identify the barriers that inhibit change. *Canadian Family Physician* 38 (1992), 309.

[27] World Health Organization et al. 2013. How to use the ICF: A practical manual for using the International Classification of Functioning, Disability and Health (ICF). *Exposure draft for comment. Geneva: WHO* (2013), 5.

[28] World Health Organization et al. 2016. Global Report on Diabetes. Geneva: World Health Organization; 2016. (2016).

[29] James O Prochaska and Wayne F Velicer. 1997. The transtheoretical model of health behavior change. *American journal of health promotion* 12, 1 (1997), 38–48.

[30] Caroline R Richardson, Kathleen S Mehari, Laura G McIntyre, Adrienne W Janney, Laurie A Fortlage, Ananda Sen, Victor J Strecher, and John D Piette. 2007. A randomized trial comparing structured and lifestyle goals in an internet-mediated walking program for people with type 2 diabetes. *International Journal of Behavioral Nutrition and Physical Activity* 4, 1 (2007), 59.

[31] Jo Salmon, Neville Owen, David Crawford, Adrian Bauman, and James F Sallis. 2003. Physical activity and sedentary behavior: a population-based study of barriers, enjoyment, and preference. *Health psychology* 22, 2 (2003), 178.

[32] Bonnie Sanderson, MaryAnn Littleton, and Lea Vonne Pulley. 2002. Environmental, policy, and cultural factors related to physical activity among rural, African American women. *Women & health* 36, 2 (2002), 73–88.

[33] Lynn Marie Schriml, Cesar Arze, Suvarna Nadendla, Yu-Wei Wayne Chang, Mark Mazaitis, Victor Felix, Gang Feng, and Warren Alden Kibbe. 2011. Disease Ontology: a backbone for disease semantic integration. *Nucleic acids research* 40, D1 (2011), D940–D946.

[34] R. Studer, V.R. Benjamins, and D. Fensel. 1998. Knowledge engineering, principles and methods. *Data and Knowledge Engineering* 25, 1-2 (1998), 161–197.

[35] John R Weisz, Mei Yi Ng, and Sarah Kate Bearman. 2014. Odd couple? Reenvisioning the relation between science and practice in the dissemination-implementation era. *Clinical Psychological Science* 2, 1 (2014), 58–74.

A Rule-based Approach to Determining Pregnancy Timeframe from Contextual Social Media Postings

Short Research Paper

Masoud Rouhizadeh
Institute for Clinical and Translational Research
Johns Hopkins University
mrou@jhu.edu

Arjun Magge
Department of Biomedical Informatics
Arizona State University
amagge@asu.edu

Ari Klein
Institute for Biomedical Informatics
University of Pennsylvania
ariklein@pennmedicine.upenn.edu

Abeed Sarker
Institute for Biomedical Informatics
University of Pennsylvania
abeed@pennmedicine.upenn.edu

Graciela Gonzalez
Institute for Biomedical Informatics
University of Pennsylvania
gragon@pennmedicine.upenn.edu

ABSTRACT

Recent advances in social media mining have opened the door to observational studies that are limited only by the capacity of systems deployed to collect and analyze the data. The significance of this power becomes important when studying specific cohorts not typically found in clinical trials or other health-related research, such as pregnant women, who are generally excluded from participating in particular studies for safety concerns. A major challenge of pregnancy studies in social media is determining the pregnancy timeframe, given that the significance of some events (e.g., medication exposure) may depend on the trimester when it occurred. Existing systems that mine pregnancy data from social media have limited coverage and generalizability and have not addressed the problem of automatically determining the estimated beginning and end of pregnancy, and general-purpose temporal taggers deployed on this dataset generate ambiguous results. We present here a rule-based system to automatically identify pregnancy timeframe based on linguistic clues about the progress of pregnancy in users' tweets. In addition, we demonstrate that we could also use this system to find and filter bots and other that repost or quote such expressions.

KEYWORDS

Social Media, Health, Natural Language Processing

ACM Reference Format:
Masoud Rouhizadeh, Arjun Magge, Ari Klein, Abeed Sarker, and Graciela Gonzalez. 2018. A Rule-based Approach to Determining Pregnancy Timeframe from Contextual Social Media Postings: Short Research Paper. In *DH'18: 2018 International Digital Health Conference, April 23–26, 2018, Lyon, France.* ACM, New York, NY, USA, 5 pages. https://doi.org/10.1145/3194658.3194679

1 INTRODUCTION

With a massive amount of language data generated daily, social media offers a unique opportunity for scientists to obtain new insights into public health directly from specific cohorts of interest. Patients are increasingly using social media for many health-related purposes, such as to seek medical advice, to share information about health conditions, treatments, medications and their side effects, or their experience with physicians and medical facilities, among others[1, 14, 18]. Studies on public health monitoring and surveillance are rapidly emerging, with a focus on utilizing the wealth of available data through social media, and developing efficient and accurate tools for social media data mining [16].

A specifically interesting population for health monitoring and surveillance through social media are pregnant women. Along with children and people with specific mental conditions, pregnant women are protected from pre-market clinical trials for fetal safety concerns [6], hence the impact of such medications cannot be examined on this particular cohort. The FDA Adverse Event Reporting System (FAERS) and other spontaneous reporting systems provide a method to report adverse reactions to post-market medications. However, previous studies suggest that these systems have many shortcomings[9, 10].

In spite of challenges in automatically extracting information from social media, we posit that deliberately designed systems that leverage social media data could serve as a complementary and unique source of health information from the patient's perspective. Recent efforts in this direction have shown the promise of these approaches. For example, De Choudhury et al. used Twitter posts to build predictive models for the impact of childbirth on the behavior and mood of new mothers, and quantified postpartum changes in 376 mothers along dimensions of social engagement, emotion, social network, and linguistic style [5]. In a follow-up study, they used Facebook posts by 165 new mothers for detecting and predicting the beginning of postpartum depression using ground truth through self-reports and psychometric tools [4]. Wang et al. present a probabilistic topic modeling method from a corpus of an online chat group of 118 pregnant women, for detecting the women's individual interests over time [18]. Oak et. al. extracted birth announcements and other life-changing events from social media, and used the extracted data to synthesize data that is on-par with actual clinical data [12].

Mining large amounts of social media data posted by pregnant women for epidemiological studies requires automatically detecting the approximate beginning and estimated end of pregnancy–the *pregnancy timeframe*–since events detected in a user's collection of posts have different significance and meaning, depending on when they happened with respect to the pregnancy timeframe (e.g., medication exposure, mentions of birth outcomes). De Choudhury et al. used linguistic patterns to identify birth events on Twitter [5]. Because their patterns use birth to distinguish the prenatal and postnatal periods, they can be used to detect only if birth has occurred. Fourney et al. studied time-dependent patterns about pregnancy and birth based on queries drawn from search engine logs[7]. They identified pregnant women by their search queries and aligned these queries to gestational weeks in order to predict due dates. Although these two studies addressed the problem, they have some limitations including that neither of them is publicly available for research purposes and do not address it in general for social media postings. The work by De Choudhury et al. is only focused on birth announcements, hence has a limited coverage and scalability. The work by Fourney et al. is essentially on search engine queries and cannot be generalized to noisy social media language straightaway.

On the other hand, existing system for resolving temporal references such as Stanford Temporal Tagger [3] cannot directly be applied in pregnancy-specific timeframe detection. They could be used as a part of such a pipeline but if we were to solely rely on them, general-domain temporal resolution methods might generate ambiguous results, hence not be independently usable given our focus on the specific domain of pregnancy. For instance, in: "I'm 12 weeks pregnant", "My due date is in 12 weeks", and "My 12-week old baby", the temporal unit "12 weeks" points to very different pregnancy events (start, due date, birth), yet are indistinguishable from each other in such systems.

In this paper, we present a deterministic system that takes as input all the social media posts made by a user who has been identified to be pregnant by a pregnancy detection system[2, 17], and, utilizing lexical cues about the progress of the pregnancy, automatically determines timeframe information for the pregnancy. The timeframe information includes: a possible beginning date for the pregnancy, the three pregnancy trimesters, and the predicted delivery date (or actual date of delivery) of the baby. To the best of our knowledge, the proposed work is without precedent in using richer linguistics patterns to extract the precise pregnancy timeframe from predominantly noisy social media data, and utilizing the extracted information to detect bots and resolve the pregnancy timeline when discrepancies are detected.

2 METHODS

2.1 Determining Pregnancy Timeframes from Tweets

We used the Twitter Streaming API to collect 199,492,503 publicly available tweets posted by 73,809 users who reported a pregnancy on Twitter [2, 17]. We tokenized the tweets using the ARK Twokenizer [13, 15] and then used hand-crafted regular expressions to identify tweets containing pregnancy-related temporal anchors–that is, indications of time that could be used to derive estimates

of the start of pregnancy (SOP) and end of pregnancy (EOP). To craft the regular expressions, we identified three types of temporal anchors and attempted to account for various linguistic patterns that tweets could use to express each of the types: (1) pregnancy duration, (2) due date, and (3) birth announcement. Table 2 illustrates the query patterns for each type of temporal anchor.

We extracted the temporal information from some of the matching tweets and the dates the tweets were posted using an extension to the Stanford Temporal Tagger (SUTime) [3], an extensible rule-based system for recognizing and normalizing time expressions distributed as part of the Stanford CoreNLP pipeline. SUTime will convert "next wednesday at 3pm" to 2018-03-07T15:00 (depending on the current time). We added rules to SUTime to respond to the specific problem of pregnancy timeframes (and social media). For example, given the tweet "I am 20 weeks pregnant" and the tweet date 05-20-2017, we defined an abstract rule of "20 weeks before today" so that SUTime would generate 12-31-2016 as the estimated SOP. To estimate the EOP, we defined a SUTime rule that adds 40 weeks to the SOP, resulting in 10-07-2017. SUTime does not recognize some of the more complex temporal representations that our regular expressions are crafted to detect. Our rule-based system normalizes the following types of temporal representations so that they can be processed with SUTime:

- *Combinations of months, weeks, and days for expressing durations*: For instance, for the phrase "My due date is in 2 weeks and 4 days", SUTime could only capture "in 2 weeks" and additional rules were implemented to add "and 4 days" to the duration phrase.
- *Month and day numbers in date*: SUTime does not recognize the combination of month and day numbers in date expressions (e.g. 4/20). This is to avoid generalization of recognizing phrases such as 2/3 (two-thirds) as date expressions. However, since our contextual patterns are precise and the occurrence locations of such expressions are meant to be the syntactic position for date expressions (e.g. "my daughter was born on 4/20"), we expanded our rule-based system to recognize such phrases as dates (currently in American usage as mm/dd).
- *Spelled out numbers*: SUTime occasionally does not capture spelled-out numbers. Our system converts spelled-out numbers into their numerical equivalent before processing with SUTime.
- *Spelling corrections and lexical variations*: To account for spelling errors, lexical variants, and abbreviations of temporal expressions in social media, we normalize our corpus using lexical mappings from two normalization lexica [8, 11] and our expanded set of normalization lexicon for time expressions.

2.2 Estimating Pregnancy Timeframes for Users

An individual user's timeline may contain multiple tweets that are matched by our regular expressions, and our system estimates a start of pregnancy (SOP) and end of pregnancy (EOP) for each tweet. These dates, even though they come from the same user, might not all be the same. To reconcile the various estimates of pregnancy pregnant, prgnt, pregnt, prgnant, prg, preg, pregs, pregg, preggs, prego, pregos, preggo, preggos, pregger, preggers, preger, pregers, due, do date, pregnancy, prgnc, pregncy, pregncy, pregnc, prgnanc, prgnancy, prgncy, birth, brth, born, brn, trimester, trimstr

Table 1: Keywords used to select pregnancy related tweets.

timeframes for a user, our system first automatically sorts estimated EOP dates chronologically and clusters them into pools of 30 days (based on variability of typical pregnancies), starting with the earliest EOP. We apply the heuristic in Algorithm 1. Users with more than three pools are marked as ambiguous, and are potentially bots rather than pregnant women.

---

if *range(all EOP dates) < 45 days* **then**
  if *distance between pools > 5 days* **then**
    | pick the bigger pool;
  else
    | merge pools;
    | take the median date +/-7 days;
  end
else
  if *pool sizes are different and there are at most three pools*
  then
    | pick the bigger pool;
  else
    | mark as ambiguous;
  end
end

Algorithm 1: Heuristic for EOP date resolution for users with multiple pools.

---

3 RESULTS

3.1 Determining Pregnancy Timeframes from Tweets

Our database includes 199,492,503 tweets from 73,809 users, of which 3,378,089 tweets (from 71,532 users) contain temporal or pregnancy-related terms or both. Our regular expressions matched 41,350 tweets posted by 16,810 users. Table 2 indicates the frequencies of specific query patterns. To evaluate our system's precision in extracting the correct start of pregnancy (SOP) and end of pregnancy (EOP) from these patterns, two annotators identified the SOP and EOP in approximately 1% of the matching tweets (394 tweets), based solely on the temporal information contained in the tweet, where *Precision = True Positives / True Positives + False Positives*. "True positives" are correct estimates of SOP and EOP, and "false positives" are incorrect estimates. Based on this evaluation, the precision of our system, at the tweet level, was calculated as 0.99. We could not, within the limitations of this study, calculate recall, given that finding temporal expressions that our patterns did not match would require mining or manually annotating the 3.3 million tweets that have a temporal or pregnancy-related term but didn't match any of the patterns.

3.2 Estimating Pregnancy Timeframes for Users

We found that 6,323 of the 16,810 users (37.61%) posted multiple tweets that were matched by our regular expressions. Of these 6,323 users, 5,014 had one pool of EOP dates, 1,055 had two pools, 108 had three pools, and 146 had four or more pools. We manually analyzed the 146 users who had four or more pools and were automatically identified as ambiguous, and all of them were determined to be "bot" accounts rather than actual users. We calculated the precision of the four-or-more-pool rule as 0.99 in detecting bots. We also manually analyzed 140 of the users with one pool (including users with one or multiple matching tweets) and found that none of them were bots. For the 1,163 users with two or three pools, our heuristic was able to reconcile various pregnancy timeframes for 770 (66.21%) of them; the pregnancy timeframes for the remaining 393 users were marked as ambiguous and will require futher analysis for understanding and resolving the discrepancies (e.g., multiple pregnancies).

4 DISCUSSION

The results outlined above describe the performance of our system at the tweet level, and at the user level. Most of the errors for estimating the correct timeframe at the pattern level were due to capturing less specific time information in the tweet instead of the more precise phrases. For instance, in *"...13 more weeks until he's here!! #2ndtrimester #pregnancy #momtobe"*, the '2nd trimester' was identified as the temporal anchor whereas '13 more weeks' was missed, since it did not match our patterns.

Based on sampling and manual analysis of the user-level outcomes of the system, we found that users with ambiguity in their pregnancy timeframe belong to one of the following categories: (1) timelines that are retrospective in nature and hence provide inconsistent temporal information (2) multiple pregnancies. Unlike bots, these are real users and hence deeper NLP analysis is required for detection and resolution of conflicts to obtain a single pregnancy timeframe with high certainty.

4.1 Limitations

The coverage of our system is significantly higher than the existing work on pregnancy timeframe detection in social media. Although our system can distinguish between bots versus real users, detecting time-related posts and redirects from Instagram (flash back to previous stages of pregnancy) remains a challenge. The coverage of our patterns is relatively limited, given it captures only about 16 thousand of the 71 thousand users (or worse, 41 thousand of 3.3 million tweets) suspected to contain hints about the pregnancy timeframe (in the form of temporal expressions and pregnancy terms). Table 2 shows a rapid decrease in the count of tweets matched by each pattern, illustrating the well-known limitation of rule-based

Query Pattern	Example	Type	Freq.
I am N months/weeks/days pregnant	i am 5 mos and 2 wks preggers	Duration	16,984
#Nmonths/weeks/dayspregnant	#25weekspregnant	Duration	10,381
#Ntrimester	#secondtrimester	Duration	4,802
N months/weeks/days from/until my due date	100 days away from my due date	Due Date	3,485
halfway through my pregnancy	1/2 way done with my prgncy	Duration	1,782
I am in my N trimester	I'm in my third trimester	Duration	997
my due date is N months/weeks/days	my due date is about five weeks away	Due Date	896
my due date is [date]	my due date is july 5	Due Date	747
my due date is tomorrow	my due date is tmrw	Due Date	357
my due date is [day]	my due date is this thurs	Due Date	272
[date] is my due date	8/3 is my due date	Due Date	165
my due date is today	my due date is today	Due Date	97
my baby/son/daughter was born [date]	my daughter was born on may 9, 2017	Birth	97
my due date is N months/weeks/days from today	my due date is three mths from today	Due Date	63
my due date was yesterday	my due dt was yesterday	Due Date	55
[day] was my due date	monday was my due date	Due Date	45
my baby/son/daughter was born N months/weeks/days ago	my son was born 1 w ago	Birth	37
N months/weeks/days from today is my due date	10 days from today is due date	Due Date	34
I gave birth on [date]	I gave birth on nov. 25	Birth	21
third of the way through my pregnancy	3rd of the way into my #pregnancy	Duration	17
my due date was [day]	my due date was last tues	Due Date	16
N months/weeks/days through my pregnancy	3m and 3d thru my pregnancy	Duration	12

Table 2: Frequent patterns and number of tweets they match in our cohort.

systems whereby a few patterns cover many cases, but coming up with all the variants becomes intractable.

4.2 Conclusion

We have presented a deterministic system for identifying pregnancy timeframes based on user's expressions on Twitter. The system generates estimates of the start and end dates of pregnancy (the pregnancy timeframe) give or take thirty days. We have shown that the system could also be used for detecting discrepancies in user's expressions of pregnancy timeframes, which in turn could be used for detecting bots. The precision of this task is specifically significant for health-related social media epidemiological studies, where determining the pregnancy timeframe is a requirement for any other study. Processing these temporal expressions could also be relevant to other studies where the length of an event is important (e.g. length of treatment or duration of the symptoms).

ACKNOWLEDGMENTS

Drs. Gonzalez Hernandez and Sarker were partially supported by the National Institutes of Health (NIH) National Library of Medicine (NLM) grant number 5R01LM011176. The content is solely the responsibility of the authors and does not necessarily represent the official views of the NLM or NIH.

REFERENCES
[1] Delroy Cameron, Gary A Smith, Raminta Daniulaityte, Amit P Sheth, Drashti Dave, Lu Chen, Gaurish Anand, Robert Carlson, Kera Z Watkins, and Russel Falck. 2013. PREDOSE: a semantic web platform for drug abuse epidemiology using social media. *Journal of biomedical informatics* 46, 6 (2013), 985–997.
[2] Pramod Bharadwaj Chandrashekar, Arjun Magge, Abeed Sarker, and Graciela Gonzalez. 2017. Social media mining for identification and exploration of health-related information from pregnant women. *arXiv preprint arXiv:1702.02261* (2017).
[3] Angel X Chang and Christopher D Manning. 2012. SUTime: A library for recognizing and normalizing time expressions.. In *LREC*, Vol. 2012. 3735–3740.
[4] Munmun De Choudhury, Scott Counts, and Eric Horvitz. 2013. Major life changes and behavioral markers in social media: case of childbirth. In *Proceedings of the 2013 conference on Computer supported cooperative work*. ACM, 1431–1442.
[5] Munmun De Choudhury, Scott Counts, and Eric Horvitz. 2013. Predicting postpartum changes in emotion and behavior via social media. In *Proceedings of the SIGCHI Conference on Human Factors in Computing Systems*. ACM, 3267–3276.
[6] FDA. 2005. Reviewer Guidance: Evaluating the risks of drug exposure in human pregnancies. (2005).
[7] Adam Fourney, Ryen W White, and Eric Horvitz. 2015. Exploring time-dependent concerns about pregnancy and childbirth from search logs. In *Proceedings of the 33rd Annual ACM Conference on Human Factors in Computing Systems*. ACM, 737–746.
[8] Bo Han, Paul Cook, and Timothy Baldwin. 2012. Automatically constructing a normalisation dictionary for microblogs. In *Proceedings of the 2012 joint conference on empirical methods in natural language processing and computational natural language learning*. Association for Computational Linguistics, 421–432.
[9] Rave Harpaz, William DuMouchel, Nigam H Shah, David Madigan, Patrick Ryan, and Carol Friedman. 2012. Novel Data-Mining Methodologies for Adverse Drug Event Discovery and Analysis. *Clinical Pharmacology & Therapeutics* 91, 6 (2012), 1010–1021.
[10] Dianne L Kennedy, Kathleen Uhl, and Sandra L Kweder. 2004. Pregnancy exposure registries. *Drug Safety* 27, 4 (2004), 215–228.
[11] Fei Liu, Fuliang Weng, and Xiao Jiang. 2012. A broad-coverage normalization system for social media language. In *Proceedings of the 50th Annual Meeting of the Association for Computational Linguistics: Long Papers-Volume 1*. Association for Computational Linguistics, 1035–1044.
[12] Mayuresh Oak, Anil Behera, Titus Thomas, Cecilia Ovesdotter Alm, Emily Prud'hommeaux, Christopher Homan, and Raymond W Ptucha. 2016. Generating Clinically Relevant Texts: A Case Study on Life-Changing Events.. In *CLPsych@ HLT-NAACL*. 85–94.
[13] Brendan O'Connor, Michel Krieger, and David Ahn. 2010. TweetMotif: Exploratory Search and Topic Summarization for Twitter.. In *ICWSM*. 384–385.
[14] Lucila Ohno-Machado. 2012. Informatics 2.0: implications of social media, mobile health, and patient-reported outcomes for healthcare and individual privacy. *Journal of the American Medical Informatics Association* 19, 5 (2012), 683–683.
[15] Olutobi Owoputi, Brendan O'Connor, Chris Dyer, Kevin Gimpel, Nathan Schneider, and Noah A Smith. 2013. Improved part-of-speech tagging for online conversational text with word clusters. Association for Computational Linguistics.
[16] Michael J Paul, Abeed Sarker, John S Brownstein, Azadeh Nikfarjam, Matthew Scotch, Karen L Smith, and Graciela Gonzalez. 2016. Social media mining for public health monitoring and surveillance. In *Pacific Symposium on Biocomputing*

(PSB). 468–79.

[17] Abeed Sarker, Pramod Chandrashekar, Arjun Magge, Haitao Cai, Ari Klein, and Graciela Gonzalez. 2017. Discovering Cohorts of Pregnant Women from Social Media for Safety Surveillance and Analysis. *Journal of Medical Internet Research* 19, 10 (2017).

[18] Tingting Wang, Zhengxing Huang, and Chenxi Gan. 2016. On mining latent topics from healthcare chat logs. *Journal of biomedical informatics* 61 (2016), 247–259.

Information Sources and Needs in the Obesity and Diabetes Twitter Discourse

Yelena Mejova

Qatar Computing Research Institute

Hamad Bin Khalifa University, Doha, Qatar

yelenamejova@acm.org

ABSTRACT

Obesity and diabetes epidemics are affecting about a third and tenth of US population, respectively, capturing the attention of the nation and its institutions. Social media provides an open forum for communication between individuals and health organizations, a forum which is easily joined by parties seeking to gain profit from it. In this paper we examine 1.5 million tweets mentioning obesity and diabetes in order to assess (1) the quality of information circulating in this conversation, as well as (2) the behavior and information needs of the users engaged in it. The analysis of top cited domains shows a strong presence of health information sources which are not affiliated with a governmental or academic institution at 41% in obesity and 50% diabetes samples, and that tweets containing these domains are retweeted more than those containing domains of reputable sources. On the user side, we estimate over a quarter of non-informational obesity discourse to contain fat-shaming – a practice of humiliating and criticizing overweight individuals – with some self-directed toward the writers themselves. We also find a great diversity in questions asked in these datasets, spanning definition of obesity as a disease, social norms, and governmental policies. Our results indicate a need for addressing the quality control of health information on social media, as well as a need to engage in a topically diverse, psychologically charged discourse around these diseases.

CCS CONCEPTS

• **Networks** → *Online social networks*; • **Applied computing** → *Consumer health*; *Health informatics*;

KEYWORDS

Information need, Misinformation, Social media, Twitter, Obesity, Diabetes

ACM Reference Format:

Yelena Mejova. 2018. Information Sources and Needs in the Obesity and Diabetes Twitter Discourse. In *DH'18: 2018 International Digital Health Conference, April 23–26, 2018, Lyon, France.* ACM, New York, NY, USA, 9 pages. https://doi.org/10.1145/3194658.3194664

1 INTRODUCTION

In the US, a majority of adults now look online for health information, according to Pew Research Center[1]. The quality of the information they may find, however, has been questioned throughout past two decades [5, 6, 15, 46]. The responsibility of evaluating online health information then falls on the shoulders of internet users, presenting a danger of misinformed decisions about health and medical treatments [12].

With the rise of social networking, health information is increasingly shared peer to peer. Major health organizations began to utilize Twitter and Facebook for communicating with the public. US Centers for Disease Control and Prevention (CDC) use their Facebook page to promote health and inform the public about emerging pandemics [45], whereas American Heart Association, American Cancer Society, and American Diabetes Association keep their Twitter followers updated on organizational news and instruct in personal health [35]. But besides these large governmental organizations promoting a healthy lifestyle, content aggregators, bots and any party with or without medical qualifications may post health-related information on social media. For instance, Facebook posts with misleading information on Zika virus were some of the most popular in the summer of 2016, with hundreds of thousands of views [42]. Either rumor-mongering, seeking clicks, or spam, such messages aim to penetrate health discussions and the social media communities around them to potential detriment of the understanding and eventual health of users coming across this information. Thus far, few attempts have been made to assess the quality and sources of health information circulating on social media, with studies focusing on particular accounts [24, 45] or events [7, 9, 42].

On the other hand, social media provides a unique opportunity to observe peoples' knowledge of and attitudes toward health issues outside of the conventional top-down institutionalized channels. For instance, it is possible to observe communities of anorexic users promoting the disease on image sharing sites like Flickr, and to measure the effect of possible interventions [55]. The attitude toward food and the perception of its desirability or healthiness can be tracked through the social interactions on Instagram [32, 33]. The spread of anti-vaccination opinions can be tracked on Twitter [13] and internet search engines [54]. Insights obtained from these sources have widespread implications from pharmacovigilance, to the design of health intervention campaigns, to public health policy.

Public perception is especially critical to the ongoing epidemics of obesity and diabetes, as these "lifestyle" diseases are connected to everyday activities, as well as psychological stressors (here we refer more to Diabetes Type II, not the largely juvenile Type I).

---

[1]http://www.pewinternet.org/2013/01/15/health-online-2013/

An astounding 39.8% of the adults in United States was obese in 2015-2016 [20] with an estimated 30.3 million people having diabetes [8]. Linked to daily diet and exercise, change in lifestyle helps manage these conditions. According to the "Transtheoretical Model" of behavior change [37], before a change in behavior can be made, a stage of awareness of the health consequences must be first achieved. Thus, gauging the awareness and attitude toward the problems of obesity and diabetes is the first step to designing effective policies for behavior change. It is especially necessary, as a powerful stigma of obesity (sometimes expressed as "fat shaming") is prevalent in the Western world [38] to the point that one survey reported that 24% of women and 17% of men said they would give up three or more years of their lives to be the weight they want [17]. Such atmosphere may further hurt the chances of individuals to lose weight, as social support and ongoing internal motivation are important factors in successful weight loss and maintenance [14].

Thus, in this paper we take a two-pronged approach to gauging the nature of discourse on obesity and diabetes:

(1) we evaluate the quality of information sources, their credentials, popularity, and the potential for them to spread through the social network;

(2) we gauge the attitudes of the participants in the conversation, including their

  (a) propensity for fat shaming,
  (b) blaming obese and diabetic people for their conditions,
  (c) exposing personal information, and
  (d) information seeking.

This study is among first of its kind to juxtapose the available information on medical conditions, in this case obesity and diabetes, with the information needs and attitudes of social media users interested in them. The mixed methods approaches applied to nearly six months of Twitter stream data comprising of 1.5 million tweets include quantitative analyses, network analysis, grounded annotation, and crowd sourcing, exemplifying the multidisciplinary content analysis indicative of the emerging fields of computational social sciences.

2 RELATED WORK

Social media has recently been acknowledged by public health community to be a valuable resource for disease outbreak detection, tracking behavioral risks to communicable and non-communicable diseases, and for health-care agencies and governments to share data with the public [26]. Non-profit organizations, for instance, use Twitter for informing the public, building a community, and encouraging individual action [30]. However, free nature of social media (and internet in general) allows for information sources not affiliated with governmental agencies, raising concerns over the provenance and quality of health and medical information they make available to the public. A recent review on "Web 2.0" urges that the community "must not easily dismiss concerns about reliability as outdated", and address the issues of authorship, information quality, anonymity and privacy [2].

Biased messages, rumors, and misinformation have been gaining attention in the literature. An analysis of anti-vaccination websites has revealed a pervasive misinformation [27]. Moreover, Dunn et

al. [13] find that prior exposure to opinions rejecting the safety or value of HPV vaccines is associated with an increased relative risk of posting similar opinions on Twitter. Recently, a tool combining crowdsourcing and text classification has been proposed to track misinformation on Twitter on the topic of Zika [18]. Another tool was proposed for crawling medical content from websites, blogs, and social media using sentiment and credibility scoring [1]. Yet another tool ranks information sources by "reputation scores" based on retweeting mechanism [53]. More generic algorithms comparing information to known sources such as Wikipedia have also been proposed [11]. Yet in medical and health domains, it is still unclear what portion of overall social media content comes from reputable sources, what other sources seek to engage with health-oriented communities, and what success these sources have in propagating their material through the social network. Our work contributes to the understanding of the quality of discourse around obesity and diabetes by evaluating the most cited resources in the relevant Twitter streams.

The breadth and reach of social media not only allowed for wider dissemination of health information, but its network features allow individuals to join communities, seek information, and express themselves on an unprecedented scale. Surveys find that consumers use social media primarily to see what others say about a medication or treatment and to find out about other peoples' experiences [41]. When they find this information, another study indicates that it largely changes what they think about the topic [43]. Moreover, the diabetes patients participating in [43] indicated willingness to discuss personal health information on online social networking sites. Another study of diabetes communities on Facebook showed that "patients with diabetes, family members, and their friends use Facebook to share personal clinical information, to request disease-specific guidance and feedback, and to receive emotional support" [19], while 27% of the posts featuring some form of promotional activity of "natural" products. Thus, social media is a marketplace for health information, where both supply and demand is captured in the same medium. In this study, we aim to examine the information needs revealed in Twitter posts concerning obesity and diabetes, as well as behaviors related to revealing one's own private health information.

In 2013, the American Medical Association (AMA) recognized obesity as a complex, chronic disease [36], prompting a debate about the effects of such a decision on weight discrimination with some claiming it "provides ammunition on 'war on obesity'," [21] while others expressing concerns that it's a sign of "abdication of personal responsibility" [47]. Public perception of obesity on social media also prompts debate. A survey in 2015 showed respondents agreeing less that people are "personally responsible for becoming obese", but more that "the cause of obesity is beyond the control" of a person who has it [28]. Further, a study of a variety of social media including Twitter, blogs, Facebook and forums showed widespread negative sentiment, derogatory language, and misogynist terms, with 92% of Twitter stream having the word "fat" [10]. Another more recent study coded the uses of the word "fat" in Twitter, finding 56.57% to be negative and 32% neutral [31]. Thus, we ask what proportion of obesity discourse contains such messages, do they similarly affect the diabetes community, and whether the institutional messaging addresses this phenomenon in its communication.

3 INFORMATION SOURCES

We begin by collecting two datasets, Obesity (tweets mentioning "obese" or "obesity") and Diabetes ("diabetes" or "diabetic") collected using Twitter Streaming API[2]. Both datasets span the period of July 19, 2017 - December 31, 2017, nearly half of a year, comprising of 1,055,196 tweets from 505,897 users in Obesity and 2,889,764 tweets from 996,486 users in Diabetes dataset. Note the conservative selection of keywords for the purposes of this analysis. Whereas other keywords may capture more of the discussion on related matters, such as "fat", "insulin", "exercise", etc., we aim to capture only the discussion on these health conditions. It is notable that whereas obesity is a more prevalent condition, for instance, in US more than one-third (36.5%) of adults have obesity [34] compared to 9.4% having diabetes [8], the Twitter stream shows nearly 3 times as many messages on the latter compared to the former, indicating either heightened interest in and/or more aggressive campaigning for the topic.

In order to understand the major sources of information within these two streams, we examine the URLs present in the tweets of each dataset. Utilizing Twitter API's "expanded url" field, we extract the original domains associated with the short URLs present in the tweet text. Note that even then some of the original URLs users type in may be shortened by some service. In total, we extract 17,511 and 43,230 domains from Obesity and Diabetes collections, respectively. For each collection, we then use Grounded Theoretic-approach to examine the first 100 domains by iteratively coding each, until a set of common codes is established.

Table 1 shows the most common codes in the two collections. Despite using expanded URLs, 13 of the top domains in each collection were shortening services. Additionally, social media managers and aggregators comprised a similar portion of content. Strikingly, a minority of the domains dealt with health: 17 and 29 in Obesity and Diabetes, respectively. Among these, the quality of the information varied greatly. In particular, we define a source as "unverified health" if it (1) publishes health-related information, but (2) has no about page describing its credentials. Second point is important, as the reader may make assumptions about the credentials of the source, in the absence of any statement. This also differentiates these sources from domains we dub "health aggregators" – websites publishing articles on topics of health which clearly state their affiliation (often a publishing company). Alternatively, if the affiliation is that of a governmental or academic institution such as National Institutes of Health (NIH) or American Diabetes Association, the domain is coded as "verified health". Note that some major websites, such as the Diabetes community site www.diabetes.co.uk may be popular, but are not associated with a governmental agency. Overall, out of the health-related domains, 23% of the ones met the criteria for "verified" for both datasets, while 41% and 50% were "unverified" in Obesity and Diabetes sets, respectively. In terms of comparative volume, unverified domains had 2.47 times more content in the Obesity stream than verified ones, similarly 2.72 for Diabetes.

As retweeting behavior is commonly used to gauge "virality" of content [23], we examine the number of retweets the content containing verified and unverified domains received in our datasets.

We begin by selecting users who are likely to be real individuals, not bots or organizations, via a two-step process. First, we filter the accounts by the number of followers and followees (maximum figures over the period of time the data was collected), selecting users having both numbers between 10 and 1000, as it has been shown that 89% of users following spam accounts have 10 or fewer followers [48]. Secondly, we use a name dictionary to identify the users having identifiable first names. These names were collected United States Social Security registry of baby names from years 1880-2016[3]. Such users comprised 36.5% of users captured in Obesity and 37.2% of Diabetes datasets. Although it is possible some bots remain in this sample, upon manual inspection, the resulting accounts looked overall likely to be used by real people.

Next, we gather statistics on the number of retweets a piece of content gathered. To make sure to catch all retweets, even if the Twitter API does not identify them as such in metadata, we clean the text of the tweet of special characters, user mentions, and urls, as well as the "RT" identifier for "retweet" to find the basic linguistic content of the tweet. Figures 1(a,b) show the kernel density (a "violin") plot of the distribution of retweets per unique piece of content for those having verified domains associated with health agencies and institutions, and all other health domains, as posted by users in the above selection. For both topics, verified domains were less likely to produce viral content, with a mean number of retweets of 1.9 for verified compared to 3.4 for other health content in Obesity dataset (difference significant at p-value < 0.01 using Welch two sample t-test) and 2.8 versus 3.8 in Diabetes (although not significant at the same level). We hypothesize that the lesser difference in Diabetes data is due to high quality websites unaffiliated with governmental agencies such as www.webmd.com and www.diabetes.co.uk. When selecting only those websites coded as "unverified", the disparity grows to 7.1 retweets for Obesity and 9.6 for Diabetes content, indicating that such websites produce an even more viral content.

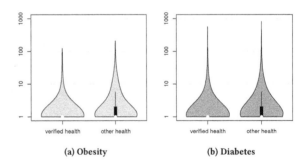

(a) Obesity   (b) Diabetes

Figure 1: Violin plots of the distributions of retweets containing domains from verified versus other sources, as posted by users likely to be real people, in the two datasets.

To further understand the impact of these information sources in the community, we create a co-citation network. In this network, an edge exists between two domains if the same user has posted urls

[2]https://developer.twitter.com/en/docs/tweets/filter-realtime/overview

[3]https://www.ssa.gov/oact/babynames/limits.html

Table 1: Domain codes for top 100 domains found in each collection, with accompanying examples.

		Obesity
num	Type	Examples
27	news	nyti.ms, www.theguardian.com, cnn.it, bbc.in, www.forbes.com, www.vox.com, wapo.st
13	shortener	bit.ly, ift.tt, goo.gl, ltl.is, tinyurl.com, snip.ly, ja.ma
8	unreachable	-
8	social media (SM)	twitter.com, youtu.be, www.facebook.com, lnkd.in
7	unverified health	atomicdinosaurenemy.com, modernlife.in, medsminders.com, peekerhealth.com
7	news aggregator	www.sciencedaily.com, movietvtechgeeks.com, www.newslocker.com
5	SM manager	ow.ly, buff.ly, paper.li, dlvr.it, po.st
4	verified health	www.ncbi.nlm.nih.gov, www.cdc.gov, nej.md, stateofobesity.org, nej.md
4	health aggregator	www.medpagetoday.com, www.medicalnewstoday.com, www.studyfinds.org
2	health personal	kylejnorton.blogspot.ca, abajardepeso.com.mx
15	others	soundcloud.com, www.nature.com, onlinelibrary.wiley.com, www.zerohedge.com
		Diabetes
num	Type	Examples
15	unverified health	diabetesmovie.net, kipaduka.com, ahealthblog.com, www.badhaai.com, diabetes-destroyer.netmd.in
13	shortener	bit.ly, ift.tt, goo.gl, ltl.is, tinyurl.com, ref.gl, j.mp
10	news	www.thenation.com, nyti.ms, dailym.ai, www.theguardian.com, bbc.in, reut.rs, futurism.com
8	social media (SM)	twitter.com, youtu.be, www.facebook.com, lnkd.in, www.instagram.com, cards.twitter.com
8	health aggregator	www.medicalnewstoday.com, www.medscape.com, www.diabetes.co.uk
8	SM manager	dlvr.it, buff.ly, paper.li, naver.me, socl.club, po.st
7	news aggregator	shareblue.com, okz.me, www.sciencedaily.com
7	verified health	www.ncbi.nlm.nih.gov, www.diabetes.org, care.diabetesjournals.org, www.idf.org, www2.jdrf.org
6	unreachable	-
1	health personal	abajardepeso.com.mx
17	others	www.change.org, www.ebay.com, etsy.me, wp.me, tacticalinvestor.com, www.soompi.com

containing them, in the same or in different posts. Due to sparsity limitations, we return to the full list of users in this experiment, which will also allow to capture the co-posting behavior of the domains and their Twitter accounts. Specifically, for each domain pair, we enumerate the users posting at some point URLs from both of the domains, which usually happens in different posts, resulting in a set of users who were interested in the content of each domain at some point during the collection period. However, this connection needs to be understood in the context of the posting frequency of each domain, with the most popular ones (such as twitter.com) potentially dominating all others. Thus, we use Jaccard similarity coefficient, having the following form:

$$Jaccard(domain_1, domain_2) = \frac{U_{domain_1} \cap U_{domain_2}}{U_{domain_1} \cup U_{domain_2}}$$

where U_{domain} is the set of users who posted at least one URL of that domain. The network is then expressed in GraphML format[4] and plotted using Gephi[5]. Figures 2(a,b) show the resulting domain co-citation networks. In both, the size of the node (domain) and its label are scaled by the number of tweets the domain appears in. The nodes are positioned using the ForceAtlas 2 force-directed algorithm such that nodes most strongly linked appear closer together while those most weakly linked appear in the periphery of the graph. Finally, the nodes are then colored by the type of domain: light blue - social media, blue - news, red - unverified health, green - verified health and health aggregators.

In both graphs, we see the green and blue dominating the center of conversation – which are the verified health institutions, health aggregators, and news. Social media is closely tied to this central cluster, but usually appears in the periphery. Notably, in both cases twitter.com appears in the corner, despite its large size, indicating that topically the content this domain provides is not central to the conversation. As Twitter provides its own shortener to the posted URLs, this finding supports that it a topically diverse domain. Notably, the unverified health domains appear in the periphery, but not too far from the center for Obesity network, and much more on the periphery for Diabetes. In the midst of the red nodes we find other domains, such www.thebingbing.com and www.grandesmedios.com. This emphasizes the difficulty of evaluating quality of content from online sources. It is possible that, despite more clear disclaimers and documentation, some domains still may be positioned in the same space as more questionable ones. Thus, using this technique, we may find candidates for further investigation into sources of health information which could have questionable provenance.

Finally, we examine the content shared by these top domains, mainly those with verified and unverified sources. For each domain,

---

[4] http://graphml.graphdrawing.org/
[5] https://gephi.org/

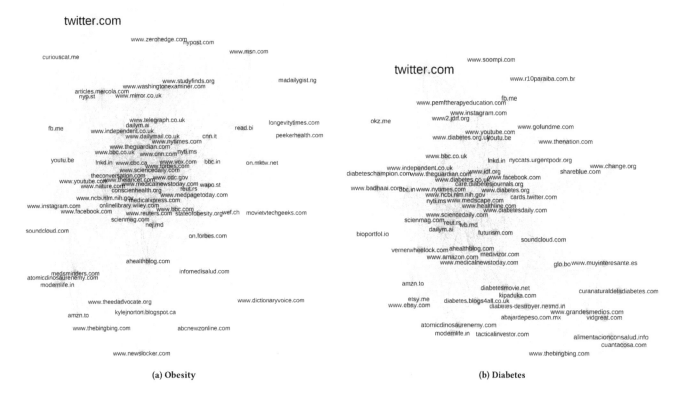

(a) Obesity

(b) Diabetes

Figure 2: Co-citation networks for top domains, excluding URL shorteners, SM managers and unreachable domains. Colors signify domain types: light blue - social media, blue - news, red - unverified health, green - verified health and health aggregators. Nodes are scaled by number of tweets containing them, and are positioned using ForceAtlas2, with the strength of a tie being Jaccard similarity in the users citing two domains.

we randomly sample up to 10 distinct tweets (de-duplicated using the method above), resulting in a sample of 40 tweets from verified and 36 unverified sources for Obesity and 70 verified and 131 unverified for Diabetes. These were then coded for major themes, iteratively coalescing to a common set of topics.

Verified sources in Obesity domain focused largely on quoting disease prevalence statistics (37%), followed by information on childhood obesity (17.5%) and therapies (12.5%) and pharmaceuticals (5%); while verified sources in Diabetes domain focused on awareness (30%), followed by diet (11%), pharmaceuticals (11%) and therapies (8%). Prevention and health education stories were also prevalent in both (at around 5%). Unverified sources, on the other hand, focused on weight loss and dieting (at around 25% in each dataset), with a substantial portion claiming Diabetes cure using superfoods and diets. Overall, the messages in Diabetes stream were more ambitious in their health claims than Obesity one, with 8% of posts claiming a diet cure, and another 3% a cure by other means. A yet another dangerous trend was of self-diagnosis advise (5%) which claimed to detect diabetes, liver disease, and even AIDS. Unfortunately, in the next section we show that this content falls far short of the information users seek and discuss on Twitter.

4 USER BEHAVIOR

The Twitter data collected for this work captures not only resources available, but also the personal views of individuals posting about diabetes and obesity. In particular, we are motivated by findings in previous studies on the use of social media for expressing opinions, information seeking, and understanding of obesity and diabetes as medical conditions. We begin by selecting tweets in English language which do not point to a URL, or external information, in attempt to exclude the information sharing aspect (which was examined in the previous section). This resulted in 136,879 documents for Obesity and 176,858 for Diabetes, out of which 1,000 tweets were randomly chosen for each dataset to be labeled.

To understand these subsets of documents, we design a crowd-sourced labeling task, run on Crowdflower[6] service. For each condition (obesity or diabetes), we ask the following four questions:

(1) Does the person posting this reveals any personal information?
(2) Does the person posting this asks a question about obesity/diabetes or some related topic (beyond rhetorical or joking ones)?

---

[6]http://www.crowdflower.com/

25

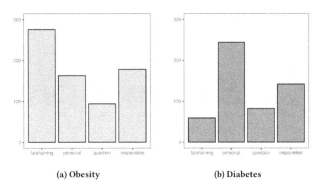

(a) Obesity (b) Diabetes

Figure 3: Distribution of labels in 1000 documents labeled for the presence of fat-shaming, sharing personal health information, asking a question about the condition, and statements people are personally responsible for their condition.

(a) Obesity (b) Diabetes

Figure 4: Co-occurrence code network for tweets expressing personal information, with nodes scaled by number of occurrences and edges weighted by number of common tweets. Layout using ForceAtlas 2.

(3) Does the person posting this states or imply people are personally responsible for being obese/diabetic?

(4) Is there fat shaming (putting someone down because of their weight)?

The instructions for the tasks include examples of each case as well as several combinations, emphasizing that the same tweet may meet several of these conditions. An additional quality control was put in place using a quiz, making sure crowd-workers understood the instructions, as well as continued test items throughout the labeling process. A worker must maintain an accuracy of at least 70% in order to continue labeling the data. For this purpose, 13 "Gold standard" questions were designed to provide unambiguous examples of correct labeling for each dataset. Finally, a minimum of 3 labels by different workers was collected for each tweet.

Out of the four questions, the third one about statements implying people are personally responsible for the condition proved to be most difficult, with annotator agreement (as measured by label overlap) at 87.8% and 88.3% for Obesity and Diabetes, respectively. Identifying personal information and fat-shaming proved to be easier, with average agreement around 91% in both tasks and datasets. Whether a question is being asked was easier for workers to agree on in the case of Obesity (at 94% agreement) than Diabetes (87.4%). However, in general the figures show a substantial agreement among the workers.

Figures 3(a,b) show the number of tweets in each category out of the 1,000 labeled, in each dataset. At a glance, we find the distributions quite different. Only 59 tweets were identified as fat-shaming in Diabetes set, while 276 in Obesity (the difference is statistically significant using 2-sample test for equality of proportions at p-value < 0.001). However, more people shared their personal information in Diabetes data, with 244 identified as having some information, compared to 163 in Obesity one (different at $p < 0.001$). Similar number of questions (94 and 82) and personal responsibility claims (178 and 142) were in the both Obesity and Diabetes datasets, respectively (not significantly different at $p < 0.001$).

Interaction between these labels can reveal interesting intersections. For instance, out of 276 fat-shaming and 163 personal-information tweets in Obesity data, 13 are in the intersection, having both labels. Combining shame and personal stories, these tweets reveal low self-image and struggles with diet and exercise (expletives removed):

"HOW AND WHY DO PEOPLE EVEN GET CRUSHES ON ME IM AN UGLY OBESE PIECE OF ****"
"i just ate a cheeseburger and fries and now i feel like i ****ing gross obese animal why did u do that?"
"My mom is making me lose 25 pounds bc she doesn't want my family in September thinking I'm obese"

Interestingly, in the Diabetes set only 2 such tweets were detected, and one of these shames another person, not self. These statistics, as well as examples, show the stigma associated with obesity, and much less with diabetes. Also note that the milder statement of responsibility of people having these conditions (rightmost bars in the Figure) are at a similar rate for both datasets.

Beyond self-image and more general evaluative statements, roughly 16% of Obesity and nearly a quarter (24.4%) of Diabetes labeled subsets contained some personal information. To understand further the nature of this information, 100 tweets were randomly selected from both sets and coded using open coding technique introduced in the domain analysis in the previous section. The resulting codes are shown in Figures 4(a,b) as co-occurrence networks, such that the weight of the edge between two codes is proportional to the number of tweets having them in common. First, the most prominent theme in both was declaration of one having the condition, more informally in Obesity, and linked to doctor visits and tests in Diabetes. At a glance, we can see the Diabetes network much more diverse, including other illnesses such as heart disease, cancer, hypoglycemia, and psychological conditions including anxiety and eating disorders. On the other hand, behavioral topics such as smoking and depression appeared in Obesity data, as well as life events concerning unemployment and education. The topic of eating is close to the center for both datasets, most often appearing as disparaging messages about own eating behavior. Thus, despite

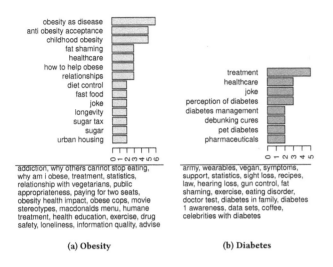

(a) Obesity

(b) Diabetes

Figure 5: Coded topics of questions in the 94 and 82 documents identified as asking a question in Obesity and Diabetes datasets, respectively.

obesity being recognized as a chronic disease by American Medical Association (AMA) [29], it is perceived much more as a personal failing than diabetes. Finally, in both sets words "obese" and "diabetic" has been used as a joke or hyperbole for instance *"I got diabetes just watching this"*. As we note in Discussion section, these terms are sometimes used even as adjectives to describe food and other activities.

Next, we examine the nature of questions present in each dataset, each having just under 10% of its documents identified by the crowd-workers as containing a question: 94 in Obesity and 82 in Diabetes ones. Unlike the personal information, questions proved to be much more diverse. Figures 5(a,b) show the main codes present in these documents, with those having only one occurrence in text below the graph. Notably, a lively discussion was taking place in Obesity data on whether obesity is a disease, with 5 posts questioning whether social "acceptance" of obesity is desirable. A similar smaller discussion took place in Diabetes data focusing on the perception of diabetics. The breadth of questions, ranging from economic policies and education, to the quality of available information, to the medical and psychological management of these conditions, exemplify the diversity of information needs of these communities.

Finally, as both conditions are known to be connected to dietary behavior [4, 39], we ask, what kinds of foods are associated with obesity and diabetes in the social media chatter? To find out, we apply a longest string matching algorithm to the text of all of the tweets (not only the subset above) to match words and phrases to a dictionary of foods along with their nutritional values. We borrow the recipe collection from [40], which contains nutrition information for both recipes (18,651) and their ingredients (1,499 unique entries). To supplement this lexicon, we take the foods listed in Lexicocalorimeter [3] and search Google for nutritional information, scraping the returned pages, resulting in 1,464 entries. The final merged list of foods contains 21,163 entries, each annotated with calorie content and other nutritional values.

The 30 most popular foods matched to the two datasets are shown in Table 2. We classify the foods in this table by caloric density, as defined by the British Nutrition Foundation[7]. It uses the ratio of kcal per gram of food and the following ranges: very low (less than 0.6 kcal/g), low (0.6 to 1.5), medium (1.5 to 4) and high (more than 4). The variability of mentioned foods reveal a dichotomy between the two themes: associating heavy foods with obesity and diabetes (in fact, using the word "diabetes" instead of "sweet"), and proposing healthier alternatives. In the minds of these Twitter users, sugar and fat seem to be most associated with both conditions, although at least in popular culture the main culprit is still undecided[8]. Also note the prominence of tea, which is the most popular remedy advertised in both datasets, especially green tea, and other "weightloss" teas (some of which may actually be effective [25]). Finally, excluded from this list is "liver", which matched a food in our dictionary, but upon a closer inspection, was actually referred to in the context of a human organ. Thus, we emphasize the diversity of the discourse captured in this data – even the supposed foods found therein may refer to widely differing content, including commentary on own state of health and behavior, questions and advise on healthy living, and commercial advertisement of goods and services.

5 DISCUSSION & LIMITATIONS

Analyzing nearly 6 months of Twitter stream about obesity and diabetes, this study explores the sources of information dominating this discourse, as well as the posting behavior of ordinary users. We find that, besides the large news websites and social media aggregators, a substantial amount of content is posted by what we dubbed "unverified" health sources, those not affiliated with any established governmental or medical organization. The situation is particularly dire in the Diabetes stream where 50% of health-related domains are of this nature. Further, we find that their content both has greater volume (at roughly 2.5 times that coming from the verified sources) and tends to be retweeted more. This is especially concerning in the case of Diabetes stream, as a substantial portion of this material claims to cure the disease. As mentioned in Related Works section, several automated and semi-automated methods have been proposed to detect misinformation [1, 11, 18, 53], but latest efforts in algorithmic correction of such material showed mixed results, such as Facebook's attempt to demote stories flagged as "fake" [44], while others like Twitter simply having no built-in algorithmic response, although third party tools are becoming more available [50, 51]. However, there are some signs that social correction may be effective in reducing misconceptions, as long as an additional reputable source of information is presented [52].

Besides misinformation, our analyses find a worrying amount of fat-shaming, including self-hate, messages, making up 27.6% of the non-URL messages mentioning obesity. Not only has social media has been shown to negatively affect body satisfaction [16], such speech may exacerbate the already largely critical body attitudes of overweight individuals, and especially young women [17]. Availability of unverified sources advertising potentially harmful weight loss programs and products compounds the danger for those

---

[7]https://www.nutrition.org.uk/healthyliving/fuller/what-is-energy-density.html
[8]https://www.newyorker.com/magazine/2017/04/03/is-fat-killing-you-or-is-sugar

Table 2: Top 30 most frequent foods in each dataset along with their energy density in kcal/gram. Foods with high energy density are in *bold italic* and medium in **bold**. Artificial sweeteners range in caloric value widely, thus "-" is used.

Obesity						Diabetes					
9.0	*fat*	3.1	**pizza**	3.7	cheese	3.8	**sugar**	3.0	raisin	0.0	ice
3.8	**sugar**	0.5	orange	2.5	**cinnamon**	9.0	*fat*	3.8	**candy**	8.8	*oil*
0.0	tea	-	artificial sweetener	2.6	**ham**	0.0	tea	2.6	**ham**	0.5	milk
0.4	soda	2.5	**honey buns**	0.0	coffee	0.0	coffee	0.5	juice	3.7	**corn**
3.0	**hamburger**	1.6	**egg**	0.8	potato	5.4	*chocolate*	0.0	stevia	2.1	**ice cream**
0.4	cola	2.0	**turkey**	2.7	**broth**	1.4	meat	0.0	salt	3.8	**cereal**
0.0	green tea	8.8	*oil*	0.0	salt	0.0	water	0.5	apple	3.7	**gluten**
1.4	meat	5.4	*chocolate*	3.7	**corn**	1.7	**milkshake**	2.7	**broth**	0.3	broccoli
0.0	water	5.1	*crackers*	1.8	**chicken**	0.4	soda	-	artificial sweetener	0.8	wine
0.4	coke	3.8	**candy**	0.7	vegetables	0.4	cola	0.4	coke	0.6	mango

prone to disordered eating [49]. It is concerning, then, that the topic of body image does not figure in Twitter content posted by verified domains, even though some agencies are aware of social media health debates. For example, the US Centers for Disease Control and Prevention published a study on #thinspo and #fitspo movements on Twitter, finding that #thinspo content (which often contained images of extremely thin women) had higher rates of liking and retweeting [22].

Although the rate of fat-shaming was much lower for diabetes data (at 5.9%), we found many misuses of the word "diabetes" to mean excessively sweet or unhealthy:

> "@user Can I have one?....I'm in the mood for some diabetes :)"

However we also find some pushback on the practice:

> "@user Love you guys but could you please stop referring to "getting diabetes" when eating sweet foods? My son is Type1D."

This attitude may be linked to an undercurrent of statements that people are responsible for their conditions (17.8% for obesity and 14.2% for diabetes non-URL streams). In fact, whether obesity is a disease is one of the most frequently asked questions, according to our sample, despite the American Medical Association (AMA) recognizing obesity as a disease in 2013 [36]. More clear messaging may be necessary to explain the complex nature of obesity, with its psychological as well as physical aspects, to the public.

Although our data collection spans nearly half of a year and contains every tweet posted in that time mentioning diabetes or obesity, this sample most certainly does not cover the entirety of conversations on these topics (especially when they are not referred to explicitly). For instance, it is likely that not all references to "fat" in Table 2 refer to food, but to people's weight. A major limitation of content analysis is, thus, the initial selection of the keywords to be considered. However, despite the sizable volume of social media posting, the majority of conversation happens offline, or in private forums and communities. For instance, one of the most popular weight loss apps LoseIt[9] had over 30 million users as of 2017, who are encouraged to network and communicate. Further, there may be ongoing campaigns outside Twitter by governmental

---

[9]http://www.loseit.com/about/

health agencies or other more local organizations. Thus, the results of this study need to be taken in the broader context of health communication.

6 CONCLUSION

This study provides an analysis of 1.5 million tweets posted in the latter half of 2017 mentioning obesity and diabetes. We examine the most cited domains, paying special attention to whether they are associated with a known governmental or health agency. Worryingly, we find a substantial volume from unverified sources, especially in the Diabetes dataset. We also find that this content tends to be retweeted more than that coming from verified sources. A complementary analysis of tweets not sharing a URL shows a strong presence of fat shaming in Obesity stream and the sharing of personal information in Diabetes one. The mismatch between the institutional messaging and the questions we have encountered in the data points to a need for better discussion of the nature of obesity and diabetes as diseases, confronting fat-shaming, and providing information other than prevalence statistics and latest medical news.

REFERENCES

[1] Ahmed Abbasi, Tianjun Fu, Daniel Zeng, and Donald Adjeroh. 2013. Crawling credible online medical sentiments for social intelligence. In *Social Computing (SocialCom), 2013 International Conference on*. IEEE, 254–263.

[2] Samantha A Adams. 2010. Revisiting the online health information reliability debate in the wake of "web 2.0": an inter-disciplinary literature and website review. *International journal of medical informatics* 79, 6 (2010), 391–400.

[3] Sharon E Alajajian, Jake Ryland Williams, Andrew J Reagan, Stephen C Alajajian, Morgan R Frank, Lewis Mitchell, Jacob Lahne, Christopher M Danforth, and Peter Sheridan Dodds. 2017. The Lexicocalorimeter: Gauging public health through caloric input and output on social media. *PloS one* 12, 2 (2017), e0168893.

[4] Susan H Babey, Allison L Diamant, Theresa A Hastert, Stefan Harvey, et al. 2008. Designed for disease: the link between local food environments and obesity and diabetes. *UCLA Center for Health Policy Research* (2008).

[5] Gretchen K Berland, Marc N Elliott, Leo S Morales, Jeffrey I Algazy, Richard L Kravitz, Michael S Broder, David E Kanouse, Jorge A Muñoz, Juan-Antonio Puyol, Marielena Lara, et al. 2001. Health information on the Internet: accessibility, quality, and readability in English and Spanish. *Jama* 285, 20 (2001), 2612–2621.

[6] Elmer V Bernstam, Muhammad F Walji, Smitha Sagaram, Deepak Sagaram, Craig W Johnson, and Funda Meric-Bernstam. 2008. Commonly cited website quality criteria are not effective at identifying inaccurate online information about breast cancer. *Cancer* 112, 6 (2008), 1206–1213.

[7] Rowena Briones, Xiaoli Nan, Kelly Madden, and Leah Waks. 2012. When vaccines go viral: an analysis of HPV vaccine coverage on YouTube. *Health communication* 27, 5 (2012), 478–485.

[8] CDC. 2017. National Diabetes Statistics Report, 2017. *National Center for Chronic Disease Prevention and Health Promotion* (2017).

[9] Cynthia Chew and Gunther Eysenbach. 2010. Pandemics in the age of Twitter: content analysis of Tweets during the 2009 H1N1 outbreak. *PloS one* 5, 11 (2010), e14118.

[10] Wen-ying Sylvia Chou, Abby Prestin, and Stephen Kunath. 2014. Obesity in social media: a mixed methods analysis. *Translational behavioral medicine* 4, 3 (2014), 314–323.

[11] Giovanni Luca Ciampaglia, Prashant Shiralkar, Luis M Rocha, Johan Bollen, Filippo Menczer, and Alessandro Flammini. 2015. Computational fact checking from knowledge networks. *PloS one* 10, 6 (2015), e0128193.

[12] Rebecca JW Cline and Katie M Haynes. 2001. Consumer health information seeking on the Internet: the state of the art. *Health education research* 16, 6 (2001), 671–692.

[13] Adam G Dunn, Julie Leask, Xujuan Zhou, Kenneth D Mandl, and Enrico Coiera. 2015. Associations between exposure to and expression of negative opinions about human papillomavirus vaccines on social media: an observational study. *Journal of medical Internet research* 17, 6 (2015).

[14] Kristina Elfhag and Stephan Rössner. 2005. Who succeeds in maintaining weight loss? A conceptual review of factors associated with weight loss maintenance and weight regain. *Obesity reviews* 6, 1 (2005), 67–85.

[15] Gunther Eysenbach, John Powell, Oliver Kuss, and Eun-Ryoung Sa. 2002. Empirical studies assessing the quality of health information for consumers on the world wide web: a systematic review. *Jama* 287, 20 (2002), 2691–2700.

[16] Jasmine Fardouly, Phillippa C Diedrichs, Lenny R Vartanian, and Emma Halliwell. 2015. Social comparisons on social media: The impact of Facebook on young women's body image concerns and mood. *Body Image* 13 (2015), 38–45.

[17] David M Garner. 1997. The 1997 body image survey results. *Psychology today* 30, 1 (1997), 30–44.

[18] Amira Ghenai and Yelena Mejova. 2017. Catching Zika fever: Application of crowdsourcing and machine learning for tracking health misinformation on Twitter. *International Conference on Healthcare Informatics (ICHI)* (2017).

[19] Jeremy A Greene, Niteesh K Choudhry, Elaine Kilabuk, and William H Shrank. 2011. Online social networking by patients with diabetes: a qualitative evaluation of communication with Facebook. *Journal of general internal medicine* 26, 3 (2011), 287–292.

[20] Craig Hales, Margaret Carroll, Cheryl D. Fryar, and Cynthia L. Ogden. 2016. Prevalence of Obesity Among Adults and Youth: United States, 2015–2016. *Centers for Disease Control and Prevention. National Center for Health Statistics* (2016).

[21] Jennifer Hansen. 2014. Explode and die! A fat woman's perspective on prenatal care and the fat panic epidemic. *Narrative inquiry in bioethics* 4, 2 (2014), 99–101.

[22] Jenine K Harris, Alexis Duncan, Vera Men, Nora Shevick, Melissa J Krauss, and Patricia A Cavazos-Rehg. 2018. Peer Reviewed: Messengers and Messages for Tweets That Used# thinspo and# fitspo Hashtags in 2016. *Preventing chronic disease* 15 (2018).

[23] Maximilian Jenders, Gjergji Kasneci, and Felix Naumann. 2013. Analyzing and predicting viral tweets. In *Proceedings of the 22nd International Conference on World Wide Web. ACM*, 657–664.

[24] Venk Kandadai, Haodong Yang, Ling Jiang, Christopher C Yang, Linda Fleisher, and Flaura Koplin Winston. 2016. Measuring health information dissemination and identifying target interest communities on Twitter: methods development and case study of the@ SafetyMD network. *JMIR research protocols* 5, 2 (2016).

[25] Yung-Hsi Kao, Hsin-Huei Chang, Meng-Jung Lee, and Chia-Lin Chen. 2006. Tea, obesity, and diabetes. *Molecular nutrition & food research* 50, 2 (2006), 188–210.

[26] Taha A Kass-Hout and Hend Alhinnawi. 2013. Social media in public health. *British Medical Bulletin* 108, 1 (2013), 5–24.

[27] Anna Kata. 2010. A postmodern Pandora's box: anti-vaccination misinformation on the Internet. *Vaccine* 28, 7 (2010), 1709–1716.

[28] T Kyle, D Thomas, A Ivanescu, Joseph Nadglowski, and Rebecca M Puhld. 2015. Indications of Increasing Social Rejection Related to Weight Bias. *ObesityWeek. Los Angeles (CA), November* 2 (2015).

[29] Theodore K Kyle, Emily J Dhurandhar, and David B Allison. 2016. Regarding obesity as a disease: evolving policies and their implications. *Endocrinology and Metabolism Clinics* 45, 3 (2016), 511–520.

[30] Kristen Lovejoy and Gregory D Saxton. 2012. Information, community, and action: How nonprofit organizations use social media. *Journal of Computer-Mediated Communication* 17, 3 (2012), 337–353.

[31] Janet A Lydecker, Elizabeth W Cotter, Allison A Palmberg, Courtney Simpson, Melissa Kwitowski, Kelly White, and Suzanne E Mazzeo. 2016. Does this Tweet

make me look fat? A content analysis of weight stigma on Twitter. *Eating and Weight Disorders-Studies on Anorexia, Bulimia and Obesity* 21, 2 (2016), 229–235.

[32] Yelena Mejova, Sofiane Abbar, and Hamed Haddadi. 2016. Fetishizing Food in Digital Age:# foodporn Around the World.. In *ICWSM*. 250–258.

[33] Yelena Mejova, Hamed Haddadi, Anastasios Noulas, and Ingmar Weber. 2015. # foodporn: Obesity patterns in culinary interactions. In *Proceedings of the 5th International Conference on Digital Health 2015. ACM*, 51–58.

[34] Cynthia L Ogden, Margaret D. Carroll, Cheryl D. Fryar, and Katherine M. Flegal. 2015. Prevalence of Obesity Among Adults and Youth: United States, 2011–2014. *NCHS Data Brief* 219 (2015).

[35] Hyojung Park, Bryan H Reber, and Myoung-Gi Chon. 2016. Tweeting as health communication: health organizations' use of twitter for health promotion and public engagement. *Journal of health communication* 21, 2 (2016), 188–198.

[36] Andrew Pollack. 2013. A.M.A. Recognizes Obesity as a Disease. *The New York Times* (2013). http://www.nytimes.com/2013/06/19/business/ama-recognizes-obesity-as-a-disease.html?smid=pl-share

[37] James O. Prochaska and Carlo C. DiClemente. 2005. The Transtheoretical Approach. *Handbook of psychotherapy integration* (2005).

[38] Rebecca M Puhl and Kelly D Brownell. 2003. Psychosocial origins of obesity stigma: toward changing a powerful and pervasive bias. *Obesity reviews* 4, 4 (2003), 213–227.

[39] Barbara J Rolls and Elizabeth A Bell. 2000. Dietary approaches to the treatment of obesity. *Medical Clinics of North America* 84, 2 (2000), 401–418.

[40] Amaia Salvador, Nicholas Hynes, Yusuf Aytar, Javier Marin, Ferda Ofli, Ingmar Weber, and Antonio Torralba. 2017. Learning Cross-modal Embeddings for Cooking Recipes and Food Images. *Training* 720 (2017), 619–508.

[41] Jane Sarasohn-Kahn. 2008. The wisdom of patients: Health care meets online social media. (2008).

[42] Megha Sharma, Kapil Yadav, Nitika Yadav, and Keith C Ferdinand. 2017. Zika virus pandemic—analysis of Facebook as a social media health information platform. *American journal of infection control* 45, 3 (2017), 301–302.

[43] Ryan J Shaw and Constance M Johnson. 2011. Health information seeking and social media use on the Internet among people with diabetes. *Online journal of public health informatics* 3, 1 (2011).

[44] Olivia Solon. 2016. In firing human editors, Facebook has lost the fight against fake news. *The Guardian* (2016). https://www.theguardian.com/technology/2016/aug/29/facebook-trending-news-editors-fake-news-stories

[45] Yulia A Strekalova. 2017. Health risk information engagement and amplification on social media: News about an emerging pandemic on Facebook. *Health Education & Behavior* 44, 2 (2017), 332–339.

[46] Besiki Stvilia, Lorri Mon, and Yong Jeong Yi. 2009. A model for online consumer health information quality. *Journal of the Association for Information Science and Technology* 60, 9 (2009), 1781–1791.

[47] Michael Tanner. 2013. Obesity is not a Disease. *National Review* (July 2013). http://www.nationalreview.com/article/352626/obesity-not-disease-michael-tanner

[48] Kurt Thomas, Chris Grier, Dawn Song, and Vern Paxson. 2011. Suspended accounts in retrospect: an analysis of twitter spam. In *Proceedings of the 2011 ACM SIGCOMM conference on Internet measurement conference. ACM*, 243–258.

[49] J. Kevin Thomson and Lauren Schaefer. 2017. Body Image, Obesity, and Eating Disorders. *Eating Disorders and Obesity: A Comprehensive Handbook* (2017), 140.

[50] Anne-Marie Tomchak. 2017. Algorithms are screwing us over with fake news but could also fix the problem. *Mashable* (2017). https://mashable.com/2017/10/05/artificial-intelligence-algorithm-neva-labs/#iQuXMaJJeaqU

[51] Amar Toor. 2016. Reuters built an algorithm to flag and verify breaking news on Twitter. *The Verge* (2016). https://www.theverge.com/2016/12/1/13804542/reuters-algorithm-breaking-news-twitter

[52] Emily K Vraga and Leticia Bode. 2017. I do not believe you: how providing a source corrects health misperceptions across social media platforms. *Information, Communication & Society* (2017), 1–17.

[53] Leila Weitzel, José Palazzo M de Oliveira, and Paulo Quaresma. 2014. Measuring the reputation in user-generated-content systems based on health information. *Procedia Computer Science* 29 (2014), 364–378.

[54] Elad Yom-Tov and Luis Fernandez-Luque. 2014. Information is in the eye of the beholder: Seeking information on the MMR vaccine through an Internet search engine. In *AMIA Annual Symposium Proceedings*, Vol. 2014. American Medical Informatics Association, 1238.

[55] Elad Yom-Tov, Luis Fernandez-Luque, Ingmar Weber, and Steven P Crain. 2012. Pro-anorexia and pro-recovery photo sharing: a tale of two warring tribes. *Journal of medical Internet research* 14, 6 (2012).

Engaging pictograms! A Methodology for Graphic Design in enhancing Player Engagement

As Applied to the Design of a Serious Game for Nepalese Women with Low Literacy

Delphine Soriano
UCL Institute for Risk and Disaster Reduction
London, United Kingdom
d.soriano@ucl.ac.uk

Abriti Arjyal and Sushil Baral
Health Research and Social Development
Kathmandu, Nepal
abriti.arjyal@herdint.com
sushil.baral@herdint.com

Andrei Boscor
UCL Institute for Risk and Disaster Reduction
London, United Kingdom
andrei.boscor.14@ucl.ac.uk

Sonja Mueller
UCL Institute for Risk and Disaster Reduction
London, United Kingdom
sonja.mueller.14@ucl.ac.uk

Gareth J. Hearn
Hearn Geoserve Ltd
United Kingdom
gareth@hearngeoserve.co.uk

Naomi M Saville
UCL Institute for Global Health
London, United Kingdom
n.saville@ucl.ac.uk

Maureen Fordham
UCL Institute for Risk and Disaster Reduction
London, United Kingdom
m.fordham@ucl.ac.uk

Virgine Le Masson
Overseas Development Institute
London, United Kingdom
v.lemasson@odi.org.uk

Patty Kostkova
UCL Institute for Risk and Disaster Reduction
London, United Kingdom
p.kostkova@ucl.ac.uk

ABSTRACT

In the graphic design of serious games, player engagement is an important consideration. We propose a new approach towards aiding the graphic designer to consider the major factors relevant to player engagement. This article describes a method for creating effective graphical content for serious games that takes into account the impact of complex pictograms on player engagement and on the learning process. We show how we applied our method to the design of a serious game for mobile phones aimed at Nepalese women in rural areas with low literacy skills. Initial results from case study suggest that our method helps designers to improve the design and the logic behind their use of imagery to the extent where the need to use text in the game's user interface was removed.

CCS CONCEPTS

• **Human-centered computing** → **Graphical user interfaces**; **HCI theory, concepts and models**; • **Applied computing** → *E-learning*;

KEYWORDS

method; engagement; graphic design; pictogram; visual complexity; abstraction; serious game; e-learning

ACM Reference Format:
Delphine Soriano, Abriti Arjyal and Sushil Baral, Andrei Boscor, Sonja Mueller, Gareth J. Hearn, Naomi M Saville, Maureen Fordham, Virgine Le Masson, and Patty Kostkova. 2018. Engaging pictograms! A Methodology for Graphic Design in enhancing Player Engagement: As Applied to the Design of a Serious Game for Nepalese Women with Low Literacy. In *DH'18: 2018 International Digital Health Conference, April 23–26, 2018, Lyon, France.* ACM, New York, NY, USA, 5 pages. https://doi.org/10.1145/3194658.3194673

1 INTRODUCTION

Player engagement or motivation appears to be linked to the learning process within a game [23]. Feeling engaged during a serious game playing session helps the learner comprehend, try again or feel a sense of satisfaction [10, 14]. Many characteristics of graphical content can have an impact on the player's experience [20]. One of the main challenges in serious game design is in designing visuals that will to satisfy a given learning objectives. Frequently this concerns making a choice between text - to maximise the precision of the information being conveyed; and images - to achieve a more emotional effect, which is considered essential to player engagement [15]. Nelson et al. [12] found that players' memory performance when presented with different styles of images (either photographs or drawings) did not vary significantly; whereas when players were presented with text, memory performance was significantly worse as compared with images. Depending on the game mechanics, using text to convey information may have a damaging effect on a serious game's effectiveness. In addition, Lan-Ting and Kun-Chou [6] have found that learners prefer images with a determinate level of visual complexity when using small screens.

Until now, these findings related to player engagement and the use of images have not been applied to serious game design. Yet this research suggests that by correctly designing and managing the use of images in our designs we can improve the experience of players. Indeed, they can inform our approach to one of the key challenges in the design of serious games (particularly educational games): that of how to produce images that are effective for driving engagement. Woodrow [22] proposes a method for the design of universal health care icons. While this is a serviceable method from the point of view of a graphic designer, it fails to take into account the context for the images (e.g. the type of screen they are displayed on), user interaction, and issues relevant to designing for player engagement in a serious game.

In the absence of research into this cross-disciplinary question of how visual design affects player engagement we propose a method for designing 2D pictograms for educational serious games [10]. Below we describe how we applied this method to the design of MANTRA, a mobile game for health designed for rural Nepalese women with a low level of literacy. We conclude with a discussion of our case study and our further works

2 BACKGROUND AND RELATED WORK

2.1 Engagement and graphical content

2.1.1 The sensation of engagement. Player engagement is commonly defined using concepts such as motivation, emotion and fun [4, 15, 17]. Brockmyer et al. [1] meanwhile, associate player engagement with the sensation of presence. According to Lombard and Ditton [7], presence occurs when players consider both themselves and the game content to be sharing the same reality. For engagement and presence, the player's emotions during and after the game constitute a major factor [1, 15]. Indeed, O'Brien and Tom [15] stress affect in their definition of player engagement and Kostkova [5] studied the importance of the concept for healthcare domain. Their approach integrates concepts such as a game's aesthetics, sensory appeal and the feedback given to user.

2.1.2 Graphical content for learning. Natkin et al. [11] have shown that certain popular and highly-engaging video games can augment players' interest in scientific topics. These are video games that include scientific content represented by the game mechanics and the game's graphical content. However, graphical content cannot be defined merely by the information that it conveys. McLaughlin et al. [9] have shown that game characters in serious games are more effective for the learning process when they are depicted in an abstract as opposed to a realistic way. But player engagement also has an impact on the learning process [23] and realistic virtual environments can increase the player's sense of presence, thereby impacting player engagement [1, 7]. Realism is defined by Lombard and Ditton [7] as the degree to which a medium produces accurate representations of objects. Abstraction is defined by McCloud [8] as the opposite of realism. He defines an abstract object as a graphic form without meaning, the visual elements of which are reduced until it retains only its essential elements. We can say, therefore, that the player's emotions, sense of enjoyment, and the game's aesthetics and success of its visual feedback all appear to be dependant on the level of player engagement, and this engagement is in turn dependant on the style of the game's graphical content (realism and abstraction). We can incorporate these considerations into a framework for the graphic designer, we must first establish an adapted terminology.

2.2 Terminology of graphic content

2.2.1 Content composed by graphic objects. Our approach requires differentiating the graphic objects that constitute the graphic design of a game according to their complexity. To this end, we have identified three key of types of an imagery: the sign, the symbol and the pictogram. The sign is defined by Rasmussen [18] as an object that triggers specific, predefined acts or behaviors he calls "rule-based-behaviours", which involve low-level perception. The symbol is an object that triggers "knowledge-based behaviour", and appears to require more experience to be understood or perceived in order to trigger a user action. The pictogram represents complex concepts. A designer creates pictograms by combining various simple graphic objects, such as graphemes and icons [21][1].

Figure 1: "Oncology" pictogram (a) [21]; high and medium level complexity (b) [6]

2.2.2 The complex pictogram paradigm. A pictogram is a more or less a stylized image that conveys complex informational content. For instance, Strauss and Zender [21] propose designing pictograms (see fig. 1-a) based on a set of concepts known by the users. They consider a pictogram to be a complex graphic object composed of elementary graphic objects such as icons and symbols. Icons, as defined by Ng and Chan [13] comprise both graphic features (colour, outline shape and size) and cognitive features (familiarity and meaningfulness) and can be characterized as having an visual appearance that has a certain effect on users.

Complexity has a cost, however. Some studies have found that the level of complexity of images has an impact on the users' memory performance (A "medium and low complexity" image might show characters but no background, for example.) [12, 16]. In addition, Lan-Ting and Kun-Chou [6] have found that learners prefer medium complexity images on mobile screens (see fig. 1-b). However, while these studies signal the importance in design of taking memory performance into consideration (for example, by stylizing the image or deleting the its background) they do not take into account the meaning of the image being displayed (as Strauss and Zender [21]).

In a serious game, pictograms must take account of both their meaning and their impact on the cognitive process of the player. In addition, must be "playable" in the context of the wider gameplay design and the way they contribute to the player's sense of engagement.

---

[1]According to Strauss and Zender [21], a grapheme is a graphic object that may or may not have meaning; an icon is composed of graphemes and represents a simple concept.

3 DESIGNING COMPLEX PICTOGRAMS

We propose a novel method for designing complex pictograms for serious games that takes into account both the impact of visual complexity on memory performance and the ways in which graphical content affects player engagement. Our method comprises two complementary frameworks: one relating to graphical intentions (symbolic, aesthetic, fact) and another relating to graphical style (realism, abstraction). We envision the designer positioning their design of a pictogram somewhere in a continuum between these attributes.

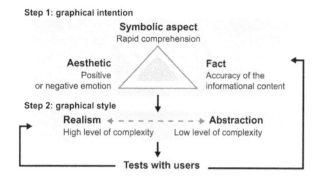

Figure 2: Method

3.1 Step 1: graphical intention

Figure 2 (step 01) shows how to emotions can be managed relative to the "quality" of the meaning and the accuracy of a pictogram's informational content. The grey area indicates the ideal positioning for a complex pictogram. Placement in this area depends on the designer's sensibilities, the intended message of the pictogram, and on the gameplay.

The term "aesthetics" in this context represents the emotional response inspired by the graphical content. According to Hunicke et al.'s three-value model for analyzing video games [3], aesthetics are the emotional responses aroused in the player during the game. This emotional element can be inspired by the graphical characteristics of a image in concert with the game mechanics and the dynamics of meaningful interaction. This "emotional part" is both an effective and a necessary factor toward achieving player engagement.

As with a game's interactive elements, symbolic elements serve to provoke player behaviors. For contexts in which the player is required to make decisions, a designer has to consider using images that draw upon the player's knowledge, as the rapid evocation of meaning is critical to ensuring smooth gameplay flow. In video games, known graphic objects or typographical signs can be used for this purpose, e.g. a question mark above the head of a quest character. Such conventions are commonly used in video games.

The "fact" component of this framework can be understood as the degree of "accuracy" used to convey information and knowledge in the game. For instance, a photograph or piece of text may be more exact or accurate than a complex pictogram but nevertheless not useful in the context of a game. "Fact" describes the serious part of a serious game.

Complex pictograms must be close to an emotional effect to improve player engagement, close to a symbolic representation for quick understanding to allow to play and close to accurate information for the serious part of the game.

3.2 Step 2: graphical style

Figure 2 (step 02) illustrates our second framework, "graphical style", which takes into account realism and abstraction[2]. These are two components that are important considerations in both in the context of player engagement and in graphic design theory [8]. For our purposes we measure realism and abstraction through the lens of complexity level, i.e. the level of visual complexity, which, as we have noted above, has an impact on memory performance.

A graphic designer must position their design between these two opposing styles considering player engagement (realism) and the learning process (abstraction). McCloud [8] emphasizes that a single image can be composed of both abstract and realistic elements. In addition, one can assume that in a serious game, the player requires more time to "read" (as opposed to understand) complex, realistic elements than more stylized ones. Finally, players tend to focus their attention on recognizable details; the designer can use this to determine how best to convey information.

3.3 Tests with users

In order to validate and understanding of meaning of each pictogram, the last step is to conduct tests with users. According to Strauss and Zender [21], use direct questions to know which graphic objects are useful for composing these pictograms is efficient (e.g. stethoscope for a doctor). Also, we believe these pictograms need to be evaluated in the context of the game (e.g delay of interactions, error rate). Depending on the required changes, a designer reviews the graphical intention of the pictogram (step 1: e.g the meaning is not clear - fact, users "dislike", reject the image - aesthetic) or/and adjusts the graphical style (step 2: e.g the designer adds a new graphical object).

4 CASE STUDY: MANTRA

The goal of MANTRA project is to use mobile technology to help increase maternal and child resilience in rural areas before, during and after disasters using mobile technology in Nepal[3].

4.1 MANTRA, the mobile game

MANTRA is a game for public health education [19]. It is designed to improve the level of health knowledge among rural Nepalese women by teaching them how to assess the level of danger posed by various situations. Because of the lack of literacy skills, the player has to make choices and progress through the game via an entirely graphical interface (as verbal cues are not used).

It is a "point and click" style of mobile game with drag-and-drop style interactions[4]. It features three playable categories: maternal health, neonatal health and geohazards. Figure 3 shows the game

[2]See section 2.1 for the definitions.
[3]Acknowledgment to the Global Challenge Research Fund (GCRF): the Natural Environment Research Council (NERC), the Arts & Humanities Research Council (AHRC), the Economic & Social Research Council (ESRC). NERC Ref.: NE/P016103/1
[4]The player uses her finger to initiate the interaction, then uses her finger to move the image to another part of the screen.

Figure 3: Second test session in Chyamrangbesi, Nepal.

interface after our test and modifications. On the left are images called "learning objective" (LO) and on the right, an image called "answer". Game difficulty is progressively increased by the inclusion of more potential responses and player progress is shown via a score bar. To start playing, the player selects what she considers to be the best LO image to match the answer and drags and drops it onto the answer image. If the player has chosen the correct LO image, she wins a point. For each successfully completed level, the player wins a flower. Overall progression is represented in terms of the number of completed flowers for each level and category.

4.2 Applying our method

In this section we explain how our method was applied to the design of complex pictograms to convey information and impart knowledge to the player toward the attainment of learning objectives (see Fig. 4-b).

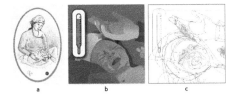

Figure 4: The baby has a fever.

4.2.1 Design workflow. The visual reference used for the creation of these illustrations produced as part of a research project[5] (see Fig. 4-a) for a card game. We used the cards to inspire and inform the visual "ambience" of our game (e.g. clothes, preferred postures). We also looked at photographs taken within the target area (e.g. skin color, vegetation). First, we created sketches that we considered to be optimal, in terms of framing, positioning, size, viewing angle, composition, and so forth. Next, we created photo montages in order to determine what the "realistic" elements might be, according to our method. Finally, we drew our pictograms, using the photo montages as reference.

4.2.2 Example: designing our "baby with fever" pictogram. To give a concrete example of how we applied our method to the game MANTRA, here we describe how we designed a pictogram called "baby with fever" (see fig. 4).

Using our "graphical intentions" framework (aesthetic, symbolic, fact) we applied an "aesthetic-emotion" intention by showing a crying baby being soothed by an adult's hand. To achieve "rapid

symbolic meaning", we used relatively few colors, linear or circular shading and simple forms. In terms of "factual/informational content", we stayed focused on the main message. For instance, we avoided using any disruptively decorative graphic objects and we used additional element to reinforce the message e.g. a red halo on the baby's forehead. See Fig. 4-b.

To apply our "graphical style" framework (realism, abstraction) while also respecting the design choices used for the first framework, we structured the pictograms into three layers of visual elements: realistic, abstract, and the background. We included the informational content we wanted to focus on the most within the more realistic layer of visual elements. For instance, the baby's face and the mother's hand are portrayed more with more realism than the other parts of the image[6] (see Fig. 4-b). We used shading, shadows and/or a larger number of vectorial points to produce this realistic layer (see Fig. 4-c and red areas). The "abstract" layer is composed of a single colour and a very small number of vectorial points. The background is a solid colour in order to lend a "medium" or "high" complexity to this pictogram [6].

4.2.3 The background. We varied the background color of the pictograms in order to limit the potential "appearance association" effect of the pictogram representing the correct answer. For 24 pictograms we used 10 randomly chosen colored backgrounds. We assumed that this system would contribute to an interface that was more visually dynamic and would focus the player's attention on the meaning of the pictogram.

4.3 Tests with users

4.3.1 Participants and method. We visited communities in Chandenimandan, Chyamrangbesi and Siddhipur in Nepal for the first session test. A total of 34 women participated in these interviews discussing the pictograms in Nepalese. Firstly, each pictogram was shown to participants on a paper (in pairs or individually, depending on group sizes). After observing their reaction, they were asked to define the meaning of the images (e.g. "what do you recognize?", "What do you think is on this image?"). Depending on the responses, correct meaning was explained. Then, participants were asked what graphical objects could be added or deleted to improve the image. Each interview covering 28 pictograms took about 30 - 40 minutes. All the comments were noted, and translated to English for the designer.

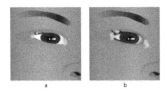

Figure 5: Before the test (a); after the modifications (b).

4.3.2 Result: an example, our design of "eyes infection". First, the participants seems to "dislike" this image - see Fig. 5-a (e.g. leave them indifferent, no particular emotion is shown). Although

[5]Mother and Infant Research Activities; funded by the Department for International Development and the Institute for Global Health, London,2016.

[6]To achieve an optimum composition and viewing angle, we drew the hand of the baby in the realistic style.

the medical case condition was recognized by most of them, we decided to reinforce the meaning of the pictogram and improve its affective aspect at the same time (step1 of our model). Our major modification was adding a red area (fact / medical symptom) and outline the eye in black [7] (aesthetic). According our model and for the step 2, we used a gradient from red colour to transparent (realistic area) - see Fig. 5-b.

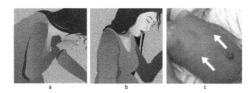

Figure 6: "vomiting" (a), "anaemia" (b), "chest indrawing" (c).

4.3.3 Discussion. Our method proved robust enough to address most of the learning objectives for our game MANTRA. Out of 28 learning objectives, only 4 could not be portrayed using our method alone. The main challenge we encountered arose when we attempted to represent diseases and symptoms such as "anaemia" (fatigue, breathlessness, pale face - see Fig. 6-b) and "chest indrawing", a symptom of pneumonia - see Fig. 6-c[8]. As breathlessness can be a symptom of both anaemia and pneumonia, a precise representation of chest indrawing, showing the precisely manner how the sick baby breathes, was necessary to be distinguished from other types of breathlessness.

5 CONCLUSIONS AND FURTHER WORKS

We propose a method for graphic design for games that enables designers to consider the impact of their design on player engagement, specifically for serious games. Our method introduces key paradigms for designing meaningful pictograms that affects player engagement into the graphic design process. Applying scientific findings about player engagement and memory performance to the design process can guide the designer's work and help the designer produce more impactful games. We have applied our method to the creation of a "visual language" used in a serious game that deals with the health risks faced by Nepalese women. Our initial results suggest that our method can directly assist designers in formalizing the main intention of each learning objective. In addition, using a bespoke method like this for conceptualizing a pictogram during the design process enhances collaboration with experts, informing the allocation of resources and shaping expectations.

For evaluating serious games, a mixed-method, cross-data analysis can be useful [4]. A next logical step could be to expand our method to include the animation process, thus widening the scope for possible representations and increasing the depth of the information able to be conveyed. Another step could be to adapt this method for the 3D design process. For example, the use of saturated, lighter colours in a 3D real-time engine is effective for evoking drama in a scene [2]; hence, for 3D interactive scenes, the saturation level should be included in any design method for serious games in order to better manage the evocation of emotion. To improve our method, it will be necessary to evaluate the impact of its use upon the effectiveness of a serious game it is used to help design.

REFERENCES

[1] Jeanne H. Brockmyer, Christine M. Fox, Kathleen A. Curtiss, Evan McBroom, Kimberly M. Burkhart, and Jacquelyn N. Pidruzny. 2009. The development of the Game Engagement Questionnaire : A measure of engagement in video game-playing. *Journal of Experimental Social Psychology* 45 (2009), 624–634.

[2] Magy Seif El-Nasr. 2006. Projecting tension in virtual environments through lighting. In *Proceedings of the 2006 ACM SIGCHI international conference on Advances in computer entertainment technology (ACE '06)*. ACM, New York, NY, USA, Article 63. https://doi.org/10.1145/1178823.1178898

[3] Robin Hunicke, Marc LeBlanc, and Robert Zubek. 2004. MDA: A formal approach to game design and game research. In *Proceedings of the AAAI Workshop on Challenges in Game AI.*

[4] K. Karadimitriou and M. Roussou. 2011. Studying Player Experience in a Collaborative Embodied Interaction Game. In *Games and Virtual Worlds for Serious Applications (VS-GAMES), 2011 Third International Conference on.* IEEE, 199–206.

[5] Patty Kostkova. 2016. User engagement with digital health technologies. In *Why Engagement Matters.* Springer, 127–156.

[6] Wang Lan-Ting and Lee Kun-Chou. 2014. The Study of Learners' Preference for Visual Complexity on Small Screens of Mobile Computers Using Neural Networks. *TOJET: The Turkish Online Journal of Educational Technology* 13, 2 (2014).

[7] Matthew Lombard and Theresa Ditton. 1997. At the Heart of It All : The Concept of Presence. *Journal of Computer Mediated Communication* 3 (1997).

[8] Scott McCloud. 1993. *Understanding Comics : The Invisible Art.* HarperCollins Publishers.

[9] Tim McLaughlin, Dennie Smith, and Irving A Brown. 2010. A framework for evidence based visual style development for serious games. In *Proceedings of the Fifth International Conference on the Foundations of Digital Games.* ACM, 132–138.

[10] Andreea Molnar and Patty Kostkova. 2013. On effective integration of educational content in serious games: Text vs. game mechanics. In *Advanced Learning Technologies (ICALT), 2013 IEEE 13th International Conference on.* IEEE, 299–303.

[11] Stephane Natkin, Delphine Soriano, Grozdana Erjavec, and Marie Durand. 2013. Could the Player's Engagement in a Video Game Increase His/Her Interest in Science? *LNCS proceedings - Advances in Computer Entertainment* 8253 (2013), 608–611.

[12] Thomas O Nelson, Jacqueline Metzler, and David A Reed. 1974. Role of details in the long-term recognition of pictures and verbal descriptions. *Journal of Experimental Psychology* 102, 1 (1974), 184.

[13] Annie Wy Ng and Alan Hs Chan. 2009. What Makes an Icon Effective? *AIP Conference Proceedings* 1089, 1 (2009), 104–114. https://doi.org/10.1063/1.3078113 arXiv:http://aip.scitation.org/doi/pdf/10.1063/1.3078113

[14] Heather O'Brien and Paul Cairns. 2016. *Why Engagement Matters: Cross-Disciplinary Perspectives of User Engagement in Digital Media.* Springer.

[15] Heather L O'Brien and Elaine G Toms. 2008. What is user engagement A conceptual framework for defining user engagement with technology. *Journal of the American Society for Information Science and Technology* 59, 6 (2008), 938–955.

[16] Kathy Pezdek, Ruth Maki, Debra Valencia-Laver, Tony Whetstone, Janet Stoeckert, and Tom Dougherty. 1988. Picture memory: Recognizing added and deleted details. *Journal of Experimental Psychology: Learning, Memory, and Cognition* 14, 3 (1988), 468.

[17] Andrew K Przybylski, C Scott Rigby, and Richard M Ryan. 2010. A motivational model of video game engagement. *Review of General Psychology* 14, 2 (2010). http://apps.isiknowledge.com.molly.ruc.dk/full_record.do?product=WOS&search_mode=GeneralSearch&qid=8&SID=Y2HD4jeAFEdPHIlllL5&page=1&doc=1

[18] Jens Rasmussen. 1983. Skills, rules, and knowledge; signals, signs, and symbols, and other distinctions in human performance models. *Systems, Man and Cybernetics, IEEE Transactions on* 3 (1983), 257–266.

[19] Ben Sawyer and Peter Smith. 2008. Serious Games Taxonomy. (Feb. 2008). http://www.seriousgames.org/presentations/serious-games-taxonomy-2008_web.pdfhttp://fr.slideshare.net/Caspianchris/taxonomy-of-serious-games

[20] J.L. Sherry, K. Lucas, BS Greenberg, and K. Lachlan. 2006. Video game uses and gratifications as predictors of use and game preference. *Playing video games. Motives, responses, and consequences* (2006), 213–224.

[21] Alisa Strauss and Mike Zender. 2017. *Design By Consensus: A New Method for Designing Effective Pictograms.* Chapter 51.2, 7–33.

[22] Jeffery Woodrow. 2016. ULOU: Universal Language of Understanding Designing a set of universal health care icons. (2016).

[23] Gabe Zichermann. 2010. Fun is the Future: Mastering Gamification. In *http://www.gamesfornature.org/.*

---

[7] The mothers outline the eyes of their babies in black in this area of Nepal.

[8] From "IMCI training video: identifying chest indrawing". The lower ribs of the chest are drawn in when the child takes a breath.

Does Journaling Encourage Healthier Choices?
Analyzing Healthy Eating Behaviors of Food Journalers

Palakorn Achananuparp
Singapore Management University
Singapore, Singapore
palakorna@smu.edu.sg

Ee-Peng Lim
Singapore Management University
Singapore, Singapore
eplim@smu.edu.sg

Vibhanshu Abhishek
Carnegie Mellon University
Pittsburgh, PA
vibs@andrew.cmu.edu

ABSTRACT

Past research has shown the benefits of food journaling in promoting mindful eating and healthier food choices. However, the links between journaling and healthy eating have not been thoroughly examined. Beyond caloric restriction, do journalers consistently and sufficiently consume healthful diets? How different are their eating habits compared to those of average consumers who tend to be less conscious about health? In this study, we analyze the healthy eating behaviors of active food journalers using data from MyFitnessPal. Surprisingly, our findings show that food journalers do not eat as healthily as they should despite their proclivity to health eating and their food choices resemble those of the general populace. Furthermore, we find that the journaling duration is only a marginal determinant of healthy eating outcomes and sociodemographic factors, such as gender and regions of residence, are much more predictive of healthy food choices.

CCS CONCEPTS

• **Applied computing** → **Health informatics**; *Consumer health*;

KEYWORDS

Healthy Eating; Eating Behaviors; Food Journals; Quantified Self

ACM Reference Format:
Palakorn Achananuparp, Ee-Peng Lim, and Vibhanshu Abhishek. 2018. Does Journaling Encourage Healthier Choices? Analyzing Healthy Eating Behaviors of Food Journalers. In *DH'18: 2018 International Digital Health Conference, April 23–26, 2018, Lyon, France*. ACM, New York, NY, USA, 10 pages. https://doi.org/10.1145/3194658.3194663

1 INTRODUCTION

Recent progress in mobile and wearable technologies has provided individuals the means to routinely track data about themselves for self-knowledge and improvement. This self-tracking practice is also known as *quantified self* or *personal informatics*. In the domain of dietary self-monitoring, mobile food journal apps, such as MyFitnessPal (MFP hereafter), are one of the most popular tracking methods widely used by millions of people. Past research has suggested that food journaling is an effective intervention in weight loss programs [9]. The act of journaling helps create increased in-the-moment awareness (mindfulness) and can encourage healthier choices [13, 14]. Understanding how the journaling practice affects eating behaviors may provide useful insights for the designs of an effective population-wide health intervention. While there is growing evidence supporting the critical role of food journals in improving weight loss outcomes, little empirical work has been done to investigate the broader impacts of the journaling practice on the individuals' healthy eating behaviors. Especially, more evidence is needed to: (1) quantitatively compare long-term healthy eating habits of food journalers with other behavioral baselines, such as the general public and the dietary recommendations; and (2) measure the influences of the journaling practice on the healthy eating outcomes with respect to other factors. From a methodological perspective, it is also an opportunity to further explore the use of a large-scale self-tracking data in conjunction with offline data sources to answer these questions.

To address the research gaps, our study aims to assess the healthy eating behaviors of food journalers by analyzing public food diary entries of MFP users and comparing their eating behaviors to those of the general populace reported in other studies. Although people tend *not* to perceive healthy eating the same ways as public-health experts [5, 41], a recent survey [13] suggests that a vast number of food journalers (past and present) generally agree with experts about the notion of healthy eating, e.g., most believe that they should eat more fruits and vegetables, lean meat, and balanced diets. Thus, it is reasonable to assume that food journalers are more likely to achieve evidence-based healthy eating outcomes, as defined by public-health experts, than the average consumers who may be less informed about healthy eating. Next, we expect active food journalers, who are likely to develop a mindful eating habit, to consciously make healthy food choices and be less influenced by the sociodemographic biases. Specifically, we formulate the following research questions:

RQ1: *Do active food journalers have healthier eating behaviors than the general populace?*

To investigate the effectiveness of journaling in encouraging healthier food choices, we aim to characterize the healthy eating behaviors of food journalers using the corresponding intakes from the dietary guidelines and the general populace as comparison data. If food journalers tend to (1) have higher intakes of healthy diets and lower intakes of unhealthy diets than the general populace and (2) consistently meet the recommended intakes per the dietary guidelines, then such findings may provide evidence supporting the notion that not only does journaling is linked to significant weight loss, but it also plays a significant role in individuals' healthier food choices.

RQ2: *How do the eating behaviors of food journalers significantly differ across sociodemographic groups?*

Mindless eating describes a situation where individuals are unaware of the influences exerted on their food choices by external factors, such as the environment and gender roles. It is generally associated with unhealthy eating habits and weight gains [45]. Here, we seek to further examine the relationship between the healthier food choices effect of journaling and the healthy eating behaviors of food journalers. Specifically, we expect food journalers of different sociodemographic backgrounds (e.g., gender, age, etc.) to be equally conscious of their food choices such that their healthy eating behavior is more homogeneous than that of the general populace. For example, male and female journalers should consume a comparable amount of fruits and vegetables. In other words, the difference in fruit and vegetable intakes between male and female journalers should not be statistically significant.

RQ3: *To what extent does the journaling practice influence the eating behaviors of food journalers?*

Past research has shown that weight loss outcomes are proportional to the journaling practice. That is, individuals who are more active in recording their food journals tend to lose more weights than the less active journalers [9]. As such, we aim to quantify the impacts of *journaling duration* and *persistence* on the healthy eating behaviors using regression analysis. If food journaling in fact encourages healthier food choices and mindful eating, we expect the journaling factors to have a higher influence on the eating behaviors than the sociodemographic factors. Such findings, together with those from the other research questions, will help demonstrate that food journaling is an effective healthy lifestyle intervention. On the other hand, unexpected results may provide us insights into the flaws of mobile food journals in affecting health behavior changes.

The main contributions of our work are as follows. *Firstly*, we thoroughly examine the relationship between food journaling, sociodemographic factors, and a variety of healthy eating behaviors in a large population of nearly 10,000 active food journalers over a six-month period. *Secondly*, we present our data preprocessing steps to automatically generate an analysis-ready dataset including: (1) identifying relevant foods and beverages from the annotated food diary entries; (2) extracting portion sizes of foods and beverages from the food diary entry text and the associated caloric value; and (3) normalizing the portion sizes of varying measurement units into standard nutritional units. *Lastly*, our findings suggest, in contrast to past studies, that the journaling duration only plays a minor role in determining healthy eating behaviors, whereas several other factors, such as gender, journaling persistence, and regions of residence, are much more influential in determining the healthy eating behaviors than the journaling duration.

In what follows, we begin by reviewing related work on food journaling and data-driven approaches to health behavior assessment. Then, we introduce the healthy eating behaviors considered in the study. Next, we describe the dataset and data preprocessing steps. In the subsequent section, we define (1) the quantitative measures of the eating behaviors; and (2) the sociodemographic and journaling factors being studied. Finally, we present the findings, discuss their significance on the food journaling practice and future design implications, and conclude the paper.

2 RELATED WORK

2.1 Personal informatics and food journaling

Much research in personal informatics has focused on characterizing the use of tools and technologies to track one's own personal data for self-discovery and behavior change in a variety of domains [19, 41]. In particular, a few researchers have explored the use of mobile food journals and other online tools for dietary self-tracking in recent years [13, 14, 18]. Cordeiro et al. identified several key challenges related to the journaling tools and practices, such as unreliable data and negative nudges [14]. To overcome tracking burden and promote mindful eating, Epstein et al. proposed a lightweight food journal [18]. Recently, Chung et al. [11] studied the practice of food tracking amongst Instagram users and the role of social support on their healthy eating pursuit.

Our work is complementary to previous food journaling research [13, 14, 18, 19]. While many studies aimed to qualitatively characterize various aspects of the self-tracking practices, few studies have taken a computational approach to examine the broader impacts of journaling on the healthy eating behaviors of food journalers. In this study, we analyze more than 1 million food diary entries to quantitatively assess the behavioral impacts of journaling.

2.2 Using online data to assess health behaviors

Data from online social media, quantified-self, and others have been used to study various aspects of health behaviors. First, a few studies [1, 15] analyzed mentions of foods in the Twitter network to track major public health issues. Next, Park et al. [39] investigated the impacts of user profile, fitness activity, and fitness network of Twitter users on the long-term engagement of fitness app users. Mejova et al. [31] analyzed food pictures shared by Instagram users to study the prevalence of obesity. Recently, a few studies have investigated the tasks of predicting diet compliance outcomes using MFP food diary data [46] together with Twitter data [17].

Our work is highly relevant to [17, 46] in which the researchers constructed computational models to predict diet compliance success using different types of features, such as words & food types identified from MFP diary entries and social and linguistic attributes extracted from the users' social media messages. While their studies particularly focused on caloric balance as the primary outcome, we examine a more comprehensive set of eating behaviors by using evidence-based healthy eating outcomes as the primary measures. Additionally, we investigate the role of sociodemographic and journaling factors, derived from the user profile and food diary data, in determining the healthy eating behaviors.

3 HEALTHY EATING BEHAVIORS

We begin by introducing the evidence-based healthy eating outcomes categorized by the consumption of: (1) fruits and vegetables; (2) animal-based protein sources, such as red and processed meat, poultry, and fish; and (3) added sugars and sugary drinks. They are identified based on growing scientific evidence from several randomized controlled trials and meta-analysis about their associations with health benefits and risks. Together, they constitute dietary intakes commonly recommended by most dietary guidelines [3, 20, 22, 36, 37, 47].

3.1 Fruits and vegetables

High intake of fruits and vegetables (abbreviated as FV) provides a variety of long-term health benefits, such as lowering the risk of cardiovascular disease [44] and cancers [30]. On the other hand, low intakes of FV are associated with the increased prevalence of obesity and diabetes [32]. Generally, a recommended daily FV intake for healthy adults is **at least 5 servings** [32] or approximately 400 - 500 grams [22, 47]. Despite numerous health benefits, the consumption of fruits and vegetables has been persistently low in the US [6] and worldwide [47] for decades. From 1994 - 2005, the average daily FV intake amongst Americans has decreased slightly from **3.43 servings** to **3.24 servings** while the percentage of people who met the recommended daily intake has remained unchanged at about **25%** [6]. In 2015, the Centers for Disease Control and Prevention (CDC) reported that **less than 15%** of Americans sufficiently met the recommendations [22].

3.2 Red and processed meat, poultry, and fish

Growing evidence suggests that processed meat is carcinogenic while red meat is probably carcinogenic [30]. High consumption of red and processed meat may increase mortality rates of type-2 diabetes [4], cardiovascular disease [42] and colorectal cancer [30]. Replacing red and processed meat with healthier protein sources such as white meat (e.g., poultry and fish) [2] may lower the risk of all-cause mortality. Most dietary guidelines recommend to limit a daily intake of red and processed meat to **1 serving** or approximately 65 - 75 grams [20]. Despite high associations with various health risks, red and processed meat still accounts for more than 50% of meat consumed in the United States with almost **2.31 servings** per day [16]. Moreover, the consumption of healthier white meat, such as fish, amongst Americans is low. On average, most adults consumed **0.17 servings** (17.28 grams) of fish a day [38], 70.59% lower than the recommended daily intake of **0.29 servings** (28.57 grams) [3].

3.3 Added sugars and sugary drinks

Added sugars are sugars not naturally occurring in foods and beverages. Asides from sweetening and adding extra calories, they provide no nutritional benefits. Sugary drinks (e.g., sodas/soft drinks, energy drinks, coffee drinks, and fruit juices) are the largest source (36%) of added sugar intake in American diets [35]. According to the recent survey by Gallup [24], **48%** of Americans drink at least 1 glass of soft drink on an average day. Ideally, sugary drink consumption should be avoided at all cost; or else an intake should be limited to **237 milliliters** a day [36]. There is strong evidence linking high consumption of added sugars and sugary drinks to increased risks for obesity and type-2 diabetes, whereas simply lowering the intake of sugary drinks can reduce weight gain and decrease prevalence of obesity [27]. Recent dietary guidelines suggest a maximum daily intake of added sugars to **25 grams** [37]. However, an American adult consumes on average **70 grams** [21] of added sugar per day, 180% higher than the recommended amount.

4 DATA

4.1 Collecting and processing MFP data

We used a public food diary dataset[1] collected from 9,896 MFP users in March 2015 by Weber and Achananuparp [46]. The dataset includes 71,715 unique food entries recorded over 1,919,024 meals from a 6-month recording period between October 2014 to March 2015. Each user recorded 59.3 days of diaries on average (S.D. = 54.6, median = 42). The majority of users were able to achieve their daily caloric goals [46]. Users who recorded at least 7 days of diary entries were treated as active users (N=8,381; 85.69% of all users in the dataset). Each food diary text was automatically annotated with categorical information describing its composition (e.g., food groups) and cooking method in the previous work [46]. In addition, basic nutritional facts (e.g., calories, protein, sugar) for each food entry were available. Next, we performed data cleaning by removing 207 outlying diary entries (0.04% of total data) whose total daily calories are: (1) greater than 6,000 kcal or 2 standard deviations away from the mean daily calories; or (2) lower than or equal to zero kcal.

For each user in the dataset, we further collected personal information from their user profile page. In total, the profile pages of 8,794 users are publicly accessible. Next, we categorized the profile attributes such as age, geographical location, and friend list into the following groups: Age group (young adults age 18-44 years old and old adults age 45 and above), social connection quartiles (Q1: 0-6 friends, Q2: 7-18 friends, Q3: 19-41 friends, and Q4: 42 or more friends), regions of residence at a global level (US and Non-US), and regions of residence within the United States as per the US census classification (Northeast, South, Midwest, and West). As we can see in Table 1, the majority of users are female (82.01%) and young adults 18 - 44 of age (79.80%). Next, more than 50% of users have less than 19 users in their friend list. Most users reside in the United States (70.88%) while the rest of the users live outside the US. Amongst US users, 33.76% live in the Southern states, whereas 18.37% live in the Northeastern states. The geographical distribution of MFP users is representative of the population distribution across US regions [8].

Table 1: Sociodemographic distributions

		Count	%
Gender	Female	7,212	82.01%
	Male	1,582	17.99%
Age group	18-44	7,015	79.80%
	45+	1,776	20.20%
Social connection	Q1 (0-6)	2,681	30.49%
	Q2 (7-18)	2,170	24.68%
	Q3 (19-41)	2,040	23.20%
	Q4 (42+)	1,903	21.64%
Global region	US	6,233	70.88%
	Non-US	2561	29.12%
US region	South	2,104	33.76%
	Midwest	1,593	25.56%
	West	1,391	22.32%
	Northeast	1,145	18.37%

---

[1] http://bit.ly/2hNzRHT

Table 2: Amounts of food equivalent to 1 serving size

	Grams	kcal
Fruit	150	75
Vegetable	75	40
Red meat	65	160
Poultry	80	160
Fish	100	160

4.2 Normalizing and extracting portion sizes

Each diary entry contains a free-text description of the food item (i.e., name and portion size) and nutritional facts, such as calories, protein, sugar. When recording a diary entry, MFP users can choose to enter the amount of food and beverage in various measurement units. For example, the measurement units for *apple* may include weights (grams, ounces, pounds, and kilograms), volumes (cup), physical sizes (small, medium, and large), and nutritional units (servings). To make it possible to directly compare the dietary intakes, we apply the following steps to normalize the portion sizes. First, we extracted quantity and unit from the diary entry text using regular expressions and convert weights and volumes from other measurement systems to grams and milliliters, respectively. Then, we used the annotated categories to identify specific types of diets. First, for solid foods containing only a category of fruit, vegetable, red meat, poultry, or fish, we determined standard serving sizes using the conversions [23] in Table 2. For example, 100 grams of *apple* is equal to 0.67 serving of fruit. If a gram-equivalent weight cannot be found in the diary entry text, the amount of corresponding calories in the diary entry was used for the conversion instead. E.g., a *320-kcal tuna* contains 2 servings of fish. Next, for composite foods typically served with grains and other types of ingredients, we subtract 240 (an average kcal for 1 regular serving of grain-based foods) from the total calories and calculate the serving sizes using the corresponding caloric values in Table 2. With these steps, we can identify 1 serving of fish from *a 400-kcal tuna sandwich*.

4.3 Caloric intake patterns

Figure 1 displays the average daily caloric intakes over time. Overall, the average daily caloric intakes, as seen in Figure 1(a) are around 1,700 kcal and 1,300 kcal for male and female users, respectively. As expected, these are much lower than the estimated calorie requirements of an average adult (2,000 - 2,200 kcal), suggesting that the users were likely dieting. Furthermore, we observe the largest interquartile range of the daily caloric intakes in December, followed by the smallest in January, a possible effect of a new year's weight-loss resolution. Lastly, we compare the daily calorie intakes between weekdays in Figure 1(b). As can be seen, the daily caloric intakes follow the weekday-weekend lifestyle pattern, trending slightly upward from Monday before reaching the largest interquartile range on Saturday.

5 METHODS

5.1 Behavioral measures

Based on the eating behaviors introduced previously, we define the following measures to quantify the behavioral outcomes for each MFP user:

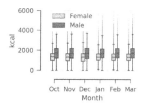

(a) Caloric intake by month

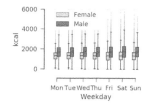

(b) Caloric intake by weekday

Figure 1: Average daily caloric intakes over time (kcal)

Journaling behaviors: Two journaling behaviors are defined to represent the journaling duration and persistence. First, *recording days* is defined as a number of days the user records food diary entries. Second, *normalized lapsing frequency* is defined as a fraction of days the user temporarily stops recording any diary entries with respect to her journaling lifetime (recording days + lapsing days).

Eating behaviors: To measure the energy intake from foods and beverages, we compute *median daily caloric intake* (in kcal). Next, for each diet type, we compute *median daily intake* (in servings for foods, grams for added sugars, and milliliters for drinks) and *normalized intake frequency* (% of days in which the diets were consumed). We used the following criteria to identify specific diet types from the annotated food diary entries. First, fruits and vegetables are selected from entries tagged with *fruit* and *vegetable* categories. Next, red and processed meats are chosen from entries tagged with *beef, pork, lamb, game* (meat from wild animals), *sausage,* and *meatball* sub-categories. Furthermore, poultry and fish are identified from entries tagged with *poultry* and *fish* sub-categories, respectively. Next, added sugars are non-zero sugar content entries tagged with the following categories and sub-categories: *beverage, dessert, snack, condiment,* and *dairy product.* Lastly, sugary drinks include any non-zero sugar content entries tagged with *beverage* category, whereas soft drinks included entries tagged with *soft drink* subcategory. This results in 14 diet-specific behavioral measures.

5.2 Sociodemographic and journaling factors

Now, we introduce the following factors known to be associated with specific healthy eating behaviors below.

Gender and age: Gender and age have been found as contributors of behavioral differences in many dietary behavior studies. For example, women tended to to eat more healthy diets than men, e.g., consuming more fruits and fiber [6]. High consumption of meat and red meat was closely associated with being male [16, 25]. Men also consumed more sugary drinks than women [7]. Next, as people get older, they tended to eat less and changed their eating behaviors. For instance, compared to younger adults, older adults were more likely to consume more fruits and vegetables [6], less red meat as well as all meat [16, 25] but more fish [16], and less sugary drink [7]. In the mean time, younger adults tended to consume more poultry [16]. In this work, we investigate (1) the behavioral differences between genders (male and female), age groups (young and old adults) in RQ2 and (2) the influences of the gender and age factors on all behavioral measures in RQ3.

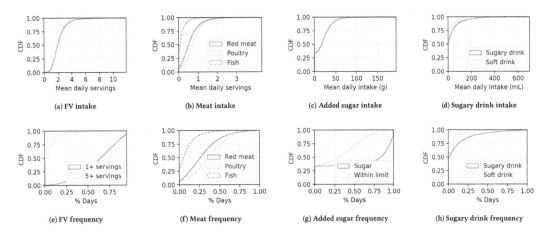

(a) FV intake   (b) Meat intake   (c) Added sugar intake   (d) Sugary drink intake

(e) FV frequency   (f) Meat frequency   (g) Added sugar frequency   (h) Sugary drink frequency

Figure 2: Average daily servings and frequencies

Social connections: Social ties have shown to have both the positive and negative influences on health behaviors [43]. For instance, daily consumption of fruits and vegetables [34] and overall weight loss [28] were associated with high levels of social support. However, having obese friends substantially increased one's own risk of obesity [10]. In this study, we explore (1) the behavioral differences between social connection quartiles in RQ2 and (3) the influence of social connections on all behavioral measures in RQ3.

Regions of residence: Differences in eating behaviors were observed amongst Americans in different regions, which could be attributed to *social norms* and *environmental contexts*. People in the Northeast and the West were more likely to consume more fruits and vegetables than those in the Midwest and the South [6]. Next, beef consumption was highest in Midwest and lowest in the South [25]. In addition, people in the Midwest and the Northeast consumed more sugary drinks than those in the South and the West [40]. Particularly, the consumption of soft drinks was the highest in the Northeast, compared to other regions [40]. In this work, we examine (1) the behavioral differences between regions of residence within the United States (Northeast, South, Midwest, and West) as well as global regions of residence (US vs. non-US) in RQ2 and (2) their influences on all behavioral measures in RQ3.

Journaling: Food journaling can promote mindful eating [13], leading to weight loss [26], and healthier behaviors [18]. Furthermore, the health benefits were greater amongst highly active journalers [9]. In this work, we explore the influence of the journaling behaviors, i.e., recording days and lapsing frequency, on all caloric and diet-specific behavioral measures in RQ3.

6 RESULTS

6.1 RQ1: Distributions of the healthy diet intakes

We first examine the average daily intake and the intake frequency of each diet type over the 6-month period. For each food type, we calculated the cumulative distribution function (CDF) of the mean daily servings and the percentage of days consumed for each user. All CDF plots are shown in Figure 2.

Fruits and vegetables: As shown in Figure 2(a), most food journalers do not consume a sufficient amount of fruits and vegetables on a daily basis. Especially, the average daily FV intake of food journalers is much lower than that of the general populace. In particular, 50% of users consume up to **1.97 servings** of FV per day, whereas only **2.18%** of users (N=183) manage to meet the recommended daily intake of 5 servings. In terms of the frequency of intake, shown in Figure 2(e), 50% of users consume fruits and vegetables up to 64.96% of the time. Furthermore, **less than 1%** of users (N=6) are able to meet the recommended intake at least 80% of the time. This is very surprising since fruits and vegetables should be an essential part of any healthy diets, particularly amongst people trying to lose weight and live a healthier lifestyle.

Red and processed meat, poultry, fish: Unlike typical American consumers, food journalers consume higher portions of healthy protein sources, especially poultry, than unhealthy red and processed meat. As shown in Figure 2(b), 50% of users consume up to **0.53 servings** of red and processed meat and **0.72 servings** of poultry per day. Moreover, the average intakes are within the recommended daily limit of 2 servings. Next, poultry is also consumed more frequently than red and processed meat. According to Figure 2(f), 50% of users consume red meat and poultry up to **26%** and **36%** of the time, respectively. However, the average daily fish intake is much lower than that of other protein sources. Similar to average consumers, food journalers consume much fewer servings of fish per day than the recommended daily intake. Particularly, 50% of users consume **0.09 servings** of fish a day, whereas only **15%** of users (N=1,444) meet the recommendation as shown in Figure 2(b).

Added sugar and sugary drinks: The average daily added sugar intake amongst food journalers is much lower than that of the general populace. According to Figure 2(c), 50% of users consume up to **16 grams** of added sugar per day. However, the top 25% of users consume higher amount of daily added sugar intake (**29.83 grams**) than the recommended limits. Furthermore, the consumption occurs very frequently. As shown in Figure 2(g), 50% of users consume added sugars up to **83%** of the time, whereas the consumption within the recommended limit only accounts for up to **30%** of the time. Next, the overall consumption of sugary

Table 3: Behavioral differences between groups.

Behavioral measure	Gender	Age	Friends	Region US	Region Global
Recording days	Male**	45+**	Q4**	Northeast**	Non-US*
Lapsing frequency	Female**	18-44**	Q1**		
Caloric intake	Male**	18-44*	Q4**		Non-US**
FV intake**	Male**		Q4*	West**	Non-US**
FV frequency	Female**		Q4**	West**	Non-US**
Red meat intake	Male**	45+**		Midwest**	Non-US**
Poultry intake	Male**	18-44**	Q4*	South**	US**
Fish intake					US**
Red meat frequency	Male**	45+**	Q4*	Midwest**	Non-US**
Poultry frequency	Male**	18-44**	Q4*	South*	US**
Fish frequency	Male**	45+**			Non-US**
Added sugar intake		18-44*	Q1**		US**
Sugary drink intake					
Soft drink intake	Male**			Midwest*	US*
Added sugar frequency	Female**		Q1**		US**
Sugary drink frequency	Female*	18-44**	Q1**		
Soft drink frequency		18-44**	Q1**	South**	US**

Significance thresholds are * p<0.05 and ** p<0.01. Caloric intake is in kcal. Food intakes are in numbers of servings. Sugar intake is in grams. Drink intakes are in mL. Intake frequencies are in percentages of days. Cell values represent groups with the highest median. Non-statistically significant results are omitted.

Table 4: Dunn's multiple comparisons for different social connections and US regions.

Behavioral measure	Friends	US regions
Recording days	12*, 13**, 14**, 23**, 24**, 34**	NS*, SM*
Lapsing frequency	14**, 24**, 34**	
Caloric intake	14*, 24**, 34**	
FV intake	24*	SM*, MW**
FV frequency	14**, 23*, 24**	NS**, NM**, SW**, MW**
Red meat intake		NS*, NM**
Poultry intake	34**	NM*, SM*
Fish intake		
Red meat frequency	14*	NS**, NM**, NW**
Poultry frequency	24**, 34**	SM*
Fish frequency		
Added sugar intake	12**, 13**, 14**, 24**, 34**	
Sugary drink intake		
Soft drink intake		
Added sugar frequency	12**, 13**, 14**, 24**, 34**	
Sugary drink frequency	13**, 14**, 24*	
Soft drink frequency	14**	NS**, SM*, SW*

Significance thresholds are * p<0.05 and ** p<0.01. Social connection groups are abbreviated as 1: Q1, 2: Q2, 3: Q3, and 4: Q4. Region groups are abbreviated as N: Northeast, S: South, M: Midwest, and W: West. Comparisons are denoted as a pair of letters, e.g., 12 represents a comparison of two social connection groups Q1 and Q2. Groups with a higher rank sum are in bold. Non-statistically significant results are omitted.

drinks and soft drinks amongst food journalers is comparable to that of the general populace. As shown in Figure 2(d), **53.25%** and **60.66%** of users do not consume any sugary/soft drinks, respectively. Amongst drinkers, the average daily intakes for both sugary and soft drinks are less than 1 glass. However, on any drinking days, the daily intake exceeds the limit most of the time.

Key insights: Unexpectedly, we find that the healthy eating behaviors of active food journalers do not differ much from those of the general populace in several areas. Given that our population is highly skewed toward females, who tend to be health-conscious, the numbers of healthy eating lapses observed are even more surprising. For example, a vast majority of food journalers did not eat enough fruits and vegetables and fish as per the dietary guidelines. Next, their sugary and soft drink consumption was about the same level as the general populace, which is a worrying trend. On a positive note, the consumption of red and processed meat and added sugars is lower in food journalers than the general populace.

6.2　RQ2: Behavioral differences

In this section, we present the differences in eating behaviors of food journalers across sociodemographic groups. Comparisons of behavioral measures, shown in Table 3, were performed by (1) Mann-Whitney U test for genders, age groups, and global regions; and (2) Kruskal-Wallis H test for social connections and US regions. Dunn's multiple comparisons, shown in Table 4, were performed for social connections and US regions for post-hoc tests.

Journaling and caloric intakes: First, significantly higher median recording days are observed amongst the following groups than other groups: males (p<0.01), older adults (p<0.01), largest social connections (p<0.01), residing in the Northeast (p<0.01), and residing outside the US (p<0.05) as shown in Table 3; pairwise differences are significant for all social connection pairs and the median

recording days of the Northeast and the Midwest are significantly higher than that of the South as displayed in Table 4. Second, median lapsing frequency are significantly higher amongst users in the following groups: females (p<0.01), younger adults (0.01), and small connections (0.01); pairwise differences are significant between smaller social connections (Q1, Q2, and Q3) vs. the largest (Q4). Significantly higher median caloric intakes are observed amongst the following groups than other groups: males (p<0.01), younger adults (p<0.05), largest social connections (p<0.01), and residing outside the US (p<0.01); pairwise differences are significant between smaller social connections (Q1, Q2, and Q3) vs. the largest (Q4).

Fruits and vegetables: Compared to the general populace, the differences in FV consumption of food journalers are associated with similar sociodemographic groups (gender, social connections, and regions of residence). First, females consume fruits and vegetables more frequently than males (p<0.01). Though, unlike the general populace, males have a significantly higher median FV intake (p<0.01). Next, the differences in FV intake and intake frequency are significant between groups with different social connections (p<0.05 and p<0.01, respectively); pairwise differences are significant between (Q2 vs. Q4) for FV intake and (Q1 vs. Q4), (Q2 vs. Q3), and (Q2 vs. Q4) for intake frequency. Moreover, significantly higher median FV intake and frequency are observed amongst those in the West (p<0.01); pairwise intake differences are significant between (South vs. West) and (Midwest vs. West), whereas pairwise frequency differences are significant between all region pairs except (Northeast vs. West) and (South vs. Midwest). In contrast to the general populace, there are no behavioral differences between age groups for FV consumption.

Red and processed meat, poultry, fish: Similar to the general populace, the differences in meat consumption amongst the MFP populace are associated with gender, age, and regions of residence.

Table 5: Coefficients (β) of 17 OLS regression models.

Predicted variable	Male	Age	Log (Friends)	Northeast	South	West	Non-US	Recording days	Lapsing frequency	Adjusted R^2
Recording days	9.470**	0.653**	7.725**	2.837	−4.292*	-2.939	2.291			0.055
Lapsing frequency	−0.047**	−0.004**	−0.019**	-0.003	0.011	0.011	-0.007			0.026
Caloric intake	343.71**	−3.458**	7.498*	-14.235	-19.207	19.598	84.805**	1.163**	−312.951**	0.219
FV intake	0.203**	-0.002	0.011	0.071	0.04	0.107*	0.198**	-0.001	−0.268**	0.012
FV frequency	−0.072**	0.001*	0.004	0.032**	0.002	0.036**	0.104**	0.0002*	−0.107**	0.069
Red meat intake	0.228**	0.004**	0.012*	−0.083**	−0.041*	-0.031	0.016	−0.0004*	-0.014	0.040
Poultry intake	0.235**	−0.006**	0.010*	0.051*	0.055**	0.039*	−0.121**	0.0001	0.0056	0.051
Fish intake	0.006	0.0003	-0.0003	0.012	0.005	0.005	0.055**	−0.0002**	-0.0193	0.011
Red meat frequency	0.057**	0.002**	0.006**	−0.037**	-0.003	-0.008	0.018*	0.0002**	−0.0561**	0.062
Poultry frequency	0.055**	−0.001**	0.004*	0.007	0.024**	0.007	−0.043**	0.0003**	−0.0718**	0.052
Fish frequency	0.009*	0.0003*	-0.001	0.006	0.007	0.004	0.047**	-0.0004	−.0309**	0.029
Added sugar intake	0.291	−0.133**	−1.454**	-0.407	-0.238	-0.439	−3.701**	−0.015*	−7.142**	0.028
Sugary drink intake	-3.066	0.117	-0.821	5.548*	5.045*	1.151	7.229**	-0.04	-6.96	0.002
Soft drink intake	6.714**	0.143	0.595	-3.613	-1.326	−6.412*	0.23	-0.042	-1.209	0.002
Added sugar frequency	−0.056**	−0.001*	−0.044**	0.008	0.013	0.021	−0.049**	−0.0008**	−0.169**	0.032
Sugary drink frequency	−0.014*	−0.001*	−0.006**	0.012	0.012	0.007	0.022**	-0.0001	−0.0293**	0.005
Soft drink frequency	0.009**	−0.0003*	0.0001	0.003	0.009*	-0.006	0.017**	-0.0003	−0.013*	0.008

Caloric intake is in kcal. Food intakes are in numbers of servings. Sugar intake is in grams. Drink intakes are in mL. Intake frequencies are in percentages of days. Intercept terms are omitted. Significance thresholds are * $p<0.05$ and ** $p<0.01$.

First, males have a significantly higher median intake ($p<0.01$) and frequency ($p<0.01$) than females, for all protein sources except fish. Second, older adults have a significantly higher fish intake frequency ($p<0.01$). In addition, poultry consumption (median intake and frequency) in younger adults is significantly higher ($p<0.01$). Next, differences in red and processed meat intake frequency are significant amongst regions of residence ($p<0.01$). Users in the Midwest generally have the highest intake and intake frequency; pairwise intake differences are significant between (Northeast vs. South) and (Northeast vs. Midwest), whereas pairwise frequency differences are significant between the followings: (Northeast vs. South), (Northeast vs. Midwest), and (Northeast vs. West). As opposed to the general populace, older adults have a significantly higher median red and processed meat intake ($p<0.01$) and frequency ($p<0.01$) than younger adults.

Added sugars and sugary drinks: Lastly, the differences in added sugar and sugary drink consumption of food journalers are associated with gender, age, and regions of residence – reflecting the overall differences in the general populace. First, males have a significantly higher median intake of soft drink ($p<0.01$) than females; however, in contrast to the general populace, females have significantly higher intake frequencies of added sugars ($p<0.01$) and sugary drink ($p<0.05$). Second, the median intake of added sugars is significantly higher in younger adults ($p<0.05$). Furthermore, younger adults have significantly higher intake frequencies of sugary drinks ($p<0.01$) and soft drinks ($p<0.01$), than older adults. In contrast to the general populace, we find that food journalers in the Midwest and the South tend to consume more soft drinks than those in the Northeast and the West. Specifically, users in the Midwest have a significantly higher median soft drink intake ($p<0.05$), whereas those in the South have a significantly higher

soft drink intake frequency ($p<0.01$) than other regions; pairwise differences are significant for the South vs. other regions for the soft drink intake frequency, whereas there are no pairwise differences between regions for the median soft drink intake.

Key insights: Overall, food journalers who are male, 45 years or older, and have the largest social network tend to have significantly longer journaling duration and more persistent in recording food journals than others. Next, the healthy eating behaviors of food journalers within the sociodemographic groups are not as homogeneous as we initially expected. As can be seen in Table 3, 58 of 85 (68%) behavioral differences are statistically significant. Furthermore, the differences in eating behaviors across sociodemographic groups are, in many cases, fairly similar to those naturally observable in the general populace. Specifically, both positive and negative eating behaviors occurred within the expected sociodemographic groups, e.g., high intake frequency of fruits and vegetables in females, high added sugar intake in younger adults, and more healthy eating behaviors in users with larger social connections, etc. The results are quite interesting as they may suggest that food journalers were not being as mindful of their healthier food choices as they should have been. We will further investigate the influences of sociodemographic and journaling factors in the next section.

6.3 RQ3: Factors influencing eating behaviors

Ordinary least squares (OLS) regression was used to assess (1) the influences of sociodemographic factors on the journaling behaviors and (2) the influences of sociodemographic and journaling factors on the caloric and diet-based behavioral measures. To that end, we built 17 regression models in which each predicted variable corresponds to each behavioral measure. For predictor variables, we included gender (dummy coded 1 for male and 0 for female), age, social connections (logarithmic scale), US region (dummy coded into 3 variables using Midwest as a reference category), global region (dummy coded 1 for non-US and 0 for US), recording days, and lapsing frequency.

Table 5 displays the predictor variables and their coefficients (β) from 17 OLS regression models. The values of adjusted R^2 of all the models vary from 0.002 - 0.219, which are fairly low. As the predicted variables are derived from a long-term (up to 6 months) consumption data, we expect the predictors of the regression models to modestly explain a small portion of variance of the predicted variables as they do not take into account the temporal variability of the behaviors. This also points to the fact that there are many other factors which could potentially influence these behaviors. In what follows, we summarize the influences of different factors on all behaviors in the order of importance (by absolute coefficient values and total number of behavioral measures influenced).

Gender: Overall, gender appears to be the most important factor in influencing most of the behaviors in the study. Being male will substantially change the value of most behavioral measures compared to being female after controlling for other variables. Specifically, gender significantly influences 14 of 17 different behavioral measures. Amongst all predictor variables, gender has the highest predictive power on 7 behavioral measures, such as recording days, lapsing frequency, and caloric intake, and the relatively high predictive power (the top-3 highest coefficients) on 7 other measures, such as FV intake, FV intake frequency, and poultry intake frequency.

Lapsing frequency: Next, lapsing frequency is the second most influential factor of eating behaviors after gender. Specifically, it has a relatively high predictive power on 10 behavior measures, such as caloric intake, FV intake, and FV intake frequency. Interestingly, it has adverse relationships with most eating behaviors as indicated by negative coefficients β. In some cases, the negative relationships seem counter-intuitive, e.g., an increase in lapsing frequency decreases median caloric intake and intakes of unhealthy diets. This could be partially explained by the fact that some food journalers may be more incline to record less and less diary entries before they temporarily stop journaling [46]. For some, this may positively indicate that they have already achieved their self-tracking goals – an example of *successful abandonment* [12]. In a recent study, De Choudhury et al. [17] concluded that this phenomenon should not be common and long-term food journalers are more likely to complete their diary entries when they choose to record a journal.

Regions of residence: Regions of residence have a substantial influence on journaling and eating behaviors, particularly global regions (US vs. Non-US). After adjusting for other factors, being outside the US will considerably affect most behavioral measures compared to being in the US. 13 of 17 behavioral measures are significantly influenced by global regions. Furthermore, it has a relatively high predictive power on 12 behavioral measures, such as caloric intake, FV intake, and FV intake frequency. More importantly, it is one of the two significant predictors of fish intake. Next, US regions of residence (Northeast, South, and West) significantly influence 10 of 17 behavioral measures. Amongst the behavioral measures, it is a relatively high predictor of red and processed meat intake (Northeast), red and processed meat intake frequency (Northeast), sugary drink intake (Northeast), recording days (South), red and processed meat intake (South), poultry intake (South), sugar drink

intake (South), soft drink intake frequency (South), and soft drink intake (West).

Age: Age is not as predictive of the healthy eating and journaling behaviors as gender, lapsing frequency, and regions of residence. Even though 13 of 17 behaviors are influenced by age, its effects (β) on these behaviors are fairly modest compared to many predictor variables. For example, a one year increase in age will increase the median red and processed meat intake by 0.004 servings after adjusting for other variables.

Recording days: Recording days is one of the least predictive factors of most dietary behaviors. A one day increase in recording days will marginally change most behavioral measures after controlling for other factors. Only half of the behavioral measures (8 of 16) are significantly influenced by recording days. In addition, it is the second worst predictor of 7 influenced measures, such as caloric intake, FV intake frequency, and red and processed meat intake. Interestingly, it is one of the two significant predictors of fish intake.

Social connections: Interestingly, social connection seems to be the least influential factor of most behavioral measures. That is, it has the least predictive power on 10 influenced behavior measures, such as recording days, lapsing frequency, and caloric intake. For instance, a 1% increase in social connections will only increase the number of recording days by 0.007725 days after adjusting for other factors.

Key insights: Between the two journaling factors considered in this study, journaling persistence is more predictive of the healthy eating behaviors than journaling duration. Moreover, the journaling duration is one of the least influential factors of behaviors compared to other sociodemographic factors. More importantly, many sociodemographic factors, especially gender and regions of residence, still play a more critical role in determining the healthy eating behaviors of food journalers than the journaling factors. Contrary to its contribution in the weight loss outcomes, the results show that the journaling duration is a marginal determinant of the healthy eating behaviors.

7 DISCUSSION

Millions of people use mobile food journals as a tool for tracking their caloric intake in order to achieve specific health goals, such as losing weight and living a healthy lifestyle. Prior findings have shown that food journals who actively record what they ate tend to meet their caloric goals [17, 46] and lose more weights [9]. However, beyond managing caloric intake and weight, we found several lapses in the food journalers' healthy eating behaviors, e.g., low consumption of fruits and vegetables and fish, and high consumption of sugary drinks and soft drinks, preventing them from fully achieving their healthy lifestyle goal. Compared to the sociodemographic factors, the journaling duration has the least amount of influence on most eating behaviors. Most journalers' healthier food choices are significantly influenced by their gender roles and environmental contexts, suggesting that their food choices are still largely subconscious [45]. Overall, our study helps to further investigate the claim about the journaling effect on healthier food choices [13, 14, 18] using a large-scale data. From the public health perspective, we find that their effectiveness in helping people achieve healthy eating behaviors as defined by evidence-based outcomes are marginal at best. Based on our findings, it appears that the calorie counting aspect of food journals is not sufficient and potentially unhelpful in facilitating sustained health behavior change. By exclusively focusing on caloric and weight control, food journals may unintentionally mislead individuals into pursuing caloric management as the only health goal and disregarding the physiological and metabolic effects of different types of diets on health and well-being. Our study also confirms findings from past study [13], suggesting that there exists a mismatch between food journalers' preconceived notions of health eating and the energy-centric design of mobile food journals, inadvertently leading to negative nudges.

Our findings have several implications to the designs of mobile food journals or other forms of *mHealth* (mobile health) interventions that can better facilitate healthy eating behaviors. First, from the goal setting perspective [33], a variety of *behavioral goals* could be suggested or posed as daily food challenges [18] to individuals by learning from their past food journal data. The aim is to: (1) supplement the existing caloric and nutrient intake goals; (2) provide a well-defined and quantifiable steps to help people achieve the healthy lifestyle goals, such as high daily FV intake; and (3) improve behavioral compliance and self-efficacy. Next, the goal-setting mechanism could incorporate individuals' backgrounds and experiences such that the behavioral goals could be dynamically and incrementally adjusted to suit them. Next, the goal-setting mechanism could be designed to focus more on targeting whole food consumption (e.g., *consuming at least 5 servings of fruits and vegetables a day*) than isolated nutrients and constituents (e.g., *consuming at least 30 grams of fiber per day*). This could effectively help educate individuals about the importance of food synergy and promote the idea of dietary variety [29]. Lastly, behavioral interventions tailored to individuals' sociodemographic backgrounds could be introduced to mobile food journals. The aim is to identify individuals who are highly susceptible to certain eating behavior lapses and provide them with additional guidance and actions relevant to their current goals. For instance, male users, who are relatively prone to infrequent fruit and vegetable consumption, could receive more targeted notification messages designed to remind and persuade them to meet their FV goals. Additionally, other complementary sources of data, e.g., social media [17], could be included to improve the adaptability and effectiveness of the interventions.

7.1 Limitations

Due to the self-reported and user-contributed natures of data, it is difficult to verify the accuracy of the MFP data [14, 17, 46]. These issues could bias the estimations of portion sizes and nutrient intakes for various diet types, especially high-sugar diets which can be deliberately omitted due to guilt [14]. Next, external data about the dietary consumption of the general populace are generally collected through traditional dietary assessment instruments, such as a Food Frequency Questionnaire (FFQ), which are more susceptible to recall bias than daily food journals. Higher prices of healthier food choices, such as fish, may also affect the healthy eating patterns. Moreover, since it is not possible to control for food journalers' personal belief and perception about food and nutrition from the MFP data, the effects (or lack thereof) of the journaling practice

may be confounded by the differences in healthy eating perception. Although most journalers generally hold the views of healthy eating which are consistent with evidence-based recommendations [13], some may choose to follow a specific dietary regimen, e.g., vegetarian diet, ketogenic diet, etc., for various reasons. Nevertheless, by allowing some noise in the data, our findings can be fairly compared to epidemiological studies'. Lastly, since our findings are obtained from online observational data, therefore they are limited in determining the causal associations between sociodemographic and journaling factors and healthy eating behaviors.

8 CONCLUSION

In this study, we investigated the healthy eating behaviors of My-FitnessPal food journalers. Despite the claim about the benefit of journaling in promoting healthier choices, we found that most food journalers did not eat more healthful diets than the general public. First, much of their dietary consumption did not meet the daily recommended intakes of healthy and unhealthy food sources. Next, their dietary patterns were not as uniform as we initially expected and the distinct patterns mostly resembled those of the general populace who may be less health conscious. Moreover, journaling duration, which was previously shown to be associated with improved weight loss outcomes, appeared to have a marginal influence on the healthy eating behaviors, whereas gender, lapsing frequency, and regions of residence are much more predictive of the healthy eating outcomes.

9 ACKNOWLEDGEMENT

This research is supported by the National Research Foundation, Prime Minister's Office, Singapore under its International Research Centres in Singapore Funding Initiative.

REFERENCES

[1] Sofiane Abbar, Yelena Mejova, and Ingmar Weber. 2015. You Tweet What You Eat: Studying Food Consumption Through Twitter. In *Proceedings of the 33rd international conference on Human factors in computing systems - CHI '15*. ACM Press, New York, New York, USA, 3197–3206. https://doi.org/10.1145/2702123.2702153

[2] Itziar Abete, Dora Romaguera, Ana Rita Vieira, Adolfo Lopez de Munain, and Teresa Norat. 2014. Association between total, processed, red and white meat consumption and all-cause, CVD and IHD mortality: a meta-analysis of cohort studies. *British Journal of Nutrition* 112, 05 (sep 2014), 762–775. https://doi.org/10.1017/S000711451400124X

[3] American Heart Association. 2016. Fish and Omega-3 Fatty Acids. (2016). Retrieved from http://www.heart.org/HEARTORG/HealthyLiving/HealthyEating/HealthyDietGoals/Fish-and-Omega-3-Fatty-Acids_UCM_303248_Article.jsp.

[4] D. Aune, G. Ursin, and M. B. Veierød. 2009. Meat consumption and the risk of type 2 diabetes: a systematic review and meta-analysis of cohort studies. *Diabetologia* 52, 11 (nov 2009), 2277–2287. https://doi.org/10.1007/s00125-009-1481-x

[5] Carole A Bisogni, Margaret Jastran, Marc Seligson, Alyssa Thompson, E.J. Lengerich, J. Atwell, and A.R. Kristal. 2009. How people interpret healthy eating: contributions of qualitative research. *Journal of Nutrition Education and Behavior* 44, 4 (jul 2009), 282–301. https://doi.org/10.1016/j.jneb.2011.11.009

[6] Heidi Michels Blanck, Cathleen Gillespie, Joel E Kimmons, Jennifer D Seymour, and Mary K Serdula. 2008. Trends in fruit and vegetable consumption among U.S. men and women, 1994-2005. *Preventing Chronic Disease* 5, 2 (apr 2008), A35. http://www.ncbi.nlm.nih.gov/pubmed/18341771http://www.pubmedcentral.nih.gov/articlerender.fcgi?artid=PMC2396974

[7] S. N Bleich, Y C. Wang, Y. Wang, and S. L Gortmaker. 2008. Increasing consumption of sugar-sweetened beverages among US adults: 1988-1994 to 1999-2004. *American Journal of Clinical Nutrition* 89, 1 (dec 2008), 372–381. https://doi.org/10.3945/ajcn.2008.26883

[8] U.S. Census Bureau. 2017. United States Population Growth by Region. (2017). Retrieved from https://www.census.gov/popclock/data_tables.php?component=growth.

[9] Lora E. Burke, Mindi A. Styn, Susan M. Sereika, Molly B. Conroy, Lei Ye, Karen Glanz, Mary Ann Sevick, and Linda J. Ewing. 2012. Using mHealth Technology to Enhance Self-Monitoring for Weight Loss. *American Journal of Preventive Medicine* 43, 1 (jul 2012), 20–26. https://doi.org/10.1016/j.amepre.2012.03.016

[10] Nicholas A. Christakis and James H. Fowler. 2007. The Spread of Obesity in a Large Social Network over 32 Years. *New England Journal of Medicine* 357, 4 (jul 2007), 370–379. https://doi.org/10.1056/NEJMsa066082

[11] Chia-Fang Chung, Elena Agapie, Jessica Schroeder, Sonali Mishra, James Fogarty, and Sean A. Munson. 2017. When Personal Tracking Becomes Social: Examining the Use of Instagram for Healthy Eating. In *Proceedings of the 2017 CHI Conference on Human Factors in Computing Systems - CHI '17*. ACM Press, New York, New York, USA, 1674–1687. https://doi.org/10.1145/3025453.3025747

[12] James Clawson, Jessica A. Pater, Andrew D. Miller, Elizabeth D. Mynatt, and Lena Mamykina. 2015. No Longer Wearing: Investigating the Abandonment of Personal Health-Tracking Technologies on Craigslist. In *Proceedings of the 2015 ACM International Joint Conference on Pervasive and Ubiquitous Computing - UbiComp '15*. ACM, 647–658. https://doi.org/10.1145/2750858.2807554

[13] Felicia Cordeiro, Elizabeth Bales, Erin Cherry, and James Fogarty. 2015. Rethinking the Mobile Food Journal: Exploring Opportunities for Lightweight Photo-Based Capture. In *Proceedings of the 33rd Annual ACM Conference on Human Factors in Computing Systems - CHI '15*. ACM Press, New York, New York, USA, 3207–3216. https://doi.org/10.1145/2702123.2702154

[14] Felicia Cordeiro, Daniel A. Epstein, Edison Thomaz, Elizabeth Bales, Arvind K. Jagannathan, Gregory D. Abowd, and James Fogarty. 2015. Barriers and Negative Nudges: Exploring Challenges in Food Journaling. In *Proceedings of the 33rd Annual ACM Conference on Human Factors in Computing Systems - CHI '15*. ACM Press, New York, New York, USA, 1159–1162. https://doi.org/10.1145/2702123. 2702155

[15] Aron Culotta. 2014. Estimating County Health Statistics with Twitter. In *Proceedings of the SIGCHI Conference on Human Factors in Computing Systems - CHI '14*. ACM Press, New York, New York, USA, 1335–1344. https://doi.org/10.1145/ 2556288.2557139

[16] Carrie R Daniel, Amanda J Cross, Corinna Koebnick, and Rashmi Sinha. 2011. Trends in meat consumption in the USA. *Public Health Nutrition* 14, 04 (apr 2011), 575–583. https://doi.org/10.1017/S1368980010002077

[17] Munmun De Choudhury, Mrinal Kumar, and Ingmar Weber. 2017. Computational Approaches Toward Integrating Quantified Self Sensing and Social Media. In *Proceedings of the 2017 ACM Conference on Computer Supported Cooperative Work and Social Computing - CSCW '17*. ACM Press, New York, New York, USA, 1334–1349. https://doi.org/10.1145/2998181.2998219

[18] Daniel A. Epstein, Felicia Cordeiro, James Fogarty, Gary Hsieh, and Sean A. Munson. 2016. Crumbs: Lightweight Daily Food Challenges to Promote Engagement and Mindfulness. In *Proceedings of the 2016 CHI Conference on Human Factors in Computing Systems - CHI '16*. ACM Press, New York, New York, USA, 5632–5644. https://doi.org/10.1145/2858036.2858044

[19] Daniel A. Epstein, An Ping, James Fogarty, and Sean A. Munson. 2015. A lived informatics model of personal informatics. In *Proceedings of the 2015 ACM International Joint Conference on Pervasive and Ubiquitous Computing - UbiComp '15*. ACM Press, New York, New York, USA, 731–742. https://doi.org/10.1145/ 2750858.2804250

[20] American Institute for Cancer Research. 2017. Lower Red Meat Consumption to Prevent Cancer. (2017). Retrieved from http://www.aicr. org/reduce-your-cancer-risk/recommendations-for-cancer-prevention/ recommendations_05_red_meat.html.

[21] Centers for Disease Control and Prevention. 2013. Consumption of Added Sugars Among U.S. Adults, 2005-2010. (2013). Retrieved from https://www.cdc.gov/ nchs/data/databriefs/db122.pdf.

[22] Centers for Disease Control and Prevention. 2015. Adults Meeting Fruit and Vegetable Intake Recommendations - United States, 2013. (2015). Retrieved from https://www.cdc.gov/mmwr/preview/mmwrhtml/mm6426a1.htm.

[23] Eat for Health. 2015. Serve sizes. (2015). Retrieved from https://www.eatforhealth. gov.au/food-essentials/how-much-do-we-need-each-day/serve-sizes.

[24] Gallup. 2012. Nearly Half of Americans Drink Soda Daily. (2012). Retrieved from http://www.gallup.com/poll/156116/ Nearly-Half-Americans-Drink-Soda-Daily.aspx.

[25] Marcia Hill Gossard and Richard York. 2003. Social Structural Influences on Meat Consumption. *Human Ecology Review* 10 (2003), 1–9. https://doi.org/10.2307/ 24707082

[26] Jack F Hollis, Christina M Gullion, Victor J Stevens, Phillip J Brantley, Lawrence J Appel, Jamy D Ard, Catherine M Champagne, Arlene Dalcin, Thomas P Erlinger, Kristine Funk, Daniel Laferriere, Pao-Hwa Lin, Catherine M Loria, Carmen Samuel-Hodge, William M Vollmer, and Laura P Svetkey. 2008. Weight loss during the intensive intervention phase of the weight-loss maintenance trial. *American Journal of Preventive Medicine* 35, 2 (Aug. 2008), 118–26.

[27] Frank B. Hu. 2013. Resolved: there is sufficient scientific evidence that decreasing sugar-sweetened beverage consumption will reduce the prevalence of obesity and obesity-related diseases. *Obesity Reviews* 14, 8 (aug 2013), 606–619. https:

//doi.org/10.1111/obr.12040

[28] Kevin O. Hwang, Allison J. Ottenbacher, Angela P. Green, M. Roseann Cannon-Diehl, Oneka Richardson, Elmer V. Bernstam, and Eric J. Thomas. 2010. Social support in an Internet weight loss community. *International Journal of Medical Informatics* 79, 1 (jan 2010), 5–13. https://doi.org/10.1016/j.ijmedinf.2009.10.003

[29] D. R Jacobs, M. D Gross, and L. C Tapsell. 2009. Food synergy: an operational concept for understanding nutrition. *American Journal of Clinical Nutrition* 89, 5 (may 2009), 1543S–1548S. https://doi.org/10.3945/ajcn.2009.26736B

[30] Paule Latino-Martel, Vanessa Cottet, Nathalie Druesne-Pecollo, Fabrice H F Pierre, Marina Touillaud, Mathilde Touvier, Marie-Paule Vasson, Mélanie Deschasaux, Julie Le Merdy, Emilie Barrandon, and Raphaëlle Ancellin. 2016. Alcoholic beverages, obesity, physical activity and other nutritional factors, and cancer risk: A review of the evidence. *Critical Reviews in Oncology/Hematology* (jan 2016). https://doi.org/10.1016/j.critrevonc.2016.01.002

[31] Yelena Mejova, Hamed Haddadi, Anastasios Noulas, and Ingmar Weber. 2015. #FoodPorn: Obesity Patterns in Culinary Interactions. In *Proceedings of the 5th International Conference on Digital Health 2015 - DH '15*. ACM Press, New York, New York, USA, 51–58. https://doi.org/10.1145/2750511.2750524

[32] Ali H. Mokdad, Barbara A. Bowman, Earl S. Ford, Frank Vinicor, James S. Marks, and Jeffrey P. Koplan. 2001. The Continuing Epidemics of Obesity and Diabetes in the United States. *JAMA* 286, 10 (sep 2001), 1195. https://doi.org/10.1001/jama. 286.10.1195

[33] Sean Munson and Sunny Consolvo. 2012. Exploring Goal-setting, Rewards, Self-monitoring, and Sharing to Motivate Physical Activity. In *Proceedings of the 6th International Conference on Pervasive Computing Technologies for Healthcare*. IEEE. https://doi.org/10.4108/icst.pervasivehealth.2012.248691

[34] Tarja Nieminen, Ritva Prättälä, Tuija Martelin, Tommi Härkänen, Markku T Hyyppä, Erkki Alanen, and Seppo Koskinen. 2013. Social capital, health behaviours and health: a population-based associational study. *BMC Public Health* 13 (jun 2013), 613. https://doi.org/10.1186/1471-2458-13-613

[35] U.S. Department of Health and Human Services. 2010. Dietary Guidelines for Americans 2010. (2010). Retrieved from https://health.gov/dietaryguidelines/ dga2010/DietaryGuidelines2010.pdf.

[36] Harvard T.H. Chan School of Public Health. 2015. Healthy Beverage Guidelines. (2015). Retrieved from https://www.hsph.harvard.edu/nutritionsource/ healthy-drinks-full-story/.

[37] World Health Organization. 2015. WHO calls on countries to reduce sugars intake among adults and children. (2015). Retrieved from http://www.who.int/ mediacentre/news/releases/2015/sugar-guideline/en/.

[38] Yanni Papanikolaou, James Brooks, Carroll Reider, and Victor L Fulgoni. 2014. U.S. adults are not meeting recommended levels for fish and omega-3 fatty acid intake: results of an analysis using observational data from NHANES 2003-2008. *Nutrition Journal* 13, 1 (dec 2014), 31. https://doi.org/10.1186/1475-2891-13-31

[39] Kunwoo Park, Ingmar Weber, Meeyoung Cha, and Chul Lee. 2016. Persistent Sharing of Fitness App Status on Twitter. In *Proceedings of the 19th ACM Conference on Computer-Supported Cooperative Work & Social Computing - CSCW '16*. ACM Press, New York, New York, USA, 183–193. https://doi.org/10.1145/ 2818048.2819921

[40] Sohyun Park, Lisa C. McGuire, and Deborah A. Galuska. 2015. Regional Differences in Sugar-Sweetened Beverage Intake among US Adults. *Journal of the Academy of Nutrition and Dietetics* 115, 12 (dec 2015), 1996–2002. https: //doi.org/10.1016/j.jand.2015.06.010

[41] John Rooksby, Mattias Rost, Alistair Morrison, and Matthew Chalmers. 2014. Personal Tracking as Lived Informatics. In *Proceedings of the SIGCHI Conference on Human Factors in Computing Systems - CHI '14*. ACM Press, New York, New York, USA, 1163–1172. https://doi.org/10.1145/2556288.2557039

[42] Mingyang Song, Teresa T. Fung, Frank B. Hu, Walter C. Willett, Valter D. Longo, Andrew T. Chan, and Edward L. Giovannucci. 2016. Association of Animal and Plant Protein Intake With All-Cause and Cause-Specific Mortality. *JAMA Internal Medicine* 176, 10 (oct 2016), 1453. https://doi.org/10.1001/jamainternmed.2016. 4182

[43] Debra Umberson, Robert Crosnoe, and Corinne Reczek. 2010. Social Relationships and Health Behavior Across the Life Course. *Annual Review of Sociology* 36, 1 (jun 2010), 139–157. https://doi.org/10.1146/annurev-soc-070308-120011

[44] Xia Wang, Yingying Ouyang, Jun Liu, Minmin Zhu, Gang Zhao, Wei Bao, and Frank B. Hu. 2014. Fruit and vegetable consumption and mortality from all causes, cardiovascular disease, and cancer: systematic review and dose-response meta-analysis of prospective cohort studies. *BMJ* 349, jul29 3 (jul 2014), g4490–g4490. https://doi.org/10.1136/bmj.g4490

[45] Brian Wansink. 2006. *Mindless Eating : Why We Eat More Than We Think*. Bantam Books. 276 pages. https://books.google.com.sg/books/about/Mindless

[46] Ingmar Weber and Palakorn Achananuparp. 2016. Insights from machine-learned diet success prediction. In *Proceedings of Pacific Symposium on Biocomputing (PSB)*.

[47] World Health Organization. 2003. Diet, nutrition and the prevention of chronic diseases: report of a Joint WHO/FAO Expert Consultation. *WHO Technical Report Series* 916 (2003).

Eat & Tell: A Randomized Trial of Random-Loss Incentive to Increase Dietary Self-Tracking Compliance

Palakorn Achananuparp
Singapore Management University
Singapore
palakorna@smu.edu.sg

Ee-Peng Lim
Singapore Management University
Singapore
eplim@smu.edu.sg

Vibhanshu Abhishek
Carnegie Mellon University
Pittsburgh, PA
vibs@andrew.cmu.edu

Tianjiao Yun
Singapore Management University
Singapore
pepperyun@smu.edu.sg

ABSTRACT

A growing body of evidence has shown that incorporating behavioral economics principles into the design of financial incentive programs helps improve their cost-effectiveness, promote individuals' short-term engagement, and increase compliance in health behavior interventions. Yet, their effects on long-term engagement have not been fully examined. In study designs where repeated administration of incentives is required to ensure the regularity of behaviors, the effectiveness of subsequent incentives may decrease as a result of the law of diminishing marginal utility. In this paper, we introduce random-loss incentive – a new financial incentive based on loss aversion and unpredictability principles – to address the problem of individuals' growing insensitivity to repeated interventions over time. We evaluate the new incentive design by conducting a randomized controlled trial to measure the influences of random losses on participants' dietary self-tracking and self-reporting compliance using a mobile web application called Eat & Tell. The results show that random losses are significantly more effective than fixed losses in encouraging long-term engagement.

CCS CONCEPTS

• **Applied computing** → **Health informatics**; *Consumer health*;

KEYWORDS

Health; Quantified Self; Food Logging; Incentives; Loss Aversion; Unpredictability; Randomized Controlled Trial

ACM Reference Format:
Palakorn Achananuparp, Ee-Peng Lim, Vibhanshu Abhishek, and Tianjiao Yun. 2018. Eat & Tell: A Randomized Trial of Random-Loss Incentive to Increase Dietary Self-Tracking Compliance. In *DH'18: 2018 International Digital Health Conference, April 23–26, 2018, Lyon, France.* ACM, New York, NY, USA, 10 pages. https://doi.org/10.1145/3194658.3194662

1 INTRODUCTION

Persistent collection of individuals' lifestyle and behavior data is instrumental in realizing precision medicine's visions of providing treatments and healthcare specifically tailored to individuals [7]. Recent advances in mobile sensors, wearable technologies, and applications (also known as apps) have greatly facilitated active and passive self-tracking of a wide range of individual behaviors, including physical activities, sleep, and dietary intake. Despite the increasing ease of tracking one own's data, continued engagement with self-tracking technology is not likely to persist long term unless the issues of individual motivation, incentives, and habit formation are also addressed. Recent findings [6, 8] have revealed that a vast number self-tracking technology adopters eventually lost their interest in self-tracking over time, leading to reduced compliance and increased abandonment rate. Many users tended to use the self-tracking data for short-term goals and migration between tools was fairly common [28].

To promote continued engagement with self-tracking health technologies, various financial and non-financial incentive designs have been proposed. For example, the designs of self-tracking applications can be improved by providing more meaningful behavioral insights from the data [6, 8] and improving social sharing to support observational learning [6]. In the context of randomized health intervention trials, financial incentives have been commonly used to motivate health behavior changes and promote self-tracking compliance [15, 25]. Several researchers [4, 16, 32, 33] argued that financial incentive is a strong motivator for improving many health-related behaviors with little to no crowding-out effect [4, 17, 26]. However, a few studies [15, 33] have also shown that achieving effective results comes with a heavy cost. In the past few years, there is a growing body of evidence supporting the use of behavioral economics principles, such as loss aversion [20], in the design of *cost-effective* incentive programs [23, 25, 32]. Particularly, financial incentives framed as loss have been proven to be a stronger motivator of health behaviors than those typically framed as gain [25, 32] (henceforth loss-framed and gain-framed incentives, respectively). This is explained by the fact that people are more likely to act to avoid loss than to acquire gain as the pain of losing is psychologically *twice* as powerful as the pleasure of gaining [20]. In many longitudinal health studies where participants are expected to be repeatedly administered interventions, e.g., being compensated on a daily basis over a long period of time, the decline in intervention effectiveness may occur due to the law of diminishing marginal utility, leading to reduced compliance. The cost-effective design of repeated financial incentives has not been fully explored, especially in the context of loss-framed incentives. Furthermore, data about individuals' day-to-day dietary choices and habits – captured via self-tracking and self-reporting – are challenging to acquire even in non precision medicine cases. The demanding nature of dietary data collection underscores the importance of incentive programs necessary for sustaining individual engagement. To our knowledge, few studies have directly examined the effectiveness of financial incentives in increasing individuals' engagement with dietary self-tracking and self-reporting tasks.

Given the research gaps, we propose a new financial incentive design called **random-loss incentive** to address the issue of declining effectiveness of repeated financial incentives. The proposed incentive incorporates the *unpredictability* principle, commonly used in Gamification [5] and behavioral reinforcement [13], into the design of a loss-framed incentive. Specifically, we hypothesize that random losses are more effective than fixed losses in promoting sustained engagement and reducing insensitivity to repeated interventions as people tend to be overpessimistic about their chance of suffering higher-than-expected losses.

We conducted a randomized controlled trial to investigate the effectiveness of the random-loss incentive to improve individuals' engagement with dietary self-tracking and self-reporting via a new mobile web application, developed as part of our research, called the **Eat & Tell** app. The app is specifically designed to facilitate the collection of dietary self-tracking and self-reported data through the food diary data import and the self-report survey components. It is also randomized trial friendly. Potential participants were asked to contribute their dietary self-reported data over a period of 30 days. Upon the successful enrollment, participants were randomly assigned to either the treatment group (random-loss incentive) or the control group (fixed-loss incentive). At the start of the study, they were given an initial S$35 worth of credit through the app, redeemable for a cash payout after 30 days. The final credit value was determined by their level of compliance with the study protocol. In the treatment condition, a random amount between S$0 to S$3 was deducted from the credit balance each day if participants failed to report their dietary intake and behavior on time. On the other hand, control participants were subjected to a fixed S$1 deduction amount if the same daily requirements had not been met. The sum of all deductions was controlled to never exceed S$35 in both conditions.

The main contributions of our work are: (1) presenting the Eat & Tell app as a unified research platform to study individuals' day-to-day dietary habits by leveraging the quantified-self ecosystems of food logging apps, integrated self-report surveys, and incentive programs; (2) introducing a comprehensive set of one-time self-report surveys to collect individual data, e.g., demographic attributes and personality measures, as well as recurring self-report surveys to collect various meal-specific contexts and daily reflection; and (3) introducing a new random-loss incentive that has been shown via a randomized trail of 245 participants to increase the compliance of dietary self-tracking and self-reporting over the fixed-loss incentive.

2 RELATED WORK

2.1 Lifestyle Data and The Quantified Self

Our study is generally related to the quantified self movement [30], an emerging practice of collecting and analyzing one's own data using a wide variety of tools and technologies, including but not limited to modern wearable devices and mobile sensors, to gain a better understanding of and improve certain aspects of daily life. Recently, several studies have explored the use of smartphone, mobile sensing, and wearable technologies to monitor individuals' physical activities and well-being. For instance, Fernandez-Luque et al. [12] examined the feasibility of capturing the quantified-self data from wearable devices and mobile applications in a weight loss camp for overweight children in Qatar. Kato-Lin et al. [21] evaluated the effectiveness of visual-based dietary tracking mobile apps in healthy eating intervention. Rahman et al. [27] proposed a sensing framework based on signal processing and machine learning to predict about-to-eat moments for just-in-time interventions. Wang et al. [34] presented the StudentLife project which employed a variety of smartphone-based mobile sensing techniques to passively and actively track well-being and academic performance of college students. Another related body of work focuses on analyzing self-tracking data in conjunction with other data sources, e.g., social media messages, to learn about individuals' health-related behaviors. For example, De Choudhury et al. [9] proposed computational methods to predict individuals' diet compliance success using linguistic, activity, and social capital features extracted from their Twitter messages. Wang et al. [35] studied weight updates automatically shared on Twitter from a Withings smart scale. In addition, social media content alone has been shown to be a useful data source for a population-level dietary lifestyle monitoring [1, 22]. Unlike recent digital health research which utilized observation data to study health-related behaviors, the results of our randomized trial are less susceptible to confounding factors.

A common issue in many health monitoring and intervention studies is the decline in self-tracking compliance over time [12, 21, 34]. One reason is that such self-tracking incentive was deliberately omitted to avoid its confounding effects on the intervention outcomes [21, 34]. Additionally, study participants are likely to experience tracking fatigue due to the demanding nature of the tasks, resulting in reduced compliance [8]. Unlike previous self-tracking studies which focus primarily on health outcomes, such as weight loss, we aim to directly address the declining compliance problem through loss-framed financial incentives. The primary goal of our study is to investigate the effectiveness of different loss-framed incentives in improving self-tracking and reporting compliance in a randomized trial. Compared to past self-tracking studies [12, 21, 34], our Eat & Tell app is the first to demonstrate an integrative approach to link self-tracking data with context-specific self-report surveys via the use of a unified research and data collection platform, leading to improved user experience.

2.2 Incentives for Health Behavior Change

Past studies have shown strong evidence of financial incentives in promoting changes in health behaviors, such as smoking cessation [16, 33], weight loss [32], exercising [4], and physical activity

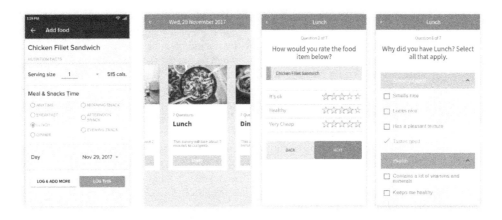

Figure 1: An example of data integration flow in the Eat & Tell app

[14, 15, 25]. Amongst these studies, behavioral economics principles, such as loss aversion [20] and commitment devices [3, 23], have been incorporated into the incentive designs to further nudge individuals toward positive behavior changes. For example, Volpp et al. [32] showed that individuals who were administered deposit contract and lottery incentives significantly lost more weights than non-incentivized individuals. In a recent study by Patel et al. [25], loss-framed financial incentives were more effective in promoting physical activity than gain-framed incentives. Milkman et al. [23] introduced a novel commitment device called temptation bundling which was shown to be effective in increasing gym attendance.

The design of our random-loss incentive is built upon the application of behavioral economics principles, specifically loss aversion and framing, in influencing health-related behavior change [25]. To our knowledge, this study is the first randomized trial to examine the impacts of unpredictability in loss-framed financial incentives on the individuals' continued engagement with dietary self-tracking and self-reporting. Prior work [19, 32] has utilized unpredictability-based designs in gain-framed incentives (e.g., lottery incentives) to exploit individuals' tendency to overestimate small probabilities of large potential rewards [20], albeit with mixed results [19]. Unlike lottery incentives where the likelihood of a payout is randomly determined, we opt for a fixed reward scheduling and introduce unpredictability during the payout stage similar to Random Rewards in Gamification [5], i.e., a randomly determined deduction amount is made for every non-compliance behavior. Lastly, our study is the first to comprehensively evaluate the influences of the incentives in dietary self-tracking studies by controlling for various personal characteristics including self-efficacy [21], grit [11], age, and gender, which intrinsically determine individuals' motivation and engagement levels.

3 EAT & TELL APP

We begin by describing the Eat & Tell app[1], a mobile web application built by the authors as a research platform for studying daily eating habits and behavior change intervention. To facilitate the data collection process and taking advantage of the quantified self and self-tracking ecosystems, the app integrates data from popular

mobile food diary apps to generate personalized self-report surveys for each user based on their food diary records. These surveys are instrumental in capturing additional behavioral and contextual information beyond what is provided by the self-tracking data. For instance, did they have breakfast alone or with other people? Did they go to a restaurant for lunch? Did they choose to have a particular meal for dinner because of sensory appeals or convenience?

3.1 Food Diary Data Integration

Food diary data from 3 mobile health and fitness apps, i.e, MyFitnessPal, Fitbit, and Healthy 365[2] can be automatically synchronized to the Eat & Tell app via web-based application programming interfaces (APIs). These mobile apps were chosen based on their popularity amongst users in Singapore where the study took place. MyFitnessPal is a popular mobile calorie counter which allows users to track their caloric balance through food and exercise diaries. Next, Fitbit is a well-known commercial service helping its users to track their physical activities, sleep, and food intakes via its activity trackers and mobile app. Lastly, Healthy 365 is a free-to-use health and diet tracking mobile app created by the Health Promotion Board of Singapore. Upon successful data synchronization, a set of self-report surveys are dynamically generated for each user based on the predefined question templates and their food diary data. Each survey is associated with meal of the day (i.e., breakfast, lunch, dinner, and snack) and contains a set of questions about meal contexts (e.g., venue, meal time, eating companions, etc.), food choices, and food items logged in the meal. Figure 1 shows an example of the data integration flow starting from (1) a user logs what he/she had for lunch in the Fitbit app, (2) the Lunch survey is generated in the Eat & Tell app from his/her Fitbit data, and (3) the user responds to the questions about the food items and (4) the meal itself.

3.2 Self-Report Surveys

We administer two major types of self-report surveys in the Eat & Tell app: **One-time surveys** and **daily surveys**. Firstly, one-time surveys are intended to be completed once and consist of standard

---

[1] https://eatntell.sg

[2] https://www.healthhub.sg/apps/25/healthy365

questionnaires about demographic information (e.g., gender, age, household income level), general health status (e.g., weight, height, blood pressure), physical activity level, and personality measures. To assess the physical activity level, we adopt questions from the Rapid Assessment of Physical Activity (RAPA) [31] for their brevity. Next, two personality measures, personality traits and grit, are administered by 50-item IPIP Big-Five Factor Markers [18] and 12-item Grit Scale [11], respectively. All users have access to the same set of one-time surveys.

Secondly, daily surveys are intended to be filled out on a daily basis and comprise: (1) a set of dynamically generated surveys (also known as food diary surveys) based on the connected food diary data; and (2) an end-of-day reflection survey. Questions about individual food items and meals of the day are included in the food diary surveys. At a food-item level, we ask users to rate each item in their diary on a 5-point Likert scale about taste (1 = hated it to 5 = loved it), healthfulness (1 = very unhealthy to 5 = very healthy), and affordability (1 = very expensive to 5 = very cheap). To lessen the self-reporting burden, our app keeps track of the users' most frequently-logged items and assign default ratings to similar items. Next, at a meal level, users provide: (1) responses to questions about meal contexts, such as time of the day, type of venue/meal location, eating companions, etc.; and (2) reasons for which a particular meal was chosen in the Food Choice questionnaire [29]. Lastly, the end-of-day surveys include self-assessment questions about the users' subjective well-being and perceived difficulty (self-efficacy) in logging food diary and completing surveys, among others. The subjective well-being questions are adopted from a 12-item Scale of Positive and Negative Experience (SPANE) [10], whereas the 5-point scale self-efficacy questions are adapted from the similar self-efficacy questionnaires used in [21]. The survey template containing all items used in this study is accessible online[3].

4 RANDOM-LOSS INCENTIVE

In this section, we describe random-loss incentive, a new loss-framed financial incentive program designed to address the issue of declining incentive efficacy caused by repeated administration of financial incentives over time. In certain longitudinal-study designs where participants are compensated on a regular basis, such as getting paid each day for achieving the goal of 10,000 steps of physical activity a day, the effectiveness of subsequent payouts of the same amount may be decreasing according to the law of diminishing marginal utility. At the start of the study, a participant may be significantly motivated to act in exchange for the first $5 payout. However, as the participant's financial gain is accumulating over the course of the study, the next $5 payout has a proportionately smaller contribution to the total gain and his/her marginal utility. Before intrinsic motivation and habit are properly developed, the same fixed-value payout may have less effect on his/her behavior than past payouts. Similar effects may also apply to loss-framed incentives. In addition to the use of standard behavioral economics principles [20], including loss aversion, the endowment effect, and framing, the design of our random-loss incentive is also inspired by Random Rewards in Gamification [5] which is based on the principles of unpredictability and curiosity. The underlying assumption of

our random-loss incentive is that people tend to be overpessimistic and emotional about their chance of suffering higher-than-expected losses and are more likely to act to avoid further misfortune than when facing predictable losses.

Let m be the length of study (m=30 days) and p be the total daily deduction budget (p=S$30), the steps to assign random losses for each treatment participant are as follows. First, we generate a probability vector l of m entries where each entry l_i is a random positive real number between 0 and 1 and the sum of all entries is one. Next, each random loss is computed by multiplying each vector entry l_i by p. Finally, we derive for the participant a sequence of m random losses which add up S$30. This method results in a non-uniform distribution of random losses which are biased toward less extreme values, making them characteristically different from lottery-based incentives. The histogram in Figure 2 shows the distribution of daily deduction amounts (SD = 0.5838) pre-generated under the random-loss incentive program for all treatment participants at the start of the study. As we can see, all random-loss based daily deductions are between S$0 and S$3.

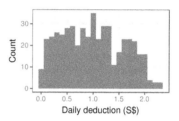

Figure 2: Distribution of daily deductions.

5 STUDY DESIGN AND PROCEDURES

5.1 Recruitment

The study was approved by the Institutional Review Board at Singapore Management University. In total, 245 participants were recruited online through the Facebook advertising platform. An advertisement campaign was launched to target Facebook users in Singapore who were 18 years or older, with access to an Android or iOS smartphone, and generally interested in mobile food diary, self-tracking, and wearable technology. To target these sets of Facebook users based on their topics of interests, the following keywords were used: "MyFitnessPal", "Fitbit", "Health Promotion Board, Singapore", "Activity Tracker", "Smartwatch", and "Wearable Technology". Based on these criteria, the campaign approximately reached 400,000 potential audience according to estimates provided by the Facebook platform. The advertisements described an opportunity to participate in a one-month research project to study individuals' daily eating habits and food choices in exchange for a cash compensation of up to S$35 and a chance to win a smartwatch (approximately S$500 in value) at the end of the study. Clicking on the advertisements redirected the users to the study website where study details, requirements to participate, and a link to the registration page were shown. The campaign ran for 24 days from May 30 - June 23, 2017. In total, the advertisements were shown 86,533 times (impressions) to 53,635 unique users (reach) yielding

---

[3] http://bit.ly/2zHcD9X

2,934 clicks on the ads or 5.47% click-through rate (CTR) per unique user. More than 80% of Facebook users who clicked on the ads were women. Ultimately, 257 website visitors from Facebook signed up to participate yielding 8.76% conversion rate per website visit at a conversion cost of S$3.84 campaign spending per sign up. Amongst the potential participants, 5 people failed to complete the registration process, whereas 7 people eventually dropped out a few days into the study by revoking their consent.

5.2 Procedures

To register for the study, participants filled out an online registration form on the Eat & Tell study website. First, they had to give consent to participate, allowing the research team to collect their personal data, online food diary records, and survey responses. Next, they provided their first name, last name, email address, and PayPal account (for receiving compensation) in the registration form. In addition, they were required to connect their online food diary account from one of the supported applications (MyFitnessPal, Fitbit, and Healthy 365) to the Eat & Tell app, giving the app a permission to access their food diary data. If they had never used an online food diary before, they were allowed to sign up for a new food diary account before resuming the registration process. To complete the registration, participants were required to confirm their identity by clicking on the verification link sent to their registered email address. No multiple sign-ups, e.g., duplicate email addresses or food diary accounts, were allowed. Additionally, we required a smartwatch winner to present a valid national identification card as proof of identity when picking up the prize in person.

Upon successful registration, participants were randomly assigned to one of the two experimental groups: **treatment** (random-loss incentive) or **control** (fixed-loss incentive), after which an introductory email was sent to their registered email address describing the start and end dates of the study and the study procedures. All participants were first instructed to log in to the Eat & Tell app and fill out a set of 5 one-time surveys about their demographic and health information, personality traits, and grit. Next, for each day in the study, participants were asked to complete a daily task involving (1) logging their food and drink intakes throughout the day in the registered food diary app; (2) synchronizing the food diary data with the Eat & Tell app and filling out surveys about food choices made in the corresponding diary entries; and (3) filling out a reflection survey about their subjective well-being and perceived task difficulty (self-efficacy) which was accessible after 5:00 PM. In total, it took about 15 - 20 minutes to complete the daily task.

Both treatment and control participants were then informed in the introductory email that a $35 online credit had been deposited to their Eat & Tell account. The credit was redeemable for real money of the same value at the end of the study, paid to them via the online payment platform Paypal. However, their online credit was still subjected to being deducted during the course of the study depending on the completion of the one-time surveys and the daily tasks. First, $1 would be deducted from their credit balance for each incomplete one-time survey for all participants. All one-time surveys were accessible until the end of the study. Next, participants in each group were told about the deduction amount for each incomplete daily task specific to their assigned

Table 1: Characteristics of participants.

Variable		Treatment	Control	All
Gender	Female	85	66	151
	Male	31	22	53
Age	18 - 24	19	22	41
	25 - 34	55	40	95
	35 - 44	21	14	35
	45 - 54	6	6	12
	55 - 64	3	0	3
	65 or older	1	0	1
Ethnicity	Chinese	111	83	194
	Indian	3	4	7
	Malay	1	0	1
	Others	1	1	2
Education	Secondary (O or N level)	8	3	11
	Junior college (A level)	7	5	12
	Vocational certificate	1	4	5
	Polytechnic diploma	17	14	31
	University or higher	80	62	142
Employment	Full-time employment	78	57	135
	Part-time employment	4	4	8
	Entrepreneur	1	2	3
	Student	17	14	31
	Homemaker	3	5	8
	Unemployed	3	4	7
	Retired	1	0	1
Marital status	Married	39	27	66
	Living with a partner	2	0	2
	Divorced	2	0	2
	Never been married	70	60	130
BMI (mean)		23.16	22.49	22.88
Grit score (mean)		2.73	2.78	2.75
Pre-treatment logging days (mean)		1.12	1.53	1.3
Number of diary entries logged per day (mean)		6.23	5.81	6.06
Caloric intake (kcal) per day (mean)		1249.05	1263.05	1254.85
Number of participants (N)		135	110	245
Number of intervention participants (N')		111	91	202

N also includes participants who did not answer/partially answered one-time survey questions. Intervention participants are those who were successfully enrolled into the study and received at least 1 deduction.

condition: (1) a random deduction between S$0 to and S$3 for the treatment group; and (2) a S$1 deduction for the control group. All daily tasks had to be completed within the next 48 hours (calendar time). Any overdue surveys were automatically made inaccessible to participants after its deadline had passed. Next, all participants were instructed that the total deduction amount would never exceed S$35 (S$5 for one-time surveys and S$30 for all daily tasks). In addition, their chance of winning a smartwatch was also proportional to their task completion rate. This was done to discourage anyone who signed up just to be in the smartwatch sweepstake but never intended to contribute to the study.

5.3 Automated Email Notifications

To facilitate participants' compliance with the study protocol, the Eat & Tell app sent an automated email reminder at 7:00 PM every day to any participants who had not yet completed the daily task, notifying them about the remaining time and a potential credit

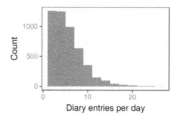

Figure 3: Distribution of daily diary entries logged.

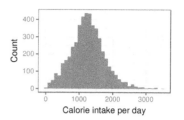

Figure 4: Distribution of daily caloric intakes (kcal).

loss. Participants were allowed to change the schedule of the email reminder by specifying the preferred time in the app. In total, two email reminders were sent before the daily task's due date. Ultimately, if participants did not complete the daily task on time, they would receive another automated email message at 8:00 AM the next day after the due date, notifying them about the recent deduction and offering short motivational messages and helpful tips on how to make the daily tasks less tedious.

5.4 Participants

All 245 participants who successfully enrolled in the study were randomly assigned to one of the two experimental groups: treatment (N=135) and control (N=110). Participant characteristics are shown in Table 1. Despite the S$5 incentive to filling out one-time surveys, not all participants complied and thus some of the participant demographics and characteristics were missing. A large portion of the study participants were female (74.02%), which was in line with other studies of the same nature [21]. There were no significant differences in the gender distribution between the conditions. Next, 50.8% of participants were 25 - 34 years old. Almost all participants (95.1%) were Chinese, which was overly represented compared to the population of Singapore [24]. Next, 70.65% of participants had a university degree or higher and 69.95% had a full-time employment. More than half of the study participants (65%) had never been married. Next, the average body mass index (BMI), calculated from participants' self-reported weight and height, of the study participants was 22.88 (SD = 5.34), which was near the normal weight and overweight boundary for Asian populations. Additionally, the BMI distribution was left-skewed, i.e., there were more normal-weight participants than overweight and obese ones. Next, the average grit score of participants in our study was 2.75 (SD = 0.58), which is considered to be moderate. Lastly, only a small portion of participants (N=25; 10.2%) had regularly logged food diaries prior to joining the study. On average, all participants logged 1.3 days (SD = 4.3; median = 0) of food diary in the last 30 days before enrolling in the study. There were no significant differences in BMI, grit score, and pre-treatment logging experience between the experimental groups.

Next, we examine the participants' food logging and eating behavior during the study. The distribution of the number of diary entries logged per day is shown in Figure 3 where the mean is 6.06 entries (SD = 3.64). On average, treatment participants logged 6.23 entries per day (SD = 3.81), whereas control participants logged 5.81 entries per day (SD = 3.38) as shown in Table 1. There is a significant difference between the experimental groups according

to the Mann-Whitney U test of diary entries (U=2704500, p<0.01). Next, to examine the participants' daily caloric intakes, we first removed 3 outlying data points whose daily caloric intakes (e.g., more than 100K kcal consumed in a single day) were higher than two standard deviations away from the participants' mean caloric intake. Upon further inspection, we found that the outliers were caused by the inaccuracy in the user-contributed food databases. Figure 4 displays the distribution of the amount of caloric intake per day. As we can see from Table 1, on average, all participants consumed 1254.85 kcal per day (SD = 508.83), whereas treatment and control participants consumed 1249.05 kcal (SD = 520.14) and 1263.05 kcal (SD = 492.4) per day, respectively. Although control participants had a slightly higher mean caloric intake than treatment participants, the difference is not statistically significant.

Lastly, at the end of the study, 202 participants (111 and 91 in the treatment and the control conditions, respectively) were considered intervention participants, i.e., those who received at least 1 deduction and therefore not having full compliance. There is no significant difference in the numbers of intervention participants between the two experimental groups.

6 ANALYSIS AND RESULTS

The primary goal of our study is to evaluate the effectiveness of random-loss and fixed-loss incentives by measuring the participants' self-tracking and self-reporting (i.e., daily task) compliance during the 30-day intervention period. Moreover, our secondary goal is to examine the effects of the two incentive programs in promoting sustained behavior change after the inventions are removed. The analysis was conducted on a modified intention-to-treat (mITT) basis. Specifically, we exclude 43 participants (24 from the treatment group and 19 from the control group) who did not receive full interventions from the analysis, i.e., those who were only briefed about the financial incentive program at the start of the study but never received any deductions and related email messages throughout the study due to full compliance. Ultimately, 202 participants are included in the analysis.

6.1 Preliminary Analysis

We first present a preliminary analysis to examine the participants' compliance in completing the daily tasks across the experimental groups. Our outcomes of interest are **compliance days**, defined as the number of days a participant completed his/her daily task, and **daily compliance users**, defined as the percentage of participants who completed the daily task on a specific day. The distribution of the number of days of completed daily tasks by participants from both treatment and control conditions is shown in Figure 5. The median number of days of completed daily tasks is 19. In total, 37 participants (18%) did not complete any daily tasks.

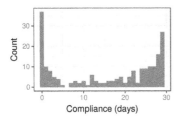

Figure 5: Distribution of the number of days participants completed daily tasks.

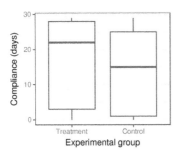

Figure 6: Compliance days by experimental group.

Figure 6 shows a box plot of compliance days for the two experimental groups. As we can see, treatment participants generally have a higher level of compliance with the study protocol than control participants. The medians compliance days of the treatment and the control groups are 22 and 15, respectively. The nonparametric Mann-Whitney U test of compliance days in the two conditions over the 30-day period shows a significant difference (H_0: treatment = control; U =4142, p<0.05). Uncontrolled, the analysis suggests that our random-loss incentive is more effective than the fixed-loss incentive in improving participants' daily task completion over 30 days.

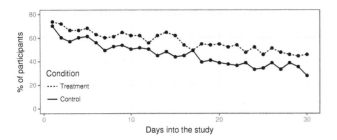

Figure 7: Daily compliance users over time.

Figure 7 depicts the percentages of daily compliance users from the start to the end of the study. On the first day, both conditions

have the similar daily compliance users (73.87% and 70.33% for treatment and control, respectively). However, the compliance trend continues to decrease over time as the study progresses. This is not surprising since the declining in compliance is consistent with past studies on longitudinal health behaviors [21, 23, 25]. Over the 30-day period, the treatment condition has consistently shown higher daily compliance users than the control condition. As we can see, 45.95% of treatment participants completed the daily task on the last day of the study, whereas only 28.09% of control participants did so.

6.2 Effectiveness of the random-loss incentive

In this section, we present the regression analysis to assess the effectiveness of our random-loss incentive. Due to the repeated measures design of the study, we model participants' daily compliance using mixed effects logistic regression, taking into account that data points from the same participant are not independent. The binary dependent variable in our models is the participants' day-to-day compliance status (1 = a participant completed the task in time on a given day, otherwise 0). Main effects for experimental condition (binary predictor; 1 = treatment, otherwise 0) and interactions between experimental condition and other predictors (e.g., the number of days into the study for a given participant) are included. Next, the models control for each participant's number of days into the study (from 1 to 30). To adjust for individuals' pre-treatment differences in self-tracking experience and self-efficacy, we also control for the number of food-diary logging days in the past 30 days before the study started and self-reported perceived task difficulty for a given day in the study, respectively. Lastly, personal characteristics, such as gender (binary predictor; 1 = male, otherwise 0), age, and self-reported grit score (from 1 to 5), are also controlled for. All analyzes were performed using the lme4 package (version 1.1.14) [2] in R (version 3.4.2).

The results are presented in Table 2. First, the uncontrolled baseline model (Model 1) shows that, on any given day, treatment participants are significantly more likely (p<0.05) to complete the daily tasks compared to control participants. This suggests that the random-loss incentive is generally more effective than the fixed-loss incentive in influencing the participants' engagement. The result is also in line with the Mann-Whitney U test of aggregated participant compliance presented in the preliminary analysis.

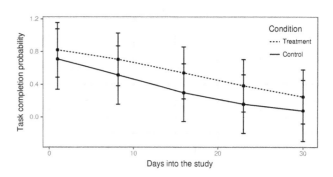

Figure 8: Interaction effect of interventions and days into the study.

Table 2: Mixed-effects logistic regressions for daily task completion.

Variables	Model 1	Model 2	Model 3	Model 4	Model 5	Model 6	Model 7	Model 8
FIXED EFFECTS:	ESTIMATE							
(Intercept)	-0.71485*	0.78933*	1.00936**	0.80661*	5.77789**	7.88429**	5.88135*	5.63715
Primary predictor variables								
Treatment	0.90950*	1.01532*	0.60770	0.62142	-1.63751†	-2.45735*	0.93464	-0.70462
Days into the study × Treatment	-	-	0.02566*	0.02585*	0.09089**	0.08749*	0.07013*	0.06986*
Male × Treatment	-	-	-	-	-	2.84370	2.14528	2.32768
Age × Treatment	-	-	-	-	-	-	-0.10341	-0.09940
Grit score × Treatment	-	-	-	-	-	-	-	0.52969
Control variables								
Days into the study	-	-0.10215**	-0.11662**	-0.11674**	-0.16769**	-0.17019**	-0.13508**	-0.13469**
Pre-treatment logging days	-	-	-	0.11290*	-0.03017	-0.03697	-0.04176	-0.04022
Perceived task difficulty	-	-	-	-	1.45901**	0.99555†	1.12445**	1.14025**
Male	-	-	-	-	-	-2.52521	-1.30442	-1.24929
Age	-	-	-	-	-	-	0.00871	0.09400
Grit score	-	-	-	-	-	-	-	0.05229
RANDOM EFFECTS:	VARIANCE							
Subjects (intercept)	8.415	10.47	10.52	10.26	9.806	12.223	3.241	3.028
Perceived task difficulty (slope)	-	-	-	-	3.073	2.206	1.334	1.312
Model statistics								
AIC	4779.5	4354.4	4350.8	4347.8	824.8	772.1	703	706.6
BIC	4799.6	4381.3	4384.3	4388	879.8	838.5	780.1	795.5
Number of observations	6050	6050	6050	6050	3316	3114	2774	2774
Number of subjects	202	202	202	202	168	150	136	136

Significance thresholds are $†$ $p<0.1$, * $p<0.05$, and ** $p<0.01$.

Next, we evaluate the significance of the decline in compliance over time, as shown in Figure 7, by controlling for the number of days since a participant has engaged with the study (Model 2) and its interaction with the experimental condition (Model 3). Figure 8 displays the interaction effect of interventions and days into the study on the participants' likelihood of completing the daily tasks. A significant interaction term ($p<0.05$), introduced in Model 3, indicates that the benefits of the treatment condition depend on the number of days a participants spent in the study. As participants spend more time in the study, their compliance tends to decline across the experimental groups. However, treatment participants are more likely to complete the tasks than control participants as the study progresses. That is, a one day increase results in the odds ratios of 0.91305 and 0.88992 for the treatment condition and the control condition, respectively. Note that the odds ratios are obtained from exponentiating the sum of the logistic regression coefficients for *days into the study* and its *treatment interaction term*

In Models 4 and 5, we further assess the main and interaction effects of the inventions by adding control variables for the participants' prior food logging experience (Model 4) as well as their current experience in engaging with the daily tasks (Model 5). After controlling for these factors, the treatment interaction effect remains significant ($p<0.01$) and the results suggest that the effectiveness of our intervention is robust even after adjusting for past experience and self-efficacy. Moreover, the difference in the odds ratios between the experimental conditions increases by 9.5% in Model 5, a considerable gain from the baseline models. As the study progresses one more day, the odds ratios of the treatment condition

and the control condition are 0.92608 and 0.84562, respectively. Unsurprisingly, we find that self-efficacy has a positive effect ($p<0.01$) on the participants' likelihood of completing the tasks, i.e., participants who consider the task to be easy/very easy on a specific day are more likely to finish it and vice versa. Interestingly, past logging experience has no significant effect on daily task completion. This may be explained by the fact that logging food diary is merely a part of the requirements for completing the daily task. Remembering to filling out all daily surveys *in time* is perhaps more demanding to most participants. Thus, having some familiarity with food logging is not an major contributor to the participants' compliance.

Lastly, we examine the main effects of personal characteristics, i.e., gender, age, and grit, and their treatment interaction effects on the participants' day-to-day compliance. These variables are included in Models 6, 7, and 8 as shown in Table 2. Unlike past studies [21], none of the personal characteristics have any significant impact on the likelihood of completing the daily tasks after adjusting for other factors. Although participants with higher grit scores are more likely to complete the daily tasks than those with lower scores, grit does not significantly impact the participants' compliance, which is surprising. As suggested by Duckworth et al. [11], grit constitutes *perseverance* and *passion* for long-term goals. Therefore, one possible explanation is that, even though the participants have voluntarily signed up for our study, they may not have strong passion for the day-to-day self-tracking and reporting tasks, making grit less effective in this context. Overall, the full model (Model 8) shows an encouraging result indicating that the effects of our random-loss incentive on day-to-day compliance is significant even after controlling for all other factors. According to the full model, the odds of completing the daily tasks for treatment participants and control participants when the time of the study increases by 1 day are 0.93723 and 0.87399, respectively.

6.3 Post-intervention self-tracking behavior

In this section, we examine the intervention effects on the participants' change in their dietary self-tracking habit before the interventions were administered and after they were removed. Approximately one month after the last participant had completed the study, we collected the food logging data from all participants in the following 30 days after their study period was over. Table 3 displays the participants' food logging behavior in the last 30 days before and after the intervention. First, there is a significantly larger number of food loggers during the post-intervention than the pre-intervention phases (40 versus 25; χ^2=3.991, p<0.05). The gain is due to changes in the participants' logging habits whereby 25 participants who had never logged any diaries during the pre-intervention phase continued to log their food intake after the study was over, whereas 10 participants who had previously logged food diaries during the pre-intervention phase became inactive thereafter. However, there is no significant difference in the numbers of *active* food loggers (defined as those who logged at least 7 days of food diary in the last 30 days) between the two periods. Amongst the treatment and the control conditions, we found no significant differences in the numbers of food loggers (21 versus 19 and) and active loggers (9 versus 10) post-intervention. Lastly, on average, all participants logged their diaries more frequently during the post-intervention than the pre-intervention phases (2.29 versus 1.3) but the difference is not significant. Within a subset of participants (N=92) who logged their diaries during both periods, there is a significant increase in the average food diary days from the pre-intervention to the post-intervention phases (3.47 versus 6.09; V=1414, p<0.01) but there is no difference between the conditions.

Table 3: Pre/post-intervention logging behavior.

Pre-intervention	Treatment	Control	All
Number of food loggers	13	12	25
Number of active food loggers	5	7	12
Number of logged diary days (mean)	1.12	1.53	1.3
Post-intervention			
Number of food loggers	21	19	40
Number of active food loggers	9	10	19
Number of logged diary days (mean)	1.84	2.84	2.29
Pre/post-intervention changes			
Number of new food loggers	12	13	25
Number of new active food loggers	2	6	8
Number of existing food loggers who gave up	4	6	10

Active food loggers are defined as users who recorded at least 7 days of food diary in the last 30 days.

7 CONCLUDING DISCUSSION

To our knowledge, this study is the first randomized trial to demonstrate that framing financial incentives as random loss is effective in increasing individuals' engagement with dietary self-tracking and self-reporting. Particularly, we show that a small unpredictable loss can serve as a fairly powerful motivator to promote compliance

and alleviate participants' insensitivity to repeated interventions. The results are encouraging especially since it is well-established that loss-framed incentive is a strong motivator for health behavior change [25, 32]. Our results indicate that individuals who were in the random-loss incentive program are significantly more likely to complete the daily tasks than those who were in the fixed-loss incentive program after controlling for time spent in the study and other personal characteristics, such as gender, age, prior self-tracking experience, self-efficacy, and grit. Unlike previous work [21], we found that the heterogeneity of participants did not affect the outcomes of the interventions. For instance, male and female participants did not differ significantly in their likelihood to complete daily tasks. More surprisingly, there is no significant difference in compliance amongst individuals with differing self-tracking experience and grit. This may be explained by the facts that: (1) prior food logging experience marginally contributes to the success of completing self-report surveys, which is arguably a more demanding requirement of the study; and (2) highly gritty participants may not necessarily be more passionate about self-tracking and self-reporting due to its tediousness nature and therefore are not more likely to persistently pursue the goals than less gritty participants. At the post-invention phase, we found no significant difference in the effectiveness of the incentives in sustaining self-tracking behavior for the next 30 days after the interventions were discontinued. Although there was an initial increase in the number of food loggers and self-tracking activities during the first post-intervention week, these numbers substantially declined in the subsequent weeks as more individuals disengaged from dietary self-tracking. The fact that the self-tracking behavior was not sustained post-intervention is not surprising. Unlike typical health intervention studies, participants in our study were not instructed to use self-tracking tools as a means to achieve specific health goals nor were they motivated beyond the primary scope of the study, i.e., contributing their lifestyle data to research about dietary habits. Consistent with recent studies [15, 25], our results confirm the importance of a long-term financial incentive program in self-tracking studies.

The results have several implications for future precision medicine and mobile-health (mHealth) studies and interventions. First, our random-loss incentive is proven to be effective in promoting long-term engagement with self-tracking regardless of individuals' personal characteristics, making it suitable for population-level intervention programs. Next, the cost-effectiveness of our incentive implies that improved compliance is attainable with relatively modest cost thanks to the effects of loss aversion and unpredictability. In our setting, the mean cost per participant, including both the cash and the smartwatch rewards, is less than S$40. Lastly, in terms of data integrity, we observe very little noise in the food diary entries and survey responses contributed by participants in our study. Apart from inaccurate nutritional facts of some food items which we discussed earlier, we find no evidence of misbehavior by our participants.

Limitations: Our study design specifically focused on dietary self-tracking and self-reporting compliance in healthy individuals and did not consider health outcomes, e.g., improved BMI, which might serve as additional motivation for participants. Understandably, this would have required a different study design and population. Although we initially aimed to representatively recruit participants from Facebook users in Singapore, the majority of participants eventually enrolled were female working adults which may potentially bias the generalizability of the findings. Lastly, future studies should further examine the effects of unpredictability (i.e., the Random Rewards design) on gain-framed and loss-framed incentives in the same settings.

8 ACKNOWLEDGEMENT

This research is supported by the National Research Foundation, Prime Minister's Office, Singapore under its International Research Centres in Singapore Funding Initiative.

REFERENCES

[1] Sofiane Abbar, Yelena Mejova, and Ingmar Weber. 2015. You Tweet What You Eat: Studying Food Consumption Through Twitter. In *Proceedings of the 33rd international conference on Human factors in computing systems - CHI '15*. ACM Press, New York, New York, USA, 3197-3206. https://doi.org/10.1145/2702123.2702153

[2] Douglas Bates, Martin Mächler, Ben Bolker, and Steve Walker. 2015. Fitting Linear Mixed-Effects Models using lme4. *Journal of Statistical Software* 67, 1 (oct 2015), 1-48. https://doi.org/10.18637/jss.v067.i01 arXiv:1406.5823

[3] Gharad Bryan, Dean Karlan, and Scott Nelson. 2010. Commitment Devices. *Annual Review of Economics* 2, 1 (sep 2010), 671-698. https://doi.org/10.1146/annurev.economics.102308.124324

[4] Gary Charness and Uri Gneezy. 2009. Incentives to Exercise. *Econometrica* 77, 3 (2009), 909-931. https://doi.org/10.3982/ECTA7416

[5] Yu-Kai Chou. 2015. *Actionable Gamification: Beyond Points, Badges, and Leaderboards*. Octalysis Media.

[6] James Clawson, Jessica A. Pater, Andrew D. Miller, Elizabeth D. Mynatt, and Lena Mamykina. 2015. No Longer Wearing: Investigating the Abandonment of Personal Health-Tracking Technologies on Craigslist. In *Proceedings of the 2015 ACM International Joint Conference on Pervasive and Ubiquitous Computing - UbiComp '15*. ACM, 647-658. https://doi.org/10.1145/2750858.2807554

[7] Francis S. Collins and Harold Varmus. 2015. A New Initiative on Precision Medicine. *New England Journal of Medicine* 372, 9 (feb 2015), 793-795. https://doi.org/10.1056/NEJMp1500523

[8] Felicia Cordeiro, Elizabeth Bales, Erin Cherry, and James Fogarty. 2015. Rethinking the Mobile Food Journal: Exploring Opportunities for Lightweight Photo-Based Capture. In *Proceedings of the 33rd Annual ACM Conference on Human Factors in Computing Systems - CHI '15*. ACM Press, New York, New York, USA, 3207-3216. https://doi.org/10.1145/2702123.2702154

[9] Munmun De Choudhury, Mrinal Kumar, and Ingmar Weber. 2017. Computational Approaches Toward Integrating Quantified Self Sensing and Social Media. In *Proceedings of the 2017 ACM Conference on Computer Supported Cooperative Work and Social Computing - CSCW '17*. ACM Press, New York, New York, USA, 1334-1349. https://doi.org/10.1145/2998181.2998219

[10] Ed Diener, Derrick Wirtz, William Tov, Chu Kim-Prieto, Dong-won Choi, Shigehiro Oishi, and Robert Biswas-Diener. 2010. New Well-being Measures: Short Scales to Assess Flourishing and Positive and Negative Feelings. *Social Indicators Research* 97, 2 (jun 2010), 143-156. https://doi.org/10.1007/s11205-009-9493-y

[11] Angela L. Duckworth, Christopher Peterson, Michael D. Matthews, and Dennis R. Kelly. 2007. Grit: Perseverance and passion for long-term goals. *Journal of Personality and Social Psychology* 92, 6 (2007), 1087-1101.

[12] Luis Fernandez-Luque, Meghna Singh, Ferda Ofli, Yelena A Mejova, Ingmar Weber, Michael Aupetit, Sahar Karim Jreige, Ahmed Elmagarmid, Jaideep Srivastava, and Mohamed Ahmedna. 2017. Implementing 360° Quantified Self for childhood obesity: feasibility study and experiences from a weight loss camp in Qatar. *BMC Medical Informatics and Decision Making* 17, 1 (dec 2017), 37. https://doi.org/10.1186/s12911-017-0432-6

[13] C. B. Ferster and B. F. Skinner. 1957. *Schedules of reinforcement*. Appleton-Century-Crofts, East Norwalk, CT, US. https://doi.org/10.1037/10627-000

[14] Eric A. Finkelstein, Derek S. Brown, David R. Brown, and David M. Buchner. 2008. A randomized study of financial incentives to increase physical activity among sedentary older adults. *Preventive Medicine* 47, 2 (aug 2008), 182-187. https://doi.org/10.1016/J.YPMED.2008.05.002

[15] Eric A Finkelstein, Benjamin A Haaland, Marcel Bilger, Aarti Sahasranaman, Robert A Sloan, Ei Ei Khaing Nang, and Kelly R Evenson. 2016. Effectiveness of activity trackers with and without incentives to increase physical activity (TRIPPA): a randomised controlled trial. *The Lancet Diabetes & Endocrinology* 4, 12 (oct 2016), 983-995. https://doi.org/10.1016/S2213-8587(16)30284-4

[16] Xavier Giné, Dean Karlan, and Jonathan Zinman. 2010. Put Your Money Where Your Butt is: A Commitment Contract for Smoking Cessation. *American Economic Journal: Applied Economics* 2, 4 (jul 2010), 213-235. https://doi.org/10.1257/app.2.4.213

[17] Uri Gneezy, Stephan Meier, and Pedro Rey-Biel. 2011. When and Why Incentives (Don't) Work to Modify Behavior. *Journal of Economic Perspectives* 25, 4 (nov 2011), 191-210. https://doi.org/10.1257/jep.25.4.191

[18] Lewis R. Goldberg. 1999. A broad-bandwidth, public-domain, personality inventory measuring the lower-level facets of several five-factor models. *Personality Psychology in Europe* 7 (1999), 7-28.

[19] Scott D Halpern, Rachel Kohn, Aaron Dornbrand-Lo, Thomas Metkus, David A Asch, and Kevin G Volpp. 2011. Lottery-based versus fixed incentives to increase clinicians' response to surveys. *Health Services Research* 46, 5 (oct 2011), 1663-74. https://doi.org/10.1111/j.1475-6773.2011.01264.x

[20] Daniel Kahneman and Amos Tversky. 1979. Prospect Theory: An Analysis of Decision Under Risk. *Econometrica* 47, 2 (jul 1979), 263-291. https://doi.org/10.1142/9789814417358_0006

[21] Yi-Chin Kato-Lin, Vibhanshu Abhishek, Julie S. Downs, and Rema Padman. 2016. Food for Thought: The Impact of m-Health Enabled Interventions on Eating Behavior. *SSRN Electronic Journal* (feb 2016). https://doi.org/10.2139/ssrn.2736792

[22] Yelena Mejova, Hamed Haddadi, Anastasios Noulas, and Ingmar Weber. 2015. #FoodPorn: Obesity Patterns in Culinary Interactions. In *Proceedings of the 5th International Conference on Digital Health 2015 - DH '15*. ACM Press, New York, New York, USA, 51-58. https://doi.org/10.1145/2750511.2750524

[23] Katherine L. Milkman, Julia A. Minson, and Kevin G. M. Volpp. 2014. Holding the Hunger Games Hostage at the Gym: An Evaluation of Temptation Bundling. *Management Science* 60, 2 (feb 2014), 283-299. https://doi.org/10.1287/mnsc.2013.1784

[24] Department of Statistics Singapore. 2017. Population Trends. (2017). Retrieved from http://www.singstat.gov.sg/docs/default-source/default-document-library/publications/publications_and_papers/population_and_population_structure/population2017.pdf.

[25] Mitesh S. Patel, David A. Asch, Roy Rosin, Dylan S. Small, Scarlett L. Bellamy, Jack Heuer, Susan Sproat, Chris Hyson, Nancy Haff, Samantha M. Lee, Lisa Wesby, Karen Hoffer, David Shuttleworth, Devon H. Taylor, Victoria Hilbert, Jingsan Zhu, Lin Yang, Xingmei Wang, and Kevin G. Volpp. 2016. Framing Financial Incentives to Increase Physical Activity Among Overweight and Obese Adults. *Annals of Internal Medicine* 164, 6 (mar 2016), 385. https://doi.org/10.7326/M15-1635

[26] Marianne Promberger and Theresa M Marteau. 2013. When do financial incentives reduce intrinsic motivation? comparing behaviors studied in psychological and economic literatures. *Health Psychology* 32, 9 (sep 2013), 950-7. https://doi.org/10.1037/a0032727

[27] Tauhidur Rahman, Mary Czerwinski, Ran Gilad-Bachrach, and Paul Johns. 2016. Predicting "About-to-Eat" Moments for Just-in-Time Eating Intervention. In *Proceedings of the 6th International Conference on Digital Health - DH '16*. Montreal, Canada.

[28] John Rooksby, Mattias Rost, Alistair Morrison, and Matthew Chalmers. 2014. Personal tracking as lived informatics. In *Proceedings of the 32nd international conference on Human factors in computing systems - CHI '14*. ACM Press, New York, New York, USA, 1163-1172. https://doi.org/10.1145/2556288.2557039

[29] Andrew Steptoe, Tessa M. Pollard, and Jane Wardle. 1995. Development of a Measure of the Motives Underlying the Selection of Food: The Food Choice Questionnaire. *Appetite* 25, 3 (dec 1995), 267-284. https://doi.org/10.1006/appe.1995.0061

[30] Melanie Swan. 2013. The Quantified Self: Fundamental Disruption in Big Data Science and Biological Discovery. *Big Data* 1, 2 (jun 2013), 85-99. https://doi.org/10.1089/big.2012.0002

[31] Tari D Topolski, James LoGerfo, Donald L Patrick, Barbara Williams, Julie Walwick, and Marsha B Patrick. 2006. The Rapid Assessment of Physical Activity (RAPA) among older adults. *Preventing Chronic Disease* 3, 4 (oct 2006), A118.

[32] Kevin G. Volpp, Leslie K. John, Andrea B. Troxel, Laurie Norton, Jennifer Fassbender, and George Loewenstein. 2008. Financial incentive-based approaches for weight loss: A randomized trial. *JAMA* 300, 22 (dec 2008), 2631-2637. https://doi.org/10.1001/jama.2008.804

[33] Kevin G. Volpp, Andrea B. Troxel, Mark V. Pauly, Henry A. Glick, Andrea Puig, David A. Asch, Robert Galvin, Jingsan Zhu, Fei Wan, Jill DeGuzman, Elizabeth Corbett, Janet Weiner, and Janet Audrain-McGovern. 2009. A Randomized, Controlled Trial of Financial Incentives for Smoking Cessation. *New England Journal of Medicine* 360, 7 (feb 2009), 699-709. https://doi.org/10.1056/NEJMsa0806819

[34] Rui Wang, Fanglin Chen, Zhenyu Chen, Tianxing Li, Gabriella Harari, Stefanie Tignor, Xia Zhou, Dror Ben-Zeev, and Andrew T. Campbell. 2014. StudentLife: Assessing Mental Health, Academic Performance and Behavioral Trends of College Students using Smartphones. In *Proceedings of the 2014 ACM International Joint Conference on Pervasive and Ubiquitous Computing - UbiComp '14*. ACM Press, New York, New York, USA, 3-14. https://doi.org/10.1145/2632048.2632054

[35] Yafei Wang, Ingmar Weber, and Prasenjit Mitra. 2016. Quantified Self Meets Social Media: Sharing of Weight Updates on Twitter. In *Proceedings of the 6th International Conference on Digital Health Conference - DH '16*. ACM Press, New York, New York, USA, 93-97. https://doi.org/10.1145/2896338.2896363

Inferring Visual Behaviour from User Interaction Data on a Medical Dashboard

Ainhoa Yera, Javier Muguerza, Olatz Arbelaitz,
Iñigo Perona
Faculty of Informatics
University of the Basque Country
Donostia, Spain
{firstname.lastname}@ehu.eus

Richard Keers, Darren Ashcroft
Division of Pharmacy and Optometry
Greater Manchester Patient Safety Translational Research Centre
University of Manchester
Manchester, United Kingdom
{richard.keers|darren.ashcroft}@manchester.ac.uk

Richard Williams, Niels Peek
Division of Informatics, Imaging and Data Sciences
Greater Manchester Patient Safety Translational Research Centre
University of Manchester
Manchester, United Kingdom
{richard.williams2|niels.peek}@manchester.ac.uk

Caroline Jay, Markel Vigo*
School of Computer Science
University of Manchester
Manchester, United Kingdom
{caroline.jay|markel.vigo}@manchester.ac.uk

ABSTRACT

Making medical software easy to use and actionable is challenging due to the characteristics of the data (its size and complexity) and its context of use. This results in user interfaces with a high-density of data that do not support optimal decision-making by clinicians. Anecdotal evidence indicates that clinicians demand *the right amount of information* to carry out their tasks. This suggests that adaptive user interfaces could be employed in order to cater for the information needs of the users and tackle information overload. Yet, since these information needs may vary, it is necessary first to identify and prioritise them, before implementing adaptations to the user interface. As gaze has long been known to be an indicator of interest, eye tracking allows us to unobtrusively observe where the users are looking, but it is not practical to use in a deployed system. Here, we address the question of whether we can infer visual behaviour on a medication safety dashboard through user interaction data. Our findings suggest that, there is indeed a relationship between the use of the mouse (in terms of clickstreams and mouse hovers) and visual behaviour in terms of cognitive load. We discuss the implications of this finding for the design of adaptive medical dashboards.

CCS CONCEPTS

• **Human-centered computing** → **Empirical studies in HCI**;
• **Applied computing** → **Health care information systems**;

---

*Corresponding author.

KEYWORDS

Medical dashboards; interaction analysis; user modelling

ACM Reference Format:
Ainhoa Yera, Javier Muguerza, Olatz Arbelaitz, Iñigo Perona, Richard Keers, Darren Ashcroft, Richard Williams, Niels Peek, Caroline Jay, Markel Vigo. 2018. Inferring Visual Behaviour from User Interaction Data on a Medical Dashboard. In *DH'18: 2018 International Digital Health Conference, April 23–26, 2018, Lyon, France*. ACM, New York, NY, USA, 5 pages. https://doi.org/10.1145/3194658.3194676

1 INTRODUCTION

The responsibility of health care professionals (especially General Practitioners) is shifting from a reactive patient-by-patient role to a proactive manager of population health. This shift requires the availability of health data and information tools that give a population-level view of such data, which allow the identification of individual patients that require intervention. Consequently, the use of medical dashboards is becoming increasingly important in using this data to improve healthcare. While the current wealth of clinical data satisfies the availability premise, it becomes, at the same time, a double-edged sword in that medical dashboards suffer from information overload. What is more, clinicians have varying levels of practical clinical experience, different problem-solving skills, and vary considerably in their IT skills. As the information density in the clinical environment is increasing rapidly and the role of medical dashboards is still at an early stage, it is of paramount importance to build smart adaptive systems that cater for the needs of clinicians and support them in the transition towards a proactive management of population health.

Before we start building smart adaptive systems that cater for the information needs of the users, we need to understand what these information needs are and whether they can be unobtrusively detected while the users interact with medical dashboards. As gaze is well known to be an indicator of interest [4], in this paper we explore if we can approximate gaze through the interactive behaviour of users including mouse clicks and mouse hovers. Previous work has explored this relationship and has found that

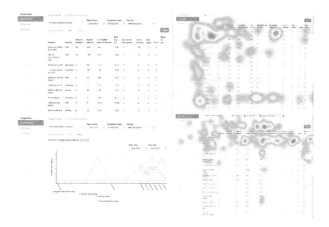

Figure 1: A sample of SMASH views: the table view (top-left) and visualisations (bottom-left). On the right, the heatmap patterns generated on the pilot study

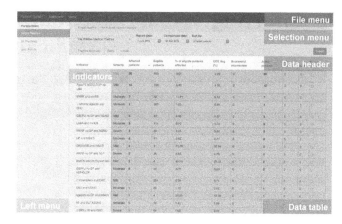

Figure 2: AOIs defined in SMASH. The remaining three AOIs correspond to pop-up dialogues (2) and charts (1)

mouse and gaze are strongly related: dwell times on specific regions are correlated with the likelihood of visiting that region with the mouse [3]. In gaze prediction models for search engine results pages (SERPs), the inclusion of the mouse coordinates, the velocity and direction of the cursor, and the time elapsed since starting to view the results achieves an accuracy of 77% [6]. However, unlike websites and SERPs, medical dashboards are constrained by grid layouts where data is displayed in a tabular fashion, which determines the variability of behaviours that can be exhibited. Given these constraints, we address the following research question: can we determine the users' visual behaviour based on their exhibited interactive behaviour?

We examine this question on the Salford Medication Safety Dashboard (SMASH), one of two vital components of a pharmacist-led information technology intervention for safe prescribing of medications in primary care, from which we collect user interaction data and whose purpose and functionalities we describe later in Section 2.1. First, we ran a user study with six clinicians in the lab where they carried out typical tasks in SMASH while gaze data was collected with an eye-tracker. Using exploratory data mining techniques we clustered the participants based on the collected interactive behaviour and we employed inferential statistics to find relationships between their visual behaviour. Second, we applied the same clustering analysis on the interaction data by adding the logged interaction of 35 clinicians in SMASH on a ten-month observational study. The ultimate objective was to ascertain whether we could reliably extrapolate the lab findings to a setting where no eye-tracking device is deployed.

2 USER STUDIES

We ran one pilot study and two user studies. The pilot study (N = 5) informed the definition of the areas of interest on the SMASH user interface prior to the laboratory study (N = 6), where we collected fixation data generated by the eye-tracker as well as user interaction data. In the observational study (N = 35) that ran for a period of 10 months we collected user interaction data. Next we describe the platform, the data we collected and the metrics we computed.

2.1 Stimulus: the SMASH Dashboard

SMASH is a web dashboard that highlights patients at risk of potentially hazardous medication safety practices in general practices [8]. SMASH incorporates a refined set of 24 prescribing indicators from the pharmacist-led information-technology based intervention (PINCER) [2]. It displays summary statistics for each of the indicators, counting how many patients are currently at risk in a given practice and relating those numbers to previous episodes and other practices. In addition, pharmacists and GPs can look up which patients are currently at risk for each indicator. The dashboard is being deployed in Salford, a city in the Greater Manchester conurbation, comprising a population of 250,000 served by primary care that uses two of the three largest GP computer systems in the UK, with additional linkage to secondary care records. The user interface of SMASH is divided into seven screens or views: (1) a landing page containing a summary of a given practice, (2) a list of patients who are affected by more than one indicator, (3) a table view displaying the indicators and (4) the graph-based visualisations of the indicators. When clicking on the number of patients affected by a given indicator on the table view, further screens are revealed including (5) the list of patients at risk for this specific indicator, (6) the trends for this indicator over time and (7) information about the selected indicator.

Figures 1–2 show the table view, which display a data table containing the number of patients who are affected by the indicators, their severity, the number of eligible patients and the percentage of patients who are affected. Indicators can be contraindications between drugs and conditions (e.g. Chronic Kidney Disease and Non-Steroidal Anti-Inflammatory drugs) or between drugs, habits and demographics. The 'Selection menu' (see Figure 2) allows the user to choose a different view of the data: the landing page, which is a small table containing the size of the practice and the number of patients affected by more than one indicator, and the 'Visualisations' view (see Figure 1, bottom-left), which is the visual representation of the table and displays the incidence of indicators as time-series through line graphs. The 'Selection menu' also contains calendar widgets for selecting reports within specific time periods.

2.2 Apparatus

The SMASH dashboard logs the user interface events triggered by the users in a database on the server. Because SMASH is a mouse-driven application the collected events are mostly mouse clicks and mouse hovers. A third event logged is the page load event, which signals navigation to a different view (e.g. from the data table to the data visualisation) that does not necessarily entail an update in the URL and is triggered by clicking on the 'Selection menu'. For each event, SMASH collects the user id, the identifier of the session (i.e. every time a user logs in, a new session is established), the timestamp, the URL where the event took place and the specific element on the user interface where the event occurred indicated by an XPATH statement.

The Tobii X2-60 eye-tracker we employed in the laboratory study logged gaze information including fixation coordinates on the screen, duration of the fixations and the saccades (movement of eyes between the fixations).

2.3 Metrics and Data Analysis Method

The gaze activity was computed using the average fixation duration (henceforth fd) in the nine Areas Of Interest (AOIs) that were defined as a consequence of the pilot study described in Section 2.5, $G = \{fd_i \mid i \in \mathbb{N}, i \leq 9\}$. Fixation duration is known to be a proxy for cognitive load [4] so our premise is that, if we want to relate visual behaviour to interactive behaviour on SMASH, cognitive load might well be an indicator to profile participants. We run Pearson correlation analysis between the G vectors in order to find participants with similar fds across the different AOIs. Consequently, a positive correlation between any two participants would entail similar visual behaviours in terms of cognitive load.

Then, we computed interaction metrics for *exploration* and *pace*.

- Exploration (e): median of the number of mouse hovers between two consecutive mouse clicks. This is based on the fact that since mouse location on screen is a proxy of gaze location [5], it can be used to quantify visual exploration.
- Pace (p): median of the elapsed time between two consecutive mouse clicks.

Using these metrics, we created two vectors per participant: $V1$ describes user interaction on all of the screens available and is computed as a vector of two attributes, the overall exploration and pace on SMASH, $V1 = \{(e, p)\}$. The second metric, $V2$, takes into consideration the above metrics in each of the seven screens of SMASH and is represented as a vector of 14 attributes per participant, $V2 = \{(e_i, p_i) \mid i \in \mathbb{N}, i \leq 7\}$. Then we applied different clustering algorithms including k-means and single-linkage method [7] to the two vectors we defined above in order to identify those users who exhibited similar interactive behaviours.

2.4 Tasks

In the pilot and laboratory study participants were assigned a specific practice and were asked to complete nine tasks classified in three ways: a) Identification of patients at risk: i.e. 'List up to three patients at risk for indicator X'; b) Identification of problems in the practice and their evolution over time: i.e. 'Identify the three indicators with the largest number of patients affected'; c) Comparison of problems between practices: i.e. 'Identify three indicators in which your practice performs worse than others'.

In the observational study no tasks were given to the participants since the SMASH dashboard was used for the purpose it was intended: the identification of those patients at risk and the promotion of good prescription practices. We expected that the participants in this study would carry out tasks of a higher ecological validity than those given in the lab setting.

2.5 Pilot Study

Five participants (3 female) who were 39 years old on average (SD = 13.5 and age range = 27–62) took part in the pilot study. All of them were computer savvy and familiar with the domain and terminology of the medication safety dashboard. Two of them were members of the Research User Group, a pool of users who frequently take part in eHealth studies, and of the remaining three: one had a degree in nursing, another one was doing a PhD in nursing and one was a medical microbiologist.

A qualitative analysis of the heatmaps of the pilot study yielded some interesting insights: the visual search strategies on the dashboard followed particular patterns. The C-shaped behaviour in Figure 1 suggests that users look at the data header, the list of indicators on the left and the values in a row belonging to a particular indicator. On the other hand, the paint drop pattern in Figure 1 indicates that users look at the header and the top rows and visual search is restricted to a few columns. This strategy can be explained by the fact that some users discovered that clicking on a header sorted the indicators based on the values of the corresponding column/variable, which was an effective strategy for completing many tasks and reduced the need for visual exploration. While the boundaries between the components of the dashboard are clear, it is difficult to establish the AOIs in a tabular environment. The patterns we found as well as the demarcation of existing user interface elements informed the design of the areas of interest, accounting for nine of them. As depicted by Figure 2 our findings suggest that the column containing the safety indicators, the table header and the remaining rows should constitute independent areas of interest.

2.6 Participants

Six participants (4 male) took part in the lab study. Five were GPs and one was a pharmacist; their average age was 38 (SD = 10 and age range = 30–56). In the observational study we collected interaction data belonging to 35 individuals who participated over a period of 10 months. Since data logging occurs unobtrusively no demographic data was collected for this study. These 35 participants are divided into the roles they play on the National Health Service: 10 pharmacists, 8 members of the Salford Clinical Commissioning Group, 8 GPs, 5 managers, and 4 other including nurses and technicians.

3 RESULTS

3.1 Interaction Data Analysis in the Lab

The k-means algorithm (k = 3 and Euclidean distance) clustered clinicians in three pair wise groups for $V1$: P4-P5, P1-P3 and P2-P6. To better understand the structure of these groups we carried out a second clustering procedure including the centroids of the clusters generated by the k-means algorithm. We then computed the distance matrix for $V1$ and then calculated the centroids using the Euclidean distance again. The resulting distance matrix can be visualized using hierarchical clustering techniques [7]. Thus, we applied the single-linkage and Ward hierarchical clustering algorithms using the Euclidean distance. Figure 3a shows the resulting dendogram for the single-linkage clustering procedure, where the height at which participants are grouped represents the distance between clusters. The arrangement of clusters in the dendogram shows three main branches that group the participants and the centroids together: P4-P5-C1, P1-P3-C2 and P2-P6-C3 which indicates that the groups discovered by k-means applied to the overall interactive behaviour of the participants remain stable.

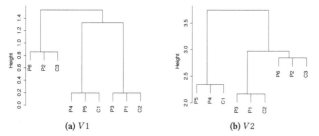

(a) $V1$ (b) $V2$

Figure 3: Single-linkage algorithm dendogram for the distance matrix and the computed centroids.

Regarding the closeness or similarity of the patterns, it can be observed that the groups of P1-P3 and P4-P5 are more compact since they are placed at the bottom of the dendrogram. To better show the proximity of the six participants, we performed a more exhaustive study of the overall interaction analysis and used the neighbour-joining tree estimation of Saitou and Nei [10] over the distance matrix of $V1$, excluding the centroids. In the resulting tree shown in Figure 4, it can be seen that P2 and P6 are some distance from the remaining participants, and P6 in particular is further than any other. This suggests that the cluster of groups P2 and P6 was not as compact as the other ones.

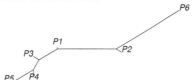

Figure 4: Neighbour joining method for the distance matrix of $V1$

We applied the same pattern discovery method on $V2$, that is, we ran the k-means algorithm (k = 3) using the Euclidean distance[1], then computed the centroids of the resulting clusters. Again, we computed the distance matrix for $V2$ and the centroids calculated in the previous step, using the Euclidean distance. Accordingly, the size of the distance matrix was of 9 x 9 measuring the distance based similarity of the six participants and the three centroids (C1-C3). Finally, we studied the proximity of the patterns discovered in $V2$, using the single-linkage algorithm [7] in the computed distance

matrix. Figure 3b shows the visual output of the single-linkage algorithm and illustrates how participants were distributed in the same form for the two clustering procedures used in $V2$, k-means and hierarchical clustering. These patterns matched the ones found for $V1$ when using the same clustering procedures. When we analysed the proximity of the patterns represented in Figure 4, we found again that P2 and P6 are quite far from the other two groups.

3.2 Eye-Tracking Data Analysis in the Lab

In order to discover groups of participants with similar visual behaviours, we paired those participants using the highest value for the Pearson correlation computed in each case – note that data was normally distributed according to the Shapiro-Wilk test ($p > 0.05$). As a result, we identified three groups (with their corresponding fixation duration patterns), which paired P1 and P3 ($\rho = 0.63, p = 0.06$), another one pairing P2 and P6 ($\rho = 0.55, p = 0.11$) and a last one pairing P4 and P5 ($\rho = 0.53, p = 0.13$). It is well known that p values are sensitive to the sample size. Since the G vectors contain 9 items, an alpha value < 0.95 is justifiable so we can say that the moderate-high correlations found show a clear tendency towards significance.

The members of the resulting groups match with the results of the cluster analysis on user interaction data. The emerging gaze patterns and the patterns discovered on user interaction data (see Figure 3) generate the same groupings. That is, those individuals having similar interactive behaviour happen to have related visual behaviour. Specifically, individuals with a similar cognitive load (as indicated by fixation durations) exhibit similar mouse use as captured by the exploration and pace metrics on SMASH ($V1$) and on its seven views ($V2$).

3.3 Interaction Data Analysis in the Observational Study

We carried out the analysis of user interaction data including the data of the lab participants and that of those who took part in the observational study. The purpose of analysing the two datasets together was to ascertain whether the emerging clusters would include the six laboratory participants in the same pairs. If the pairs of users fell again in the same clusters we could speculate that those participants belonging to the same cluster would have similar search behaviour to their lab counterparts. We therefore re-run our analysis (i.e. k-means and Euclidean distance) on $V1$, which this time accounted for 41 participants (i.e. 35 from the observational study + 6 from the lab).

Table 1 below shows the distribution of the lab study participants in the generated clusters[2]. The results indicate that the six laboratory participants are grouped in a similar way. P2 was the only participant falling in a different group, as instead of belonging to the same pair as P6, they were a member of P1 and P3's group. Taking into account the proximity analysis carried out for $V1$ (see Figure 4) this finding was not surprising given that P2 and P6's clustering was unstable. Hence, the fact that P2 switched groups would be understandable.

---

[1] A silhouette analysis on Cluster Validity Indexes [1] indicates that k = 3 is the most appropriate cluster configuration when compared to k = 4 and k = 5. Scores are 0.51, 0.20 and 0.003 respectively for $V1$, and 0.002, -0.011 and -0.046 for $V2$.

[2] A silhouette analysis on Cluster Validity Indexes indicates, again, that k = 3 is the most appropriate cluster configuration for all ks, where $3 \leq k \leq 10$.

Table 1: Results of k-means (k = 3, d = Euclidean) for $V1$ when merging the participants of the lab and the observational study

	Clusters		
	1	2	3
Lab participants	P6	P4, P5	P1, P2, P3
Number of participants from the observational study	2	19	14

4 DISCUSSION AND CONCLUSIONS

The clustering analysis on the vectors containing exploration and pace metrics generated clusters with the same members when the analysis considered the whole platform ($V1$) and when the screens were factored in the analysis ($V2$). This may mean that, within the generated clusters, the users' interactive behaviour was similar across all views of SMASH. Alternatively, if the behaviour was different (i.e. a specific view led to a different behaviour) this also changed similarly across the participants within the clusters. There are implications as far as user modelling is concerned in that this finding suggests that incorporating the specific view in the user model may not make any difference to the way pace and exploration metrics are used in the model.

The analysis of the fixation duration in the nine areas of interest of SMASH yields the same groups as the ones generated by the analysis of user interaction. This indicates that those participants who exhibited a particular interactive behaviour in terms of pace and exploration had a similar visual behaviour in terms of fixation duration on the AOIs. Prior work suggests that gaze is a proxy of attention and, at the same time, attention precedes action: this relationship is transitive and the delay from gaze to cursor action is between 250–700 milliseconds [6]. Therefore we can say that these groupings are not incidental and the exhibition of particular interactive behaviours might be determined, to some extent, by the duration of fixations on specific areas of interest.

We evaluated the robustness of the laboratory analysis by including the interaction data of another 35 participants who used SMASH as part of their daily activities. The results show that the resulting clusters are stable across the two settings despite the fact that different tasks were conducted. This adds further evidence to the initial research question about whether we can infer visual behaviour from interactive behaviour. Without having gaze data from the participants of the observational study, we can hypothesise that their visual behaviour might be similar to that of the laboratory participants who were grouped in their respective clusters. Future work will certainly pursue this lead.

This has promising consequences in that visual behaviour could be inferred using interactive data alone. Interaction data analysis can be carried out in real time in the browser. The processing and analysis of interaction data is straightforward –provided that the right metrics are being monitored– and the deployment of eye-tracking devices beyond laboratory settings is not to be expected in the medium term. Since we found that there is a relationship between exploration and pace, and fixation durations (and, consequently, cognitive load), these metrics can be used 1) to infer usability problems in real-time and 2) to inform adaptations on the user interface. These adaptations could be implemented as views on the data to reduce the information overload of medical dashboards. This could be accomplished by enabling the direct manipulation of data tables [11] and the use of transient visualisations [9].

ACKNOWLEDGMENTS

Ethical approval for the study was granted by the School of Computer Science Ethics Committee (reference number CS 152b) and University of Manchester Research Ethics Committee.

This research was funded by the National Institute for Health Research Greater Manchester Primary Care Patient Safety Translational Research Centre (NIHR Greater Manchester PSTRC) and the MRC Health eResearch Centre, Farr Institute, UK (MR/K006665/1). The views expressed are those of the author(s) and not necessarily those of the NHS, the NIHR or the Department of Health.

Funded by the University of the Basque Country UPV/EHU (grant PIF15/143); by the research group ADIAN that is supported by the Department of Education, Universities and Research of the Basque Government, (grant IT980-16); and by the Ministry of Economy and Competitiveness of the Spanish Government, co-founded by the ERDF (PhysComp project, TIN2017-85409-P).

The authors have declared that no competing interests exist.

REFERENCES

[1] Olatz Arbelaitz, Ibai Gurrutxaga, Javier Muguerza, Jesús M. Pérez, and Inigo Perona. 2013. An extensive comparative study of cluster validity indices. *Pattern Recognition* 46, 1 (2013), 243 – 256. https://doi.org/10.1016/j.patcog.2012.07.021

[2] Anthony J Avery, Sarah Rodgers, Judith A Cantrill, Sarah Armstrong, Kathrin Cresswell, Martin Eden, Rachel A Elliott, Rachel Howard, Denise Kendrick, Caroline J Morris, et al. 2012. A pharmacist-led information technology intervention for medication errors (PINCER): a multicentre, cluster randomised, controlled trial and cost-effectiveness analysis. *The Lancet* 379, 9823 (2012), 1310–1319.

[3] Mon Chu Chen, John R. Anderson, and Myeong Ho Sohn. 2001. What Can a Mouse Cursor Tell Us More?: Correlation of Eye/Mouse Movements on Web Browsing. In *CHI '01 Extended Abstracts on Human Factors in Computing Systems (CHI EA '01)*. ACM, New York, NY, USA, 281–282. https://doi.org/10.1145/634067.634234

[4] Claudia Ehmke and Stephanie Wilson. 2007. Identifying Web Usability Problems from Eye-tracking Data. In *Proceedings of the 21st British HCI Group Annual Conference on People and Computers (BCS-HCI '07)*. British Computer Society, Swinton, UK, 119–128.

[5] Qi Guo and Eugene Agichtein. 2010. Towards Predicting Web Searcher Gaze Position from Mouse Movements. In *CHI '10 Extended Abstracts on Human Factors in Computing Systems (CHI EA '10)*. ACM, New York, NY, USA, 3601–3606. https://doi.org/10.1145/1753846.1754025

[6] Jeff Huang, Ryen White, and Georg Buscher. 2012. User See, User Point: Gaze and Cursor Alignment in Web Search. In *Proceedings of the SIGCHI Conference on Human Factors in Computing Systems (CHI '12)*. ACM, New York, NY, USA, 1341–1350. https://doi.org/10.1145/2207676.2208591

[7] Anil K. Jain and Richard C. Dubes. 1988. *Algorithms for clustering data*. Prentice-Hall, Inc., Upper Saddle River, NJ, USA.

[8] RN Keers, R Williams, C Davies, N Peek, and DM Ashcroft. 2015. Improving medication safety in primary care: developing a stakeholder-centred electronic prescribing safety indicator dashboard. *Pharmacoepidemiology and Drug Safety* (2015). https://doi.org/10.1002/pds.3812 Online Supp.

[9] Charles Perin, Romain Vuillemot, and Jean-Daniel Fekete. 2014. A Table!: Improving Temporal Navigation in Soccer Ranking Tables. In *Proceedings of the 32nd Annual ACM Conference on Human Factors in Computing Systems (CHI '14)*. ACM, New York, NY, USA, 887–896. https://doi.org/10.1145/2556288.2557379

[10] N Saitou and M Nei. 1987. The neighbor-joining method: a new method for reconstructing phylogenetic trees. *Molecular Biology and Evolution* 4, 4 (1987), 406–425. https://doi.org/10.1093/oxfordjournals.molbev.a040454

[11] Romain Vuillemot and Charles Perin. 2015. Investigating the Direct Manipulation of Ranking Tables for Time Navigation. In *Proceedings of the 33rd Annual ACM Conference on Human Factors in Computing Systems (CHI '15)*. ACM, New York, NY, USA, 2703–2706. https://doi.org/10.1145/2702123.2702237

Impact of Cyberchondriasis on Polycystic Ovarian Syndrome Patients Searching Health Information Online

Mehak Soomro
Saima General Hospital
Gulshan e Hadeed, Karachi Pakistan
std_15272@iobm.edu.pk

Ather Akhlaq
Center for Health Information
Institute of Business Management
Karachi Pakistan
ather.akhlaq@iobm.edu.pk

ABSTRACT

Cyberchondriasis is the name given to the health anxiety of patients catalyzed by reading literary material available on the internet. This research finds the impact of cyberchondriasis on polycystic ovarian syndrome (PCOS) patients searching health information online. This study was carried out using a survey with a sample size of 100 PCOS patients in Karachi, Pakistan. Participants were selected from an academic institute and a private hospital. We used the cyberchondriasis scale that included five different factors namely; 'compulsion', 'distress', 'excessiveness', 'reassurance' and 'mistrust' to measure its effect searching health information online by PCOS patients. These five factors of cyberchondriasis were taken as independent variables whereas 'searching health information online' was taken as dependent variable. Exploratory factor analysis and binary logistic regression were applied on the data collected. Factor analysis reduced the cyberchondriasis scale into three factors, from which we retained two, 'compulsion' and 'mistrust'. Binary logistic regression concluded that 'compulsion' increased the odds of searching health information online by PCOS patients.

KEYWORDS

Cyberchondriasis; health anxiety; online health information; polycystic ovarian syndrome

ACM Reference format:
Mehak Soomro and Ather Akhlaq. Impact of Cyberchondriasis On Polycystic Ovarian Syndrome Patients Searching Health Information Online. In *DH'18: 2018 International Digital Health Conference, April 23-26, 2018, Lyon, France.* ACM, NY, NY, USA, 5 pages.
https://doi.org/10.1145/3194658.3194685

1 INTRODUCTION

The Internet has become the primary source of health information and has increased anxiety levels of patients searching health information online. A survey conducted among 12,000 participant in 12 different countries showed that 75% of the participants used the Internet for searching health information [1]. Internet has enabled people to search for health information instead of getting information from doctor. They examine and prescribe medicine themselves using the Internet and hardly visit doctors. Due to the availability of health information online, people has become more sensitive to symptoms and perceive themselves to be unnecessary ill when they self-diagnoses themselves and increase their health anxiety [2].

Cyberchondriasis is the health anxiety caused by reviewing health information online [1]. Rao [3] showed that people searching the Internet regarding any illness or symptoms also read about its effects and hazards, which in turn increase their health anxiety [2].

Polycystic ovary syndrome (PCOS) is the most common endocrinopathy among adult women all over the world and is characterized by anovulation, androgen excess (primarily ovarian, but also adrenal in origin) and the appearance of polycystic ovaries (on ultrasound) [4]. The most common symptoms of PCOS are infertility and irregular menstrual cycle, hirsutism and increased hair growth, weight gain and difficulty losing weight. Every one in five women faces severe PCOS and 80% of women who have reached puberty exhibited symptoms of PCOS [2]. Additionally, these patients were more susceptible to develop anxiety disorders, depression, personality and other psychological disorders [5] that may lead to several health issues such as changes in appearance, irregular or absent menstrual periods, and disturbances in sexual attitudes and behavior [6].

According to the data of Google Trends, keywords such as "Polycystic Ovary Syndrome" and/or "PCOS" have been increasingly used since January 2015 [7].

Interestingly, regions with most online searches for PCOS are Caribbean islands followed by Middle East and Africa, Asia, United States and Australia.

This study conducted in Karachi, Pakistan finds the impact of cyberchondriasis on PCOS patients searching health information online

2 HYPOTHESES DEVELOPMENT

Cyberchondriasis severity scale is a multidimensional measure of cyberchondria comprising of 40 items, each with a Likert-scale, prepared and validated by McElroy and Shevlin [8] (see

Appendix). The scale included five latent factors, namely 'compulsion', 'distress', 'excessiveness', 'reassurance' and 'mistrust'.

'Compulsion' referred to the interruption of daily online and offline activities when people or patients repeatedly search online for medical conditions and symptoms [8, 9]. Similarly, the extensive patterns of online searching for PCOS as per data given by the Google Trends (see Figure 1) led to our first hypothesis:

H1: Compulsion has an effect on online search for PCOS.

Moreover, 'Distress' referred to the inner feelings of anxiety associated with online health research [8, 9] whereas 'excessiveness' referred to the multiple and repeated online searches for health information [8, 9]. Google data reflected that a great number of people with possible PCOS symptoms had searched for PCOS. By searching health information online, people subsequently increased their anxiety level [10]. Therefore, we hypothesize the following two hypotheses:

H2: Distress has an effect on online search for PCOS.

H3: Excessiveness has an effect on online search for PCOS.

'"Reassurance"' referred to the need to consult with doctor [8, 9]. In a nonclinical study, it was found that around 40% of the people experienced increased health anxiety whereas 50% of them experienced reduced health anxiety as a result of using the Internet [11]. The Internet is not designed to reassure its users, therefore, the outcome of seeking reassurance are sometimes high and sometimes low [1]. This has led to our fourth hypothesis:

H4: Reassurance has an effect on online search for PCOS.

"Mistrust" referred to the distrust of medical services from healthcare providers or distrust of medical services [8, 9]. Turkiewicz [12] showed that searching online health information weakened doctor-patient relationship, as patients conducted self-diagnosis with tools available online and do not pay attention to doctors' advice. This has led to our fifth hypothesis:

H5: Mistrust has an effect on online Search for PCOS

3 METHODS

The data were collected through cyberchondriasis scale using purposive and convenience sampling. The 100 PCOS patients were recruited from an academic institute and a private hospital, in Karachi, Pakistan. The study population were patients who had access to internet and searched health information on PCOS online. The questionnaire contained three demographic variables such as age, marital status and qualification and a section on the cyberchondriasis factors. Likert-scale responses ranged from strongly disagree through agree neutral to strongly agree. Ethics approval was taken from the hospital and the academic institute prior the study

4 DATA ANALYSIS

Exploratory Factor Analysis (EFA) was conducted on the 40 items of cyberchondriasis factors for construct validity and to measure indicators of the latent factors [1, 8]. Kaiser-Meyer-Olkin (KMO) and Bartlett's test were run to check the suitability of factor analysis on the collected data. Internal consistency and reliability were determined using cronbach α values [13]. Finally the binary logistic regression analysis was conducted to investigate the association of online search with cyberchondriasis factors. SPSS version 23.0 was used for data analysis.

5 RESULTS

The mean age of 100 females surveyed was 27.78±4.94 ranging from 17-37 years. Table 1 shows marital status of PCOS patients, Table 2 shows their education status and Table 3 shows type of information searched by them.

Table 1. Marital Status

Marital Status	Percentage
Single	35%
Married	53%
Divorced	7%
Widowed	5%

Table 2. Education Status

Education Status	Percentage
High School	2%
College	17%
Bachelor's Degree	38%
Master's Degree	42%
Other education (e.g. diploma, training)	1%

Table 3. Type of Information Searched Online

Type of information searched online for PCOS (multiple options)	Percentage
Possible Causes of PCOS	60.6%
Treatment Of PCOS	22.2%
Available Health Services	11.1%
Undiagnosed Medical Conditions	5.1%
General Search Engine (E.G. Google, Bing, Yahoo , Ask Jeeves)	72.2%
Medical Search Engine (E.G. Health Line	21.2%
Health Related Websites (E.G. NH's Direct, Patient Uk)	4%
Help from Support Groups	2%

5.1 Reliability Analysis

The overall reliability of the cyberchondriasis constructs was 0.91.

5.2 Factor Analysis

The KMO test gave the value of 0.716 indicating that factor analysis was suitable to run on this data set. The Bartlett's test of sphericity was also found significant. Three factors were formed through EFA, we selected 'compulsion' and 'mistrust' for further analysis and dropped the third factor which was a composition of 'distress', 'excessiveness' and 'reassurance'

5.3 Logistic Regression Model

We have applied binary logistic regression to investigate the association of online search with cyberchondriasis factors. Table 5 represents univariate and multivariate model.

Table 5. Univariate and multivariate model.

Associated Factors	Univariate Model	P-value	Multivariate Model	P-value
	Odds ratio (95% C.I)		Odds ratio (95% C.I)	
Compulsion	9.12(1.67,49.94)	0.01*	4.15(1.44,12)	0.009*
Mistrust	0.59(0.18,1.92)	0.37	0.68(0.39,1.19)	0.17
Dependent Variable: Online Search (Yes/No) , Predictors: Compulsion, Mistrust scores. *P-value <0.05 was considered significant.				

Below is the summary of hypotheses rejected/not rejected (see Table 6)

Table 6. Summary of Result

Hypotheses	Rejected/ Not Rejected
H_3: Compulsion has an effect on Online search for PCOS	Rejected
H_5: Mistrust has an effect on Online Search for PCOS	Not rejected

Compulsion was found significant both in the univariate model and the multivariate model. This showed that compulsion has increased the odds by nine times for searching health information online by PCOS patients.

6 DISCUSSION

6.1 Overview of Findings

The impact of cyberchondriasis on searching health information has been studied among PCOS patients that showed a strong association of compulsion with searching health information online. High health anxiety makes individuals search more information on PCOS, thus disturbing their offline chores and online activities.

6.2 Strengths and Weaknesses

Strengths of this study included a cyberchondriasis validated scale [8] and research conducted in the biggest metropolitan city (Karachi) of Pakistan. Moreover, participants recruited were familiar with technology and online searching.

Weaknesses included a small sample size as it was difficult to recruit PCOS patients as most of them were not willing to disclose their health status. Also, data collected from one city of Pakistan would make generalization of findings difficult

7 CONCLUSIONS

This study investigated the impact of cyberchondriasis on PCOS patients searching health information online. The study concluded that 'compulsion', one of the factors of cyberchondriasis, increased the odds of searching health information online by nine times, thus increasingly interrupting their social and official activities online and offline. Other factors of cyberchondriasis may also have an effect on searching health information online but our small size was not able to explain any other associations. Studies with large sample size would better explain the impact of cyberchondriasis on PCOS patients searching health information online

APPENDIX

Questionnaire

Name: [   ]   Age: [   ]
Marital Status: □ Single □ Married □ Divorced □ Widowed □ Don't want to disclose

Education: □ High School □College □Bachelor's Degree □Master's Degree □Other

Occupation: _____
1. What type of information do you search for when using the internet as a source of information about health?

[ ] Possible causes of symptoms (e.g. headaches)

[ ] Information on treatment options

[ ] Information on an undiagnosed medical condition (e.g. cancer)

[ ] Information about health services available

[ ] Information about a diagnosed medical condition (e.g. asthma)

☐ Descriptions of others' experiences of illness

☐ Other (please state)

2. Where do you typically go to look for information about your health on the internet?

☐ A general search engine (e.g. Google or Ask Jeeves?)

☐ A medical search engine (e.g. health line) (please state)
_____

☐ Health related websites (e.g. NHS direct, patient UK etc.) (Please State)
_____

☐ Message boards / support groups (please state)
_____

☐ Other (please state)
_____

Answer the following as
- o Strongly disagree
- o Disagree
- o Neither agree nor disagree
- o Agree
- o Strongly Agree

3. Researching (polycystic ovarian syndrome) PCOS online interrupts my online leisure activities (e.g. streaming movies).

4. Researching PCOS online interrupts my time spent on social networks.

5. Researching PCOS interrupts my offline work activities.

6. Researching PCOS distracts me from reading news/sports/entertainment articles online.

7. Researching PCOS interrupts or slows my online communication (e.g. Instant Messaging, Skype).

8. Researching PCOS online interrupts my work (e.g. writing emails, working on word documents or spreadsheets).

9. Researching PCOS online interrupts my offline social activities (reduces time spent with friends/family).

10. Researching PCOS online interrupts other research (e.g. for my job/college assignment/homework).

11. I have troubled relaxing after researching PCOS online.

12. I find it hard to stop worrying about PCOS that I have researched online.

13. I have troubled getting to sleep after researching PCOS online.

14. I feel more anxious or distressed after researching PCOS online.

15. I start to panic when I read online that PCOS I have are found in a rare/serious condition.

16. I think I am fine until I read about a serious condition online.

17. I am more easily annoyed or irritated after researching PCOS online.

18. I lose my appetite after researching PCOS online.

19. I read different web pages for my condition.

20. I read the same web pages about my condition on more than one occasion.

21. I enter the same symptoms into a web search on more than one occasion.

22. Ranking of the web search results reflects how common an illness is.

23. When researching PCOS online I visit both trustworthy sources.

24. When researching PCOS online, I visit forums where individuals discuss symptoms

25. If I notice an unexplained bodily sensation I will search for it on the Internet.

26. I visit trustworthy sources only when PCOS symptoms online.

27. I discuss my online medical findings with my GP/health professional.

28. Discussing online info about my condition with my GP reassures me.

29. Researching PCOS online leads me to consult with other medical specialists (e.g. consultants).

30. Researching PCOS online leads me to consult with my doctor (GP).

31. I find myself thinking: "I would not have gone to the doctor if I had not read about those symptoms online".

32. I suggest to my GP/medical professional that I may need a diagnostic procedure that I read about online (e.g. a biopsy/a specific blood test).

33. I trust my GP/medical professional's diagnosis over my online self-diagnosis.

34. I take the opinion of my GP/medical professional more seriously than my online medical research.

35. When my GP/medical professional dismisses my online medical research, I stop worrying about it.

REFERENCES

[1] Starcevic, V. and D. Berle, Cyberchondria: towards a better understanding of excessive health-related Internet use. Expert Review of Neurotherapeutics, 2013. 13(2): p. 205-213.

[2] Homburg, R., What is polycystic ovarian syndrome? A proposal for a consensus on the definition and diagnosis of polycystic ovarian syndrome. Human Reproduction, 2002. 17(10): p. 2495-2499.

[3] Rao, P., Wired and Worried: Understanding Users' Emotions while Web Searching for Health Information. Procedia Computer Science, 2016. 84: p. 132-136.

[4] Stein, I.F. and M.L. Leventhal, Amenorrhea associated with bilateral polycystic ovaries. American Journal of Obstetrics & Gynecology, 1935. 29(2): p. 181-191.

[5] Sahingöz, M., et al., Axis I and Axis II diagnoses in women with PCOS. General hospital psychiatry, 2013. 35(5): p. 508-511.

[6] Elsenbruch, S., et al., Quality of life, psychosocial well-being, and sexual satisfaction in women with polycystic ovary syndrome. The Journal of Clinical Endocrinology & Metabolism, 2003. 88(12): p. 5801-5807.

[7] GoogleTrends. Google Trends. 2017 [cited 2017 25 March]; Available from: https://trends.google.com/trends/explore?q=PCOS.

[8] McElroy, E. and M. Shevlin, The development and initial validation of

the cyberchondria severity scale (CSS). Journal of anxiety disorders, 2014. 28(2): p. 259-265.

[9]   Fergus, T.A., The Cyberchondria Severity Scale (CSS): an examination of structure and relations with health anxiety in a community sample. Journal of anxiety disorders, 2014. 28(6): p. 504-510.

[10]   Trent, M.E., et al., Fertility concerns and sexual behavior in adolescent girls with polycystic ovary syndrome: implications for quality of life. Journal of pediatric and adolescent gynecology, 2003. 16(1): p. 33-37.

[11]   White, R.W. and E. Horvitz. Experiences with web search on medical concerns and self diagnosis. in AMIA annual symposium proceedings. 2009. American Medical Informatics Association.

[12]   Turkiewicz, K.L., The impact of cyberchondria on doctor-patient communication. 2012: The University of Wisconsin-Milwaukee.

[13]   Cronbach, L.J., Coefficient alpha and the internal structure of tests. psychometrika, 1951. 16(3): p. 297-334.

DrinkWatch: A Mobile Wellbeing Application Based on Interactive and Cooperative Machine Learning

Simon Flutura, Andreas Seiderer, Ilhan Aslan, Chi Tai Dang, Raphael Schwarz, Dominik Schiller
and Elisabeth André
University of Augsburg
Augsburg, Germany
{lastname}@hcm-lab.de

ABSTRACT

We describe in detail the development of DrinkWatch, a wellbeing application, which supports (alcoholic and non-alcoholic) drink activity logging. DrinkWatch runs on a smartwatch device and makes use of machine learning to recognize drink activities based on the smartwatch's inbuilt sensors. DrinkWatch differs from other mobile machine learning applications by triggering feedback requests from its user in order to cooperatively learn the user's personalized and contextual drink activities. The cooperative approach aims to reduce limitations in learning performance and to increase the user experience of machine learning based applications. We discuss why the need for cooperative machine learning approaches is increasing and describe lessons that we have learned throughout the development process of DrinkWatch and insights based on initial experiments with users. For example, we demonstrate that six to eight hours of annotated real world data are sufficient to train a reliable base model.

CCS CONCEPTS

• **Human-centered computing** → **Ubiquitous and mobile computing systems and tools**;

KEYWORDS

Mobile Social Signal Processing, interactive Machine Learning

ACM Reference Format:
Simon Flutura, Andreas Seiderer, Ilhan Aslan, Chi Tai Dang, Raphael Schwarz, Dominik Schiller and Elisabeth André. 2018. DrinkWatch: A Mobile Wellbeing Application Based on Interactive and Cooperative Machine Learning. In *DH'18: 2018 International Digital Health Conference, April 23–26, 2018, Lyon, France.* ACM, New York, NY, USA, 10 pages. https://doi.org/10.1145/3194658.3194666

1 INTRODUCTION

Utilizing mobile devices to collect personal behavioral data has many benefits, such as concisely informing medical professionals of

a patient's "in the wild" behavior, and help in identifying appropriate intervention methods. However, there are still multiple technical and conceptual concerns, considering the mobile collection and processing of health related data. A paradigmatic example is the concern for privacy. Other concerns relate to data processing approaches based on machine learning (ML) in mobile settings. While mobile ML can be a powerful tool, its downsides include potential performance issues in learning individual and contextual differences (e.g. [19]), and negative user experiences due to a lack of system transparency and loss of user control (e.g. [1, 12]). We believe that many of the concerns associated with mobile ML applications can be addressed by taking inspiration from Horvitz's idea of mixed-initiative systems [13] and implementing a cooperative style of ML, in which users are interactively integrated into the ML process. In addition, by enabling cooperative ML completely on a mobile device, one would be able to address privacy-related user concerns associated with outsourcing data storage and processing to non-personal devices and unknown locations.

Because of the important role that ML approaches for mobile (health) applications will play in the foreseeable future, there is a need to explore human-centered techniques and paradigms towards balancing human needs and experiences with "machine autonomy". The increasing importance of designing for wellbeing and contributing factors, such as (perceived) human autonomy and competence is highlighted by researchers, such as Calvo and Peters [7], who promote a paradigm shift towards "Positive Computing" and away from designing solely to increase productivity. While ML is a well studied field with many fellow researchers working on improving ML's performance and its impact on productivity increase for various domains, the field of mobile cooperative ML is rather unexplored. Towards exploring the potential benefits and limitation of mobile cooperative ML applications, we came to understand that an initial, but important step is exposing ourselves to the process of developing an exemplary application and gathering initial insights with users.

In the following section, we provide background on previous research including descriptions of relevant forms of ML. Then we present in detail the development process of the smartwatch application DrinkWatch as an exemplary mobile cooperative ML application, which aims to provide logging support of drink activities (i.e. taking alcoholic or non-alcoholic liquids) throughout a day as a behavior. We conclude by discussing lessons learned and guidelines for the development of mobile cooperative ML applications, such as how the performance of different ML algorithms (i.e. Naive Bayes vs. linear SVM from LibLinear) is related to their learning curve with simulated user interaction.

2 BACKGROUND

Arguably, the advent of mobile and ubiquitous technology has disrupted how we (as users) envision technology's role in our everyday life. While originally mobile devices were perceived as personal information management tools, and thus as *tools* in a traditional sense, today's mobiles have access to a vast amount of knowledge from which they can learn, and seemingly become a companion capable to contest a user's agency and autonomy.

There are some benefits of this ongoing shift of agency and capabilities towards mobiles or technology in general, such as technology becoming able to recognize harmful behavioral habits of users and assist users in reflecting on their habits and hopefully provide support in adopting positive habits. Be it to regularly taking a walk or drinking enough, behavior change bears great potential towards improving wellbeing. Most new year's intents, for example, will have been given up by the time you read this paper.

In the following, we summarize related work in human activity recognition, which is an essential part in recognizing human behavior, and describe different ML approaches with regard to their characteristics and application domains.

2.1 Human Activity Recognition

Over the last two decades, research in Human Activity Recognition (HAR) has been focusing on a wide range of applications, such as surveillance and security [29], ambient intelligence [23] (e.g. to assist older adults [31]), or health care [38]. In particular, in ubiquitous computing environments or smart home environments, Human Activity Recognition is a key feature, for example, to monitor daily activities of users or provide assistance [39].

The rapid technical development of mobile devices and wearables, such as smartphones and smartwatches, has further expanded the possibilities for HAR. Mobile devices are equipped with a plethora of sensors and are worn or carried around all day. Thus, many activities of users can potentially be recognized. Consequently, a lot of research that investigated methods and applications [37] for HAR has emerged, in particular, research employing inertial sensors of smartphones [19, 28].

In more detail, HAR is used to automatically recognize a person's activities from a stream of sensor data, for example to pro-actively provide assistance, log daily routines, or to initiate necessary procedures (such as calling an ambulance or neighbors in case a person has fallen [5]). This makes them an important entity among today's e-health topics, be it detecting stereotyped movements in children with developmental disabilities [17] or automatic monitoring of rehabilitation processes [30] or using smart cups to track the behavior of residents of an inpatient nursing care facility [41]. In comparison to smartphones, smartwatches have a decisive advantage, which makes them particularly suitable for HAR. They are body-mounted and therefore always at the same place (i.e. constantly attached to the user's arm throughout a day). The human arm is actively involved in most of daily activities, whereas movements of the body can be smaller and may only reveal few activities.

Smartphones usually detect only movements related to the whole body due to their typical placement in the pocket. Therefore, the number of identifiable activities with smartphones is limited. Examples from the literature include walking, running, jogging, standing, sitting, walking up/down stairs, or using an elevator [11, 19, 20]. In contrast, smartwatches or wrist-worn wearables have the potential to detect more activities than with smartphones, such as drinking, smoking, typing on the keyboard, or eating with a knife and fork. Thus, new application areas can be addressed, such as food/drink reminders and related habit awareness applications (e.g. [22, 28]). The fact that smartwatches record the subtleties of each individual's arm movements in turn allows ML algorithms to generate personalized models for activity recognition. Personalized models usually result in higher precision of recognition algorithms and require less amount of sample data than user-independent models.

With the rapid development of smartwatch technology, HAR on smartwatches is an ascending topic [4, 27]. In contrast to previous work that utilizes smartwatches, the work at hand combines online learning and interactive ML to continuously improve activity recognition models. Moreover, the complete learning process is done solely on the smartwatch without access to any online resources or requiring network connectivity.

2.2 Machine Learning

2.2.1 Interactive and Cooperative Machine Learning. Another very active field of research in Human Activity Recognition addresses interactive machine learning (iML) on mobile devices [19, 27]. Interactive ML distinguishes from classical ML by directly involving users in the ML process. Training of models is part of the deployed product (continuously improving models) and not just applied during the development process (static and previously trained models). For this reason, iML bears great potential for applications that have to continuously adapt to a user.

Ware et al. [36] describe an approach in which the user interacts with an ML system by selecting individual attributes for the creation of a decision tree. In their case, the user requires a certain amount of expertise in ML. In contrast, we aim to involve non-expert users in the ML process to exploit the fact that the user can judge for his/her activities best. Fails et al. [9] showed a similar approach for design tools using perceptual interfaces.

The work of Shahmohammadi et al. [27] evaluated iML based on smartwatch sensor data for Human Activity Recognition and found that only few training samples are required to achieve high recognition accuracy. They demonstrated that personalized models from iML performed significantly better than classic learning approaches. In comparison to their work, we make use of online learning approaches which require less computing resources and thus enable us to run the whole application solely on the smartwatch without the need to stream data to more powerful devices for further processing. By this means, our system increases mobility and makes the application independent of external dependencies or permanent reliable and stable network connections. We also rely on naturally recorded annotated sensor data instead of data based on instructions given to users to perform specific actions.

Similar to iML, *Cooperative Machine Learning* (cML) aims to leverage the capabilities of human and machine to solve an ML problem. Here, the focus lies on the effort required for labeling recorded data. Not the deployed model is handed over to the user for modification, but the human annotators are supported by the machine to speed up their work [40]. To implement such a cML

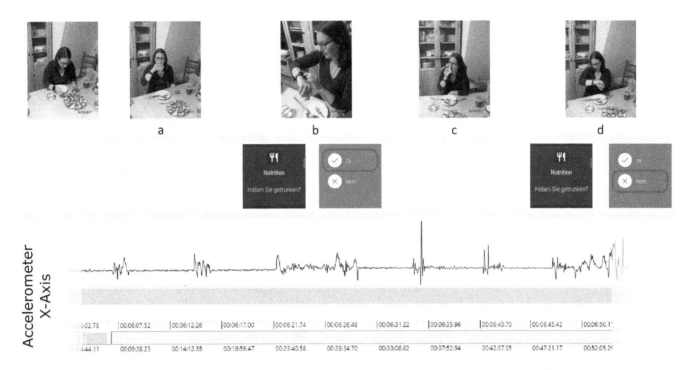

Figure 1: An exemplary health application scenario presenting the interaction and cooperation between a user and the Drink-Watch application. The second row provides screenshots of the DrinkWatch application and the third row presents raw accelerometer data of one movement axis as exemplary sensor data, which are used to recognize the drink activity.

approach the tight integration between an annotation software and the respective ML platform is crucial. In our previous work, this integration is provided by the NOVA annotation tool which has been developed by Baur et al. [3]. This tool makes use of the Social Signal Interpretation framework (SSI) [35] as an ML framework to speed up the annotation of social signals [34]. More specifically, the combination of both platforms enables users to train a new model based on only a few annotations from a recorded session and subsequently use this model to automatically predict annotations for the remaining part of the session. The annotator then only needs to correct the system's prediction which is potentially much less time-consuming than annotating the data from scratch. In an initial simulated study, we demonstrated a reduction of the labeling effort by 40 %. Following a similar approach, we make use of both tools in order to simulate the cooperative ML process of our mobile implementation as described in Section 4.2. They form the basis of the mobile implementation of Section 3.3.

2.2.2 Active Learning. Miu et al. [19] presented an Online Active Learning framework and studied how to collect user-provided annotations to bootstrap personalized activity models. They demonstrated that generating personalized Human Activity Recognition models can be achieved on-the-fly and does not require expert supervision or retrospective annotation of sample data. While Miu et al. made use of a smartphone app to query the user, our work queries annotations through a smartwatch interface. A smartwatch app has the benefit that queries on a smartwatch can be handled

more comfortably and quickly since smartwatches don't require users to get it out of the pocket first.

Active Learning has been investigated for different models and classification types (e.g. Support Vector Machines [32]) as well as different types of query strategies. An overview is given by Settels et al. [25]. The most widely used approach and therefore selected for our applied entry point in Section 3.3.5 is Uncertainty Sampling [18] or Query on Uncertainty. In these approaches, a labeling system picks up samples for which the target class cannot be determined with a high certainty. This way the system is not locked into just learning from data that it already handles well. According to Lewis et al. [18], this approach performs better than relevance sampling which picks high confidence samples for relabeling.

Also common is the approach called Query on Committee [26], where multiple models, that have a strongly different way of operating, are grouped into a committee. Those samples are chosen for labeling by an oracle, where the individual models disagree most. Other query methods are focused on error reduction [25]. They either directly try to maximize the expected error reduction with the selected sample or they look at the expected model change that is expected from all possible labels of the sample.

To the best of our knowledge, only few recent works on HAR have investigated iML based on a smartwatch [27, 28] or online learning with a smartwatch [19], but no one has attempted to combine both approaches to realize interactive online machine learning solely on a smartwatch independent of external computing resources. We designed and built a smartwatch application prototype that implements this combination of approaches and present insights from a technical evaluation.

3 DRINKWATCH PROTOTYPE

Across all the state-of-the-art and off-the-shelf mobile devices, smartwatches seem most suitable in providing least intrusive and immediate feedback in mobile settings, and thus, allowing users to reflect on their immediate activities and contextual habits. While their form factor and small size is indeed an advantage when considering their integration in everyday situations, it is also often challenging to design and to develop interactive applications for smartwatches. For example, smartwatches provide only a very small-sized screen which limits the amount of information that can be presented to users. This limitation is, however, not relevant for the intended use case of our system as we mainly make use of the smartwatch's movements for hand activity logging. Our system only occasionally shows notifications to users and asks them for feedback related to activities. The prototype system further aims to reduce the complexity and amount of interaction (required to recognize and log drink activities) through automation.

DrinkWatch aims at recognizing drink activities (by means of inertial sensor data of the smartwatch) and tracks each drink activity for later analysis (see Figure 1). If DrinkWatch senses "interesting data", which potentially represent a drink activity worth learning from (Figure 1a), the smartwatch queries the user for assigning a label to the recorded sample data (Figure 1b). Thereby, the user is actively involved in the ML process and may choose to adapt the drink activity model or not. Consequently, not only drinking, but also activities, such as blowing one's nose or wiping one's mouth (Figure 1c) may lead to a query to the user (Figure 1d).

DrinkWatch serves three main functions. First, it offers a graphical *user interface* for querying the user for annotations and for reviewing recognized/logged activities.

Second, DrinkWatch continuously collects data samples from the watch's accelerometer and other potential data sources. In our prototype, we included a smartscale which is outlined in Section 3.2.2. This data collection, our *corpus* (Section 3.2), serves as the basis for a *warmstart model* in our ongoing cML process. For the purpose of later evaluations, all collected data samples are also locally logged on the smartwatch. However, this is not required for the online learning approach since the learning process requires only the latest annotated sample, see Section 3.3.4.

Third, Drinkwatch integrates an *ML logic*, which runs as a service on the smartwatch. While most of the logic, such as the online learning classifier, are implemented in the C++ programming language, part of the logic is embedded in a thin Java layer connecting the ML logic with the Android system (e.g. user interface) via JNI.

In the following, we describe each of the three parts of the DrinkWatch, including the implementation of the ML logic (see Section 3.3) in detail.

3.1 User Interface

DrinkWatch is implemented as a stand-alone application that runs on the smartwatch Asus ZenWatch 2, which is using the mobile

Figure 2: Cooperative Learning Interface on the smartwatch. The first two buttons enable the user to start or stop the recognition pipeline. Whenever a drink activity is detected, the user can inform the system whether the recognition was correct ("Yes") or incorrect ("No"). Additionally, with the last button, the user is able to indicate whether a drink activity was not detected.

operating system Android Wear 2 (Figure 2). Beneath the up-to-date OS, it can be charged and programmed fast using a USB connection, which is handy for development and experiments. There are hardware solutions with a wider range of sensors or fitted input hardware, such as a bezel, that might be more attractive for long-term use. We designed a minimal user interface on the watch (see Figure 2) to handle queries to the user and to start and stop the learning pipeline. Thus, users have control over when and whether to provide labels. The simple interface allows non-expert users to easily provide feedback on the go. Drink activities that lie within the desired confidence range of the iML model trigger a request/notification. Notifications are given by playing the standard notification sound of the watch and displaying a text ("Have you been drinking?" instead of "Waiting on Event"). In our current prototype implementation, we had to turn off the vibration function of the watch as it influenced its accelerometer sensor. This issue will be solved in a next iteration by disabling sensor reading while a vibration is being executed by the watch.

3.2 Corpus for the Warmstart Model

3.2.1 Recording setup. In contrast to many other studies on activity recognition, we do not ask people to perform specific actions, but rather record sample data in everyday situations to label them afterwards based on a ground truth. Our recording setup was slightly different from session to session. Recording of acceleration data from the wrist was always performed using an Asus Zenwatch 2. In addition, the setup also included a camera to record video of the user when possible. The number of users per session varied from three to one, while 22 sessions (out of 25) had only a single user (see Figure 3). Every user was asked to wear the watch on their preferred hand. All recordings, except for five sessions, contained smartscale data, which can be used by our iML approach to speed up the annotation process.

Figure 3: Recording setup with up to three people wearing smartwatches to record labeled accelerometer data for the initial classification model. The weight of one person's drinking vessel acquired by a smartscale and video data were additionally recorded to be able to annotate drink activities afterwards.

3.2.2 Smartscale. The smartscale prototype [24] in our system (see Figure 4) continuously broadcasts weight data of vessels placed on it via Bluetooth 4.0 to every receiver that is nearby. In our case, the smartwatch received and recorded the data whenever the watch was in reach of the smartscale.

Figure 4: A glass of apple juice standing on the smartscale.

Figure 5 exemplary shows recorded data of the smartscale. The graph resulted from drinking from two 0.5 l PET bottles (one by one). After each drink activity the bottle was placed on the smartscale. When the first bottle was empty it was replaced by a full one. The plot shows that the first bottle was not completely full and has not been placed on the sensor after being empty.

Whenever someone wants to drink out of a vessel placed on the scale, he or she usually first takes the vessel from the smartscale (weight is 0 g), drinks out of the vessel, and places the vessel back on the smartscale. The weight is now lower than before. The mass can increase if additional fluid is filled into a vessel or another vessel is being used which is heavier and/or contains more fluid.

In comparison to accelerometer data, the weight data of the smartscale is easier to interpret so that an annotator can quickly detect a drink activity, but also enables automated annotations. The video data can be used to validate the labeled time segments but does not have to be completely watched.

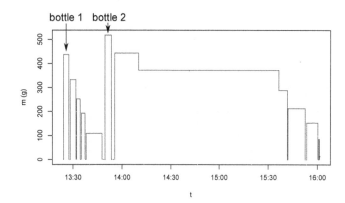

Figure 5: Weight data of the smartscale. Two filled 0.5 ml PET bottles have been drunken during this session. Whenever the drinking vessel is lifted the weight is 0 g (short lifting is omitted). After drinking the weight is reduced.

3.2.3 Dataset. We recorded 25 sessions, which consist of 16 hours and 30 minutes of every day activities containing 5117 samples of drink activities and 26288 samples of non-drink activities. One sample consists of a 1 second frame step together with 7 seconds of overlapping preceding data. A typical snippet of a drink activity is shown in Figure 7. Such an activity is characterized by three phases: picking up, bringing the vessel to the mouth and back as well as finally putting the vessel down. We employed random under-sampling to balance both classes in the training process. Acceleration data were recorded with 25 samples per second using the accelerometer sensor of an Asus ZenWatch 2. As ground truth we synchronously recorded video and smartscale data. An annotation session containing all data can be found in Figure 9. Furthermore, the Android system provides a so-called *linear acceleration sensor*, which represents the raw acceleration sensor exempt from the earth gravitation influence. Our prototype makes use of this linear acceleration sensor as it provides better performance for HAR [27]. These data were used to simulate a cML process and to gain a warmstart model for further iML, see Section 4. Thus, the data set is an important input for the ML module. The ML module is described in the following.

3.3 Implementation of the ML Module

We employ activity recognition to reduce manual logging effort that is required by the user when using a notebook or a conventional logging app. To this end, we continuously track the user's wrist activities in order to detect specific time windows (frames) that may be interpreted as an indicator of drinking. In case of high confidence, a drink event is automatically registered by a higher level app, e.g. a nutrition logging app. In case of low confidence, the system has to decide whether to ask the user for confirmation

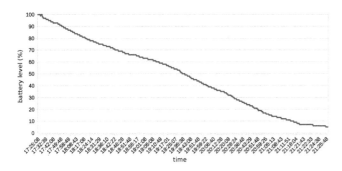

Figure 6: Battery level of Asus ZenWatch 2 running the mobileSSI iML pipeline

- Mean
- Std. deviation
- Variance
- Energy
- Interquartile range (IQR)
- Mean absolute deviation (MAD)
- Root mean square (RMS)
- Min
- Max

Additionally following features are generalizing over all axes:

- Correlation between XY, XZ, YZ axis
- Mean, Std. deviation, Min, Max, IQR on length of per sample vector over all axes (magnitude)

This results in overall 35 features calculated on the previously described 1 + 7 seconds containing 200 samples.

3.3.3 Normalization. Normalization is scaling all features' data range to fit a certain range, in our case within 0 and 1. This is, for example, done by using the accelerometer's maximum output value that can be queried using the Android API. Compared to a classical approach in mobileSSI and many other implementations of classical ML, the responsibility of data normalization is moved from the training process, iterating over all samples in the data set, to the feature calculation, on the current chunk of data. This is necessary because with low initial sample count determining the minimum and maximum on already known data might not be representative for future data. There are alternatives to feature based normalization, such as adaptive scaling. While normalization is not strictly necessary for Gaussian Naive Bayes it is recommended to keep features with higher values from dominating features with small values. Our pipeline provides a feature vector of dimension 35 that is fed into the following online classifier component every second.

or not. We consider information gain as well as the user's situation, as discussed by Amershi et al. [1]. For example, the user should not be disturbed if the expected information gain is very low.

The maximum runtime of the system without WiFi is about four hours, as can be seen in the graph of Figure 6. In case of low battery (2 %), our prototype app stops the ML pipeline in order to properly finish the session. From the two days maximum battery life under optimized circumstances, this means a strong reduction.

Our prototype relies on mobileSSI [10]. It is open source and available on Github[1]. While mobileSSI already has ML capabilities for a range of classifiers, implementation follows a classic non-interactive approach. Our extensions include online learning capabilities (see Section 3.3.4) that enable the user to interact with the model using a simple user interface while the model actively (see Section 3.3.5) queries the user. Our prototype also shares parts with a classic ML pipeline, such as data collection and feature extraction, which are described in the following.

A brief overview of the pipeline and application concept is given in Figure 8. The red arrows mark continuous streams with a fixed sample rate kept in sync by the SSI framework. Blue dotted arrows mark events that are sporadic, but contain a time stamp and duration. Gray components are either future work, the user moderation and context component, or not described in this paper, namely the integration with the nutrition logging app.

3.3.1 Frame Size. In order to continuously process data, segmentation of the data has to be addressed. We selected a fixed window size of 1 second together with an overlap of preceding 7 seconds. This allows us to capture the whole event in most cases while having a reactive system, giving quick feedback. Given our chosen sample rate of 25 Hz we gain 200 raw data points in three dimensions, as our accelerometer has three axes.

3.3.2 Feature Selection. Accelerometer data are widely used in Human Activity Recognition and a lot of features have been experimented with. Features are needed to simplify the classification process in contrast to end-to-end learning. Our feature set is based on related work. In particular, we selected a range of features that are known to work well on acceleration data [2, 8, 14, 16, 21] and have been used for the recognition of drink activities.

On each axis/dimension, the following features were calculated:

3.3.4 Online Learner. Classification of the current data frame is handled by our pipeline, as it would be the case in a classic ML pipeline. Our main objective is to continuously improve learned models for fluid intake based on tracked data and user input. Online learning enables us to learn a new model from scratch in the deployed application. Furthermore, the model can be improved at the moment the user provides new labeled data and the next input can be analyzed with the improved model without the need to restart or stop the application. To speed the process up, a classically trained model is used as a starting point for further incremental training. This procedure is called warm-start.

We chose Naive Bayes which can be easily adapted for online learning (see e.g. the implementation used in MOA [6]). The online learning variant of Naive Bayes incrementally calculates mean, variance and standard derivation and additionally stores the sample count to be able to adjust with new data proportionally. The algorithm is described in detail by Knuth [15] on page 115. The calculations are executed per feature and class, thus our model consists of 210 float values and a sample count. As Naive Bayes classification results into confidence values, it enables us to query the user based on the level of uncertainty. Furthermore, it is fast in training and execution. This makes Naive Bayes a good option for restricted platforms, such as smartwatches. Moreover, it offers an

---

[1]https://github.com/hcmlab/mobileSSI

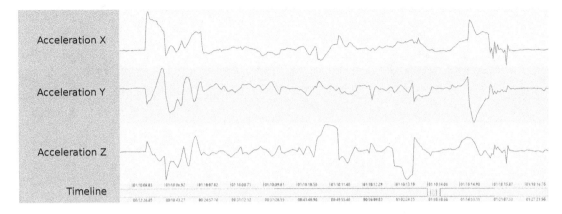

Figure 7: Three axis accelerometer data of a drink activity. The start and end of the signal describe the movement of the drinking vessel to and from the mouth. In the middle of the signal the rotation of the vessel by turning the wrist takes place.

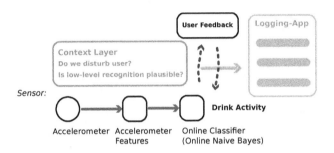

Figure 8: Overview over iML Pipeline and future system components.

advantage in data security, as no other data that can give an insight in user behavior or health related information are permanently saved to the watch.

At this point LibLinear is only integrated without online learning capabilities, but a solution exists according to Tsai et al. [33]. The future integration of LibLinear as additional online learning library depends on the result of our evaluation, see Section 4.

3.3.5 Active Learning. Our Active Learning implementation uses query on uncertainty for sample selection, see Section 2.2.2 for further background. We can specify the credibility range that triggers user requests, thus supports relevance sampling as well as uncertainty sampling. The option is part of an online classifier component shown in Figure 8. It manages the assembly of sample lists from user annotations and data streams as well as the training process of our online model. The model's predictions are also handled by the online classifier. Both, requests and predictions, are handled as events instead of streams with fixed sample rate.

4 EVALUATION AND RESULTS

Following system implementation and data collection, three steps of evaluation are presented in this section: the static evaluation of the fully annotated data set in Section 4.1, the evaluation of different learning strategies in Section 4.2, and the interactive run performed with end users in Section 4.3.

4.1 Evaluation of Static Models

To give an overview of our collected data and provide an impression of what accuracy fully trained models are able to achieve, Table 1 shows results of Naive Bayes and linear SVM (implementation: LibLinear) models trained on the full data set, evaluated on the fixed test set that is also used for the simulation of cooperative ML.

	Results of full Training	
	Naive Bayes	**linear SVM**
Drinking	81.4%	84.9%
Not drinking	71.6%	79.8%
Unweighted Average	**76.5%**	**82.3%**

Table 1: Results of training on all annotations contained in the training set, evaluated on the test set.

Our results are in line with other results on drink activity recognition found in literature. The linear SVM model shows a six percent points lead over Naive Bayes, which again is as expected. While there is a difference on the "drinking" class, it is larger on the "not drinking" class. As "not drinking" is by far larger and more complex, Naive Bayes meets its limitations in describing it.

4.2 Learning Strategy Simulation

As we aim to utilize the learning process within an end user application that is designed to continuously adapt to the specific activity patterns of the user, it makes sense to not only evaluate the complete model, but also the relative improvements of the classifier when increasing the amount of training data. To evaluate this continuous refinement of the classification system, we simulated the iterative training process by using the NOVA [3] toolkit.

First of all, we trained our base model on a small stack of eight annotations from one session. From there on we used this baseline classifier to predict the rest of the training data. Subsequently, we took the first label where the confidence is equal or greater than the lower end of a predefined confidence interval. In case the confidence value lies within the interval we queried the oracle to correct our

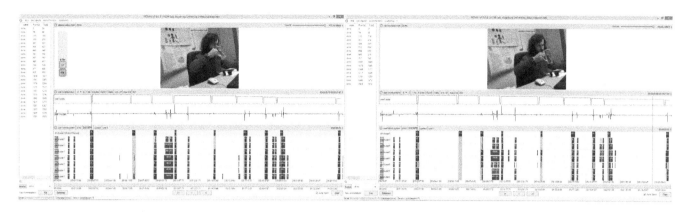

Figure 9: Cooperative Machine Leaning in NOVA: Predictions of LibLinear (left) and Naive Bayes (right) on one session. Video, smartscale and acceleration data are followed by annotations. The first line contains the hand labeled annotation and is followed by predictions of models with increased number of training data. Areas marked in green are drink activity.

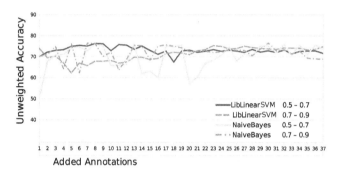

Figure 10: Training progression using different confidences and models

answer. The oracle is simulated by the full hand-labeled annotation. In case the confidence value of the prediction is higher than the upper limit of the interval we assume that the classification of the sample is correct, and forwarded to the logging application. Afterwards we add our newly annotated sample to the training data and retrain our classifier before repeating the same steps again. This process continues iteratively until all available data has been annotated. While in theory the classifier could learn from data with high classification confidence and improve without explicit user input, we stick to user (oracle) labeled data only because those are guaranteed to be true positive samples as long as the user gives correct feedback.

The study has been conducted by applying an uncertainty sampling strategy which utilizes a low confidence interval ranging from 0.5 to 0.7 as well as a relevance sampling strategy using a high confidence interval from 0.7 to 0.9, see Figure 10. While one would expect the unweighted average accuracy to increase steadily with the number of available training data our simulation results paint a different picture as shown in Figure 10. Naive Bayes is clearly more unstable than LibLinear's linear SVM. Obviously, it is less robust against variations across sessions and users as well as untypical drink activities, for example, those with long pauses while holding the vessel.

All models stabilize over the course of the simulation. By the time 30 additional labels are added to the base stock, the variations in accuracy narrow down to five percent points for Naive Bayes and three percent points for LibLinear, when adding new labels to the training process. While low confidences seem to be preferred by the LibLinear SVM model, queries based on high confidences seem to be the better choice for Naive Bayes. The progress of both models is best judged using predictions, as shown in Figure 9. One can see where the classifier triggers and with what confidence, as indicated by hatching and color. The first line contains the hand labeled annotation and is followed by predictions of models with increased number of training data. Areas marked in green are drink activities. Naive Bayes changes in accuracy, seen in Figure 10 manifest themselves as low confidence, red bars on the right.

4.3 Interactive Machine Learning Sessions

We recruited two users who used DrinkWatch for one hour to track their drink activities. For this experiment, we picked the high confidence range (0.7 to 0.9) as it promises an earlier stabilization for Naive Bayes. To create a reliable base model, we used at least 40 annotations.

One can judge the quality of the model by the appropriateness and frequency of queries. While both users had the impression that drink activities were accurately recognized in general (e.g. "Five out of six" stated by one of our two users), there were many wrong positives due to the unbalanced nature of both classes. The unfiltered requests were described as annoying by the users and made the system unusable.

The behavior of the system appeared transparent to users. They noted that moving a vessel containing fluid, slow and steady was a key trigger for recognizing drink activities. It was also easy for them to mimic activities triggering the model, describing properties of the movement that lead to requests.

4.4 Discussion

In the beginning we have motivated the need for mobile interactive and cooperative ML approaches by highlighting shortcomings of traditional ML approaches, considering (i) difficulties in getting authentic data of every day living, and (ii) a deficit of transparency and user control. We have also argued that interactively integrating users into the ML process would have the potential to address both issues, allowing users to label their own activities, to gain some understanding of and control over machine functionalities, and to ultimately peek behind the curtain of automation and to leave users with a feeling of competence and self-efficacy.

Since mobile cooperative learning is a novel research area with many conceptually and technically open issues, we have exposed ourselves into the process of developing the DrinkWatch application and its integration with smart data sources, such as the smartscale. Our intention and aim was to become able to infer limitations and potentials of future mobile cooperative ML application. After developing the core functionalities of the DrinkWatch application, we spent a time period of six months iterating the application based on multiple tests, including a longer period of time testing the application with ourselves and short episodes collecting insights from letting colleagues and friends try the application. Consequently, our main contribution is DrinkWatch as a hardware and software solution, demonstrating technical feasibility, providing detailed information for scientific reproduction, and last but not least initial user impressions and insights considering how we expect users will experience DrinkWatch. We also hope to have provided fellow researchers a methodological scheme, which can be reused and adapted for developing and evaluating other interactive and cooperative ML applications.

By building and testing DrinkWatch, we have learned that interactive cooperative machine learning is already feasible on today's state of the art smartwatches. We believe the feedback provided by the model (i.e. the machine intelligence) as a direct consequence to a drink activity is intuitively graspable by users even when feedback is provided through simple audio notifications. Based on the model performance in recognizing drink activities, we believe (as it is typical with many ML based models) that it can be adopted easily to recognize other hand-based activities.

LibLinear's linear SVM does not only show higher accuracy compared to Naive Bayes, but also a smoother learning curve. Since both models have opposing tendencies when it comes to confidence intervals, fusing both models in a Query on Committee [26] implementation, seems promising. The committee might also be accompanied by static models, such as the warmstart model or save points that can be created by the user as well.

As also described in the interactive ML paradigm [1], we believe that queries should be forwarded to the user with care since wrong positives cause frustration and users tend to describe the experience associated with wrong positives as "annoying". When it comes to adaptability to new health-related hand activities, we presented several observations that can be used as reference points. The minimal strength of the Naive Bayes warmstart model for our problem can be set at circa 40 overall annotations, this equals about eight hours of recording in our case while the linear SVM stabilizes at about 30 overall annotations or six hours of recording.

We introduced the smartscale as an option to integrate data from other data sources, in the hope to improve the (initial) quality of the model. The use of a smartscale reduced the annotation effort drastically and we came to understand that it is a suitable physical object to facilitate logging of fluid intake as well as to support

annotation and online learning on smartwatches in a stationary setting.

4.4.1 Limitations and Future Directions. We have focused on single user scenarios, investigating the question of how DrinkWatch can provide users with "power" over their ML applications. However, in many health applications, the user is not the only person who should interact with the ML application. Furthermore, there are places and contexts in which desired and available autonomy of users may vary. For example, in hospitals or retirement homes, the environment may impose autonomy constraints. A patient's behavior may need to be observed more intensively, and observation and interaction responsibility in hospitals may be distributed among patients and others (such as nurses and medical doctors), resulting in a nurse that helps observe patient behavior and label data. While on the go the integration of additional data sources comes with challenges (due to privacy issues), in (smart) homes the performance of ML applications may be improved by integrating additional knowledge sources, such as smartscales.

There is no doubt that ML-based automation in health monitoring applications will increase, resulting in a larger number of everyday user interactions with "smart" applications, which observe user behavior and query user feedback. One of the future challenges will be to integrate multiple applications and systems and to regulate not only the pure amount, but also the nature of user-system interactions. We therefore plan to integrate a context-aware mediator layer, filtering requests and learning when is a good point in time to bother the user with queries. As the query frequency will then be changed, the unfiltered query frequency can be transported to the user by other modalities, such as volume, length or pattern of the notifications' sound or vibration. In our immediate future work, we aim to study when to trigger user feedback on smartwatches in order to explore how modality and timing of notifications interfere with user experience and willingness for cooperation. Using the refined prototype, DrinkWatch can be employed "In the Wild" with a larger group of users for deeper insights.

5 CONCLUSIONS

In this paper we presented the adoption of cooperative machine learning on a smartwatch. We evaluated a prototype via simulation and initial interactive sessions. Our approach shows that today's smartwatches are capable of executing interactive machine learning for activities of daily life. The model generates sufficient feedback to let the user judge its state by means of query frequency and time. Smartwatches enable the user to intuitively mimic recognized behavior and explore the model's capabilities. From here a variety of options are open for future research, be it refining the machine learning process, integration into existing logging applications, or studying and refining how the system interacts with the user.

REFERENCES

[1] Saleema Amershi, Maya Cakmak, W. Bradley Knox, and Todd Kulesza. 2014. Power to the People: The Role of Humans in Interactive Machine Learning. *AI Magazine* (December 2014).
[2] Ling Bao and Stephen S. Intille. 2004. *Activity Recognition from User-Annotated Acceleration Data*. Springer Berlin Heidelberg, Berlin, Heidelberg, 1–17. https://doi.org/10.1007/978-3-540-24646-6_1

[3] Tobias Baur, Gregor Mehlmann, Ionut Damian, Florian Lingenfelser, Johannes Wagner, Birgit Lugrin, Elisabeth André, and Patrick Gebhard. 2015. Context-Aware Automated Analysis and Annotation of Social Human-Agent Interactions. *ACM Transactions on Interactive Intelligent Systems (TiiS)* 5, 2 (2015), 11.

[4] Sourav Bhattacharya and Nicholas D. Lane. 2016. From smart to deep: Robust activity recognition on smartwatches using deep learning. In *2016 IEEE International Conference on Pervasive Computing and Communication Workshops, PerCom Workshops 2016, Sydney, Australia, March 14-18, 2016.* 1–6. https://doi.org/10.1109/PERCOMW.2016.7457169

[5] Noemi Biancone, Chiara Bicchielli, Fernando Ferri, and Patrizia Grifoni. 2016. Falls Detection and Assessment. In *Proceedings of the 8th International Conference on Management of Digital EcoSystems.* ACM, New York, NY, USA, 204–207. https://doi.org/10.1145/3012071.3012088

[6] Albert Bifet, Geoff Holmes, Richard Kirkby, and Bernhard Pfahringer. 2010. MOA: Massive Online Analysis. *J. Mach. Learn. Res.* 11 (Aug. 2010), 1601–1604. http://dl.acm.org/citation.cfm?id=1756006.1859903

[7] Rafael A Calvo and Dorian Peters. 2014. *Positive Computing: Technology for Wellbeing and Human Potential.* MIT Press.

[8] Yen-Ping Chen, Jhun-Ying Yang, Shun-Nan Liou, Gwo-Yun Lee, and Jeen-Shing Wang. 2008. Online classifier construction algorithm for human activity detection using a tri-axial accelerometer. *Appl. Math. Comput.* 205 (2008), 849–860.

[9] Jerry Alan Fails and Dan R. Olsen, Jr. 2003. Interactive Machine Learning. In *Proceedings of the 8th International Conference on Intelligent User Interfaces (IUI '03).* ACM, New York, NY, USA, 39–45. https://doi.org/10.1145/604045.604056

[10] Simon Flutura, Johannes Wagner, Florian Lingenfelser, Andreas Seiderer, and Elisabeth André. 2016. MobileSSI: Asynchronous Fusion for Social Signal Interpretation in the Wild. In *Proceedings of the 18th ACM International Conference on Multimodal Interaction (ICMI 2016).* ACM, New York, NY, USA, 266–273. https://doi.org/10.1145/2993148.2993164

[11] Arindam Ghosh and Giuseppe Riccardi. 2014. Recognizing Human Activities from Smartphone Sensor Signals. In *Proceedings of the 22Nd ACM International Conference on Multimedia.* ACM, New York, NY, USA, 865–868. https://doi.org/10.1145/2647868.2655034

[12] Tad Hirsch, Kritzia Merced, Shrikanth Narayanan, Zac E. Imel, and David C. Atkins. 2017. Designing Contestability: Interaction Design, Machine Learning, and Mental Health. In *Proceedings of the 2017 Conference on Designing Interactive Systems.* ACM, New York, NY, USA, 95–99. https://doi.org/10.1145/3064663.3064703

[13] Eric Horvitz. 1999. Principles of Mixed-initiative User Interfaces. In *Proceedings of the SIGCHI Conference on Human Factors in Computing Systems (CHI '99).* ACM, New York, NY, USA, 159–166. https://doi.org/10.1145/302979.303030

[14] Tâm Huynh and Bernt Schiele. 2005. Analyzing Features for Activity Recognition. In *Proceedings of the 2005 Joint Conference on Smart Objects and Ambient Intelligence: Innovative Context-aware Services: Usages and Technologies.* ACM, New York, NY, USA, 159–163. https://doi.org/10.1145/1107548.1107591

[15] Donald E. Knuth. 1985. *The Art of Computer Programming, Volume 2 (2nd Ed.): Seminumerical Algorithms.* Addison-Wesley Longman Publishing Co., Inc., Boston, MA, USA.

[16] O. D. Lara and M. A. Labrador. 2013. A Survey on Human Activity Recognition using Wearable Sensors. *IEEE Communications Surveys Tutorials* 15, 3 (Third 2013), 1192–1209. https://doi.org/10.1109/SURV.2012.110112.00192

[17] YeongJu Lee and Minseok Song. 2017. Using a Smartwatch to Detect Stereotyped Movements in Children With Developmental Disabilities. *IEEE Access* 5 (2017), 5506–5514.

[18] David D. Lewis and William A. Gale. 1994. A Sequential Algorithm for Training Text Classifiers. In *Proceedings of the 17th Annual International ACM SIGIR Conference on Research and Development in Information Retrieval.* Springer-Verlag New York, Inc., New York, NY, USA, 3–12. http://dl.acm.org/citation.cfm?id=188490.188495

[19] T. Miu, P. Missier, and T. Plötz. 2015. Bootstrapping Personalised Human Activity Recognition Models Using Online Active Learning. In *2015 IEEE International Conference on Computer and Information Technology; Ubiquitous Computing and Communications; Dependable, Autonomic and Secure Computing; Pervasive Intelligence and Computing.* 1138–1147. https://doi.org/10.1109/CIT/IUCC/DASC/PICOM.2015.170

[20] Yunyoung Nam, Seungmin Rho, and Chulung Lee. 2013. Physical Activity Recognition Using Multiple Sensors Embedded in a Wearable Device. *ACM Trans. Embed. Comput. Syst.* 12, 2, Article 26 (Feb. 2013), 14 pages. https://doi.org/10.1145/2423636.2423644

[21] Nishkam Ravi, Nikhil Dandekar, Preetham Mysore, and Michael L. Littman. 2005. Activity Recognition from Accelerometer Data. In *Proceedings of the 17th Conference on Innovative Applications of Artificial Intelligence - Volume 3.* AAAI Press, 1541–1546. http://dl.acm.org/citation.cfm?id=1620092.1620107

[22] Reza Rawassizadeh, Blaine A. Price, and Marian Petre. 2014. Wearables: Has the Age of Smartwatches Finally Arrived? *Commun. ACM* 58, 1 (Dec. 2014), 45–47.

https://doi.org/10.1145/2629633

[23] Natalia Díaz Rodríguez, M. P. Cuéllar, Johan Lilius, and Miguel Delgado Calvo-Flores. 2014. A Survey on Ontologies for Human Behavior Recognition. *ACM Comput. Surv.* 46, 4, Article 43 (March 2014), 33 pages. https://doi.org/10.1145/2523819

[24] Andreas Seiderer, Simon Flutura, and Elisabeth André. 2017. Development of a Mobile Multi-device Nutrition Logger. In *Proceedings of the 2Nd ACM SIGCHI International Workshop on Multisensory Approaches to Human-Food Interaction.* ACM, New York, NY, USA, 5–12. https://doi.org/10.1145/3141788.3141790

[25] Burr Settles. 2010. Active learning literature survey. *Computer Sciences Technical Report* 1648 (2010).

[26] H. S. Seung, M. Opper, and H. Sompolinsky. 1992. Query by Committee. In *Proceedings of the Fifth Annual Workshop on Computational Learning Theory.* ACM, New York, NY, USA, 287–294. https://doi.org/10.1145/130385.130417

[27] F. Shahmohammadi, A. Hosseini, C. E. King, and M. Sarrafzadeh. 2017. Smartwatch Based Activity Recognition Using Active Learning. In *2017 IEEE/ACM International Conference on Connected Health: Applications, Systems and Engineering Technologies (CHASE).* 321–329. https://doi.org/10.1109/CHASE.2017.115

[28] Muhammad Shoaib, Stephan Bosch, Ozlem Durmaz Incel, Hans Scholten, and Paul J. M. Havinga. 2016. Complex Human Activity Recognition Using Smartphone and Wrist-Worn Motion Sensors. *Sensors* 16, 4 (2016). http://www.mdpi.com/1424-8220/16/4/426

[29] C. Stauffer and W. E. L. Grimson. 2000. Learning patterns of activity using real-time tracking. *IEEE Transactions on Pattern Analysis and Machine Intelligence* 22, 8 (Aug 2000), 747–757. https://doi.org/10.1109/34.868677

[30] Christina Strohrmann, Rob Labruyère, Corinna N. Gerber, Hubertus J. van Hedel, Bert Arnrich, and Gerhard Tröster. 2013. Monitoring motor capacity changes of children during rehabilitation using body-worn sensors. *Journal of NeuroEngineering and Rehabilitation* 10, 1 (30 Jul 2013), 83.

[31] Kristin Taraldsen, Sebastien F.M. Chastin, Ingrid I. Riphagen, Beatrix Vereijken, and Jorunn L. Helbostad. 2017. Physical activity monitoring by use of accelerometer-based body-worn sensors in older adults: A systematic literature review of current knowledge and applications. *Maturitas* 71, 19 (2017). https://doi.org/10.1016/j.maturitas.2011.11.003

[32] Simon Tong and Daphne Koller. 2002. Support Vector Machine Active Learning with Applications to Text Classification. *J. Mach. Learn. Res.* 2 (March 2002), 45–66. https://doi.org/10.1162/153244302760185243

[33] Cheng-Hao Tsai, Chieh-Yen Lin, and Chih-Jen Lin. 2014. Incremental and Decremental Training for Linear Classification. In *Proceedings of the 20th ACM SIGKDD International Conference on Knowledge Discovery and Data Mining.* ACM, New York, NY, USA, 343–352. https://doi.org/10.1145/2623330.2623661

[34] J. Wagner, T. Baur, Y. Zhang, M. F. Valstar, B. Schuller, and E. André. 2018. Applying Cooperative Machine Learning to Speed Up the Annotation of Social Signals in Large Multi-modal Corpora. *ArXiv e-prints* (Feb. 2018). arXiv:cs.HC/1802.02565

[35] Johannes Wagner, Florian Lingenfelser, Tobias Baur, Ionut Damian, Felix Kistler, and Elisabeth André. 2013. The social signal interpretation (SSI) framework: multimodal signal processing and recognition in real-time. In *ACM Multimedia Conference, MM '13, Barcelona, Spain, October 21-25, 2013.* 831–834.

[36] Malcolm Ware, Eibe Frank, Geoffrey Holmes, Mark Hall, and Ian H. Witten. 2002. Interactive Machine Learning: Letting Users Build Classifiers. *Int. J. Hum.-Comput. Stud.* 56, 3 (March 2002), 281–292. http://dl.acm.org/citation.cfm?id=514412.514417

[37] Che-Chang Yang and Yeh-Liang Hsu. 2010. A Review of Accelerometry-Based Wearable Motion Detectors for Physical Activity Monitoring. *Sensors* 10, 8 (2010), 7772–7788. https://doi.org/10.3390/s100807772

[38] Jun Yang. 2009. Toward Physical Activity Diary: Motion Recognition Using Simple Acceleration Features with Mobile Phones. In *Proceedings of the 1st International Workshop on Interactive Multimedia for Consumer Electronics.* ACM, New York, NY, USA, 1–10. https://doi.org/10.1145/1631040.1631042

[39] Mi Zhang and Alexander A. Sawchuk. 2012. USC-HAD: A Daily Activity Dataset for Ubiquitous Activity Recognition Using Wearable Sensors. In *Proceedings of the 2012 ACM Conference on Ubiquitous Computing.* ACM, New York, NY, USA, 1036–1043. https://doi.org/10.1145/2370216.2370438

[40] Zixing Zhang, Eduardo Coutinho, Jun Deng, and Björn Schuller. 2015. Cooperative Learning and Its Application to Emotion Recognition from Speech. *IEEE/ACM Trans. Audio, Speech and Lang. Proc.* 23, 1 (Jan. 2015), 115–126. https://doi.org/10.1109/TASLP.2014.2375558

[41] C. Zimmermann, J. Zeilfelder, T. Bloecher, M. Diehl, S. Essig, and W. Stork. 2017. Evaluation of a smart drink monitoring device. In *2017 IEEE Sensors Applications Symposium (SAS).* 1–5. https://doi.org/10.1109/SAS.2017.7894061

COMPETING INTERESTS

The authors have declared that no competing interests exist.

ML Approach for Early Detection of Sleep Apnea Treatment Abandonment: A Case Study

Matheus Araujo, Rahul Bhojwani, Jaideep Srivastava

[arauj021,bhojw005,srivasta]@umn.edu

University of Minnesota

Louis Kazaglis, Conrad Iber

[lkazagl1,ciber]@fairview.org

Fairview Health Systems

Minneapolis, Minnesota

ABSTRACT

Sleep apnea is a growing problem in the country, with over 200,000 new cases being identified each year. Continuous positive airway pressure (CPAP) is the best treatment for obstructive sleep apnea (OSA), but is limited by low adherence to treatment. Fairview's Sleep program actively tracks CPAP usage and outcomes and employs tele-health coaching to improve adherence. This labor-intensive protocol is applied to those who are failing to meet early adherence targets. However, the implementation of this is based on heuristic rules which may not be matched to actual outcomes, contacting some patients too late and others unnecessarily. Machine learning can facilitate efficient contact strategies through early and accurate identification of therapy trajectories based on patient history, including EHR data, health information, questionnaires, and daily PAP metrics. Prediction models for classification of patients regarding CPAP adherence at a clinically-important time of 6 months of regular use were built. Using data from the first 30 days of CPAP usage, and a more aggressive decision scenario from the first 13 days of usage, the proposed approach results in an improvement in prediction significantly better than the current approach used by the hospital. Further, it is shown that a hospital can utilize this precise and earlier prediction by implementing appropriate actions based on the patient's predicted risk level.

KEYWORDS

Machine Learning, Health Informatics, Sleep Apnea Treatment, CPAP Adherence.

ACM Reference Format:

Matheus Araujo, Rahul Bhojwani, Jaideep Srivastava and Louis Kazaglis, Conrad Iber. 2018. ML Approach for Early Detection of Sleep Apnea Treatment Abandonment: A Case Study. In *DH'18: 2018 International Digital Health Conference, April 23–26, 2018, Lyon, France.* ACM, New York, NY, USA, Article 0, 5 pages. https://doi.org/10.1145/3194658.3194681

1 INTRODUCTION

Sleep apnea is a sleep disorder in which patients have flow-limited respiration during sleep, due to upper airway narrowing or collapse, leading to low oxygen levels and repeated awakenings. Symptoms

of sleep apnea include poor quality non-restorative sleep, frequent and unexplained nighttime awakenings, and daytime sleepiness. This condition can lead to high blood pressure, chronic heart failure, atrial fibrillation, stroke, and other cardiovascular problems; and is associated with type 2 diabetes and depression. It is estimated that 22 million Americans suffer from sleep apnea with more than 200,000 cases being added every year. Around 80% of those cases are moderate or severe, meaning patients will have more than 15 respiratory-related awakenings per hour [2].

Optimal treatment of sleep apnea incorporates lifestyle changes, such as weight loss and exercise, since excess body weight is one controllable risk factor [16]. However, lifestyle counseling is typically ineffective at resolving sleep apnea, requiring other treatment options. The most effective treatment is use of a continuous positive airway pressure (CPAP) machine [7]. CPAP is a device that is worn nightly during sleep, and consists of an oronasal or nasal mask which is connected to a flow generator and provides a positive flow of air into the airway in order to prevent collapse. In severe cases of sleep apnea, surgery is also considered an option [1].

CPAP is the standard of care for obstructive sleep apnea but is limited by poor adherence rates (as low as 60% of patients adhering to the regimen) [18]. There is growing evidence that frequent and focused contact can improve long-term adherence to therapy, thus converting potentially non-adherent patients into adherent patients. However, due to financial constraints of medical practice patients are often not seen until several months into CPAP therapy. Fairview Health Systems' Sleep Therapy Management (STM) program has been working on solving this issue using a telemedicine intervention approach. Patients receive scheduled feedback and counseling at 3, 14, and 30 days to assist in overcoming difficulties and enhance their motivation for device usage [17].

The STM protocol is labor-intensive, and is currently applied uniformly to all patients; resulting in high, and often unnecessary, cost. What is desired is an automated methodology to identify target patients with high probability of non-adherence, in order to take appropriate actions which may alter their treatment trajectory. The current methodology to identify the patients has two main challenges. First, the algorithm to identify the potential "churning" patients has low precision, and it does not take into account several pieces of information from the patient such as EHR data and daily CPAP usage signals. Second, further intervention occurs based on patient classification only available after the first 30 days of usage, which in many cases is too late. Earlier telemedicine contact is made at 2 weeks, and with an earlier classification patients truly requiring advice can be the focus. A decision procedure that addresses these two needs, namely of **high decision accuracy**, and **early decision making**, will reduce wasted effort on the side of both hospital staff and patients, resulting in cost reduction and improved patient satisfaction.

2 THE PROBLEM AND CURRENT SOLUTIONS

The main challenge of CPAP therapy is that a patient needs to use the device nightly and continuously during sleep. Previous studies have shown threshold effects on therapy, including data suggesting that at least 4 hours of usage per night is necessary to significantly improve outcomes [6]. Compliance is influenced by symptom improvement, but maximal improvement in symptoms may not occur until 6 months of therapy [11]. Formally, patients who used the CPAP device for more than 4 hours in at least 70% of the days between the 151st day and 180th day after first use, are considered to have successfully adapted to CPAP therapy. Regular and long-term nightly use of CPAP is difficult due to the burden of care and a host of other reasons, and unfortunately, patients often stop therapy or churn out of adherent treatment groups.

In order to address the problem of identifying patients who are likely to cease CPAP treatment, the following mathematical formulation can be used: Given the input matrix X with patient history data such that $X_i \in R_d$, and output array y such that $y_i \in \{0, 1\}$, find a function $H(X, \theta)$ which minimizes the cost, defined as:

$$COST = (\frac{1}{N}) * \sum_{i}^{N} Loss(y_i, H(X_i, \theta))$$

where θ stands for all parameters that need to be tuned subject to constraints and N is the total number of patients. This formulates an optimization problem based on the relation of $H(X, \theta)$. In the rest of the paper, the proposed procedure to find the best H and θ, and it's respective comparison results with Fairview baseline, is presented.

2.1 Data

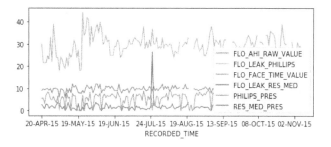

Figure 1: Example of patient's data from CPAP device.

Fairview Health Systems sleep program actively tracks patient characteristics and CPAP usage data. The dataset used for this study contains 3588 unique patients. Figure 1 shows an example of the raw CPAP signals from April 2015 to November 2015 for one patient. The recorded signals have daily granularity. The daily variables included 95% pressure (measurement of the upper limit of pressure delivered by CPAP), AHI value (Apnea-Hypopnea Index) which represents the residual number of sleep apnea events per hour as a metric for effectiveness of applied pressure, time on face (time that the machine detects breathing as opposed to time the machine

is running), and air pressure leakage in L/min (a measure of the quality of mask fit).

The shared dataset is a combination of CPAP usage data and relevant electronic health record (EHR) data linked by a unique identifier. Previous studies have demonstrated that patient characteristic data can influence CPAP adherence[9]. Therefore, the health record feature set was also used, including information on medical diagnoses, medications, questionnaire, health care encounters, gender, BMI, age, blood pressure, and data from sleep studies.

2.2 Current Fairview Model

To address the goal of predicting long-term adherence and engagement, Fairview uses a simple approach customized to the care model based on predictability of failure based on early adherence behavior and logical markers for treatment failure. The care model consists of telemedicine coaching visits on days 3, 14, and 30, with targeted early interventions followed by a continuous monitoring. On day 3, contact is primarily to ensure patient has started therapy. Early subjective problems, such as mask discomfort or mouth dryness, are often identified within 14 days of use. The final scheduled contact on day 30 was chosen based on insurance and regulatory requirements; most insurers require patients to demonstrate high levels of adherence for a 30 day window between days 31 and 90 of therapy to authorize continued payment for care. Patients failing to reach benchmarks for subjective tolerance [lack of improvement on therapy, low self-reported use, discomfort due to therapy air pressure, dryness, mask comfort, and general complaints], adherence [minutes per day of use], and effectiveness of therapy [residual breathing events per hour, excessive mask leak in liters per minute], are sent to a two week recurrence of coaching and subsequent face-to-face visit with a sleep specialist for targeted individualized care. At that visit, the specialist reviews usage and determines if CPAP therapy should continue or if the patient should transition to an alternative option, based on the likelihood of long-term adherence.

The **baseline model** used by Fairview examines the daily usage time (facetime attribute) for each patient each day after initiation of CPAP therapy. After 30 days, if the percent of days in which the patient uses the device for 4 or more hours is less than 70% (i.e. ≤21 days) [18], patients undergo more extensive individualized review over 2 weeks, and subsequently are directed to a face to face visit if benchmarks are not achieved. Day 30 is chosen as the decision point based on the timing of the last telemedicine contact unless patients are found to have abandoned the device or fail to meet the adherence target. This is to allow for further recommendations at the telemedicine contact and to suggest a trajectory at the subsequent face-to-face visit. This baseline model serves as the control for the present study.

Despite being computationally simple, the baseline approach has serious drawbacks. This ruled-based system ignores the vast majority of the data available, including all of the health record information. Furthermore, by waiting until day 30 to classify patients, there is an increased risk of complete patient disengagement from care. Accurate predictions in an earlier treatment window, in particular before the 14th day, would allow for early treatment diversions or more tailored counseling at the fixed 14-day telemedicine contact, as well as reducing the number of non-reimbursed contacts.

Finally, there is a need to find better methods that can help tele-health prioritize care. The current model does not allow Fairview to stratify patients based on the likelihood of adherence. Rather, all patients are contacted uniformly at a specified time.

3 OUR PROPOSED APPROACH

Machine learning based predictive modeling is used to address multiple drawbacks of the current methodology mentioned in section 2. It helps in classifying the patients more accurately even at a very early stage in their treatment journey as compared to the current approach. And using the distance of the points from the class boundary allows ranking the patients based on risk factor, leading to a reasonable and actionable list. It learns from the patterns in the data, so is adaptable to changes in user behavior over time. These strengths, when functional in the clinical process, can reduce cost and human effort.

The entire approach defined below was applied to two different scenarios. First, the data of the initial 30 days of the patient's journey is used to predict their adherence usage by the end of the 180th day (6th month of treatment). This has the goal to improve the current model (baseline) discussed above. The second scenario addresses the same classification but using the data only till the end of the 13th day of the patient's journey. The latter aims to assess the patients before their meeting with the doctor, which is after the second week of the treatment. Previous studies have shown that information from the early stage of treatment can give sufficient information about patient's adherence to treatment. [3].

Figure 2 shows the methodology used to implement a machine learning solution for the problem. The input data includes the daily signals from CPAP devices and the EHR data of the patients. The combined input stream is passed to a feature selection layer, where the optimal set of features is selected based on feature selection techniques. The final dataset is then passed to 10 fold cross-validation process, dividing the data into 90:10 ratio to training and test data respectively. The training data is passed through a sampling layer which generates a class balanced dataset with the technique mentioned in Section 3.3. A set of models are then trained on the training data and the results are measured by evaluating their performance on the test data. Various model evaluation measures were used to compare the model performance, as described in Section 4.

3.1 Feature Extraction

As common in machine learning tasks with raw data, different potential signals were explored, that could be underlying in the dataset, before proceeding to solve the problem [10].

It was observed that patients do not have a uniform use of CPAP devices through their treatment, and there are days with missing record values. Since the missing values are on days that patients do not use the CPAP, it is a signal that cannot be ignored. In fact, as discussed in [13], it should be treated as missing data not at random (MNAR). MNAR exists when the value of the variable that is missing is related to the reason it is missing (e.g. a person with depression would not like to fill a form about his depression [5]). Thus, the missing value percent is used as a new feature for detecting compliance with the device.

Other hidden features in the data were explored by positing hypotheses guided by subject matter expertise and testing the effect on the results. For example, Figure 3 shows the average facetime usage in hours (Y-axis) per day (X-axis) during their first 30 days of CPAP treatment. We plotted in **solid** the values for patients who keep with the treatment for at least 180 days and in **broken** the values for the "churning" patients. The mean and standard deviation in this cases are a good signal to identify the correct patient category. The mean of facetime usage for compliant patients (solid line) is 42% higher than "churning" patients. Also, the mean standard deviation is 5x greater on the "churning" case. These features were used in training the model. To capture the trend, the interval mean and standard deviation after each time window of few days was taken. This led us to expand the feature space and retain more trend information. Also, this led to the use of window interval as a hyper-parameter which was tuned during the process.

3.2 Feature selection

After having an expanded feature space the model was optimized based on the cost function and generated test results. In total, for the 30th day predicting model, there were 46 features derived from the CPAP device signals and 72 EHR data features. Thus, the final dataset had 118 features. Similarly, for the 13th day predicting model, there were 85 total features, divided into 22 and 63 for CPAP and EHR, respectively. To avoid the curse of dimensionality feature selection was used. NSpecifically, ANOVA F-value was used as the feature selection technique to select K best features to be used in the model, where K was kept as a hyper-parameter and was selected based on cross-validation on the models.

3.3 Imbalanced class problem

In the dataset, 1045 patients out of 3588 total were labeled as not compliant with the treatment, which leads to an imbalanced distribution of the data. A generic model might not learn good separation boundaries and parameters because of the imbalance and low information on the minority class. A possible solution to address this issue is either by under-sampling or oversampling the training data. Because of the lack of available data, we decided to go for oversampling of the minority, using SMOTE [4] [12]. It is important to highlight that the distribution of the test data was not altered.

3.4 Machine Learning Methods

After generating the class balanced training data with selected features, the machine learning experimentation module was run to explore different techniques to learn the best definition of function $H(X, \theta)$, that minimizes the cost, mentioned in section 2. Initially, simple linear and tree-based models like linear/logistic regression and Decision Tree were tried. Next, a parameter optimization approach to SVM was explored. These models gave negligible improvements over the baseline model. Subsequently, ensemble tree models like Random Forest and boosting trees like XGBoost were tried. These models provided a significant improvement in results, as described in section 4. Model implementations were performed using the **sci-kit learn** toolkit[14]. Deep feedforward network, CNN and LSTM for time series classification were considered. However, the results of these experiments are omitted in this work since no interesting learning pattern could be detected. Intial assessment is that these models did not perform well compared to the shallow

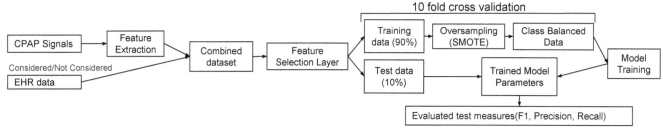

Figure 2: Flowchart of our approach

models because of the lack of data. This remains a promising area for further exploration.

4 ANALYSIS AND RESULTS

For the purpose of experimentation, different type of machine learning methods along with the EHR data usage flag, are shown in Table 1. And the results of our approach for two different scenarios, as discussed in Section 3, are presented. For the first scenario, data from the 1st to the 30th day of the patients' treatment was used to predict their compliance, as the baseline does. For the second scenario, data from 1st to the 13th day of treatment was used.

To evaluate the results four different metrics were considered: F1-Score, Precision, Sensitivity (recall of positive class) and Specificity (recall of negative class). Positive class are those patients who are compliant with the treatment, and negative class are those patients who did not accomplish minimum usage of the device. Since F1-Score and Precision are sensible by what is considered as the positive or negative class, the results for both are shown. The columns **F1(-)** and **Precision(-)**, represent the F1 score and the precision for the negative class respectively. More information about these metrics are discussed in [15].The Precision(-), also known as NPV, is a commonly used metric for this domain. Also, it helps in understanding the results better, as explained in the end of this section. The following observations were made as a result of experiments conducted during the analysis.

Table 1, summarizes the results obtained. Given **Scenario 1**, the proposed approach is better for all but **Precision(-)** and **Sensitivity** than the baseline regardless of the model or the use of EHR data. The XGBoost model combined with the patient EHR data gives the best result. Compared to the baseline we have the following results variation: **F1**(+8%), **F1(-)**(+7%), **Precision**(+15%), **Precision(-)**(-10%), **Sensitivity**(-1%) and **Specificity**(+19%). The use of demographic data from patients did not show a significant improvement and may not be incorporated in a production model for simplification reasons. Nonetheless, these results shows a higher accuracy in terms of classification using machine learning.

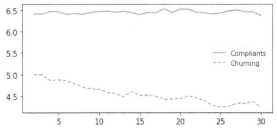

Figure 3: Average facetime usage during first 30 days

For **Scenario 2**, the same technique was used. However, only the features available on the 13th day were considered. Again, XGBoost with EHR data gave the best results. It is better than baseline for **F1**(+6%), **Precision**(+12%), **Specificity**(+8%). However, it is worse than baseline for: **F1(-)**(-1%), **Precision(-)**(-15%) and Sensitivity(-2%). It shows that similar precision and recall for both positive and negative class can be obtained two weeks earlier than what is implemented today.

Given the criticality of the use case, the model is performing better in all the metrics but the **Precision (-)**. However, examining the **F1(-)**, the results show a much higher performance in Situation 1 and almost the same in Situation 2, which is because recall for the negative class (**Specificity**) is better than the baseline. This means that more people are being captured in the "Churn" bucket then the baseline, with some loss of precision. In a health treatment context, this loss of precision is no harm, since they end up getting extra care. A worse scenario would be if an approach mis-classifies someone as likely to continue in the treatment even though they are going to churn. But that's been taken care by the proposed model with better precision and recall for the positive class.

5 HOW CAN THESE RESULTS BE OPERATIONALIZED

Figure 4: Operationalization given models output

The combination of machine learning techniques and a robust data aggregation system of patient data allows the identification of the likelihood of compliance to CPAP therapy. Health-care systems like Fairview can intervene earlier and with higher accuracy. Moreover, as classifying machine learning models can be analyzed to get the distance of each data point from class division boundaries, it can further be used to order each data point(patient in this case) based on their risk factor of compliance. For probabilistic models like Random Forest and XGBoost discussed here, we proposed to look at the probability difference from the class threshold and use that as the distance. The predicted negative class will have negative distance and the positive class will have positive distance.

Figure 4 shows a possible approach to operationalize a trained model in hospital computed systems. The vertical arrow going from

Methodology	Model	EHR data	F1	F1 (-)	Precision	Precision (-)	Sensitivity	Specificity
Baseline (Scenario 1 - 30 days)			0.79	0.57	0.72	0.72	0.88	0.48
M.L. Models (Scenario 1 - 30 days)	XGB	No	0.84	0.62	0.84	0.63	0.85	0.61
	XGB	Yes	0.85	0.61	0.83	0.65	0.87	0.57
	RF	No	0.84	0.60	0.83	0.62	0.85	0.58
	RF	Yes	0.84	0.60	0.83	0.64	0.86	0.57
M.L. Models (Scenario 2 - 13 days)	XGB	No	0.82	0.54	0.80	0.58	0.85	0.51
	XGB	Yes	0.84	0.56	0.81	0.61	0.86	0.52
	RF	No	0.82	0.52	0.79	0.57	0.85	0.48
	RF	Yes	0.83	0.55	0.80	0.61	0.87	0.50

Table 1: Machine learning models results compared to Fairview baseline

bottom to top shows a ranking of patients based on the distance from the "compliance" class divided into three groups of risk. Patients towards the bottom, labeled as High Risk, are at high risk of not being compliant, and are unlikely to continue CPAP therapy. These are the patients predicted as negative class and they will have negative distance from the threshold, as mentioned above. This group is least likely to have a telemedicine contact change their trajectory. Several other options exist for this High-Risk category, falling into alternative therapies, such as surgery or a mandibular advancement device, or intensive interventions, like working with a behavioral counselor.

Similarly, patients in the Low-Risk category would be expected to continue CPAP therapy long-term. They would not need tailored interventions, and could be cared for using automated methods. Options such as web-based contact or automated phone calls and emails can be used to maintain the status quo [8].

The focus of the telemedicine contact program would be the Medium Risk category, as they would theoretically be the ideal patient population for brief interventions. Assuming patients closer to the Low Risk boundary are more likely to be compliant than those closer to the High Risk boundary, several options for prioritization exist. One approach would be to rank contact based on distance to Low Risk division boundary, and thus concentrate the interventions on the patients most likely to be compliant (low-hanging fruit approach). A complementary approach would be to focus on the patients closest to the High Risk border (at-risk approach), concentrating effort on those that appear distinct from the High Risk group to try to maximize compliance.

6 CONCLUSION

Our team, in partnership with the Fairview sleep program, has created a solution to the problem of identifying patients who are unlikely to continue CPAP therapy for sleep apnea.

These initial machine learning efforts improved performance over standard predictors though several metrics. We highlight the XGBoost algorithm which presented a significntly better model to solve the problem compared to the baseline. Also, it could provide results so good as the baseline 2 weeks earlier (using less than 50% of the same data). We believe that further refinement will improve performance using different weighting/cost functions, advanced learning methods, and non-dichotomous models.

Data aggregation in electronic health records is growing rapidly. Nonetheless, this type of model is easily localized and implementable in most EHRs. Developing predictors of long-term adherence will allow for tailoring of follow-up and timely care. Using this approach, we have been able to significantly improve upon standard

compliance prediction. Prospective evaluation and alternative care pathways are the next steps to capitalizing on these models.

We acknowledge the Fairview Health Systems for sharing the dataset and knowledge that made this study possible.

REFERENCES

[1] [n. d.]. CPAP: Treating Sleep Apnea. ([n. d.]). https://sleepfoundation.org/sleep-disorders-problems/continuous-positive-airway [Online; 27-Jan-2018].
[2] [n. d.]. Sleep Apnea Information for Clinicians. ([n. d.]). https://www.sleepapnea.org/learn/sleep-apnea-information-clinicians/ [Online; 27-Jan-2018].
[3] Rohit Budhiraja, Sairam Parthasarathy, Christopher L Drake, Thomas Roth, Imran Sharief, Pooja Budhiraja, Victoria Saunders, and David W Hudgel. 2007. Early CPAP use identifies subsequent adherence to CPAP therapy. Sleep 30, 3 (2007).
[4] Nitesh V. Chawla, Kevin W. Bowyer, Lawrence O. Hall, and W. Philip Kegelmeyer. 2002. SMOTE: Synthetic Minority Over-sampling Technique. J. Artif. Int. Res. (June 2002).
[5] Wikipedia contributors. 2017. Missing data — Wikipedia, The Free Encyclopedia. (2017). https://en.wikipedia.org/w/index.php?title=Missing_data&oldid=816369302 [Online; accessed 27-January-2018].
[6] Heather M Engleman, Sascha E Martin, and Neil J Douglas. 1994. Compliance with CPAP therapy in patients with the sleep apnoea/hypopnoea syndrome. Thorax 49, 3 (1994), 263–266.
[7] Jan Magnus Fredheim, Jan Rollheim, Rune Sandbu, Dag Hofsø, Torbjørn Omland, Jo Røislien, and Jøran Hjelmesæth. 2013. Obstructive sleep apnea after weight loss: a clinical trial comparing gastric bypass and intensive lifestyle intervention. Journal of clinical sleep medicine: JCSM 9, 5 (2013), 427.
[8] Dennis Hwang, Jeremiah W Chang, Adam V Benjafield, Maureen E Crocker, Colleen Kelly, Kendra A Becker, Joseph B Kim, Rosa R Woodrum, Joanne Liang, and Stephen F Derose. 2018. Effect of Telemedicine Education and Telemonitoring on Continuous Positive Airway Pressure Adherence. The Tele-OSA Randomized Trial. American journal of respiratory and critical care medicine 197, 1 (2018).
[9] Anne Roed Jacobsen, Freja Eriksen, Rasmus Würgler Hansen, Mogens Erlandsen, Line Thorup, Mette Bjerre Damgård, Martin Glümer Kirkegaard, and Klavs Würgler Hansen. 2017. Determinants for adherence to continuous positive airway pressure therapy in obstructive sleep apnea. PloS one 12, 12 (2017), e0189614.
[10] Michel Jambu. 1991. Exploratory and multivariate data analysis. Elsevier.
[11] Clete A Kushida, Deborah A Nichols, Tyson H Holmes, Stuart F Quan, James K Walsh, Daniel J Gottlieb, Richard D Simon Jr, Christian Guilleminault, David P White, James L Goodwin, et al. 2012. Effects of continuous positive airway pressure on neurocognitive function in obstructive sleep apnea patients: the Apnea Positive Pressure Long-term Efficacy Study (APPLES). Sleep 35, 12 (2012).
[12] Guillaume Lemaître, Fernando Nogueira, and Christos K. Aridas. 2017. Imbalanced-learn: A Python Toolbox to Tackle the Curse of Imbalanced Datasets in Machine Learning. Journal of Machine Learning Research 18, 17 (2017), 1–5.
[13] Roderick JA Little and Donald B Rubin. 2014. Statistical analysis with missing data. Vol. 333. John Wiley & Sons.
[14] F. Pedregosa, G. Varoquaux, A. Gramfort, V. Michel, B. Thirion, O. Grisel, M. Blondel, P. Prettenhofer, R. Weiss, V. Dubourg, J. Vanderplas, A. Passos, D. Cournapeau, M. Brucher, M. Perrot, and E. Duchesnay. 2011. Scikit-learn: Machine Learning in Python. Journal of Machine Learning Research 12 (2011), 2825–2830.
[15] David Martin Powers. 2011. Evaluation: from precision, recall and F-measure to ROC, informedness, markedness and correlation. (2011).
[16] Naresh M Punjabi. 2008. The epidemiology of adult obstructive sleep apnea. Proceedings of the American Thoracic Society 5, 2 (2008), 136–143.
[17] David Sparrow, Mark Aloia, Deborah A DeMolles, and Daniel J Gottlieb. 2010. A telemedicine intervention to improve adherence to continuous positive airway pressure: a randomised controlled trial. Thorax 65, 12 (2010), 1061–1066.
[18] Terri E Weaver and Amy M Sawyer. 2010. Adherence to continuous positive airway pressure treatment for obstructive sleep apnea: implications for future interventions. The Indian journal of medical research 131 (2010), 245.

Screening Dyslexia for English Using HCI Measures and Machine Learning

Luz Rello
HCI Institute
Carnegie Mellon University
Pittsburgh, USA
luzrello@cs.cmu.edu

Enrique Romero
Department of Computer Science
Universitat Politècnica de Catalunya
Barcelona, Spain
eromero@cs.upc.edu

Maria Rauschenberger
Web Science and Social Computing
Research Group
Universitat Pompeu Fabra
Barcelona, Spain
maria.rauschenberger@upf.edu

Abdullah Ali
Information School
University of Washington
Washington, USA
xyleques@uw.edu

Kristin Williams
HCI Institute
Carnegie Mellon University
Pittsburgh, USA
krismawil@cs.cmu.edu

Jeffrey P. Bigham
HCI & LTI Institutes
Carnegie Mellon University
Pittsburgh, USA
jbigham@cs.cmu.edu

Nancy Cushen White
Department of Pediatrics
University of California San Francisco
San Francisco, USA
nancycushen.white@ucsf.edu

ABSTRACT

More than 10% of the population has dyslexia, and most are diagnosed only after they fail in school. This work seeks to change this through early detection via machine learning models that predict dyslexia by observing how people interact with a linguistic computer-based game. We designed items of the game taking into account *(i)* the empirical linguistic analysis of the errors that people with dyslexia make, and *(ii)* specific cognitive skills related to dyslexia: *Language Skills, Working Memory, Executive Functions,* and *Perceptual Processes*. . Using measures derived from the game, we conducted an experiment with 267 children and adults in order to train a statistical model that predicts readers with and without dyslexia using measures derived from the game. The model was trained and evaluated in a 10-fold cross experiment, reaching 84.62% accuracy using the most informative features.

CCS CONCEPTS

• **Computers and Society**; • **Social Issues**; • **Assistive Technologies for persons with disabilities**;

KEYWORDS

Dyslexia, screening, early detection, diagnosis, linguistics, serious games, machine learning

ACM Reference Format:
Luz Rello, Enrique Romero, Maria Rauschenberger, Abdullah Ali, Kristin Williams, Jeffrey P. Bigham, and Nancy Cushen White. 2018. Screening Dyslexia for English Using HCI Measures and Machine Learning. In *DH'18: 2018 International Digital Health Conference, April 23–26, 2018, Lyon, France.* ACM, New York, NY, USA, 5 pages. https://doi.org/10.1145/3194658.3194675

1 INTRODUCTION

More than 10% of the population has dyslexia [11, 26]. The *DSM-V* [1] defines dyslexia as a *specific learning disorder* with a neurological basis. According to the *World Federation of Neurology* it occurs in children who, despite conventional classroom experience, fail to attain the language skills of reading, writing, and spelling commensurate with their intellectual abilities [28]. In summary, dyslexia is frequent, universal and related to school failure. However, it remains under-diagnosed. For instance, in the UK, a country that effectively treats dyslexia as compared with other countries, only 5% of the individuals with dyslexia are diagnosed and given appropriate help, and [7]. It is estimated that over 85% of adult illiterates have dyslexia [7].

Yet, early detection is crucial for addressing dyslexia and effective remediation. Often, students are under-diagnosed because current procedures for diagnosis are expensive [16, 21] and require professional oversight [3, 8]. Our goal is for anyone to know as early as possible if they might have dyslexia in an inexpensive way.

To achieve this goal, we have created a computer game that records a wide variety of web-page interaction measures to screen dyslexia for English. We conducted a user study with 267 participants to collect data to train a machine learning model that is able to correctly determine if a person has (or does not have) dyslexia with 84.62% accuracy.

2 BACKGROUND AND RELATED WORK

The complexity of administering paper-based diagnostic tools, and the time they require, have led educators to turn towards computer based screening methods to derive a quick assessment.

2.1 Commercial Software

Among the available commercial software to detect dyslexia in English there is *Lexercise Screener* [13] and *Nessy* [17]. We could not find studies behind these commercial applications, although they are widely used in practice. To our knowledge, they are not based on a machine learning model predictive of dyslexia, and we have not found publication of their accuracy.

2.2 Computer Based Games

There are a number of computer games designed to screen for dyslexia, but they do not use machine learning models.

Lyytinen *et al.* [15] created the computer game *Literate*, later called *GraphoGame* [14], to identify children at risk in Finland. The game was tested with 12 and 41 children between 6 and 7 years old -with statistically significant differences.

There are three other on-going projects for early risk detection of dyslexia that have not yet reported significant results yet: one approach for Italian tested with 24 pre-schoolers [9], and a language-independent approach *MusVis* evaluated with German, English and Spanish children [19, 24].

2.3 Machine Learning Approaches

Machine learning approaches to predict dyslexia are more recent. In 2015, the first method to screen dyslexia in Spanish was introduced; it used eye-tracking measures from 97 subjects (48 with dyslexia) [21]. Later in 2016, eye-tracking measures were also used to predict dyslexia for Swedish (185 subjects, 97 of then with high-risk of dyslexia)[2]. Both methods used *Support Vector Machines*. Another study detected dyslexia subtypes in the Hebrew language using data derived from existing medical records [12].

The only approach we are aware of to predict risk of dyslexia using features derived from computer-based measures is the game *Dytective* for Spanish. The screener, *Dytective*, was first evaluated with 343 people (95 with diagnosed dyslexia) and attained 83% accuracy in a held-out test set with 100 participants using Support Vector Machines [23]. Later, the model was improved by applying a neural network model (Long Short-Term Memory Networks (LSTMs) [10]) to a larger dataset–4,335 participants (763 with professional dyslexia diagnosis)–attaining 91.97% accuracy [22]. This model was integrated into a free online tool *Dytective* which has been used over 100,000 times.[1] An earlier study piloted *Dytective's* screening measures with 60 English speaking children and found the feature set was promising, but the study did not fully incorporate machine learning methods [25].

We advance these approaches by *(i)* extending these methods to the English language and *(ii)* include a wider number of items targeting cognitive indicators predictive of dyslexia.

3 USER STUDY

We conducted a within-subject study (267 participants) with all participants exposed to the same linguistic items integrated into an online game *Dytective*.

3.1 Procedure and Ethics Statement

Participants completed the experiment remotely, through a computer at home, school, or in a specialized center in the USA (mainly from the states of Pennsylvania, New York and Texas). All participants agreed to participate through an online consent form, and children provided assent along with their parent or legal guardian following protocols approved by our institutional review board (IRB). Parents/legal guardians were specifically warned that they could not help their children complete the study exercises. When schools and specialized centers oversaw participation, parental/legal guardian consent was obtained in advance, and the study was supervised by the school counselor or therapist.

The first part of the study consisted of a questionnaire collecting demographic data. This questionnaire was completed by the participant's supervisor (school counselor or therapist) in cases when the participant was under 18 years of age. Then, following oral instructions, participants were given 20 minutes to complete the test exercises.

3.2 Participants

We recruited 267 participants from one specialized center, three schools, and from individuals with dyslexia who knew about our study through our public call online.

Subjects ranged in age from 7 to 60 years old. We classified these participants into three groups. Of the participants, 52 were diagnosed with dyslexia -Class *D (dyslexia)*- (28 female, 24 male, $M = 11.16, SD = 6.31$) and 206 without a diagnosis of dyslexia served as a control group -Class *N (Not-Dyslexia)*- (94 female, 112 male, $M = 11.89, SD = 5.11$). There were 9 participants at risk of having dyslexia or suspected of having dyslexia -Class *M (Maybe)*- (4 female, 5 male, $M = 17.66, SD = 16.17$).[2]

The first language of all participants was English, although 84 participants spoke another language (mostly Spanish in the Texas area). A total of 224 participants reported having trouble with language classes at school.

3.3 Dependent Measures

Participants' performance was measured using the following *dependent measures* for each of the exercises: (i) Number of *Clicks* per item; (ii) *Hits* (*i.e.*, the number of correct answers); (iii) *Misses* (*i.e.*, the number of incorrect answers); (iv) *Score* (*i.e.*, the sum of correct answers for each stage's problem type); (v) *Accuracy* (*i.e.*, the number of *Hits* divided by the number of *Clicks*; and (vi) *Miss Rate* (*i.e.*, the number of *Misses* divided by the number of *Clicks*).

We later used these performance measures together with the demographic data as features of our prediction model's dataset (see Section 4).

---

[1]https://dytectivetest.org/

[2]All were either adults or children under observation by professionals, the step before having an official diagnosis.

Language Skills	Working Memory
Alphabetic Awareness	Visual (alphabetical)
Phonological Awareness	Auditory (phonology)
Syllabic Awareness	Sequential (auditory)
Lexical Awareness	Sequential (visual)
Morphological Awareness	**Executive Functions**
Syntactic Awareness	Activation and Attention
Semantic Awareness	Sustained Attention
Orthographic Awareness	Simultaneous Attention
Perceptual Processes	
Visual Discrimination and Categorization	
Auditory Discrimination and Categorization	

Table 1: Indicators used for the design of the test items.

3.4 Materials

We integrated test items into a software game to serve as the primary material of our study.

3.4.1 Design and Implementation. Dytective is a cross-platform web-based game built in *HTML5, CSS, JavaScript* and a *PHP* server and a *MySQL* database. It was designed with a high level of abstraction to make it easily portable for future native implementations.

The interface design of the game implements the guidelines that, according to the latest findings in accessibility research, ensure the best on-screen text readability for this target group. Text is presented in black using a mono-spaced typeface *Courier* and a minimum font size of 14 points [20].

3.4.2 Playing Dytective. At each phase, the player's goal is to accumulate points by solving a linguistic problem type as many times as possible in a 25-second time window. For example, the player hears the target, non-word *crench* and then a board is shown on screen containing the target non-word as well as distractors that are particularly difficult for people with dyslexia to differentiate (See Figure 1 (a)). After each time window, the player continues on to the next item corresponding to a new linguistic problem type.

3.4.3 Content Design. The test items are composed of a set of attention and linguistic exercises addressing three or more of the following indicators belonging to different types of *Language Skills, Working Memory, Executive Function,* and *Perceptual Processes.* These indicators are related to dyslexia [5, 6, 27].

The exercises were designed according to linguistic knowledge and the expertise of dyslexia therapists (specific to the English language). In addition, to assist item selection (exercises) we used the following criteria:

(i) linguistic analyses of 833 confusion sets[3], created from the errors of people with dyslexia writing in English [18]; and

(ii) Performance measures from the linguistic exercises of an online game called *Piruletras.*[4] This game is part of previous work targeting children with dyslexia to improve spelling performance [24]. We selected exercises that were more challenging for the players (those with higher error rates and need for more time to be solved) since those exercises were more likely to manifest dyslexia difficulties.

---

[3]A confusion set is a small group of words that are likely to be confused with one another–such as *weather* and *whether.*
[4]https://itunes.apple.com/us/app/dyseggxia/id534986729?mt=8

4 DATASET

The dataset is composed of 226 features per participant (i.e., total of 60,342 data points. Each participant from the dataset was marked as *D* if the participant has dyslexia, *N* if not, and *M* (maybe) if the participant suspects that he or she has dyslexia but is not diagnosed. From the dataset we extracted the following features:

1. **Gender** of the participant. A binary feature with two values, *female* and *male.*
2. **Age** of the participant ranging from 7 to 60 years old.
3. **Second language.** A binary feature with two values, *no* and *yes,* when the participant had a second language in case of bilingualism.
4. **Language subject.** This is a binary feature with two values, *no* and *yes,* when the participant declares that she has trouble with language classes at school.

Features from **5** to **226** are **performance measures**; they correspond with the six dependent measures (*Clicks, Hits, Misses, Score, Accuracy,* and *Missrate*) per level played (37 levels).

These features target some of the skills presented in Table 1. Note that all the exercises involve attention, so all these features target the *executive functions* **activation and attention**, and **sustained attention**. In addition, some of them also target **simultaneous attention** when the participant pays attention to a number of sources of incoming information at the same time.

5-28 These features are performance measures related to **alphabetic awareness** and **visual discrimination and categorization**. For these tasks the participant hears the name of a letter, *e.g., d,* and identifies it from among the distractors (orthographic and phonetically similar letters, *e.g. b, q, p*) within a time frame, using a Whac-A-Mole-style game interaction.

29-52 These features relate to **phonological awareness** and **auditory discrimination and categorization**. The participant listens to the sound (phoneme) of a letter and identifies it from among distractors. For example, the participant hears the phoneme /n/ and then a board is shown containing the target <n> as well as distractors. We use distractors that are particularly difficult for people with dyslexia to differentiate (*i.e.,* other phonemes that share phonetic features, such as. nasal and sound consonants.

53-88 These features target **syllabic awareness** and **auditory discrimination and categorization**. The players hear the pronunciation of a syllable (*e.g., /prin/*) and identify its spelling from among orthographic distractors <pren> <prein>, <prain>, <prean>, and <pryn>.

89-112 These features correspond to a set of exercises where participants identify a word's spelling after hearing its pronunciation (*e.g., /greet/* by discriminating among phonetically and orthographically similar words and/or non-words (*e.g.,* <create>, <greate>, <great>, <grete>, <greit>, <creet>, <crete>, <creat>. These features target **lexical awareness, auditory working memory,** and **auditory discrimination and categorization.**

113-136 These performance features correspond to exercises targeting **visual discrimination and categorization**, by requiring participants to find as many different letters as possible

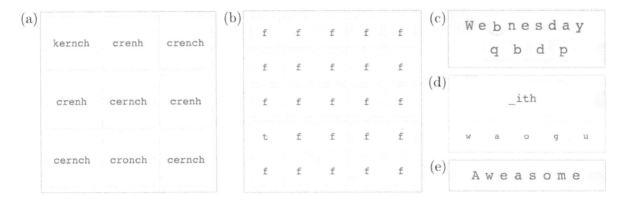

Figure 1: Screenshots of the exercises requiring the player to click on the target non-word listed among the distractors; (a) select the different letter; (b) build a correct word by substituting a letter, (c) selecting a letter, (d) or deleting a letter (e).

within a time frame in a visual search task (*e.g. E/F, g/q, c/o, b/d* or *p/q*). See Figure 1, exercise (b).

137-160 These features were extracted from a set of exercises requiring players to listen to a non-word and choose its spelling (*e.g. /lurled/*) from among distractors (*e.g. <rurled>, <larled>, <lurded>, <lurleb>, <lorled>*). These features target **sequential auditory working memory**, and **auditory discrimination and categorization**. See Figure 1, exercise (a).

161-172 These performance features target **lexical, phonological,** and **orthographic awareness;** They are derived from exercises requiring participants to supply a missing letter [161-166] or delete an extra letter in a target word [167-172]. See Figure 1, exercises (d) and (e), respectively.

173-178 These performance features target **morphological** and **semantic awareness.** They are collected from exercises requiring participants to find a morphological error in a sentence when there is also a semantic error. For example, in the sentence, *The affect of the wind was to cause the boat's sails to billow.* (The word *affect* should be *effect*).

179-184 These features relate to **syntactic awareness.** Participants find an error in a sentence related to a grammatical or function word that changes, (*e.g., of* instead of *on* in *"Smoking is prohibited of the entire aircraft"*).

185-190 This set of features relates to **phonological, lexical,** and **orthographic awareness.** These exercises require to find an error in a sentence and correct it by choosing a letter from a set of distractors. See Figure 1, exercise (c).

191-202 This set of features -**phonological, lexical** and **orthographic awareness (Features 191-196)**-require participants to rearrange letters to spell a real word (*e.g., b e c u a s e*) or to rearrange syllables to spell a real word (*e.g., /na/ /na/ /ba/*) -**syllabic, lexical,** and **ortho- graphic awareness** (Features **197-202**).

203-208 This set of features, addressing **phonological, lexical** and **orthographic awareness** requires players to separate words to make a meaningful sentence, *e.g.* Change *sheranupthehill* to *e.g. she ran up the hill.*

209-214 This set of features targets **sequential visual working memory** and **visual discrimination and categorization** since they are gathered from exercises where players see a

	Score
Accuracy	84.62%
Precision – *Class D (Dyslexia)*	63.76%
Recall – *Class D (Dyslexia)*	80.24%
Precision – *Class N (Not-Dyslexia)*	93.88%
Recall – *Class N (Not-Dyslexia)*	85.83%

Table 2: Classifier accuracy in the cross validation experiment, using the optimized feature set.

sequence of letters for 3 seconds and then write the sequence discriminating targets from distractors.

215-226 This set of features (**215-220**) targets **lexical** and **orthographic awareness** and requires participants to listen and write a word (*e.g., /make/*) or targets **sequential auditory working memory** and **phonological awareness (221-226)** and requires participants to listen and write a non-word (*e.g., /smay/*).

5   RESULTS AND DISCUSSION

To determine whether it is feasible to detect whether a user may have dyslexia, we set up a machine learning experiment. We carried out an experiment with a binary classifier of LIBSVM [4] in the Gaussian Support Vector Machine (SVM) setup. An SVM is a method for supervised machine learning that analyzes data and finds patterns for classification. As other Machine Learning algorithms, given a set of training examples, each marked as belonging to a category, an SVM training algorithm builds a model that assigns new examples into the categories. The particular bias of SVMs is that of constructing a hyperplane (either in the original space or in a transformed one) for the classification output. This hyperplane is constructed by combininig the original input examples with the aim of maximizing the functional margin. Our SVM is trained on the dataset as the one described in Section 4.

We performed a 10-fold cross validation experiment by dividing the data into 10 different roughly equal subsets (10% of the data in each subset). Then, we trained a statistical model on the rest of the data (90%) and tested on the corresponding fold by iterating 10 times; at the end, all data was tested independently. We used 10-fold cross validation because it is normally recommended for smaller datasets when a single train-development test split might not be informative enough.

We randomized the data and used stratified sampling to ensure a similar distribution of data categories in all folds. Participants marked as *M (Maybe)* were assigned to the class *D (Dyslexia)*. Outliers' values in the number of *Clicks* and *Misses* were limited to a maximum fixed value. Subsequently, the data were scaled to zero mean and unit variance.

We analyzed the data for features whose distributions were different between dyslexic and non-dyslexic participants. To that end, a *Kolmogorov-Smirnov* test was performed. The number of *Hits* and *Misses* showed different distributions for a number of exercises.

Table 2 shows the accuracy of the SVM model (Gaussian kernel). This result suggests that the model is able to predict players with dyslexia quite accurately with a final result of 80.24% by using a subset of informative features. Note that the baseline (the percentage of subjects assigned to the class Dyslexia in the data set) is 22.85%.

The most informative features were a set of 10 features composed of *Hits* and *Misses*, *Misses* being the most informative ones at an individual level. These features are performance measures belonging to exercises that target **Alphabetic Awareness**, **Phonological Awareness**, **Visual Discrimination and Categorization** and **Auditory Discrimination and Categorization**. More concretely, these features come from exercises where the participant was required to map (or associate) a letter name or a letter sound with a grapheme (letter or letters). This is consistent with previous literature on dyslexia that focus on the deficit on the phonological component in dyslexia [26, 27].

6 CONCLUSIONS AND FUTURE WORK

We presented a method to screen for risk of dyslexia among English speakers that combines machine learning and web-based interaction data collected from a linguistic game. The method was evaluated with 267 participants and attained 84.62% accuracy on its prediction. These results build on earlier findings from the first version of *Dytective* [23], where only Spanish was considered.

These results should be taken as preliminary, since the model was trained on a small dataset. Further experiments with more participants under other less controlled conditions are needed. Our next step will be to conduct a large-scale study. With positive results, we will integrate the model in a tool to screen risk of dyslexia online. Since estimations of dyslexia are much higher than the actual diagnosed population, we believe this method has potential to make a significant impact.

ACKNOWLEDGMENTS

This paper was developed under a grant from the US Department of Education, NIDRR grant number H133A130057; and a grant from the National Science Foundation (#IIS-1618784).

We thank the *Valley Speech Language and Learning Center in Brownsville* in Texas, and the schools *Winchester Thurston School* (Pittsburgh, PA), and *Ellis School* (Pittsburgh, PA). . We thank the volunteers who participated (Adam Brownold, Elsa Cárdenas-Hagan, Anne Fay, Susan Freudenberg) in supervising the participants. Thanks to Lola Álvarez, Susanne Burger, Debbie Meyer, and Regina Rash for their help with recruiting participants

REFERENCES

[1] American Psychiatric Association. 2013. *Diagnostic and statistical manual of mental disorders, (DSM-V)*. American Psychiatric Publishing, Arlington, VA.
[2] Mattias Nilsson Benfatto, Gustaf Öqvist Seimyr, Jan Ygge, Tony Pansell, Agneta Rydberg, and Christer Jacobson. 2016. Screening for Dyslexia Using Eye Tracking during Reading. *PloS one* 11, 12 (2016), e0165508.
[3] Elizabeth Carrow-Woolfolk. 1995. *OWLS, Oral and Written Language Scales*. NCS Pearson Incorporated.
[4] Chih-Chung Chang and Chih-Jen Lin. 2011. LIBSVM: A library for support vector machines. *ACM Transactions on Intelligent Systems and Technology* 2 (2011), 27:1–27:27. Issue 3. Software available at http://www.csie.ntu.edu.tw/~cjlin/libsvm.
[5] F. Cuetos and F. Valle. 1988. Modelos de lectura y dislexias (Reading models and dyslexias). *Infancia y Aprendizaje (Infancy and Learning)* 44 (1988), 3–19.
[6] Robert Davies, Javier Rodríguez-Ferreiro, Paz Suárez, and Fernando Cuetos. 2013. Lexical and sub-lexical effects on accuracy, reaction time and response duration: impaired and typical word and pseudoword reading in a transparent orthography. *Reading and Writing* 26, 5 (2013), 721–738.
[7] Dyslexia Research Institute. 2015. Dyslexia, Identification. http://www.dyslexia-add.org/issues.html. (January 2015).
[8] Angela Fawcett and Rod Nicolson. 2004. *The Dyslexia Screening Test: Junior (DST-J)*. Harcourt Assessment.
[9] Ombretta Gaggi, Giorgia Galiazzo, Claudio Palazzi, Andrea Facoetti, and Sandro Franceschini. 2012. A serious game for predicting the risk of developmental dyslexia in pre-readers children. In *Proc. ICCCN'12*. IEEE, 1–5.
[10] Sepp Hochreiter and Jürgen Schmidhuber. 1997. Long short-term memory. *Neural Computation* 9, 8 (1997), 1735–1780.
[11] Interagency Commission on Learning Disabilities. 1987. *Learning Disabilities: A Report to the U.S. Congress*. Government Printing Office, Washington DC.
[12] Yair Lakretz and Michal Rosen-zvi. 2015. Probabilistic Graphical Models of Dyslexia. In *Proc. SIGKDD'15*. 1919–1928.
[13] Lexercise. 2016. Dyslexia Test - Online from Lexercise. http://www.lexercise.com/tests/dyslexia-test. (2016). [Online; accessed 18-September-2017].
[14] Heikki Lyytinen, Jane Erskine, Janne Kujala, Emma Ojanen, and Ulla Richardson. 2009. In search of a science-based application: A learning tool for reading acquisition. *Scandinavian journal of psychology* 50, 6 (2009), 668–675.
[15] Heikki Lyytinen, Miia Ronimus, Anne Alanko, Anna-Maija Poikkeus, and Maria Taanila. 2007. Early identification of dyslexia and the use of computer game-based practice to support reading acquisition. *Nordic Psychology* 59, 2 (2007), 109.
[16] Dennis L Molfese. 2000. Predicting dyslexia at 8 years of age using neonatal brain responses. *Brain and language* 72, 3 (2000), 238–245.
[17] Nessy. 2011. Dyslexia Screening - Nessy UK. https://www.nessy.com/uk/product/dyslexia-screening/. (2011). [Online; accessed 18-September-2017].
[18] J. Pedler. 2007. *Computer Correction of Real-word Spelling Errors in Dyslexic Text*. Ph.D. Dissertation. Birkbeck College, London University.
[19] Maria Rauschenberger, Luz Rello, Ricardo Baeza-Yates, Emilia Gomez, and Jeffrey P. Bigham. 2017. Towards the Prediction of Dyslexia by a Web-based Game with Musical Elements. In *W4A'17*. 4–7. https://doi.org/10.1145/3058555.3058565
[20] L. Rello and R. Baeza-Yates. 2013. Good Fonts for Dyslexia. In *Proc. ASSETS'13*. ACM Press, Bellevue, Washington, USA.
[21] L. Rello and M. Ballesteros. 2015. Detecting Readers with Dyslexia Using Machine Learning with Eye Tracking Measures. In *Proc. W4A '15*. ACM, Florence, Italy.
[22] L. Rello and M. Ballesteros. 2017. Data Processing System to Detect Neurodevelopmental-Specific Learning Disorders. *United States Patent and Trademark Office* filed in on April 20, 2017, as application 15/493,060 (2017).
[23] L. Rello, M. Ballesteros, A. Ali, M. Serra, D. Alarcón, and J. P. Bigham. 2016. Dytective: Diagnosing Risk of Dyslexia with a Game. In *Proc. Pervasive Health'16*. Cancun, Mexico.
[24] Luz Rello, Enrique Romero, Maria Rauschenberger, Abdullah Ali, Kristin Williams, Jeffrey P. Bigham, and Nancy Cushen White. 2018. Towards language independent detection of dyslexia with a web-based game. In *W4A'18*. Lyon, France. https://doi.org/10.1145/3192714.3192816
[25] Luz Rello, Kristin Williams, Abdullah Ali, Nancy Cushen White, and Jeffrey P. Bigham. 2016. Dytective: Towards Detecting Dyslexia Across LanguagesUsing an Online Game. In *Proc. W4A'16*. ACM Press, Montreal, Canada.
[26] S.E. Shaywitz, M.D. Escobar, B.A. Shaywitz, J.M. Fletcher, and R. Makuch. 1992. Evidence that dyslexia may represent the lower tail of a normal distribution of reading ability. *New England Journal of Medicine* 326, 3 (1992), 145–150.
[27] F. R. Vellutino, J. M. Fletcher, M. J. Snowling, and D. M. Scanlon. 2004. Specific reading disability (dyslexia): What have we learned in the past four decades? *Journal of Child Psychology and Psychiatry* 45, 1 (2004), 2–40.
[28] World Federation of Neurology (WFN). 1968. Report of research group on dyslexia and world illiteracy. Dallas: WFN. (1968).

Talking to Ana: A Mobile Self-Anamnesis Application with Conversational User Interface

Kerstin Denecke
Bern University of Applied Sciences
Höheweg 80, Biel
Switzerland
kerstin.denecke@bfh.ch

Sandra Lutz Hochreutener
Zurich University of Arts
Pfingstweidstrasse 96, Zürich
Switzerland
sandra.lutz@zhdk.ch

Annkathrin Pöpel
Sanatorium Kilchberg
Alte Landstrasse 70, Kilchberg
Switzerland
Annkathrin.Poepel@sanatorium-kilchberg.ch

Richard May
Bern University of Applied Sciences
Höheweg 80, Biel
Switzerland
richard.may@bfh.ch

ABSTRACT

Normally, a physician is collecting a patient's medical history under time pressure during the initial patient interview. This leads to incomplete, erroneous data with negative effects on treatment and patient safety. The objective of this work is to introduce a concept for a self-anamnesis realized as a mobile application for patients. We implement the concept for the concrete example of self-anamnesis in music therapy. For this purpose, requirements are collected in discussions with music therapists. A conversational user interface is chosen to simulate the patient-therapist conversation. The self-anamnesis application is equipped with 63 questions that are asked subsequently to the user. We have chosen a rule-based approach for realizing the chat conversation and used the Artificial Intelligence Markup Language (AIML) for encapsulating the questions and responses of the chatbot. In contrast to digital questionnaires, the application of a conversational user interface in the context of collecting information regarding a patient's medical history, provides several benefits: the user can be encouraged to complete all queries and can ask clarifying questions in case something is unclear.

CCS CONCEPTS

• **Information systems** → **Mobile information processing systems** • *Information systems* → *Decision support systems* • **Human-centered computing** → **Natural language interfaces**

KEYWORDS

Mobile Application; Patient Empowerment; Anamnesis; Decision Support System; Conversational User Interface

ACM Reference format:

K. Denecke, S. Lutz Hochreutener, A. Pöpel, R. May. 2018. Talking to Ana: A Mobile Self-Anamnesis Application with Conversational User Interface. In *DH'18: 2018 International Digital Health Conference, April 23-26, 2018, Lyon, France.* ACM, NY, NY, USA, 5 pages. https://doi.org/10.1145/3194658.3194670

1 INTRODUCTION

Information on a patient's medical history is essential for the diagnosis and therapy decision process. In the first appointment with a physician, he or she is asking the patient many questions to get to know the medical history of the person. The accuracy of this information affects significantly the quality of the diagnostic process [1]. One of the main causes of misdiagnoses is an incomplete medical history [2]. Beyond, studies show that certain health problems remain unrecognized in the patient-doctor conversation. For example, 50% of psychosocial and psychiatric problems are not recorded in the anamnesis [3]. 54% of problems and 45% of concerns are neither reported by the patient nor revealed by the attending physician [4].

A digital medical history entered by a patient himself can improve this situation and helps avoiding unnecessary duplication of data, as long as the medical history data is available for the different actors in the health care process. Self-anamnesis is a procedure in which the patient answers questions about the personal medical history without direct interaction with a doctor or medical assistant. A digital representation of the anamnesis enables a structured and thus more complete recording of the information [5]. In the course of the implementation of the eHealth Act in Switzerland and in other countries, a digital medical history can be stored in future in the electronic patient record, which avoids unnecessary duplication of data.

Several means exist already for fetching the medical history of a patient in a digital manner by means of electronic questionnaires or tools like AnaBoard (http://anaboard.de). It has been proven that such electronic gathering helps to improve the correctness and completeness of the data compared to the traditional paper-based anamnesis survey [6, 7]. The data quality of a digital acquisition is therefore potentially better than the traditional data collection process. In existing approaches, however, it turned out to be a problem to motivate patients to answer an often comprehensive catalogue of medical history questions [8].

In this paper, we want to address this challenge by exploiting a dialog-oriented user interface for a mobile application that offers the possibility to interact with the user already during the medical history survey. More specifically, the main research question for this work is: Can a self-anamnesis be realized as a mobile application with conversational user interface? As specific use case, we have chosen the field of music therapy.

Music therapy uses specifically selected music in the therapeutic process to promote, maintain and restore mental, physical and mental health. A complete, systematic history of experiences with music and of the music taste of a patient to be treated plays an important role in therapeutic process [9, 10]. The therapy plan and in particular music selection is made based on the music biography that is collected in the first meetings with the patient. The aim of application is not to replace the therapist or physician and the first consultation, but to provide a better and higher quality information base for the first consultation with the therapist or physician as well as for the following decision making process.

2 RELATED WORK

A conversational user interface or chatbot system is a computer program that interacts with users using natural language. Different terms are used for a chatbot such as machine conversation system, virtual agent, dialogue system, conversational user interface and chatterbot. The purpose of a chatbot system is to simulate a human conversation. Chatbots are usually text-driven, with images and unified widgets, which make it easy to start interacting with a bot. There are two types of chatbots: Unintelligent chatbots interact using a predefined conversation flow. Intelligent chatbots use machine learning to automatically generate responses on the fly.

Already in 1966, Weizenbaum presented ELIZA [11], a program that allows a natural language conversation with a computer. ELIZA stored its knowledge directly into the application code. Later, the design language Artificial Intelligence Markup Language (AIML) was used to manage the knowledge-based data ("chatbot brain") [12].

Chatbots have been reported in the literature for health related applications for example for student education, patient advice, information access, to achieve health behaviour change [13] or disease self-management. Lokman and Zain [14] introduced a chatbot that serves as a virtual dietitian for diabetic patients. The chatbot asks questions and gives at the end a diet advice suitable for the current diabetic situation. The conversation is going along a path that is remembered by the system to consider all answers

in the decision-making. VPbot, an SQL-based chatbot for medical applications is a chatbot that takes advantage of relational database model design to store, manage and use the SQL language to perform the matching process within the chatbot conversation. eMMA, the electronic medication assistant, is a mobile application developed to support a patient in the medication management. The app is equipped with a chatbot for providing information on interactions between food and medications and to collect compliance data [15].

Several chatbots have been implemented in the health domain and are available in the app stores even though no scientific publication is available. The existing systems provide a triage, search functionalities or support to a certain extent disease management or conversation with doctors (e.g. Ada, https://ada.com/). Babylon Health (https://www.babylonhealth.com/) provides a triage function via a conversational user interface that is intended to supplement or replace the telemedicine hotline in the English health care system. So far, there is no application with conversational user interface available that is fully integrated in the treatment process such as a self-anamnesis chatbot. Our self-anamnesis concept aims at improving the data collection at the beginning of the diagnosis and treatment process. In contrast to existing systems, our concept foresees the integration of the collected data into the treatment process.

3 METHODS

In this section, we are describing the methodology for concept development and the main technology underlying our system.

3.1. Requirements gathering and questionnaire generation

For developing the concept, we first retrieved requirements in discussions with music therapists and by reviewing literature. Additionally, we collected requirements for a mobile self-anamnesis used in other medical domains. Next, we established a set of queries for self-anamnesis. After interviewing several music therapists as well as performing a web and literature search for standard anamnesis questionnaires in the field of music therapy, we found out that there is no such standardized questionnaire available. Instead, we identified some sets of queries that have been published by music therapists [9, 16, 17]. These query sets were reviewed by two music therapists who selected questions to be integrated in our application. A selection criteria was the suitability of a query for a self-anamnesis: the queries should not create any negative emotions in a patient.

3.2. Conversational user interface and AIML

We decided to implement the application using a conversational user interface since this offers several advantages compared to a regular digital questionnaire: 1) The patient can ask the chatbot for explanations if a question was not understandable to him and 2) The chatbot can encourage the patient to answer the questions by means of appropriate messages. In contrast to standard questionnaires, a chatbot-guided tour through the anamnesis ensures a systematic and complete collection of responses.

To represent the chatbot's brain, we use AIML [12]. This language is a derivative of Extensible Mark-up Language (XML) and has been developed to store knowledge underlying chatbot systems. AIML is a recursive language that allows breaking down natural language text input to match a response that the chatbot can send. It consists of data objects called AIML objects, which are made up of units called topics and categories. A topic is an optional top-level element, has a name attribute and a set of categories related to that topic. Categories are the basic unit of knowledge in AIML. Each category is a rule for matching an input and converting to an output, and consists of a pattern, which matches against the user input, and a template, which is used in generating the chatbot answer. A set of possible user inputs is modeled using AIML and, for each one of these sentences (stimuli), pre-programmed answers were built to be shown to the user.

The Program AB (https://github.com/lumenrobot/program-ab) used in this work is an AIML interpreter that identifies the best match between all AIML categories stored in a database using PHP's SimpleXML/XPATH functions. More details on the matching can be found in the AIML working draft [18].

3 RESULTS

This section summarizes the collected requirements and the questionnaire that forms the basis for our system. Further, the concept for a mobile self-anamnesis is described and the implementation of our application *Ana*, the self-anamnesis application.

3.1 Requirements

We could not identify any requirements that are specific only for gathering the music biography of a patient through a mobile application. Instead, the following requirements are valid for such tool applied in any medical subdomain including music therapy. In the systematic requirements analysis, intuitive operation and accessible data storage, e.g. on an eHealth platform, have been identified as essential requirements. Currently, a re-use of anamnesis data collected by a physician is impossible since this data is neither systematically stored nor transferred to another treating physician. The relevance of data sharing depends on the medical specialty, e.g. the music biography is probably irrelevant for the family practitioner. But a specialist might be interested in the anamnesis of the family practitioner. The interaction between the mobile application and the patient should be as simple as possible. A self-anamnesis tool could help by enabling the patient in a more comfortable situation and with time constraints to answer relevant questions. To avoid negative effects, only questions should be asked that cannot produce negative feelings in a patient. In order to be accessible for the physician or therapist, the collected anamnesis data need to be available in the information system or accessible through another kind of frontend.

3.2 Questionnaire

The questionnaire comprises 63 questions and is structured into three categories: demographic information, general questions on experiences with music, specific questions for several stages of life (pregnancy, infancy, age groups 5-6, 7-12, 13-16, 16-20, adulthood: 21-30, 31-40 etc.). Specific questions per age group comprise questions on stylistics, frequency of the activity and favorite pieces for four groups of activities: listening to music, singing, playing an instrument and moving / dancing. Some examples are shown in table 1.

Table 1: Examples for questions on the music biography

Category / stage in life	Possible questions
Early experiences with music	Listening to lullabies, Christmas songs...? Played an instrument? Singing as a child? Experiences with music at school?
Experiences as youth	Kind of music listening to Positive experiences with music
Current habits in music consumption	Playing an instrument? How often listening to music? Recognized effects when listening to music

3.3 Self-anamnesis concept

In this section, we describe the concept of the self-anamnesis application and its integration into the care process. This concept is valid also for medical disciplines outside music therapy. The self-anamnesis application is integrated as follows in the care process (see figure 1): when a patient makes an appointment with a physician, he or she is pointed to the link of the self-anamnesis application. The patient is asked to fill out the questionnaire already at home or he/she can do this in the waiting room when coming for the appointment. For this purpose, the patient is interacting with *Ana*, the self-anamnesis application, who is asking the questions on the patient's medical history. Once all questions are completed, the responses are stored in a structured manner on an eHealth platform, for example MIDATA [19]. MIDATA.coop has developed an open source IT platform for the secure storage, management and sharing of personal health data of any sort. A developer's guide is available at the website [19]. It explains the general architecture of the platform and how mobile apps and plugins can interact with it. Through a frontend, a therapist or physician can access the medical history stored on the eHealth platform of the patient or it can be imported into the physician's information system to be integrated in the local patient record.

3.3 Implementation

We decided to use the Pandorabots playground (https://www.pandorabots.com/) as a framework for implementing and testing AIML files before integrating them into the application. Pandorabots supports the latest version of AIML and offers the opportunity of experimenting with all XML-based AIML tags.

To connect the chatbot to our mobile application and to guarantee that the chatbot will work offline, we exploit a special interpreter as an AIML reference implementation for Java, the Program AB. This interpreter is integrated as a library to our Java-based Android application. Program AB allows to use 37 given standard tags with different features to customize a chatbot. An example is given in table 2.

Table 2: Example for AIML categories

```
<category>
  <pattern>I AM *</pattern>
  <that>WHAT IS YOUR NAME</that>
  <template>Hallo   <set   name="username"><star/></set>.
How
        old are you?
      <learnf>
          <category>
            <pattern>NAME</pattern>
            <template>Username:
<eval><star index="1"/> </eval>
  </template>
          </category>
        </learnf>
  </template>
  </category>

<category>
  <pattern>My NAME IS *</pattern>
  <that>WHAT IS YOUR NAME</that>
  <template><srai>I AM <star/></srai></template>
</category>
```

The conversation patterns in the current version of the app have been developed in German. Within a developing time of five months, we have implemented more than 600 categories using nearly 30 different tags. Within these categories and tags we encapsulated 63 anamnesis questions for music therapy and possible answers to react adequately to a user's input. The answers of the chatbot as well as the user's messages were embedded into a messenger user interface to ensure an intuitive conversational user interface, which the patient can use like a common messenger (see figure 2). In its current implementation, *Ana* poses the questions of the anamnesis questionnaire and allows modifying previously given responses to selected queries. Audio output is supported, while audio input remains open for the future. Depending on the question, the answer is requested as free text entry by the user, by selecting a value on a scale or by selecting a button referring to a predefined answer (e.g. when asking for the sex of the patient).

4 DISCUSSION

Health dialogue differs from typical information-seeking conversation as supported in conversational agents such as Siri or Cortana: 1) data validity and accuracy is critical in many health applications, 2) confidentiality is crucial, 3) continuity of interactions (support for a longer period of time) is requested, and 4) user engagement has to be maintained. We addressed some of these issues by developing a rule-based intelligent assistant, and a secure data storage on an eHealth platform. In order to engage a user during the anamnesis collection, motivation statements are posted by the chatbot and queries can be posed by the patient.

With respect to ensure continuity of interactions, the application needs to be extended by additional query opportunities for the patient where he/she can ask *Ana* for information or explanations. We can thus confirm that a self-anamnesis can be realized as a mobile application with conversational user interface.

In a first user study, we collected open issues and technical problems with the app. The initial feedback was that the anamnesis conversation with the system is comfortable due to the animating comments of the bot. In a systematic usability study, we just started to study the quality of the chatbot, to identify limitations of the user interface and to improve the interaction facilities. Once the system has been optimized, a comprehensive study will be run to answer the question, whether the self-anamnesis application leads to a more complete medical history. It remains open for the future to assess in a clinical study whether the limitations of the current anamnesis process can be reduced by the application, i.e. assessing whether the patient feels more comfortable, is more open and to what extent duplication of data is avoided when using *Ana*.

For adapting the system to other medical fields, it requires a set of anamnesis questions that need to be reformulated to create an engaging conversation. AIML patterns need to be generated manually for query / answer pairs.

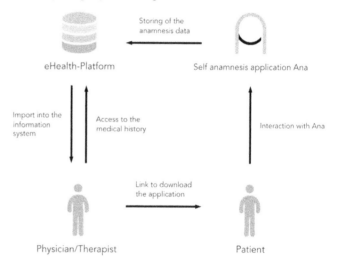

Figure 1. Concept of the self-anamnesis application and its integration into the care process

There are several use cases and possibilities for extending the application introduced in this paper. Saarikallio et al. introduced a healthy-unhealthy music scale [9] as an instrument for screening musical engagement that is indicative of proneness for depression in youth. Such data collection could be realized by our application. Additionally, the tool offers the opportunity for a music therapy home program for patients as suggested by Denecke [20]. The systematic collection of the music biography provides also means for researching effects of music to certain health conditions.

Studies show that the medical history of a patient is the most correct when the replies are given for the first time [21]. For this reason, it could be useful, when the first anamnesis can be shared among the treating physicians, which in turn requires a data storage of the collected medical history. Our concept foresees the data storage on an eHealth platform from which the health care team can access the data. However, a structured format for the medical history is required, which is still unavailable.

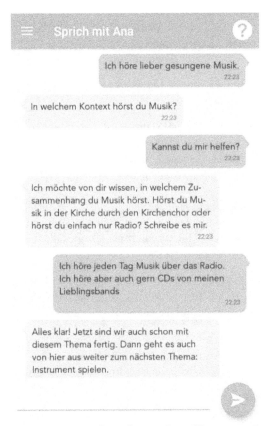

Figure 2. Screenshot of Ana, the self-anamnesis application, aksing for specific experiences of the patient with music.

ACKNOWLEDGEMENT

This research is part of the project entitled "A chatbot for self-anamnesis with an example in music therapy", partially founded by the Hasler foundation.

REFERENCES

[1] Kassirer JP. Imperatives, expediency, and the new diagnosis. Diagnosis 1(1):2015; 11–12

[2] Moonen PJ, Mercelina L, Boer W, Fret T. Diagnostic error in the Emergency Department: follow up of patients with minor trauma in the outpatient clinic. Scand J Trauma Resusc Emerg Med. 2017 Feb 14;25(1):13. doi: 10.1186/s13049-017-0361-5.

[3] Davenport S, Goldberg D, Millar T. How psychiatric disorders are missed during medical consultations. Lancet. 1987 Aug 22;2(8556):439-41.

[4] Palermo TM, Valenzuela D, Stork PP. A randomized trial of electronic versus paper pain diaries in children: impact on compliance, accuracy, and acceptability. Pain. 2004 Feb;107(3):213-9.

[5] Hayna S., Schmücker P. e-Anamnese ein einrichtungs-, sektoren- und berufsgruppenübergreifender Lösungsansatz für die Elektronische Anamnese, Telemedizinführer Deutschland, Bad Nauheim, 2009

[6] Dale O, Hagen KB. Despite technical problems personal digital assistants outperform pen and paper when collecting patient diary data. J Clin Epidemiol. 2007 Jan;60(1):8-17. Epub 2006 Aug 30.

[7] Tiplady B, Crompton GK, Dewar MH, Bollert FGE, Matusiewicz, Campbell LM: The use of electronic diaries in respiratory studies. Drug Information Journal, 1997; 31:759-64

[8] Slack WV, Kowaloff HB, Davis RB, Delbanco T, Locke SE, Safran C, and Bleich HL: Evaluation of computer-based medical histories taken by patients at home. J Am Med Inform Assoc. 2012 Jul-Aug; 19(4): 545–548.

[9] Saarikallio S, Gold C, and McFerran K. Development and validation of the Healthy-Unhealthy Music Scale. Child Adolesc Ment Health. 2015 Nov; 20(4): 210–217.

[10] Zeitler W, Auditive Music Therapy. tredition (Verlag), Hamburg, 2016

[11] Weizenbaum J. ELIZA-a Computer Program for the Study of Natural Language Communication Between Man and Machine. Commun. ACM 9, 1 (Jan. 1966), 36–45. https://doi.org/10.1145/365153.365168

[12] das Gracas M Marietto B, de Aguiar RV, de Oliveira Barbosa G, Botelho WT et al. Artificial Intelligence Markup Language: A Brief Tutorial, 2013

[13] Fadhil A, Gabrielli S. Addressing Challenges in Promoting Healthy Lifestyles: The AI-Chatbot Approach. Pervasive Health Workshop on Challenges and Opportunities in Pervasive Health-enabled Telemedicine. Barcelona, Spain, May 2017

[14] Lokman AS, Zain JM. An architectural design of Virtual Dietitian (ViDi) for diabetic patients. Computer Science and Information Technology, International Conference on (2009), 408–411. https://doi.org/doi.ieeecomputersociety.org/10.1109/ICCSIT.2009.5 234671

[15] Dorner T, Tschanz M, Denecke K: eMedication Meets eHealth with the Electronic Medication Management Assistant (eMMA) In: Dieter Hayn, Günter Schreier (eds): Stud Health Technol Inform, 2017;236:196-203

[16] Frohne-Hagemann I. Das musikalische Lebenspanorama. In: Fenster zur Musiktherapie, Wiesbaden: Reichert Verlag , 2001

[17] Spychiger M: Das musikalische Selbstkonzept. Wer ich bin und was ich kann in der Musik. Üben & Musizieren 6_13. Mainz: Schott Musikpädagogik GmbH, 2013.

[18] Wallace RS: AIML 2.0 Working Draft, Revision 1.0.2.22, https://docs.google.com/document/d/1wNT25hJRyupcG51aO89UcQ EiG-HkXRXusukADpFnDs4/pub

[19] MIDATA developer guide. URL: https://test.midata.coop/#/developer/guide. Accessed: 2017-06-02.

[20] Denecke K. A Mobile System for Music Anamnesis and Receptive Music Therapy in the Personal Home, Stud Health Technol Inform. 2017;245:54-58

[21] Ravishankar K. The art of history-taking in a headache patient. Ann Indian Acad Neurol. 2012 Aug; 15(Suppl 1): 7–14. doi: 10.4103/0972-2327.99989

ZIKΛ: A New System to Empower Health Workers and Local Communities to Improve Surveillance Protocols by E-learning and to Forecast Zika Virus in Real Time in Brazil

Juan D. Beltrán
Institute for Risk and Disaster Reduction
University College London, UK
juan.beltran@ucl.ac.uk

Andrei Boscor
Institute for Risk and Disaster Reduction
University College London, UK
andrei.boscor.14@ucl.ac.uk

Wellington P. dos Santos
Department of Biomedical Engineering
Federal University of Pernambuco
Brazil
wellington.santos@ufpe.br

Tiago Massoni
Department of Systems and Computing
Federal University of Campina Grande, Brazil
massoni@computacao.ufcg.edu.br

Patty Kostkova
Institute for Risk and Disaster Reduction
University College London, UK
p.kostkova@ucl.ac.uk

ABSTRACT

The devastating consequences of neonates infected with the Zika virus makes it necessary to fight and stop the spread of this virus and its vectors (*Aedes* mosquitoes). An essential part of the fight against mosquitoes is the use of mobile technology to support routine surveillance and risk assessment by community health workers (health agents). In addition, to improve early warning systems, the public health authorities need to forecast more accurately where an outbreak of the virus and its vector is likely to occur. The ZIKΛ system aims to develop a novel comprehensive framework that combines e-learning to empower health agents, community-based participatory surveillance, and forecasting of occurrences and distribution of the Zika virus and its vectors in real time. This system is currently being implemented in Brazil, in the cities of Campina Grande, Recife, Jaboatão dos Guararapes, and Olinda, the State of Pernambuco and Paraiba with the highest prevalence of the Zika virus disease. In this paper, we present the ZIKΛ system which helps health agents to learn new techniques and good practices to improve the surveillance of the virus and offer a real time distribution forecast of the virus and the vector. The forecast model is recalibrated in real time with information coming from health agents, governmental institutions, and weather stations to predict the areas with higher risk of a Zika virus outbreak in an interactive map. This mapping and alert system will help governmental institutions to make fast decisions and use their resources more efficiently to stop the spread of the Zika virus.

The ZIKΛ app was developed and built in Ionic which allows for easy cross-platform rendering for both iOS and Android. The system presented in the current paper is one of the first systems combining public health surveillance, citizen-driven participatory reporting and weather data-based prediction. The implementation of the ZIKΛ system will reduce the devastating consequences of Zika virus in neonates and improve the life quality of vulnerable people in Brazil.

CCS CONCEPTS

• **Information systems ~ Location based services**
• **Information systems ~ Geographic information systems**

KEYWORDS

Zika virus; big data; surveillance; forecasting; e-learning

ACM Reference Format

Juan D. Beltrán, Andrei Boscor, Wellington P. dos Santos, Tiago Massoni, Patty Kostkova. 2018. ZIKA: A New System to Empower Health Workers and Local Communities to Improve Surveillance Protocols by E-learning and to Forecast Zika Virus in Real Time in Brazil. In 2018 Digital Health Proceedings, April 23–26, 2018, Lyon, France. ACM, NY, NY, USA, 5 pages. https://doi.org/10.1145/3194658.3194683

1 INTRODUCTION

The Zika virus (ZIKV) has devastating consequences in neonates [1, 2], and its spread has alarmed international organizations [3]. It is critical to fight and stop the spread of the ZIKV and its vectors [4]. The ZIKV is usually spread by *Aedes* mosquitoes [5, 6]. The ZIKV can also be transmitted by transfusions of contaminated blood, via unprotected sex [7] and from mothers to unborn children (perinatal transmission) [8, 9].

The ZIKV is associated with microcephaly and severe deformities in children who have been infected by perinatal transmission [1, 2]. There is no vaccine available at the moment to prevent ZIKV infection. The fact that ZIKV affects the health and life quality of newborns makes the ZIKV a public health problem that needs constant surveillance.

The latest outbreak occurred in the Americas, when in 2015 the Brazilian Ministry of Health confirmed autochthonous infections in the Bahia region [10, 11]. However, phylogenetic analyses of the DNA of the virus suggested that it was introduced in 2013 [12]. Since then, the virus has spread to countries in South and Central America and tropical territories of the US, perhaps associated with the El Niño effect in 2015-2016 [13].

In Brazil more than 1.5 million cases have been reported and this is the largest outbreak of ZIKV [14]. In Brazil other viruses are co-occurring such as Dengue virus (DENV) and Chikungunya virus (CHIKV). In February 2016 the World Health Organization declared the ZIKV a public health emergency and a matter of international concern [3].

In order to fight the ZIKV it is necessary to implement a surveillance protocol which empowers local communities to avoid bad practices to decrease the prevalence of ZIKV. In addition, it is necessary to understand the population dynamics of the vector in real time (*Aedes* mosquitoes; in particular *A. aegypti*) to alert governmental institutions to allocate resources in areas with higher risk. The present study is focused on Brazil (in particular in the cities of Campina Grande, Recife, Jaboatão dos Guararapes, and Olinda, the State of Pernambuco and Paraiba) because Brazil is the country with the highest number of reported ZIKV cases in the world.

The elimination of the vector requires cooperation of governments and healthcare agencies setting the disease control strategies with general population. However, in Brazil the situation is more complex: the local "community health workers" (health agents) volunteers deliver care alongside professional healthcare workers but are often disregarded when it comes to engagement and training which makes combating vectors very challenging. How can community health agents in primary care, who are often geographically dispersed in poor and hard to reach regions, better fight the mosquito outbreaks?

Considering the potential of engagement of games like Pokemon Go©, gamified applications like Waze©, and the popularization of smartphones among individuals of all social classes in Brazil, there is a great potential to train health agents in practical knowledge using medical training apps and serious games. In this paper we propose the development of a gamified system to engage community health workers to help in the surveillance of ZIKV in the States of Pernambuco and Paraiba.

2 MONITORING THE DISTRIBUTION OF MOSQUITOES AND ZIKV IN REAL-TIME

Understanding the location of the most vulnerable areas for the ZIKV infections in real time is a priority for early warning and rapid response. The use of real-time spatial-temporal big data is needed to model and to predict the distribution of the virus and its vector. The most recent literature concerning the potential distribution of the ZIKV and its vectors have focused on a global scale using historical data [9]. For example, the potential distribution of the ZIKV, DENG and their vectors have been assessed using Random Forest and Artificial Neural Networks [9,

15, 16]. The global scale and the temporal scale that the previous studies used make it difficult to draw any inference at regional, local scale or real time, where the governmental institutions have to make decisions to allocate their resources efficiently to fight the virus.

The potential distribution and prediction of the ZIKV vectors and the ZIKV in the cities of Campina Grande, Recife, Jaboatão dos Guararapes, and Olinda require the use of finer-scale variables (such as, the use of daily weather variations, vectors population density, and presence-absence ZIKV data). These variables are relatively easy to obtain using mobile devices and can establish critical information such as ZIKV suspected, potential and confirmed cases, based on the surveillance protocol established by the WHO in 2016.

Other applications such as Mosquito Alert© have focused on reporting the presence of mosquitos in real time. Mosquito Alert© has been used mainly in Spain and has not been used much in the Americas where the most recent ZIKV outbreak has occurred. Monitoring mosquitoes is a very important part of the surveillance process. However, in order to evaluate the risk of infection in a geographical context it is necessary to model both mosquitoes and the presence of the virus in the States of Pernambuco and Paraiba in Brazil.

3 ZIKA SYSTEM - THE THEORETICAL FRAMEWORK

This paper proposes a novel surveillance system using a medical app to train (e-learning) health agents improving the surveillance of ZIKV in Brazil. In addition, by using other sources of data (governmental institutions, weather and climatic data, laboratory records, among others) the system can establish the potential areas of the ZIKV and its vectors. With that information is possible to assess the risk of the localities in the cities mentioned in section 2. The databases described in Fig. 1 improve the e-learning platform which helps health agents to identify mosquitoes' species and where the help is most critically needed, and good practices to reduce the spread of the virus. In addition, it will help to build and recalibrate the forecasting of ZIKV in real time.

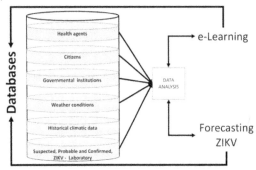

Figure 1. Schematic representation of the different databases and the construction of the forecasting of ZIKV and the e-learning app. Some datasets are updated every day and therefore the forecasting and the e-learning algorithms are recalibrating based on the ZIKV forecasting.

The distribution model of the virus and the vector is currently under construction and validation. The first model to assess both distributions only took into account historical climatic data and the scale is ~30 arc-sec (1 km^2). That model is used as an *a priori* model to build the most robust model (ZIVK Model).

The ZIVK Model integrates the databases from the health workers, governmental institutions, weather daily conditions and laboratory records (Fig. 2). The ZIKV Model is in constant recalibration, on a daily basis, from the databases described in Fig. 1. Health agents have been actively collecting data by visiting houses or other properties in vulnerable neighborhoods and uploading new data to the distribution model of the ZIKV and its vectors. The ZIKV Model uses georeferenced information provided by the health agent in combination with weather conditions associated with the georeferenced location of the health agent.

The output of the ZIKV Model is based on two distribution models (the virus and the vector) mapped in a geographical context, giving an associated risk index (Fig. 2). Random forest and Artificial Neural Networks have been used to model the species distributions of the genus Aedes [15, 16]. In the ZIKΛ system the models are still under construction and evaluation. The output of the ZIKV Model can be visualized by health agents and governmental institutions. To incentive the active participation of the health agent, a series of electronic rewards are included (this part of the app is still under construction).

The proposed system is unique because it combines healthcare surveillance and big data prediction in a single system. The system will empower local communities in the cities of Recife, Jaboatão dos Guararapes, and Olinda and give tools to governmental institutions to act more precisely by attending more vulnerable areas.

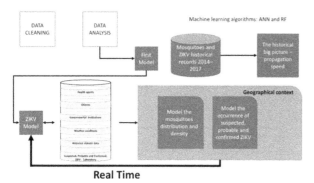

Real Time

Figure 2. Schematic representation of the construction of the First Model and ZIKV Model.

4 ZIKΛ APP ARCHITECTURE AND IMPLEMENTATION

The ZIKΛ app was built in Ionic which allows for easy cross-platform rendering for both iOS and Android. The code was written in Angular and then compiled into iOS and Android apps. This allows for easy testing as code is written only once. Any platform-specific wrappers are added by Ionic automatically.

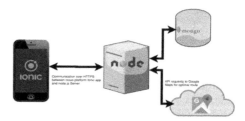

Figure 3. ZIKΛ app architecture showing the Google Maps API and the connection with the databases stored in MongoDB.

The server is built with Express.js, a node.js framework that allows the creation of a RESTful API by defining routes and running specific functions for the routes. This allows us to create protected paths that require an authentication token. This ensures that our database cannot become corrupted by anyone abusing the API. This also ensures that the user can only modify the specific database objects that they have access to. The ZIKΛ app architecture is represented in Fig. 3.

5 DATABASE MODELS

The ZIKΛ app uses email as the username and requires it to be unique within the database. Furthermore, instead of storing the actual password of the user, the ZIKΛ app only stores the hashed version. In terms of security, if the database is hacked, no sensitive information is leaked.

The activities are created with latitude, longitude, address and a photo as well as a list of assigned health agents to that property. This effectively allows managers to link individual properties to agents. This also allows for a very efficient lookup time by using MongoDB object IDs.

The forms that the health agents are required to fill out are stored as separate MongoDB objects with references to the ObjectID of the user as well as references to the ObjectID of the Property (Activity) they belong to. In this sense, it is very efficient to create functions that gives us information regarding the number of forms filed by an agent or the number of forms belonging to a property.

6 AUTHENTICATION AND SECURITY

The username and password are sent to the API endpoint 'auth/login'. This is done over HTTPS and the login function in the back-end will return two tokens. The first is a long-lived refresh token and the second is an authentication token. The second token is short lived, with a life span of 10 minutes. The second token is used to authenticate the user at every request. It does not hold any sensitive information and is signed with a secret only known to the server. When it has expired, the front-end requests a new authentication token using the refresh token. If this fails, the user is asked to authenticate again. The refresh token is kept within the database and can be invalidated and regenerated at any time. Furthermore, the tokens are JSON web tokens which are self-contained and are signed with a secret only available to the back-end server to ensure that they have not been tampered.

7 RELEASE, TESTING AND CONTINUOUS INTEGRATION

The Ionic app was compiled and bundled into an '.apk' file for Android and an '.ipa' file for iOS. Any future improvements require an update to these files.

The back-end Node.js server is hosted on Heroku and is using continuous integration testing to ensure that only a stable version is being served to the users at all times.

In order to test the code of both the app and the back-end we used the following: Mocha, Karma, and Chai.

These allowed us to test all functions within both the front-end and back-end with assertions. This method ran the tests multiple times and in different browsers to ensure stability.

8 ZIKΛ APP DESIGN AND FLOW

At the moment, the workflow of the health agents is to visit as many properties as they can each day. From our observations before the implementation of the ZIKΛ app, we noticed that the process without the app was very inefficient. Health agents often communicated over telephone and wrote the reports of visited properties on paper which were later digitized manually. Therefore, the vision of the app is for this process to be automated (reducing the burden on health agents).

The setup process is as follows: health agents register on the app and managers will then be able to assign properties to individual agents by simply linking the address with the health agent's name.

All the properties a particular agent should visit are shown as cards, ordered by the Google Maps API based on their current location. This allows for the agent to visit more properties than before as the routes are now optimized. They can then add information about the property by simply clicking the "+" button. This might be modified taking into account the risk of areas where the properties are located.

Figure 4. Multi-step form to be completed by health agents. The previous paper forms are now electronic, and each form could be completed during the inspection. An optimized route is given to visit properties by the health agent based on relative closeness and priority.

As seen in Fig. 4, the form is now multi-step with a progress bar and selectable options. This allows the agents to quickly complete the form and submit the information about the property they are visiting. The form is sent and stored in the database of health agents.

After selection of critical areas and to increase route optimization, the properties to visit are shown as numbered markers on the map. The users can then click on the map and add information about the property or redirect them to Google Maps for directions. This visualization allows health agents to quickly decide where to go to next. Additionally, the health agents can modify their information at any time easily and it will be updated in the database.

9 DISCUSSION AND FUTURE WORK

It is necessary to characterize the data streams given the great diversity of data sources [17]. The variety of data sources raises issues relating to high noise in real-time datasets, especially, including issues in public health such as swine flu, vaccines rumors, and even social media issues related with ZIKV [18–24].

The health agent's database is obtained by the daily use of the application by the health agents. The whole app has been designed to share their data in an automatic way. All reports from the health agents are georeferenced and validated using Google Maps API. The e-learning and gamified environment ensure that the data collection is situation-aware. All data collected by the app is structured. The health agents' reports are essential to validate the ZIKV Model described in Fig. 2.

One of the key innovations of the present system is the integration of citizens' data (collected by health agents) and official data in order to improve the current ZIKV surveillance and to forecast the occurrence of ZIKV. The governmental data includes density of citizens, number of hospitals per locality and also the official records of confirmed ZIKV outbreaks. Data offered by governmental institutions is sometimes outdated but contains the historical true positives of ZIKV and is therefore important to be included in the ZIKV Model.

Another key innovation of the present system is the combination of weather data to predict in real time the distribution of the ZIKV and mosquitoes. The timeliness of the weather data is perhaps the most finer scale database. The system uses the API from GlobalWeather.com to associate weather conditions for each report. The weather database is georeferenced and structured.

Perhaps one of the most fundamental parts of validating the models is to corroborate whether a suspected or a probable ZIKV case will be confirmed. To establish that condition it is necessary to conduct laboratory tests to find the ZIKV traces in the blood. This task takes several days. To improve that step we propose the use of a cost-effective and portable graphene-enabled biosensor described recently by the heath agents [25]; this issue is still under consideration by the government institutions. The use of this portable sensor will help to reach remote areas that could be in high risk.

Part of the validation of the model is to establish ZIKV presence when the citizens have been preventing the infection by avoiding bad practices. To do that, samples of water in high risk areas have been taken to analyze the presence of the virus in the larvae of the mosquitoes.

The ZIKV Model is currently under construction and evaluation and will be recalibrated on a daily basis given the new true positives, the true negatives, the changes in weather and the reports from the health agents and citizens. Combining the big data analysis and the gamified applications we could empower the local communities and health agents to fight and stop the spread of ZIKV using the ZIKΛ app.

10 CONCLUSIONS

This paper presents the ZIKΛ system which combines public health surveillance, citizen-driven participatory reporting with weather data-based prediction. The main characteristic of the system is to empower health agents by a gamified app that will also be a platform to share data and to visualize the output of the forecasting. The engagement of different actors to build robust forecasting and improve surveillance will help to stop the spread of the ZIKV. This will reduce the devastating consequences of ZIKV in neonates and improve the life quality of vulnerable people in Brazil.

ACKNOWLEDGMENTS

This work was supported by the British Council Newton Fund No. 280860230.

REFERENCES

[1] Martines RB, Bhatnagar J, Keating MK, Silva-Flannery L. Notes from the field: evidence of Zika virus infection in brain and placental tissues from two congenitally infected newborns and two fetal losses-Brazil, 2015. MMWR Morb Mortal Wkly Rep. 2016; 65:159–60.
[2] Oliveira Melo AS, Malinger G, Ximenes R, Szejnfeld PO. Zika virus intrauterine infection causes fetal brain abnormality and microcephaly: tip of the iceberg? Ultrasound Obstet Gynecol. 2016; 47:6–7.
[3] Gulland A. WHO urges countries in dengue belt to look out for Zika. BMJ. 2016; 352:i595.
[4] Attar N. Zika virus circulates in new regions. Nature Rev Microbiol. 2016; 14: 62.
[5] Javed F, Manzoor KN, Ali M, Haq IU, Khan AA, Zaib A, Manzoor S. Zika virus: What we need to know? J Basic Microbiol. 2017; 2017:3–16
[6] Fauci AS, Morens DM. Zika virus in the Americas—yet another arbovirus threat. N Engl J Med. 2016; 374: 601–604
[7] Musso D, Roche C, Robin E, Nhan T. Potential sexual transmission of Zika virus. Emerg Infect Dis. 2015; 21:359–61.
[8] Alam A, Imam N, Farooqui A, Ali S. Recent trends in ZikV research: a step away from cure. Biomed Pharmacother. 2017; 91:1152–9.
[9] Carlson CJ, Dougherty ER, Getz W. An Ecological Assessment of the Pandemic Threat of Zika Virus. 2016. PLoS Negl Trop Dis. 10:e0004968.
[10] Campos GS, Bandeira AC, Sardi SI. Zika virus outbreak, Bahia, Brazil. Emerg Infect Dis. 2015; 21:1885–6.
[11] Zanluca C, Melo VC, Mosimann AL, Santos GI. First report of autochthonous transmission of Zika virus in Brazil. Mem Inst Oswaldo Cruz. 2015; 110:569–72.
[12] Faria NR, Azevedo RSS, Kraemer MUG, Souza R, Cunha MS, Hill SC, Thézé J, Bonsall MB, Bowden TA, Rissanen I, Rocco IM. Zika virus in the Americas: Early epidemiological and genetic findings. Science. 2016; 352: 345–349.
[13] Paz S, Semenza JC. El Niño and climate change–contributing factors in the dispersal of Zika virus in the Americas? Lancet. 2016; 387: 745.
[14] Kindhauser MK, Allen T, Frank V, Santhana RS. Zika: the origin and spread of a mosquito-borne virus. Bull World Health Organ. 2016; 94:86–67
[15] Messina JP, Kraemer MUG, Brady OJ, Pigott DM, Shearer FM, Weiss DJ, Golding N, Ruktanonchai CW, Gething PW, Cohn E, Brownstein JS. Mapping global environmental suitability for Zika virus. eLife. 2016; 5: e15272.
[16] Samy AM, Thomas SM, El Wahed AA, Cohoon KP, Peterson AT. Mapping the global geographic potential of Zika virus spread. Mem Inst Oswaldo Cruz. 2016; 111:559–560.
[17] Kostkova P. A roadmap to integrated digital public health surveillance: the vision and the challenges. ACM Proceedings of the 22nd International Conference on World Wide Web 2013. 2013; 1:687–694.
[18] Szomszor M, Kostkova P, De Quincey E. # Swineflu: Twitter predicts swine flu outbreak in 2009. International Conference on Electronic Healthcare 2010. 2010; 1:18–26.
[19] De Quincey E, Kostkova P. Early warning and outbreak detection using social networking websites: The potential of twitter. International Conference on Electronic Healthcare 2009. 2009; 1: 21–24.
[20] Kostkova P. Grand challenges in digital health. Frontiers in Public Health. 2015; 3:134.
[21] Barata G, Shores K, Alperin JP. Local chatter or international buzz? Language differences on posts about Zika research on Twitter and Facebook. PLoS ONE. 2008; 13: e0190482.
[22] McGough SF, Brownstein JS, Hawkins JB, Santillana M, Simeone R, Hills S. Forecasting Zika incidence in the 2016 Latin America outbreak combining traditional disease surveillance with search, social media, and news report data. PLoS Negl Trop Dis. 2017;11: e0005295.
[23] Kostkova P, Szomszor M, St Louis C. #swineflu: The use of Twitter as an early warning tool and for risk communication in the 2009 swine flu pandemic. ACM Transactions on Management Information Systems. 2014; 5: 8.
[24] Kostkova P, Mano V, Larson HJ, Schulz WS. Who is Spreading Rumours about Vaccines?: Influential User Impact Modelling in Social Networks. ACM Proceedings of Digital Health 2017. 2017; 1: 48–52.8
[25] Afsahi S, Lerner MB, Goldstein JM, Lee J, Tang X, Bagarozzi Jr DA, Pan D, Locascio L, Walker A, Barron F, Goldsmith BR. Novel graphene-based biosensor for early detection of Zika virus infection. Biosensors and Bioelectronics. 2018:15:85–8.

Learning about Hygiene and Antibiotic Resistance through Mobile Games

Evaluation of Learning Effectiveness

Andreea Molnar
Lancaster University
Lancaster, United Kingdom
andreea.molnar@lancaster.ac.uk

Patty Kostkova
University College London
London, United Kingdom
P.Kostkova@ucl.ac.uk

ABSTRACT

Edugames4all MicrobeQuest! is a mobile game that aims to teach microbiology and create awareness about important healthcare issues among 9 to 12 years old. This article presents the game, discusses the game design and integration of the learning objectives into the game mechanics. A pilot study has been performed to assess the game effectiveness in teaching the learning objectives integrated into the game. The study showed that the game can teach the learning objectives, however, the knowledge difference has not been statistically significant across all three learning objectives.

CCS CONCEPTS

• **Applied computing** → **Interactive learning environments**; *Computers in other domains*;

KEYWORDS

antibiotic resistance; children; health; hygiene; learning; mobile apps; serious games

ACM Reference Format:
Andreea Molnar and Patty Kostkova. 2018. Learning about Hygiene and Antibiotic Resistance through Mobile Games: Evaluation of Learning Effectiveness. In *DH'18: 2018 International Digital Health Conference, April 23–26, 2018, Lyon, France.* ACM, New York, NY, USA, 5 pages. https://doi.org/10.1145/3194658.3194682

1 INTRODUCTION

Currently, there is an increased ownership of mobile devices among children [1]. They could be used to complement teaching in an enjoyable manner through games. This paper will present a mobile game, edugames4all MicrobeQuest! [20], aimed at improving children knowledge about healthcare issues such as hygiene, infection prevention and responsible antibiotic use. A review of serious games for health [4] aimed at games that address interventions associated with infections and infection prevention and control has shown that the research in this area is still emerging with most studies focusing on the inception and development stages. In this

study, we want to address part of the evaluation gap and present an evaluation of existing games for health.

A previous version of this game exists as a desktop version and the desktop version has previously been evaluated [9]. The mobile version of the game had only been evaluated for usability [21]. There are several challenges that can occur in using mobile devices for learning including the possibility of cognitive overload [23]. Therefore, the evaluation of the desktop version does not necessarily guarantee the same results as the mobile version, an evaluation of the mobile version of the game also being necessary. This research will focus on exploring whether the mobile game version improves the player's learning outcome.

In order to address this aim, the paper is organised as follows. The next section presents existing research on educational mobile games. The following section describes the Edugames4all Microbe-Quest!, what learning objectives are covered and how they have been integrated into the game mechanics. This section is followed by the evaluation and the results. This research ends with a presentation of the study's conclusion and proposed future work.

2 GAMES FOR HEALTH

Among STEM educational games, games that teach about healthcare issue are the most popular [3]. It is probably not surprising as serious games were embraced early by the medical community and are aimed at improving directly or indirectly the physical, mental and well-being of individuals.

Mobile games have been used to facilitate healthy living, rehabilitation or awareness about healthcare issues, such as improving medication compliance for elders [6], as a means to research the nutritional choices [12], promoting physical activity [13] or as part of telerehabilitation programs [7]. Positive results have been reported in the literature for improved medication compliance (tested in an 18 weeks user study), an improvement which has been higher for participants that had a previous interest in games [6]. OrderUP! [10], a game that aims to improve understanding of healthy eating, has shown to lead to players showing early engagement changing their eating habits [10].

As opposed to the above games, our game focuses on creating awareness about hygiene and responsible antibiotic use among children. Hand hygiene significantly reduces illness related absences [22], whereas antibiotic resistance is an ongoing concern and responsible antibiotic use could help alleviate this issue [8]. With the aim of addressing these issues, the desktop version of the game has been adapted [9] for play on mobile devices as an app [19]. This would allow us to assess how effective the app is in delivering the

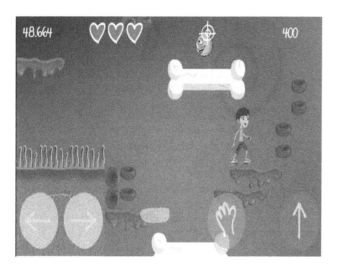

Figure 1: Player exploring the human body

Figure 2: Player exploring the kitchen

educational message and the game's appeal for children in our age group.

A review of serious games for health [4] aimed at games that address interventions associated with infections and infection prevention and control has shown that the research in this area is still in emerging form with most studies focusing on the inception and development stages. Games that were evaluated and have been focused on educating children about antibiotic resistance [11], [18] have shown mixed results regarding their effectiveness. This research aims to address this gap and to focus on the effectiveness of the game on educating and creating awareness about hygiene and antibiotic awareness, as children are one of the population categories often ignored by the existing healthcare campaigns [16].

3 EDUGAMES4ALL MICROBEQUEST!

Edugames4all MicrobeQuest! is aimed at creating awareness about microbe transmission; food, body and hand hygiene; and responsible antibiotic use [20]. The game was designed to focus on learning objectives that would be covered in the primary school curriculum, however, some of its content could be useful for the general public.

The game is organised across different missions, starting with a tutorial mission aiming to familiarise the player with the game mechanics. This was motivated by two principles. First, there is empirical support showing that text based tutorials are not too effective [2, 17], especially when working with children [17]. Second, having a *tutorial* level that slowly introduces the players to the game mechanics has been shown to be effective in teaching the game mechanics in other educational games aimed at children [17].

At the beginning of the game, the player is asked to select an avatar. The selected avatar then shrinks up to the size of a microorganism, allowing the player to interact with different microbes, bacterias and viruses (see Figure 1 and Figure 2). By shrinking the player, we can see the effect of different actions such as: what happens with the microorganism on the hand after washing them with soap, how the milk becomes yoghurt with the help of a bacteria, or what is the effect of not following the doctor's instructions when using antibiotics.

The game missions facilitate the exploration of different environments such as: human hand, human body (see Figure 1) or the food in the kitchen (see Figure 2). During these explorations, the player is taught the learning objectives through game mechanics and text incorporated into the game. For example, in order to teach the following learning objective: *Our bodies have natural defences that protect us*, through the game mechanics the player avatar, shrunken to the size of a microorganism and explores inside of the human body. Through the journey, the player encounters harmful microorganism. In order to protect the body and the player not to lose his game *life* s/he has to collect white blood cells and throw them at the harmful microorganism. The same learning objective would be reinforced through text, by displaying to the player: *There are good and bad microbes. Good microbes can turn milk into yoghurt. That's how yoghurt gets made. Amazing isn't it?.*

To facilitate the educational content assessment, the game allows for a similar integrated assessment of the educational content as the desktop version of the game [14]. The game allows assessing the player knowledge before and after being exposed to the learning objectives in games, though a quiz similar with "How to be a millionaire". This could be used to assess the effectiveness of the game without the need for additional questionnaires being delivered to the students outside the game but also to determine what aspects of the game are more effective in delivering the educational message and what others need to be improved. An evaluation of this kind of assessment on the desktop version of the game has shown that 63% of the players preferred it, as opposed to questionnaire before and after the game play [14]. Moreover, the quiz provides an opportunity to provide the players formative and summative assessment and feedback on their progress.

Table 1: Statements of the Questions used to assess Player's Knowledge

Q. No.	Question
Q1	If you cannot see a microbe it is not there
Q2	Bacteria and viruses are the same
Q3	Soap can be used to wash away bad bugs
Q4	You should wash your hands after handling raw meat
Q5	We use good microbes to make things like bread and yogurt
Q6	Antibiotics can harm our good bacteria as well as bad bacteria
Q7	Bacteria, viruses and fungi can be found in different enviroments
Q8	Bacteria, viruses and fungi come in different shapes and sizes
Q9	"Bad" microbes can make us ill
Q10	Not all microbes are harmful
Q11	Our bodies have defences to fight off disease
Q12	Antibiotics can be used ot fight off bacterial infections
Q13	If antibiotics are taken, it is important ot finish the course
Q14	Vaccines can be used to obtain immunity to viral diseases
Q15	Vacciness can be used to obtain immunity to viral diseases where the body's natural defences alone are not enough
Q16	Bacteria are becoming resistant to many antibiotics due to antibiotic misuse (not finishing the course)

4 EVALUATION

The evaluation questionnaire was designed to cover the learning objectives presented in the section above. Learning objectives were assessed through a multiple choice questionnaire. These questions have also been used to assess the same learning objectives in other studies [9]. Table 1 presents the question's statements. The player had to state whether they agree with a given affirmation and had to choose between the following options: *True, False* and *Don't know*.

Paired sample t-test [5] was used to check whether there was a statistically significant difference between the players' answers to the questionnaire assessing their knowledge before the game (pre-test) and the questions assessing their knowledge after the playing session (post-test).

4.1 Participants

A total of 19 participants from different socio economic backgrounds and age groups took part in the study. The participants were recruited from schools in the UK and an after-school computer club. The children were recruited to match the age group the game was aimed for. Their average age was 9.2 years old, standard deviation 0.91. Most of the participants were female (n=11) and most of them were playing computer games on a regular basis.

4.2 Set-Up and Methodology

Before taking part in the study, consent was obtained from the school and after-school club, and from the parents of the children that took part in the study. All were provided with written information about the study. During the experimental section, the children were explained the study again (by the teacher and/or the researcher that carried out the study). They were given the opportunity to ask questions and were given the option to leave the study at any time (none of the participants opted for this and all

of them fully participated in the study). Afterwards, they asked to complete a questionnaire collecting demographic information (age and gender) and assessing their previous knowledge of the learning objectives covered in the game. Next, the participants were given a mobile phone (Samsung Galaxy S4), that had the game already pre-installed. They were asked to play the game for thirty minutes. Afterwards, they were asked to fill a questionnaire that comprises of questions assessing their learning performance. The questions assessing the knowledge before playing the game were the same questions which assessed the knowledge after the game play.

4.3 Results and Discussions

To assess how much the players have learned we have compared the study participants responses to the pre-test questionnaire (administered before they played the game) to those of the post-test questionnaire (administered after the playing session). Figure 3 presents the player's answers to the pre-test knowledge questions. It presents how many players answers on average correct, incorrect or reporting that they do not know the answer to the given questions.

The Student t-test was used to determine whether there is a significant difference between the answer to the questions before and after playing the game, considering a 95% confidence interval. The results showed that for one of the learning objectives, *Q8 - Bacteria, viruses and fungi come in different shapes and sizes*, the difference was statistically significant (see Table 1). For the other learning objectives, the difference between the pre and post test was not statistically significant. There are four reasons which might have contributed to these results. **First**, the results could be explained by the fact that the most of the players already know some of the concepts covered in the game (see Figure 3 for the participants answers to the questionnaire administered prior to the study). For example, all students knew the correct answer to the questions four before

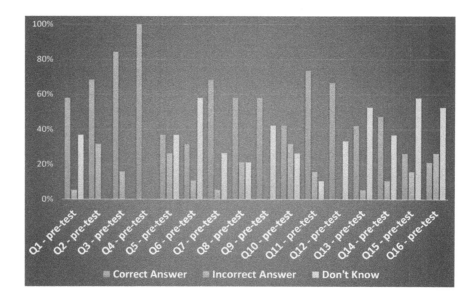

Figure 3: Players' answers to the pre-test questions

Table 2: Paired t-test Results

Q. No.	Mean	Std. Deviation	Std. Error Mean	t	p
Q1	-0.11	0.99	0 .24	-0.48	0.63
Q2	-0.056	0.72	0.17	-0.32	0.74
Q3	0.11	0.85	0.20	0.56	0.57
Q4	0.11	0.47	0.11	1.00	0.33
Q5	0.05	0.99	0.23	.23	0.81
Q6	0.38	0.77	0.18	2.12	0.05
Q7	-0.11	0.75	0.17	-.62	0.54
Q8	-0.44	0.85	0.20	-2.20	0.04
Q9	-0.16	0.70	0.16	-1.00	0.33
Q10	-0.38	1.09	0.25	-1.51	0.14
Q11	-0.11	0.58	0.13	-0.80	0.43
Q12	0.17	0.63	0.15	1.14	0.26
Q13	-0.11	0.99	0.24	-0.48	0.63
Q14	0.35	1.11	0.27	1.30	0.21
Q15	0.11	0.83	0.19	0.56	0.57
Q16	-0.05	0.93	0.22	-0.25	0.80

playing the game: *You should wash your hands after handling raw meat.* **Second**, it might be due to the difficulty in executing some game mechanics in the game [20]. As a result, not all the students advance to the next level and were not exposed to all the learning objectives. **Third**, the traditional education is more effective for the children/young adults who do not usually play video games, and the gaming profile could affect the interest and motivation towards

learning with a certain type of game [15]. **Fourth**, our sample was relatively small (n=19) and a larger sample size might have led to better results.

5 CONCLUSIONS AND FUTURE WORK

We presented edugames4all MicrobeQuest!, a mobile game aimed at teaching children microbiology. The game uses a combination of text and game mechanics to teach and reinforce the learning objectives. The learning objectives covered in the game are based on the primary school curriculum. This paper presented the results of a study assessing primary school children learning with the game. The results showed that the game could teach but the learning across all learning objectives was not statistically significant. As the sample size was small, we cannot confirm the hypothesis in one direction or another.

We are currently attempting to get a larger sample size and determine whether the difference in learning outcomes among different learning objectives still persist. We want to perform an experimental study assessing the differences in learning with mobile vs PC games both in formal and informal learning environments. We plan to take steps to increase the sense of immersion even further by complementing the teaching done through game mechanics not only through text but also through speech, as the children, especially those on the younger side found reading the text explanation tiring and often skipped over it. On a longer term, we want to assess whether the game leads to changes in children's attitude and behaviour towards hygiene and responsible antibiotic use.

6 ACKNOWLEDGMENTS

Our thanks go to Fariz Benchaoui, Charlie Green and Jonny Wildey for developing the mobile app. Christina, Daly, Lucy Milner, Nikki Chester, Alison Minall and Nancy Clunie with helping with organising the study. The children who took part in the study and volunteered their feedback on the application. This research was partially supported by the University of Portsmouth Research Accelerator Fund and GADSA, Grant No: ES/P004733/1. The desktop version of the game was initially implemented as part of the e-bug, a European Commission funded project, DG SANCO, Grant no: 2005211.

7 COMPETING INTERESTS

The authors have declared that no competing interests exist.

REFERENCES

[1] 2014. One in Three Children has their own Tablet Computer. (2014). http://media.ofcom.org.uk/news/2014/media-lit-audit-oct2014/ [Online; accessed 29-January-2015].

[2] Erik Andersen, Eleanor O'Rourke, Yun-En Liu, Rich Snider, Jeff Lowdermilk, David Truong, Seth Cooper, and Zoran Popovic. 2012. The impact of tutorials on games of varying complexity. In *Proceedings of the SIGCHI Conference on Human Factors in Computing Systems*. ACM, 59–68.

[3] Elizabeth A Boyle, Thomas Hainey, Thomas M Connolly, Grant Gray, Jeffrey Earp, Michela Ott, Theodore Lim, Manuel Ninaus, Claudia Ribeiro, and João Pereira. 2016. An update to the systematic literature review of empirical evidence of the impacts and outcomes of computer games and serious games. *Computers & Education* 94 (2016), 178–192.

[4] Enrique Castro-Sánchez, Yiannis Kyratsis, Michiyo Iwami, Timothy M Rawson, and Alison H Holmes. 2016. Serious electronic games as behavioural change interventions in healthcare-associated infections and infection prevention and control: a scoping review of the literature and future directions. *Antimicrobial Resistance & Infection Control* 5, 1 (2016), 34.

[5] Louis Cohen, Lawrence Manion, and Keith Morrison. 2013. *Research methods in education*. Routledge.

[6] Rodrigo De Oliveira, Mauro Cherubini, and Nuria Oliver. 2010. MoviPill: improving medication compliance for elders using a mobile persuasive social game. In *Proceedings of the 12th ACM International Conference on Ubiquitous Computing*. ACM, 251–260.

[7] Marcus Dithmer, Jack Ord Rasmussen, Erik Grönvall, Helle Spindler, John Hansen, Gitte Nielsen, Stine Bæk Sørensen, and Birthe Dinesen. 2016. The Heart Game: Using Gamification as Part of a Telerehabilitation Program for Heart Patients. *Games for health journal* 5, 1 (2016), 27–33.

[8] Julia Fahrenkamp-Uppenbrink. 2015. Countering antibiotic resistance. *Science* 347, 6226 (2015), 1109–1111.

[9] David Farrell, Patty Kostkova, Julius Weinberg, Lisa Lazareck, Dasun Weerasinghe, Donna M Lecky, and Cliodna AM McNulty. 2011. Computer games to teach hygiene: An evaluation of the e-Bug junior game. *Journal of Antimicrobial Chemotherapy* 66, suppl 5 (2011), v39–v44.

[10] Andrea Grimes, Vasudhara Kantroo, and Rebecca E Grinter. 2010. Let's play!: mobile health games for adults. In *Proceedings of the 12th ACM international conference on Ubiquitous computing*. ACM, 241–250.

[11] Alexander R Hale, Vicki Louise Young, Ann Grand, and Cliodna Ann Miriam McNulty. 2017. Can Gaming Increase Antibiotic Awareness in Children? A Mixed-Methods Approach. *JMIR serious games* 5, 1 (2017).

[12] Maria L Hwang and Lena Mamykina. 2017. Monster Appetite: Effects of Subversive Framing on Nutritional Choices in a Digital Game Environment. In *Proceedings of the 2017 CHI Conference on Human Factors in Computing Systems*. ACM, 4082–4096.

[13] Ruud H Knols, Tom Vanderhenst, Martin L Verra, and Eling D de Bruin. 2016. Exergames for Patients in Acute Care Settings: Systematic Review of the Reporting of Methodological Quality, FITT Components, and Program Intervention Details. *Games for health journal* 5, 3 (2016), 224–235.

[14] Patty Kostkova and Andreea Molnar. 2014. Educational Games for Creating Awareness about Health Issues: The Case of Educational Content Evaluation Integrated in the Game. In *Medicine 2.0 Conference*. JMIR Publications Inc., Toronto, Canada.

[15] Borja Manero, Javier Torrente, Clara Fernandez-Vara, and Baltasar Fernandez-Manjon. 2017. Investigating the impact of gaming habits, gender, and age on the effectiveness of an educational video game: An exploratory study. *IEEE Transactions on Learning Technologies* (2017).

[16] Andreea Molnar. 2017. Children as agents of change in combatting antibiotic resistance. *Journal of Health Services Research & Policy* (2017). https://doi.org/1355819617701512

[17] Andreea Molnar and Patty Kostkova. 2014. Gaming to master the game-game usability and game mechanics. In *Serious Games and Applications for Health (SeGAH), 2014 IEEE 3rd International Conference on*. IEEE, 1–7.

[18] Andreea Molnar and Patty Kostkova. 2015. Learning through interactive digital narratives. In *Interactive digital narrative: history, theory and practice*. Routledge, 200–210.

[19] Andreea Molnar and Patty Kostkova. 2015. Mind the Gap: From Desktop to App. In *Proceedings of the 5th International Conference on Digital Health 2015*. ACM, 15–16.

[20] Andreea Molnar and Patty Kostkova. 2016. Ubiquitous bugs and drugs education for children through mobile games. In *Proceedings of the 6th International Conference on Digital Health Conference*. ACM, 77–78.

[21] Andreea Molnar and Patty Kostkova. 2018. Teaching Hygiene and Responsible Antibiotic Use through a Mobile Game for Children. In *Mobile Apps Engineering: Architecture, Design, Development and Testing*.

[22] Inge Nandrup-Bus. 2009. Mandatory handwashing in elementary schools reduces absenteeism due to infectious illness among pupils: a pilot intervention study. *American journal of infection control* 37, 10 (2009), 820–826.

[23] Lung-Hsiang Wong and Chee-Kit Looi. 2011. What seams do we remove in mobile-assisted seamless learning? A critical review of the literature. *Computers & Education* 57, 4 (2011), 2364–2381.

Foursquare to The Rescue:
Predicting Ambulance Calls Across Geographies

Anastasios Noulas
New York University
New York, USA
noulas@nyu.edu

Colin Moffatt
De Montfort University
Leicester, UK
syrphus7@gmail.com

Desislava Hristova
New York University
New York, USA
desii.hristova@gmail.com

Bruno Gonçalves
New York University
New York, USA
bgoncalves@gmail.com

ABSTRACT

Understanding how ambulance incidents are spatially distributed can shed light to the epidemiological dynamics of geographic areas and inform healthcare policy design. Here we analyze a longitudinal dataset of more than four million ambulance calls across a region of twelve million residents in the North West of England. With the aim to explain geographic variations in ambulance call frequencies, we employ a wide range of data layers including open government datasets describing population demographics and socio-economic characteristics, as well as geographic activity in online services such as Foursquare. Working at a fine level of spatial granularity we demonstrate that daytime population levels and the deprivation status of an area are the most important variables when it comes to predicting the volume of ambulance calls at an area. Foursquare check-ins on the other hand complement these government sourced indicators, offering a novel view to population nightlife and commercial activity locally. We demonstrate how check-in activity can provide an edge when predicting certain types of emergency incidents in a multi-variate regression model.

ACM Reference Format:
Anastasios Noulas, Colin Moffatt, Desislava Hristova, and Bruno Gonçalves. 2018. Foursquare to The Rescue: Predicting Ambulance Calls Across Geographies. In *Proceedings of Eighth International Digital Health Conference (DH'18)*. ACM, New York, NY, USA, 10 pages. https://doi.org/10.475/123_4

1 INTRODUCTION

Effectively predicting the demand for ambulances across regions can both improve the operational capacity of emergency services as well as reduced costs by optimizing resource utilization and providing an optimal spatial deployment and duty planning of paramedic crews. This results in quicker response times in attending emergency incidents reducing fatalities. Moreover, as ambulances play a critical role as first responders, calls to the ambulance service provide precious real time epidemiological information traces that can assist population health monitoring at scale and lead to improved policy design in healthcare.

Past studies aiming to explain geographic variations in the volume of calls for emergencies [2, 13, 19, 22] have been limited to examining epidemiological patterns across very broad geographic scales (national level). Enabling predictions at finer spatial scales, e.g. at the level of city neighborhoods, can generate intelligence that will allow the targeting of healthcare interventions in a more accurate manner, specializing treatment to the characteristics of populations in need. The importance of geography for health in fact has been highlighted through works pointing out that postal code may be a better predictor, compared to genetic information, when it comes to explaining the well being of local populations [3, 11].

In this work, our aim is to estimate the volume of ambulance calls at the level of individual Lower Super Output Areas (LSOA) in the North West of England. We investigate various environmental, socio-economic and demographic factors that can contribute to the rise of emergency incidents at a given *locale*. In this setting, we note how a population's level of deprivation has a deterring impact on its health status with deprived urban areas being those where the number requests for emergency medical attention surges. Additionally, we identify regional population volume dynamics as one of the primary drivers for emergency calls to take place, showing how health incidents are likely to occur in areas where people become active and not simply those where they are registered as residents according to census. *Critically to the novelty of the present work, we exploit place semantics and mobility patterns in location based-service Foursquare to infer population activity trends at local areas and attain more accurate predictions of the volume of calls an area will experience.* Our research findings are described in more detail next:

- **Ambulance calls concentrate in urban areas and form patterns of spatial co-occurrence:** in Section 3 we show how the spatial distribution of calls to emergency services is highly skewed, with a large fraction of activity being concentrated in major urban centers. Furthermore, there are strong patterns in terms of how incident types spatially co-occur. For instance, *overdose/poisoning* cases are highly correlated across geographies with *convulsions/seizures* and *unconscious/fainting* incidents. On the other hand *breathing problems* tend to correlated more with *chest pain* complaints and *sick person* cases.

- **Higher regional levels of deprivation imply higher volumes of ambulance calls:** In Section 4.3 characterize geographic areas using various socio-economic indicators accessed through open government datasets, including we scores of geographic regions [18]. We find that *breathing problems*, *chest pain* and *psychiatric/suicide* related incidents are more common in areas with higher crime rates and lower income levels.

- **Daytime population levels are a better predictor of ambulance calls than residential population:** In Section 4.2 we define a variable to estimate *daytime population* levels. This is the sum of the number of workers at an area, younger (below 16 year old) and older (above 65 year old). We describe the stark differences between the spatial-distribution of *daytime* and *residential* populations showing how the former yields a much higher correlation score (pearson's $r = 0.68$ vs $r = 0.18$) with the total number of calls in an area and is key to explaining variations for a set of incidents types including *traumatic/injuries* and *uconscious/fainting*.

- **Foursquare activity patterns at urban regions contribute to better predictions in ambulance calls for an area:** Finally, in Section 5 we formulate a prediction task where our goal becomes to combine the various information sources discussed above and assess their relative importance in predicting the number of ambulance calls at an area. Daytime population levels are the most significant factor in explaining variations in ambulance calls, followed by the index of multiple deprivation for an area and foursquare check-in activity. The importance of each variable however, depends on the type of incident considered. Daytime population level best explain high number in *falls* and *traumatic injuries* whereas calls at areas with increased levels of *unconscious/fainting* and *overdose/poisoning* incidents are best approximated using check-in frequencies from location-based service Foursquare. The service proves to be a useful proxy of population activity at Food and Nightlife places.

Our work demonstrates how traditional, yet critical, sectors in healthcare may be improved through the integration of digital datasets from online sources. Location-based technologies could improve the operational efficiency of emergency services through more refined descriptions of population activities at fine geographic scales. From an epidemiological perspective they can be integrated with socio-economic and demographic indicators to offer a deeper understanding on population health patterns.

2　RELATED WORK

Health Geography and environmental epidemiology. Spatial analysis and health geography trace their roots back to 1854 London when John Snow famously drew maps with markers of health incidents to locate the source of a cholera outbreak [26]. Spatial epidemiology has ever since contributed to our understanding of how diseases spread and appear geographically [10] tracing its

roots on spatial statistics and quantitative geography [9]. The state-of-the-art in statistical epidemiology of non-infectious disease usually treats occurrences as a spatio-temporal point process[7, 8, 17]. This family of techniques however focuses on predicting incident frequencies of a single disease and does not provide interpretations on the environmental and demographic factors that may drive the spatio-temporal occurrence of medical incidents. They trace their roots in methods such as kriging [27] and they effectively reduce the problem of modeling the spatio-temporal occurrences of epidemiological incidents to a form of interpolation.

More recently, research literature in the field of health geography has focused on explaining geographic variations in emergency requests in terms of census and demographics data which has become available on a national level [20]. Deprivation levels of urban communities (e.g. accessibility to employment) or differences between rural and urban areas have been projected to partially explain geographic variations in the volume of calls for emergencies [19, 22]. Our work considers urban deprivation factors in explaining call variations at a fine level of spatial granularity of areas with a few hundred residents. Moreover, we investigate the interplay of environmental, demographic and urban activity factors across different incident types (e.g. psychiatric, assault, fall etc.).

Social media in health analytics. In terms of related work in the area of social media in health analytics, the field of digital health has risen in recent years thanks to the proliferation of the web as well as mobile sensing technologies [24]. Despite their biases [14], web and online social media sources, provide ample opportunity to break away many of the barriers that characterize traditional experimental methodology in medical studies. These include being able to track users health behavior in a social context and anonymously [5, 6], or at large population scales [21] while retaining the benefits of fine spatio-temporal views on user behavior [16]. An aspect of novelty in the present work regards the incorporation of information from social media services to understand ambulance demand regionally. Geo-referenced datasets from services like Foursquare have the advantage of providing us with place semantics and mobility patterns described at fine spatial scales.

3　OPERATIONAL SCOPE & DATA

3.1　The North West Ambulance Service

The North West Ambulance Service NHS Trust (NWAS)[2] is the second largest ambulance trust in England, providing services to a population of seven million people across a geographical area of approximately 5,400 square miles. The organisation provides a 24 hour, 365 days a year accident and emergency services to those in need of emergency medical treatment and transport, responding to hundreds of thousands emergency calls per year. Highly skilled staff provide life-saving care to patients in the community and take people to hospital or a place of care if needed. Calls that result in an ambulance dispatch may come via the 999 (The Europe-wide 112 also results in a 999 call). The call operator will ask the caller a series of questions to ascertain the degree of emergency and will assign a dispatch code to the call. Dispatch codes are numeric and correspond to a broad classification of incidents (e.g. falls, traumatic

---

[2]http://www.nwas.nhs.uk/

Source	Variable Description
Lower Super Output Area Boundaries (data.gov.uk)	LSOA shapefile polygons
2011 Census; Table PHP01 (data.gov.uk)	#People residing in LSOA
Communal Population (CmmnlRs)	#People in communal establishments
Area size	LSOA area in hectares
Average Household Size (AvHshlS)	#persons in household (mean)
Workplace Population 2011[1]	Employed People 16-74
LSOA Mid-Year Population Estimates 2011 (ons.gov.uk)	# Persons at each age in years
English Indices of Multiple Deprivation (www.gov.uk)	Deprivation scores for a local area
Foursquare check-in data	logged check-ins and place categories by LSOA

Table 1: Summary of external data sets used. In cases where abbreviations have been used they are put in parentheses in the first column.

injuries, assualt, psychiatric etc.). If the call requires a response, an appropriate team receives the instruction, and then swiftly makes its way to the incident location, using an onboard satelite navigation system.

3.2 Datasets

We next describe the characteristics of the data employed in the present work. The primary source of data, the ambulance calls, has been collected by the North West Ambulance Service (NWAS). We employ numerous datasets to design a number of variables from demographic, socio-economic and web sources (Foursquare). These data layers will let us assess the efficacy of various information sources in predicting geographic variations in ambulance calls.

Ambulance calls dataset. The data provided by NWAS are those routinely collected as an emergency call operator receives a call where it is anticipated an ambulance may be required. The data is comprised of 4.4 million calls the service has responded to from April 2013 to March 2017. Each incident has a *dispatch code* which corresponds to the type of the medical condition or cause that led to the call (e.g. suicide, fall, traffic incident etc). Codes range from 1 to 35 though other codes for rare cases may also be used. We exploit the incident number to stratify ambulance calls by nature and ask the question whether different incident types are associated with different factors. Critically to the present work, we exploit geographic information on where the incident took place at the administrative level of *lower super output areas* (LSOAs) which in the UK corresponds to the first four letters of the zip code. We explain LSOAs in detail next.

Spatial boundaries, populations, demographics and socio-economic indicators. Table 1 summarizes the additional data sets in terms of the variables that we utilise. The Lower Super Output Areas (LSOAs) are the fundamental unit of spatial aggregation considered in this work. Output areas were originally created such that populations were approximately similar socially and in size [4]. LSOAs were assembled to maintain such similarity with a target population size of around 1500, but naturally, there is some variation as we demonstrate in the next section.

In terms of population data, we use information on the number of people residing in each LSOA, the number of people in communal establishments (communal population) and average household size. The workplace population corresponds to an enumeration of the

people that work in an LSOA. In Section 4 we combine workplace population with residential population of young and older age groups (non working populations) to define the *daytime population* variable, which becomes one of the best predictors for ambulance calls.

In terms of socio-economic indicators, we employ *The Index of Multiple Deprivation* (IMD) which is a score calculated by the government in the UK to characterize areas through the consideration of a set of deprivation and quality of life indicators. These include income and crime levels, accessibility to education, health deprivation and disability, barriers to housing as well as the quality of the living environment. IMD has been shown to be a very important discriminative signal when aiming to predict the dynamics of complex urban processes including gentrification [12]. The number of *healthcare providers* corresponds to an enumeration of health services that are present in an area, which includes hospitals, general practioners (GPs) and social support facilities amongst others.

Location-based services. Finally, we employ a dataset of public Foursquare check-ins pushed on Twitter, collected over 11 months in 2011. For every check-in information about the place the user has checked-in becomes available, including its location in terms of latitude and longitude coordinates. Additionally, for every Foursquare venue we know the category of it (Coffee Shop, Italian Restaurant etc.). For the purposes of the present work we use the higher level Foursquare categories (Food, Nightlife, Travel & Transport, Residences, Arts & Entertainmens, Shops, College & University Outdoors & Recreation, Professional & Other places.)[3]. Overall in the area covered by the North West Ambulance service, we have observed approximately 240 thousand check-ins over the 11 month period considered. We observe significant practical correlations between the Foursquare and ambulance call datasets despite the the fact that their time windows do not overlap (2011 versus 2013-2017). Finally, we have associated every Foursquare venue with an LSOA through a spatial join of the venues dataset with the polygons describing the boundaries of the LSOAs.

3.3 Spatial distribution of calls

The main focus of the present work is to predict the geographic variations of ambulance calls and the identification of the factors that drive their increase. To highlight the relevance of the question,

---

[3]https://developer.foursquare.com/docs/resources/categories

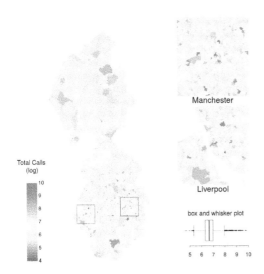

Figure 1: Choropleth map for (natural log) for all calls with location of hospitals circled with zoomed Manchester and Liverpool areas. Bottom right shows a box and whisker plot of the data.

LSOA code	LSOA name	calls	x mean
E01005316	Manchester 053D	13274	14.7
E01033658	Manchester 054C	10216	11.3
E01033653	Manchester 055B	8401	9.3
E01018326	Cheshire Wes 034A	7846	8.7
E01012681	Blackpool 006A	7797	8.6
E01005948	Tameside 013A	7397	8.2
E01033760	Liverpool 060C	7095	7.9
E01012736	Blackpool 010D	6833	7.6
E01005758	Stockport 014B	6703	7.4
E01033756	Liverpool 061C	6294	7.0

Table 2: Top 10 LSOAs for call volume over the 4 year period. Right column shows how many times greater than the mean of all LSOAs.

we provide views on how ambulance calls are skewed across different geographic regions (LSOAs) in the North West of England. The choropleth map for the total number of calls across the whole four year period is shown in Figure 1, using the natural logarithm to represent the number of calls in each LSOA. One can see that the sizes of the LSOAs vary considerably to maintain approximately similar population sizes, with urban centres corresponding to smaller geographic areas of higher population density. The squares on the main map show areas zoomed in to reveal more detail in the two main urban centers of the region, Manchester and Liverpool. As can be observed, there is a significant variation in calls across areas. Table 2 shows the ten of those LSOAs with the highest numbers of calls. The highest rated is the LSOA with Manchester Airport, followed by a number of urban areas that are known to concentrate high commercial activity.

Dispatch Code	Complaint	%
35	Healthcare Practitioner Referral	16.2
17	Falls	13.3
6	Breathing Problems	10.8
10	Chest Pain	9.1
31	Unconscious/Fainting	7.6
26	Sick Person	7.1
12	Convulsions/Seizures	4.7
25	Psychiatric/Suicide	4.0
23	Overdose/Poisoning	3.0
30	Traumatic Injuries	2.5

Table 3: Ten most frequent dispatch codes ranked by frequency.

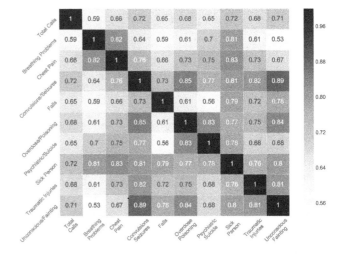

Figure 2: Pearson correlation scores between variables representing pairs of health incidents.

4 ANALYSIS OF SPATIAL EPIDEMIOLOGICAL PATTERNS

In this section, we investigate to what extent socio-economic and demographic factors, together with population related variables and data from location-based services (Foursquare) are associated with different types of ambulance incidents. We perform a correlation-driven analysis reporting pearson correlation scores between pairs of variables across the various information layers. We have applied the Bonferroni correction when measuring the statistical significance of all correlation measurements and they were all significant for the corresponding thresholds.

4.1 Incident frequencies and associations

The ten most frequent dispatch code call for each age group resulted in a combined list of ten dispatch codes as given in Table 3. They accounted for 78.3% of all calls. Healthcare practitioner referral (Dispatch Code 35) is the most frequent and corresponds to calls made by doctors at healthcare facilities to transfer a patient to a hospital. In the analysis that follows next, we have filtered out calls that correspond to this incident code from the data as they relate

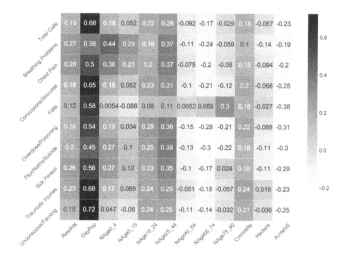

Figure 4: Correlation matrix reporting pearson's r correlation scores between variables describing medical incidents attended by ambulances and a number of population, demographic and geographic variables.

may yield different epidemiological incidents in nature and hence the question becomes whether it is possible to identify the characteristics that makeup those areas and are contributing to these patterns.

4.2 Residential versus daytime populations

In answering the question *what geographic and demographic features influence the number of calls to an ambulance service?*, it seems reasonable to expect that, to some degree, the size of the population would be relevant. We present two population-based maps here. While LSOAs were created with a goal of their being equal in population size (and therefore, varying in area), there was some considerable variation as Figure 3 shows. In fact, population size ranged from 988 (an urban area in Southport) to 6137 (a largely rural area south of Lancaster but which contains the university campus of Lancaster University), with a median of 1520. The city centres of Manchester and Liverpool show one or two higher than average populations, but in general green colours which correspond to lower population areas dominate.

Populations fluctuate constantly as people move about their daily activities. A characteristic example of such process is commuting, where typically large populations move from the more peripheral areas towards urban centers. In the present context, we can hypothesize that ambulance calls are likely to happen in the areas where people are active and not simply in the areas where their residence is registered. With this in mind we have designed a new variable, namely *daytime population* which is the sum of the *workplace population* (described in the previous section) with residents younger than 16 and older than 74 year old. This aims to provide a proxy to the number of people active at a geographic area during working hours. Figure 3 shows the distribution of this feature geographically. Note that the colour scale is different from the previous plot showing residential population levels, with the

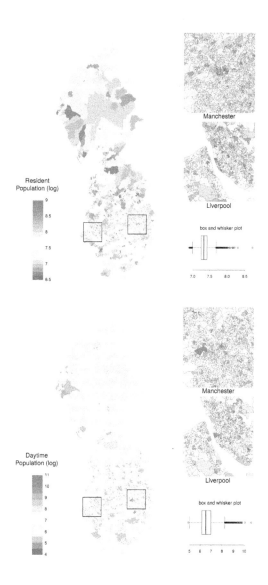

Figure 3: (a) Choropleth map and box-and-whisker plot of (log of) resident population size. (b) Choropleth map and box-and-whisker plot of (log of) daytime population size.

primarily to operations within the health service (e.g. transfering patients to a hospital with more beds) and not to epidemiological traces we are interested in in the present work.

Figure 2 shows the pearson's r correlation scores between the frequencies of all calls (Total Calls) per LSOA and the most frequent incident types (dispatch codes). A higher correlation score between two incident types implies a higher chance of them co-occuring spatially. *breathing problems* and *chest pain* correspond to one of the most related pairs (pearson's $r = 0.82$). As suggested by a correlation score of $r > 0.83$, *overdose/poisoning* related incidents are more likely to associate with the occurrence of *psychiatric/suicide*, *convulsion/seizuers* and *unconscioous/fainting* cases. *breathing problems* are more associated with *chest pain* incidents and *sick person* cases. These figures already indicate that different geographic areas

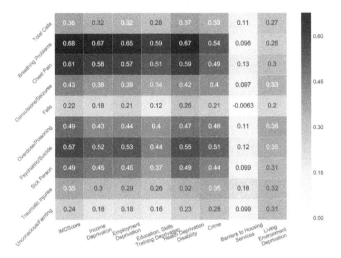

Figure 5: Correlation matrix reporting pearson's r correlation scores between variables describing medical incidents attended by ambulances and a number of socio-economic indicators.

range of daytime population being rather larger; from 132 in West Cumbria to 42357 in the City Centre of Manchester. Some areas of relatively low resident population have a much higher working population, with the reverse also being a possibility. Daytime and residential populations capture different temporal instances of population whereabouts and as we demonstrate in the following paragraphs are both important to estimating calls to the ambulance service. The daytime population levels appears to be a much more important indicator to residential population levels as noted by the corresponding pearson's r with the total number of calls ($r = 0.68$ for daytime population versus 0.18 for residential). Daytime population is strongly associated with the frequency of *unconscious/fainting* incidents ($r = 0.72$), which are followed closely by *traumatic injuries* ($r = 0.68$), *convulsions/seizures* $r = 0.65$) and *falls* ($r = 0.58$). In terms of how different age group resident numbers explain ambulance call variations, the age group 25-44 sticks out as the one that contributes consistently across different incident types (for most cases we have an $r > 0.3$), with young kids of age 0-4 being associated to breathing problem related incidents ($r = 0.44$) and the number of older people being the group mostly associated with *falls* (pearson's $r = 0.3$), in line with previous studies that have associated this age group with higher fall risk due to the presence of specific risk factors (e.g. weakness, unsteady gait, confusion and certain medications) [23].

4.3 Socio-economic indicators

We now investigate the relationship, between the index of multiple deprivation (IMD), the seven constituent metrics that it is comprised of and the frequencies and types of calls per LSOA. The pearson correlation scores between the different pairs of variables is shown in Figure 5. The Index of Multiple Deprivation (IMD) scores a pearson's r of 0.68 with respect to *breathing problems* which is the most highly correlated incident type, followed by *chest pain* incidents

$r = 0.61$ and *psychiatric/suicide* incidents ($r = 0.57$). While the overall index provides a general notion of the deprivation levels of an area, its constituent metrics can shed light on the more specific factors that relate to ambulance calls. Income, employment, health and crime deprivation correlate highly with the incidents types noted above. Note that interestingly, the IMD score of an area does not yield an as high correlation score when considering other types of incidents such as *falls, traumatic injuries* or *fainting*. These results highlight how population in deprived areas are essentially more likely to suffer a serious medical condition, perhaps due to lack of access to preemptive care and lifestyle related factors. Links between deprivation of living standards have been identified before in the literature [1, 15, 25] with reported correlation score values in the range of 0.4 − 0.5 across large geographic regions at national scale. Here we demonstrate that the link between deprivation and population health not only persists in smaller geographic scales, but in this case the geographic divide that exists amongst regions becomes larger.

4.4 Digital traces of human mobility

With the goal of understanding to what extent mobile web proxies of human urban activity such as Foursquare could capture geographic variations in ambulance calls we visualise the two sources of data in Manchester in Figure 6. For a set of LSOAs in the center of the city, we plot the predominant categories of calls and check-ins respectively. Distinctive geographical patterns of the types of incidents can be observed for both cities, with *unconscious/fainting* being the predominant epidemiological trend in the dense urban cores, whereas other types of emergencies are more characteristic of the peripheral areas. With comparison to human activity as derived from Foursquare check-ins, we can also note some activities which are more typical for the core as opposed to the periphery of the city such as *nightlife* and *shopping*.

We further quantify these relationships in Figure 7, where a correlation matrix of call types and check-in types is presented for the whole North West region whereas the ambulance service operates. We notice that specific types of human activity tend to be associated with particular calls on the small-scale of LSOAs. For example, the most common type of activity associated with the total number of calls is *professional* places. *breathing problems* tend to be called in areas with a high number of *shopping* and *food* check-ins, similar to *chest pain*. Cases of *convulsions/seizures* are mostly associated with *food, nightlife, shops* and work environments, as well as cases of *falls, overdose/poisoning, traumatic injuries* and reports of *sick person*. To a lesser extent, travel and outdoor activities were also related to such cases. However, the highest correlations found were between the *food* and *nightlife* categories and calls related to loss of consciousness (Pearson's $r = 0.72$ and $r = 0.67$ respectively). Overall, most types activities correlate with the *unconscious* category of calls to a varying extent which was most expressed in dense urban centers where most calls are made (see Figure 1).

5 PREDICTING AMBULANCE CALLS

Our aim next becomes to predict the number of ambulance calls for each location by considering a set of the variables discussed in the previous section in an ordinary least squares (OLS) linear

Figure 6: Most common types of health incidents in central Manchester (top) and Liverpool (bottom) visually compared with the most popular categories in terms of number of check-ins in the same area. Areas with no check-in activity are colored in grey.

regression model. Formally, given an area i and then the number of calls that originated from the area, y_i is set to be approximated by the linear following relationship:

$$y_i = \mathbf{x_i}^T \beta + \epsilon_i \tag{1}$$

where x_i represents a predictor variable, and where β is a $p\times 1$ vector of unknown parameters where p is the number of input variables. ϵ_i in this setting are unobserved scalar random variables (errors) which account for the discrepancy between the actually observed responses y_i and the predicted outcomes. To alleviate colinearity effects we have not used variables that are inherently related (e.g. age group frequencies and residential population). All variables have been standardized by substracting the corresponding mean and dividing by the standard deviation. As a metric of assessment

for the prediction task we use the adjusted R^2 which provides an indication of how much of the variance is explained by the model compared to the total variance of variable y taking into account the number of independent variables. Overall, we examine ten prediction tasks, one for the overall number of calls in an area, and one for each of the nine most popular incidents types.

Evaluation results. In Table 4 we present the coefficients of the variables of the linear regression models built for four out of ten prediction tasks considered. The adjusted R^2 values are considerably high in most cases with an $R^2 = 0.702$ being achieved when the total number of calls is considered as the dependent variable. The model attains an $R^2 = 0.645$ for *breathing problems* and for cases of *chest pain* and *sick person* incidents the values of R^2 remained above 0.6. The lowest number was recorded for the cases of *falls* with an $R^2 =$

All Calls: $AdjR^2 = 0.702$

	coef	std err	t	P>|t|
IMDScore	0.0784	0.003	24.563	0.000
Checkins	0.2369	0.025	9.547	0.000
DayPop	0.8359	0.022	37.676	0.000
Resdnts	0.0989	0.013	7.514	0.000
CmmnlRs	0.0311	0.023	1.347	0.178
AvHshlS	-0.0413	0.010	-4.199	0.000
Hectars	-0.0392	0.011	-3.647	0.000

Breathing problems: $AdjR^2 = 0.645$

	coef	std err	t	P>|t|
IMDScore	0.3077	0.005	57.846	0.000
Checkins	-0.0095	0.042	-0.229	0.819
DayPop	0.7904	0.037	21.292	0.000
Resdnts	0.4577	0.022	20.920	0.000
CmmnlRs	-0.2449	0.039	-6.339	0.000
AvHshlS	-0.1286	0.016	-7.858	0.000
Hectars	-0.1677	0.018	-9.433	0.000

Chest Pain: $AdjR^2 = 0.645$

	coef	std err	t	P>|t|
IMDScore	0.2096	0.004	49.674	0.000
Checkins	0.1346	0.033	4.084	0.000
DayPop	0.8262	0.029	28.055	0.000
Resdnts	0.3181	0.017	18.328	0.000
CmmnlRs	-0.1038	0.031	-3.386	0.001
AvHshlS	-0.0779	0.013	-6.002	0.000
Hectars	-0.0764	0.014	-5.414	0.000

Convulsions: $AdjR^2 = 0.645$

	coef	std err	t	P>|t|
IMDScore	0.0958	0.003	33.775	0.000
Checkins	0.4229	0.022	19.101	0.000
DayPop	0.6123	0.020	30.940	0.000
Resdnts	0.0874	0.012	7.495	0.000
CmmnlRs	0.0443	0.021	2.151	0.032
AvHshlS	-0.0560	0.008	-6.929	0.000
Hectars	-0.0378	0.009	-3.986	0.000

Falls: $AdjR^2 = 0.448$

	coef	std err	t	P>|t|
IMDScore	0.0358	0.004	9.335	0.000
Checkins	0.2065	0.030	6.901	0.000
DayPop	0.6573	0.027	24.576	0.000
Resdnts	0.1099	0.016	6.970	0.000
CmmnlRs	-0.0283	0.028	-1.018	0.309
AvHshlS	-0.2200	0.012	-18.658	0.000
Hectars	-0.0278	0.013	-2.170	0.030

Overdose: $AdjR^2 = 0.616$

	coef	std err	t	P>|t|
IMDScore	0.0867	0.002	36.193	0.000
Checkins	0.4574	0.019	24.476	0.000
DayPop	0.2700	0.017	16.166	0.000
Resdnts	0.0872	0.010	8.849	0.000
CmmnlRs	0.0916	0.017	5.270	0.000
AvHshlS	-0.0884	0.007	-11.999	0.000
Hectars	-0.0409	0.008	-5.108	0.000

Psychiatric: $AdjR^2 = 0.553$

	coef	std err	t	P>|t|
IMDScore	0.1766	0.004	40.795	0.000
Checkins	0.2215	0.034	6.555	0.000
DayPop	0.5762	0.030	19.083	0.000
Resdnts	0.2015	0.018	11.309	0.000
CmmnlRs	0.0103	0.031	0.328	0.743
AvHshlS	-0.1679	0.013	-12.604	0.000
Hectars	-0.0923	0.014	-6.385	0.000

Sick person: $AdjR^2 = 0.609$

	coef	std err	t	P>|t|
IMDScore	0.1414	0.004	35.303	0.000
Checkins	0.4558	0.031	14.579	0.000
DayPop	0.6434	0.028	23.028	0.000
Resdnts	0.2833	0.016	17.207	0.000
CmmnlRs	-0.0639	0.029	-2.198	0.028
AvHshlS	-0.1747	0.012	-14.186	0.000
Hectars	-0.1063	0.013	-7.947	0.000

Traumatic injuries: $AdjR^2 = 0.618$

	coef	std err	t	P>|t|
IMDScore	0.0914	0.004	25.758	0.000
Checkins	0.4481	0.028	16.175	0.000
DayPop	0.8070	0.025	32.593	0.000
Resdnts	0.1253	0.015	8.582	0.000
CmmnlRs	0.1084	0.026	4.210	0.000
AvHshlS	-0.0607	0.011	-5.559	0.000
Hectars	0.0335	0.012	2.825	0.005

Unconscious: $AdjR^2 = 0.685$

	coef	std err	t	P>|t|
IMDScore	0.0371	0.002	17.467	0.000
Checkins	0.5552	0.017	33.448	0.000
DayPop	0.4430	0.015	29.865	0.000
Resdnts	0.0445	0.009	5.095	0.000
CmmnlRs	0.0372	0.015	2.409	0.016
AvHshlS	-0.0496	0.007	-7.590	0.000
Hectars	-0.0211	0.007	-2.972	0.003

Table 4: Summary of linear regression results.

0.447 whereas the rest of the incident types were predicted with values above 0.5. In all cases, with the sole exception of breathing problems the Foursquare variable (check-ins) corresponded to a statistically significant case and in all such cases the sign of the variable was positive implying that a higher number of check-ins in an area is in general associated with a higher number of calls.

To assess the importance of the different information signals in explaining the variance of different types of incidents we run the

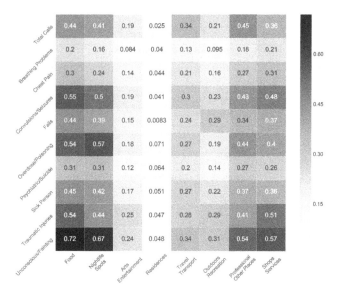

Figure 7: Correlation matrix reporting Pearson's r scores between Foursquare categories and frequent types of medical incidents.

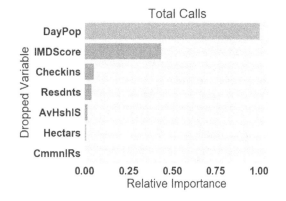

Figure 8: Relative importance of variables to the prediction of the total number of calls.

following experiment. For each incident type, we removed each of the variables and measured the reduction in R^2. To obtain then the *relative importance* of a variable we simply measured the reduction in R^2 associated to it with respect to the maximum reduction attained by any of the variables. The barplot in Figure 8 show the relative importance of each predictor for the total number of calls, whereas in Figure 9 we plot the results for all nine types of incidents. Notably, the index of multiple deprivation appears to be the most important variable in the majority of cases with *daytime* population explaining best *falls* and *traumatic injuries* cases. Foursquare check-ins correspond to the third most important variable when considering the total number of calls, whereas for incidents of *unconscious/fainting* it becomes the most important indicator. An explanation for the performance of the Foursquare variable is the

fact that most *unconscious/fainting* incidents occur in the city centers and the service's usage patterns tend to be associated with activity in commercial, food and nightlife areas. Its importance for the *overdose/poisoning* case of incidents where it scores higher even than *daytime* population activity points in this direction.

6 CONCLUSION

Our results highlight the opportunity that arises from using data from online media sources and the mobile web to power the operation of medical services critical for citizens. Limitations in using such data sources in the present context relate to biases in mobile application usage patterns amongst others. Daytime population levels have been an important predictor of ambulance calls and a clear improvement to simply using residential population information, yet it still represents a static signal about the activity levels of an area. Populations fluctuate constantly and so a promising future direction would be to exploit real time digital datasets from location-based services to model medical incident activity not only across geographies, but also over time. The importance of deprivation indicators in explaining geographic variations of ambulance calls provide an additional reminder of the large divides that exist in our society. Providing evidence through data driven analysis of population activity and government collected socio-economic indicators as we have done in the present work is an important step to bridge this gap by informing relevant policies.

REFERENCES

[1] S. Bernard and L. K. Smith. 1998. Emergency Admissions of Older People to Hospital: A Link with Material Deprivation. *Journal of Public Health* 20, 1 (March 1998), 97–101. https://doi.org/10.1093/oxfordjournals.pubmed.a024727

[2] M W Carter and S D Lapierre. 2001. Scheduling emergency room physicians. *Health Care Management Science* (2001).

[3] R Chetty, M Stepner, S Abraham, S Lin, B Scuderi, N Turner, A Bergeron, and D Cutler. 2016. The association between income and life expectancy in the United States, 2001-2014. *Jama* 315, 16 (2016), 1750–1766.

[4] S Cockings, A Harfoot, D Martin, and D Hornby. 2011. Maintaining existing zoning systems using automated zone-design techniques: methods for creating the 2011 Census output geographies for England and Wales. *Environment and Planning A* 43, 10 (2011), 2399–2418.

[5] M De Choudhury and S De. 2014. Mental Health Discourse on reddit: Self-Disclosure, Social Support, and Anonymity.. In *ICWSM*.

[6] M De Choudhury, E Kiciman, M Dredze, G Coppersmith, and M Kumar. 2016. Discovering shifts to suicidal ideation from mental health content in social media. In *Proceedings of the 2016 CHI Conference on Human Factors in Computing Systems*. ACM, 2098–2110.

[7] PJ Diggle and PJ Ribeiro. 2007. *Model-Based Geostatistics*. Springer.

[8] P. Diggle, B. Rowlingson, and T. Su. 2005. Point process methodology for on-line spatio-temporal disease surveillance. *Environmetrics* 16, 5 (2005), 423–434.

[9] A S Fotheringham, C Brunsdon, and M Charlton. 2000. *Quantitative geography: perspectives on spatial data analysis*. Sage.

[10] A C Gatrell, T C Bailey, P J Diggle, and B S Rowlingson. 1996. Spatial point pattern analysis and its application in geographical epidemiology. *Transactions of the Institute of British geographers* (1996).

[11] Garth N Graham. 2016. Why Your ZIP Code Matters More Than Your Genetic Code: Promoting Healthy Outcomes from Mother to Child. *Breastfeeding Medicine* 11, 8 (2016), 396–397.

[12] D Hristova, M J Williams, M Musolesi, P Panzarasa, and Cecilia Mascolo. 2016. Measuring Urban Social Diversity Using Interconnected Geo-Social Networks. In *Proceedings of the 25th International Conference on World Wide Web*. International World Wide Web Conferences Steering Committee, 21–30.

[13] D Jones, S Bates, S Warrillow, H Opdam, D Goldsmith, G Gutteridge, and R Bellomo. 2005. Circadian pattern of activation of the medical emergency team in a teaching hospital. *Critical Care* 9, 4 (2005), 1.

[14] D Lazer, R Kennedy, G King, and A Vespignani. 2014. The parable of Google Flu: traps in big data analysis. *Science* 343, 6176 (2014), 1203–1205.

[15] G McCartney, C Hart, and G Watt. 2013. How Can Socioeconomic Inequalities in Hospital Admissions Be Explained? A Cohort Study. *BMJ Open* 3, 8 (Aug. 2013),

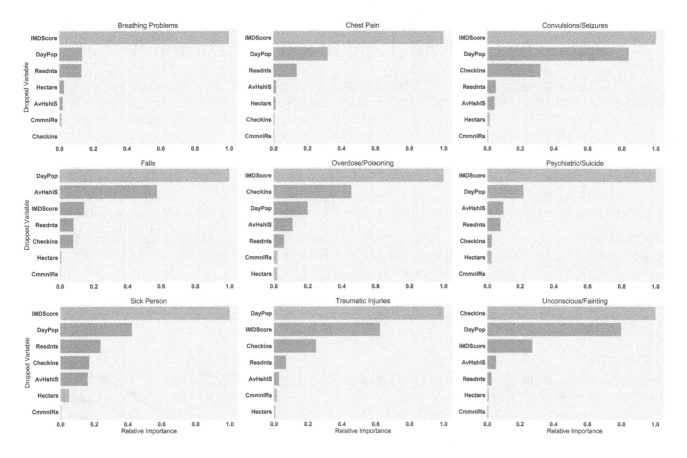

Figure 9: Relative importance of variables to the prediction for different types incidents.

e002433. https://doi.org/10.1136/bmjopen-2012-002433

[16] Y Mejova, H Haddadi, A Noulas, and I Weber. 2015. # FoodPorn: Obesity patterns in culinary interactions. In *Proceedings of the 5th International Conference on Digital Health 2015*. ACM, 51–58.

[17] J Møller, A R Syversveen, and R P Waagepetersen. 1998. Log gaussian cox processes. *Scandinavian journal of statistics* 25, 3 (1998), 451–482.

[18] M Noble, G Wright, G Smith, and C Dibben. 2006. Measuring Multiple Deprivation at the Small-Area Level. *Environment and Planning A* 38, 1 (Jan. 2006), 169–185. https://doi.org/10.1068/a37168

[19] A O'cathain, E Knowles, R Maheswaran, T Pearson, J Turner, E Hirst, S Goodacre, and J Nicholl. 2013. A system-wide approach to explaining variation in potentially avoidable emergency admissions: national ecological study. *BMJ Qual Saf* (2013), bmjqs-2013.

[20] M EH Ong, F SP Ng, J Overton, S Yap, D Andresen, D KL Yong, S Lim, and V Anantharaman. 2009. Geographic-time distribution of ambulance calls in Singapore: utility of geographic information system in ambulance deployment (CARE 3). *Annals Academy of Medicine Singapore* (2009).

[21] Michael J Paul, Abeed Sarker, John S Brownstein, Azadeh Nikfarjam, Matthew Scotch, Karen L Smith, and Graciela Gonzalez. 2016. Social media mining for public health monitoring and surveillance. In *Biocomputing 2016: Proceedings of the Pacific Symposium*. 468–479.

[22] P J Peacock and J L Peacock. 2006. Emergency call work-load, deprivation and population density: an investigation into ambulance services across England. *Journal of Public Health* 28, 2 (2006), 111–115.

[23] L Z Rubenstein. 2006. Falls in older people: epidemiology, risk factors and strategies for prevention. *Age and ageing* 35, suppl_2 (2006), ii37–ii41.

[24] S Servia-Rodríguez, K K Rachuri, C Mascolo, PJ Rentfrow, N Lathia, and Gillian M Sandstrom. 2017. Mobile sensing at the service of mental well-being: a large-scale longitudinal study. In *Proceedings of the 26th International Conference on World Wide Web*. International World Wide Web Conferences Steering Committee, 103–112.

[25] T. Smith. 1992. The Relative Effects of Sex and Deprivation on the Risk of Early Death. *Journal of Public Health Medicine* 14, 4 (Dec. 1992), 402–407. WOS:A1992KE30000010.

[26] John Snow. 1855. *On the mode of communication of cholera*. John Churchill.

[27] ML Stein. 2012. *Interpolation of spatial data: some theory for kriging*. Springer Science & Business Media.

Using Mathematical Modeling to Simulate Chagas Disease Spread by Congenital and Blood Transfusion Routes

Edneide Ramalho
UFRPE
Recife, PE, Brazil
edneide.ramalho@gmail.com

Daniel López Codina
UPC
Castelldefels, Spain
daniel.lopez-codina@upc.edu

Clara Prats
UPC
Castelldefels, Spain
clara.prats@upc.edu

Claudio Cristino
UFRPE
Recife, Brazil
ctcristino@deinfo.ufrpe.br

Virginia Lorena
FIOCRUZ
Recife, PE, Brazil
lorena@cpcam.fiocruz.br

Jones Albuquerque
UFRPE/LIKA-UFPE
Recife, PE, Brazil
jones.albuquerque@pq.cnpq.br

ABSTRACT

Chagas disease is an important health problem in Latin America. Due to the mobility of Latin American population, the disease has spread to other countries. In this work, we used a mathematical model to gain insight into the disease dynamics in a scenario without vector presence as well as to assess the epidemiological effects provided by control strategies.

KEYWORDS

Chagas disease; mathematical modeling; simulation; blood transfusion transmission; congenital transmission

ACM Reference Format:
Edneide Ramalho, Daniel López Codina, Clara Prats, Claudio Cristino, Virginia Lorena, and Jones Albuquerque. 2018. Using Mathematical Modeling to Simulate Chagas Disease Spread by Congenital and Blood Transfusion Routes. In *DH'18: 2018 International Digital Health Conference, April 23–26, 2018, Lyon, France*. ACM, New York, NY, USA, 1 page. https://doi.org/10.1145/3194658.3194661

1 INTRODUCTION

According to the World Health Organization, around 8 million people are infected by Chagas world-wide. Around 30-40% of infected people develop cardiomyopathy, digestive megasyndromes, or both. Demographic data of Spain were used on simulations because it is the European country which hosts more Latin Americans immigrants and possible diseases carriers. As there is no vector presence, the only transmission routes are by congenital transmission or by blood transfusion.

2 MATERIALS AND METHODS

We introduce a deterministic compartmental model for Chagas transmission distinguishing people from countries with and without vector presence, as well as men and women to take into account

the vertical transmission. Consequently, population was classified into eight compartments.

3 RESULTS

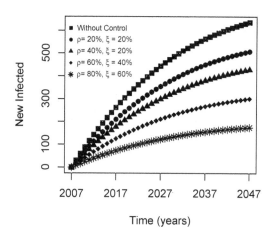

Figure 1: Epidemiological effect of control strategies. ρ: proportion of treatment in infected newborns and, ξ: effective surveillance in blood transfusion.

4 CONCLUSIONS

Mathematical models can be used as valuable tools to explore different scenarios and to justify decision making in public health policies for control and treatment of the disease.

ACKNOWLEDGMENTS

The first author would like to thank CAPES (Coordenação de Aperfeiçoamento de Pessoal de Nível Superior) for the scholarship (88881.133410/2016-01).

Hearts and Politics: Metrics for Tracking Biorhythm Changes during Brexit and Trump

Luca Maria Aiello
Nokia Bell Labs
luca.aiello@nokia-bell-labs.com

Daniele Quercia
Nokia Bell Labs
quercia@cantab.net

Eva Roitmann
Nokia
eva.roitmann@nokia.com

ABSTRACT

Our internal experience of time reflects what is going in the world around us. Our body's natural rhythms get disrupted for a variety of external factors, including exposure to collective events. We collect readings of steps, sleep, and heart rates from 11K users of health tracking devices in London and San Francisco. We introduce measures to quantify changes in not only volume of these three bio-signals (as previous research has done) but also synchronicity and periodicity, and we empirically assess how strong those variations are, compared to random expectation, during four major events: Christmas, New Year's Eve, Brexit, and the US presidential election of 2016 (Donald Trump's election). While Christmas and New Year's eve are associated with short-term effects, Brexit and Trump's election are associated with longer-term disruptions. Our results promise to inform the design of new ways of monitoring population health at scale.

ACM Reference Format:
Luca Maria Aiello, Daniele Quercia, and Eva Roitmann. 2018. Hearts and Politics: Metrics for Tracking Biorhythm Changes during Brexit and Trump. In *DH'18: 2018 International Digital Health Conference, April 23–26, 2018, Lyon, France*. ACM, New York, NY, USA, 6 pages. https://doi.org/10.1145/3194658.3194678

1 INTRODUCTION

Our body pulses in cycles: we sleep or waken, are hungry or full, are alert or tired. The most dominant period in a person's rhythms is the circadian cycle. Major departures from the normal range of the period have been associated with endogenous factors (e.g., illness) or exogenous ones (e.g., an external event inducing fear). Previous work has explored the relationship between circadian cycles and external factors, linking prolonged disruption of rhythms to pathological conditions, including cancer [18, 21]. Nowadays, "the alternation of sleep and walking and all the bodily cycles attendant on those states" [13] can be measured based on the use of social media [1, 6, 25], of augmented-reality games [3, 9], and, more reliably, of activity trackers [2, 19].

Yet, previous research has rarely ventured into: *i)* studying activity metrics beyond their volume; and *ii)* linking these metrics'

changes to global events. This study aims at exploring these two aspects for the first time, and it does so by relying on large-scale data collected data from Nokia Health monitoring devices used by 11,600 customers who live in London (67% of users) and San Francisco (33%) over the course of 1 year (from 1st April 2016 to 30th April 2017). Our users are 44% female, and their median age is 42 years. All users opted-in for research studies, and their data has been processed in an anonymized form. We consider three types of *activities*: total number of *steps* walked during the day; *sleep duration* measured in number of minutes slept at night; the estimated *sleep time* when the user went to bed for the night (hour and minutes, adjusted for timezone); and the average *heart rate* (beats per minute) measured once per day. Steps and sleep are measured by Nokia Health devices (e.g., former Withings wristbands and smart watches). All activities are measured at daily level for each user. For heart rates, when multiple measurements are available on the same day, we average them out. Our users represent a sample of the larger user population and are selected based on the number of days they used their devices: indeed, to reduce sparsity, we consider users who, for at least 90% of the days, measured their heart rates. This leaves us with 3.8M+ daily activity summaries.

By drawing from previous physiological and psychological studies, we derive metrics that relate walking, sleeping, and heartbeat to well-being. We characterize those three activities in terms of their *volume* (the raw value of the signal over time, §2), *synchronicity* (the degree to which the cycles of different people are in phase, §3) and *rhythm* (the activity periodicity, §4). We show how these metrics vary over the entire year, and how such variations represent distinctive signatures for four collective events: Christmas, New Year's Eve, Brexit, and the US election of 2016. We find that users slept more than usual during the Christmas period and, as one expects, slept less than usual during Brexit, the US election, and New Year's eve. Brexit and the US election are also associated with long-term disruptions in two main ways. First, in terms of sleeping patterns: users became heavily out-of-sync in the weeks after Brexit and even more so after the US election. Second, in terms of heart rates, we found major shifts in rhythm and volume, especially in the months around the US presidential election. These results suggest that our three metrics effectively capture how our biorhythms change during large-scale events, opening up new ways of monitoring population health at scale[1].

2 VOLUME

The amount of steps, hours of sleep and the dynamics behind heart rates have all been related to health outcomes. Physical activity boosts the levels of immune cells, and that results in a considerable reduction of sick days – from children to elderlies [15]. Sleep

---

[1]Additional material is on http://goodcitylife.org/health

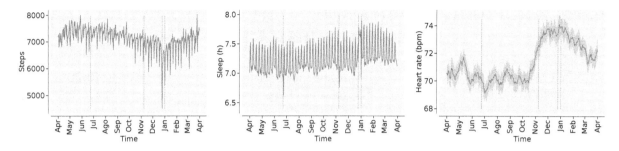

Figure 1: Daily average number of steps, hours slept, and heart rate (with 95% confidence interval). The dates of the following four events are marked by horizontal lines (left to right): the Brexit referendum, the US presidential election, Christmas and New Year's Eve.

deprivation has been found to make people accident-prone on the road, unproductive at work [27], and subject to brain aging [8, 27]. Sleep deprivation also increases the chances of ailments such as hypertension [23], cancer [5], diabetes, and obesity [16], and, as such, increases mortality rates [7]. In this work, to capture the amount of steps, sleep, and heart rates, given the measurement of an activity A (e.g., steps), we denote the activity of user u on day t with $A_u(t)$, and compute the average activity during day t at population level as $\overline{A}(t) = \frac{\sum_{u \in U} A_u(t)}{|U|}$.

In Figure 1, we plot the average daily number of steps, hours of sleep, and heart rates for the whole year. The plots of steps and hours of sleep are spiky, and that comes from our typical weekly patterns: during weekends, people usually walk less and sleep more. Some of the spikes are much more prominent than the others though, and correspond to four major events (marked with dashed lines in the plots): the "Brexit" referendum in which the UK electorate voted to leave the EU on the 23th of June 2016, the US presidential election on the 8th of November 2016, and Christmas and New Year's Eve of the same year. For steps (first plot in Figure 1), there are two low points, which correspond to Christmas and New Year's Eve. For hours of sleep (second plot), there are three low points, which correspond to Brexit, the US election, and New Year's Eve. Finally, for heart rates (third plot), there are a few peaks and low points but they are limited – the most remarkable trend is represented by a considerable collective increase of heart rate just around the US election. These results might suggest that increases in heart rates are in a cause-and-effect relationship with the US election. However, before considering causation, we need to rule out alternative explanations:

New users. If new users are suddenly introduced in the sample, heart rate volume could increase. That does not apply to our case since, for the whole duration of the year, we study the very same set of users whose heart rate is monitored almost continuously throughout the year (90%+ of the days).

Software/hardware update. Device and software updates might impact measurements. During the year of observation, our devices' software that measured heart rates did not change, and all measurements showed high consistency.

Physical Activity. Heart rates could increase as a result of increased physical activity. However, there was no substantial change in daily number of steps at the time of the US election (a person did, on

average, 6794 steps a day in October, 6750 in November, and 6660 in December).

Temperature. In cold weather, to keep the body warm, the heart beats faster. The temperature in the months concerning the US election was stable (Figure 2D), ruling out temperature as co-founding factor. *Seasonality.* People's rhythms are seasonal [1]. However the observed heart rate increases are steady and are not seasonal. If they were, given the comparable weather conditions (Figure 1), the heart rate levels in April 2016 would be the comparable to those in April 2017 – but they are not.

Upon observational data, it is hard to argue what caused heart rate increases. However, the strongest association appears to be with the US election, and that is because of three main reasons:

(i) Alternative Explanations. We have just ruled out the most plausible explanations other than the US election.

(ii) External Validity. Increases in heart rates have been found to be associated with emotional regulation and stress [10, 22, 24]. It should come as no surprise that the US election *caused* (self-reported) stress in a considerable part of the electorate. Based on a representative sample on 1,000+ US residents, a survey commissioned by the American Psychological Association found that more than half of the interviewees experienced the political climate around the presidential campaign as a significant source of stress [4].

(iii) Dose-response relationships. Dose-response patterns on observational data are necessary (but not sufficient) for considering causation. In our case, we indeed observe that events are strongly linked to biorhythm responses. To see how, contrast Londoners with San Franciscans: San Franciscans experienced rapid heart rate increases the last two months of the US political campaign (Figure 2C), experienced a peak exactly on the election day, and slept the least during the US election night (Figure 2B); by contrast, Londoners slept less the night after Brexit (Figure 2A), and started to experience heart rate increases on the US election day (Figure 2C), suggesting that their response was shifted compared to the US counterpart, as one expects. Therefore, dose-response relationships are observed for both the US election and Brexit.

3 SYNCHRONICITY

So far we have captured the volume of steps, hours slept, and heart rates. To go beyond volume, we now focus on temporal patterns.

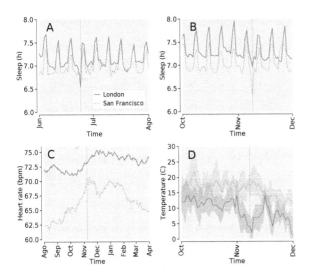

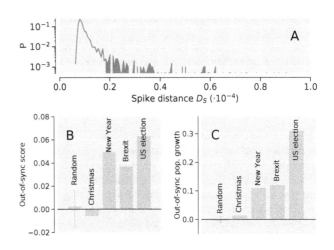

Figure 2: (A) Number of hours slept in the weeks around Brexit. (B) Number of hours slept for the US presidential election. (C) Average heart rate around the US presidential election. (D) Temperature changes for the US presidential election (the average temperature curve is enclosed within the *min* and *max* curves).

Figure 3: (A) Frequency distribution of the spike distance D_S over the whole population during the full year. The tail (the set of points that are 2 standard deviations away from the median) is marked with a solid blue area under the curve. (B) Out-Of-Sync score (OOS) for the four events plus the random model computed with a 95% confidence interval. (C) Out-Of-Sync population growth ($OOS^\uparrow$) for the four events plus the random model computed with a 95% confidence interval.

The timing of behavior has always been a strong expression of the style of individuals and entire populations [13]. Nowadays that timing can be reliably captured by smart devices. Our sleep data, for example, includes the time at which users go to bed every day. This can be interpreted as an ordered sequence of timestamps, which is also called *spike train*. For the purpose of this study, we are interested in measuring the degree of synchronization between two users, that is, between two spike trains $s_1 = \{t_1^{(1)}, ..., t_n^{(1)}\}$ and $s_2 = \{t_1^{(2)}, ..., t_m^{(2)}\}$, within an interval $[0, T]$ of, say, one year. The SPIKE-distance function D_S provides a parameter-free way of doing that [14]. It is defined as the integration of an instantaneous spike function $S(t)$ over time: $D_S(0, T) = \frac{1}{T} \int_0^T S(t)dt \in [0, 1]$.

The spike function at time t is defined as:

$$S(t) = \frac{|\Delta t_P(t)| \cdot \langle x_F^{(n)}(t) \rangle_n + |\Delta t_F(t)| \cdot \langle x_P^{(n)}(t) \rangle_n}{\langle ISI \rangle_n} \quad (1)$$

where $\Delta t_P(t)$ is the difference between the two spikes $t_P^{(1)}(t)$ and $t_P^{(2)}(t)$ that immediately precede time t in the two trains; $\Delta t_F(t)$ is the difference between the spikes following t; $x_P^{(n)}(t)$ is the distance between t and the previous spike in the nth train; $ISI^{(n)}$ is the mean inter-spike interval in the nth train; and $\langle \bullet \rangle_n$ denotes the average over the two trains. When $D_S = 0$, the two trains have no distance between them, meaning that their spikes are perfectly synchronized; when $D_S = 1$, the two trains are completely out-of-phase. The formulation of D_S for the bivariate distance (for 2 users) can be extended to a multivariate case (for 2+ users) by averaging the distances of all the pairs of spike trains in the set. We compute that quantity and denote it with $\overline{D_S}$.

Each user's sleep patterns for the entire year have been converted into a spike train. This consists of the sequences of times at which the user went to sleep. The level of de-synchronization in the population is then computed as the average spike distance score $\overline{D_S}$ over all user pairs. Even if theoretically bounded in $[0, 1]$, the D_S variable takes values from 0 to 10^{-4} in our data (Figure 3A). That is because $\overline{D_S}$ is quite low for events influenced by exogenous events (e.g., it is rare to find a considerable number of people who sleep in the middle of the afternoon). To quantify the extent to which synchronization changes after each of our four events, we compare the average spike distance $\overline{D_S}$ over all user pairs in the week before the event, and in the week after the event. More formally, we define the *Out-Of-Sync score* (OOS) of an event e occurring at time t as $OOS_{e@t} = \overline{D_S}(t, t + \alpha) - \overline{D_S}(t - \alpha, t)$,

where t is the time of event e, and α is a buffer time window, which, in our case, we set to be of one week. If the event's score is above zero, then this means that, after the event, the population became, on average, less synchronized. If it is below zero, then the population became more synchronized. To make sure that an event's score is not due to chance, we contrast it to a null/random model, that is, we contrast it to what the score would be if computed at random days. More specifically, we compute OOS with α of one week at 100 random days along the whole year, obtaining 100 scores. We then average those scores out to obtain the random model's score, which is supposed to be zero. By definition, the accuracy of the D_S measure (and, consequently, that of OOS) suffers in the presence of missing data points, which is the case for our data, since our devices are not perfectly reliable. As such, to get robust measurements, we filter out all users whose spike trains are not complete in the weeks before each event, and in the weeks after it.

This step turns out to exclude at most a few hundred individuals for each event.

After this filtering, we compute the out-of-synch scores OOS. We find that, at random days, the scores are close to 0, as one expects. By contrast, the scores are subject to changes during three of our four events. More specifically, they do not change in a statistically significant way during Christmas, but they do considerably change during New Year's Eve, Brexit, and the US election, suggesting that several users became out-of-sync after these three events (Figure 3B). To quantify the fraction of the population who slipped considerably out-of-sync after each event, we consider the frequency distribution of out-of-sync scores (Figure 3A): its right tail represents those user pairs who are heavily out-of-sync with each other. Using a standard practice in outlier identification [12], we consider all the points that are at least 2 standard deviations (2σ) higher than the median ($\tilde{\mu}$) as outliers: $\text{outliers}(D_S(t, t + \alpha)) = \int_{\tilde{\mu}+2\sigma}^{1} f_{D_S(t,t+\alpha)}(x)dx$,

where α is the considered time window (i.e., one week), and f is the probability density function computed for the variable D_S in the time period $[t, t + \alpha]$. To then measure the impact of an event e, we compute the value for the previous expression of outliers() after e minus its value before e, and normalize the result:

$$OOS^{\uparrow}_{e@t} = \frac{\text{outliers}(D_S(t, t + \alpha)) - \text{outliers}(D_S(t, t - \alpha))}{\text{outliers}(D_S(t, t - \alpha))} \quad (2)$$

The resulting value is the *Out-Of-Synch population growth* ($OOS^{\uparrow}$): it is the relative increase in the portion of user pairs that are heavily out-of-sync. From Figure 3C, one sees that the value increased by 10% after New Year's Eve and Brexit, and by as much as 30% after the US election. The random baseline shows no increase.

4 RHYTHMS

As a final metric, we consider circadian rhythm. This is a roughly 24 hour cycle in the physiological processes of living beings, including humans. Although circadian rhythms are endogenous ("built-in"), they are adjusted to the local environment by external cues such as light and temperature. Disruptions in a person's circadian rhythm for sleep and heart rates have been found to have negative health consequences [20] and lead to pathological conditions [18, 21]. To see how to track circadian rhythms on our data of sleep patterns and heart rates, consider that any activity signal over time can be interpreted as a *time series*, an ordered sequence of activity measurements. To extract the period of an activity time series, one can use the Discrete Fourier Transform. This decomposes the temporal signal into a number of discrete frequencies which, if recombined, compose the original signal. The *Power Spectral Density (PSD)* is the distribution of relative power of those frequencies; we extract it using the Welch method [26]. To make the results more interpretable, we transform the frequencies of the PSD into periods (*period(PSD)*), which denote the amplitudes of the wave originated by those frequencies, expressed in number of days (e.g., a period of 7 days denotes a weekly pattern). More formally, given a user u's time series in a period $[t_1, t_2]$, we define its characteristic *rhythm* as the period with the maximum PSD value in $[t_1, t_2]$: $rhythm_u(t_1, t_2) = \arg\max(period(PSD(t_1, t_2)))$.

Our goal is to go beyond individual users and quantify the *rhythm shift* associated with an event in the entire population. To this end,

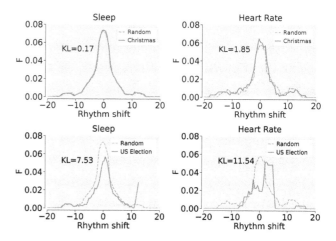

Figure 4: The frequency distributions of the rhythm shifts for sleep and heart rates after Christmas and the US presidential election. The KL-divergence between the observed distribution and the random model's is our *rhythm disruption*.

for any given event e that took place at time t, we first compute the rhythm shift an individual user u experienced before and after the event, within a temporal window α: rhythm shift$_{u, e@t}$ = $rhythm_u(t, t + \alpha) - rhythm_u(t - \alpha, t)$.

We then aggregate the rhythm shift values across all users by computing their frequency distribution $f_{\text{rhythm shift}_{e@t}}$. To make sure our shift values are not due to chance, we resort to a null/random model. We compute such model's score value by computing "rhythm shift" scores for 100 random days: we first compute *individual* shift scores around those days (rhythm shift$_{u, rand@t}$), and then compute the distribution over all users and days ($f_{\text{rhythm shift}_{rand@t}}$).

Finally, to estimate the entire population's rhythm disruption associated with e, we compare the observed distribution for e with the distribution for random days: rhythm disruption$_{e@t}$ = $D_{KL}(f_{\text{rhythm shift}_{e@t}}, f_{\text{rhythm shift}_{rand@t}})$. This is the KL divergence between the two frequency distributions [11]. The higher it is, the higher the rhythm shift that is associated with the event compared to random expectation (zero for no shift).

Figure 4 shows the distribution of rhythm shift for sleep and heart rates around Christmas and the US election. Each distribution is shown together with the corresponding null/random model's distribution, and the difference between the observed distribution and the random one (called 'rhythm disruption') is also reported and denoted with "KL". After Christmas and New Year's Eve, the shifts for both sleep and heart rates are limited. Instead, after the US election and Brexit, the shift for sleep is considerable, and that for heart rates is disruptive[2].

5 CONCLUSION

Based on all the results, one might hypothesize that each of our metrics could offer a way of profiling large-scale events. In reality,

---

[2]Due to page restrictions, we show the results for Christmas and the US election here and invite the reader to visit http://goodcitylife.org/health for more.

Event	Volume			OOS	OOS↑	Rhythm Disruption		
	Steps	Sleep	Heart	Sleep	Sleep	Steps	Sleep	Heart
Brexit	7564	6.6	69.6	$37 \cdot 10^{-3}$	12%	0.06	0.37	9.61
US	7042	6.7	70.7	$62 \cdot 10^{-3}$	32%	0.43	7.53	11.5
Christmas	4531	7.7	71.5	$-6 \cdot 10^{-3}$	10%	0.13	0.17	1.85
New Year's	5370	6.9	71.1	$49 \cdot 10^{-3}$	1%	0.12	0.17	1.64
Random	7129	7.2	71.4	$49 \cdot 10^{-3}$	0%	0.0	0.0	0.0

Table 1: Average values for each of our metrics for our four events.

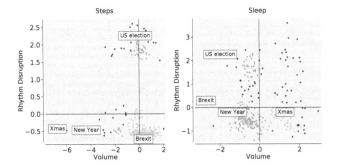

Figure 5: Clusters of the days of the year under study based on the volume and rhythm disruption for steps and sleep. Each dot corresponds to a day, and the colors encode the different (DBSCAN) clusters (black dots are outliers and, as such, do not belong to any cluster). The days in which our four main events happened are marked with labels. Values on both axes are standardized.

no individual metric considered in separation would be sufficient. For example, from Table 1, one can see that volume alone is not a reliable marker for distinguishing the four events under consideration: Brexit is indistinguishable from New Year's Eve, for instance. By contrast, considering our metrics in combination is sufficient for distinguishing the four events. Indeed, by plotting the daily average number of steps in a "rhythm disruption by volume" plot (Figure 5A), the four events are separable (i.e., they form distinctive clusters), suggesting that rhythm disruption and volume are, in our case, reliable markers for event classification. The same applies to daily average number of hours slept (Figure 5B). This is further supported by a DBSCAN clustering of those points, which returns a silhouette value (clustering quality value [17]) of ~0.35.

Taken all together, our results are very promising, yet three main limitations hold. First, our users are not representative of the general population. Second, our metrics suffer from data sparsity and, to be generalizable, they need to be furthered researched. Finally, our results do not speak to causation. Still, despite those limitations and based on the dose-response nature of the relationships between events and biorhythm measurements, we can conclude that, with our metrics at hand, one is able to capture "how we experience time" in unobtrusive ways. Synchronization and rhythms seem to be present in all living beings. They generally serve to keep the inner organisms working and keep the body coordinated with the external world. A failure of synchronization puts the body out-of-sync and under stress. Nowadays smart health trackers are able to

capture that experience, and are able to do so at an unprecedented scale.

REFERENCES

[1] Scott A Golder and Michael W Macy. 2011. Diurnal and Seasonal Mood Vary with Work, Sleep, and Daylength Across Diverse Cultures. (2011).
[2] Tim Althoff, Jennifer L Hicks, Abby C King, Scott L Delp, Jure Leskovec, et al. 2017. Large-scale physical activity data reveal worldwide activity inequality. *Nature* (2017).
[3] Tim Althoff, Ryen W White, and Eric Horvitz. 2016. Influence of Pokémon Go on physical activity: study and implications. *JMIR* (2016).
[4] Sophie Bethune and Elizabeth Lewan. 2016. *Stress in America*. Technical Report. American Psychological Association.
[5] Scott Davis, Dana Mirick, and R G Stevens. 2001. Night Shift Work, Light at Night, and Risk of Breast Cancer. (2001).
[6] Munmun De Choudhury, Mrinal Kumar, and Ingmar Weber. 2017. Computational Approaches Toward Integrating Quantified Self Sensing and Social Media. In *CSCW*. ACM.
[7] Daniel F Kripke, Lawrence Garfinkel, Deborah L Wingard, Melville R Klauber, and Matthew Marler. 2002. Mortality Associated With Sleep Duration and Insomnia. (2002).
[8] Jane Ferrie, Martin Shipley, Tasnime Akbaraly, Michael Marmot, Mika Kivimäki, and Archana Singh-Manoux. 2011. Change in Sleep Duration and Cognitive Function: Findings from the Whitehall II Study. (2011).
[9] Eduardo Graells-Garrido, Leo Ferres, Diego Caro, and Loreto Bravo. 2017. *The effect of Pokémon Go on the pulse of the city: a natural experiment*. *EPJ Data Science* (2017).
[10] Nis Hjortskov, Dag Rissén, Anne Katrine Blangsted, Nils Fallentin, Ulf Lundberg, and Karen Søgaard. 2004. The effect of mental stress on heart rate variability and blood pressure during computer work. *European Journal of Applied Physiology* (2004).
[11] S. Kullback and R. A. Leibler. 1951. On Information and Sufficiency. *Annual Mathematics and Statistics* (1951).
[12] Christophe Leys, Christophe Ley, Olivier Klein, Philippe Bernard, and Laurent Licata. 2013. Detecting outliers: Do not use standard deviation around the mean, use absolute deviation around the median. *Journal of Experimental Social Psychology* (2013).
[13] K. Lynch. 1972. *What Time is this Place?* MIT Press.
[14] Mario Mulansky, Nebojsa Bozanic, Andreea Sburlea, and Thomas Kreuz. [n. d.]. A guide to time-resolved and parameter-free measures of spike train synchrony. In *Event-based Control, Communication, and Signal Processing (EBCCSP)*. IEEE.
[15] David Nieman. 2000. Exercise effects on systemic immunity. (2000).
[16] John Reilly, J Armstrong, and A.R. Dorosty. 2005. Early life risk factors for childhood obesity: Cohort study. (2005).
[17] Peter J Rousseeuw. 1987. Silhouettes: a graphical aid to the interpretation and validation of cluster analysis. *Journal of computational and applied mathematics* (1987).
[18] Saurabh Sahar and Paolo Sassone-Corsi. 2011. Regulation of Metabolism: The Circadian Clock dictates the Time. (2011).
[19] Ali Shameli, Tim Althoff, Amin Saberi, and Jure Leskovec. 2017. How Gamification Affects Physical Activity: Large-scale Analysis of Walking Challenges in a Mobile Application. In *WWW*. ACM.
[20] Joseph Takahashi, Hee-Kyung Hong, Caroline Ko, and Erin L McDearmon. 1960. Biological Clocks in Medicine and Psychiatry: Shock-phase hypothesis. (1960).
[21] Joseph Takahashi, Hee-Kyung Hong, Caroline Ko, and Erin L McDearmon. 2008. The genetics of mammalian circadian order and disorder: implications for physiology and disease. (2008).
[22] Julian F Thayer, Fredrik Åhs, Mats Fredrikson, John J Sollers III, and Tor D Wager. 2012. A meta-analysis of heart rate variability and neuroimaging studies: implications for heart rate variability as a marker of stress and health. *Neuroscience & Biobehavioral Reviews* (2012).
[23] Céline Vetter, Elizabeth E. Devore, Lani R. Wegrzyn, Jennifer Massa, Frank Speizer, Ichiro Kawachi, Bernard Rosner, Meir J. Stampfer, and Eva Schernhammer. 2016. Association Between Rotating Night Shift Work and Risk of Coronary Heart Disease Among Women. (2016).
[24] Tanja GM Vrijkotte, Lorenz JP Van Doornen, and Eco JC De Geus. 2000. Effects of work stress on ambulatory blood pressure, heart rate, and heart rate variability. *Hypertension* (2000).
[25] Yafei Wang, Ingmar Weber, and Prasenjit Mitra. 2016. Quantified Self Meets Social Media: Sharing of Weight Updates on Twitter. In *Digital Health*. ACM.
[26] Peter Welch. 1967. The use of fast Fourier transform for the estimation of power spectra: a method based on time averaging over short, modified periodograms. *IEEE Transactions on audio and electroacoustics* (1967).
[27] R. Wiseman. 2014. *Night School: The Hidden Science of Sleep and Dreams*. Pan Macmillan.

When Less is Better: A Summarization Technique that Enhances Clinical Effectiveness of Data

P Durga*
Amrita Vishwa Vidyapeetham

Rahul Krishnan Pathinarupothi[†]
Amrita Vishwa Vidyapeetham

Ekanath Srihari Rangan[‡]
Amrita Vishwa Vidyapeetham

Prakash Ishwar[§]
Boston University

ABSTRACT

The increasing number of wearable sensors for monitoring of various vital parameters such as blood pressure (BP), blood glucose, or heart rate (HR), has opened up an unprecedented opportunity for personalized real-time monitoring and prediction of critical health conditions of patients. This, however, also poses the dual challenges of identifying clinically relevant information from vast volumes of sensor time-series data and of storing and communicating it to health-care providers especially in the context of rural areas of developing regions where communication bandwidth may be limited. One approach to address these challenges is data summarization, but the danger of losing clinically useful information makes it less appealing to medical practitioners. To overcome this, we develop a data summarization technique called RASPRO (Rapid Active Summarization for effective PROgnosis), which transforms raw sensor time-series data into a series of low bandwidth, medically interpretable symbols, called "motifs", which measure criticality and preserve clinical effectiveness benefits for patients. We evaluate the predictive power and bandwidth requirements of RASPRO on more than 16,000 minutes of patient monitoring data from a widely used open source challenge dataset. We find that RASPRO motifs have much higher clinical efficacy and efficiency (20 – 90% improvement in F1 score over bandwidths ranging from 0.2–0.75 bits/unit-time) in predicting an acute hypotensive episode (AHE) compared to Symbolic Aggregate approXimation (SAX) which is a state-of-the-art data reduction and symbolic representation method. Furthermore, the RASPRO motifs typically perform as well or much better than the original raw data time-series, but with up to 15-fold reduction in transmission/storage bandwidth thereby suggesting that *less is better*.

---

*The first and second authors have contributed equally to this work.

[†]P. Durga and R.K. Pathinarupothi are with Amrita Center for Wireless Networks & Applications (AmritaWNA), Amrita School of Engineering, Amritapuri, Amrita Vishwa Vidyapeetham, India. email: rahulkrishnan@am.amrita.edu.

[‡]E. S. Rangan is with School of Medicine, Cochin, Amrita Vishwa Vidyapeetham, India.

[§]P. Ishwar is with the ECE department, Boston University, Boston, MA, USA 02215.

DH'18, April 23–26, 2018, Lyon, France
© 2018 Association for Computing Machinery.
ACM ISBN 978-1-4503-6493-5/18/04...$15.00
https://doi.org/10.1145/3194658.3194674

CCS CONCEPTS

• **Information systems** → **Decision support systems**; *Mobile information processing systems*;

KEYWORDS

Predictive health monitoring, personalization, data analytics

ACM Reference Format:
P Durga, Rahul Krishnan Pathinarupothi, Ekanath Srihari Rangan, and Prakash Ishwar. 2018. When Less is Better: A Summarization Technique that Enhances Clinical Effectiveness of Data. In *DH'18: 2018 International Digital Health Conference, April 23–26, 2018, Lyon, France*. ACM, New York, NY, USA, 5 pages. https://doi.org/10.1145/3194658.3194674

1 INTRODUCTION

We are witnessing an exponential growth in the adoption of vitals monitoring sensors among the general population as well as the patient community [4]. Despite offering multiple advantages to the patients and healthcare providers in terms of continuous monitoring and reduced healthcare delivery costs, the challenge lies in mining the large amount of data that comes from these sensors to make sensible and timely diagnosis of critical health conditions such as myocardial infarctions, strokes, hypotensive episodes, or syncopes. Towards this end, the research community has been actively looking at various data summarization techniques [11]. In addition to storage and communication bandwidth savings, data reduction can potentially improve prediction power by improving the signal-to-noise ratio and eliminating redundant and uninformative signal dimensions. However, a concern of medical practitioners is that data reduction may result in either loss of feature details that could be clinically relevant or may produce reduced representations that are difficult to interpret medically [11]. In this paper, we propose a novel technique, which by utilizing medical knowledge to summarize voluminous sensor data, not only retains medical interpretability and reduces bandwidth, but also improves the efficacy of predicting diseases.

This technique, that we call as RASPRO (Rapid Active Summarization for effective PROgnosis), transforms raw sensor data to patient health status "motifs". These motifs are easily readable health summaries of the patient, and they directly help doctors and caretakers gauge the urgency of the patient's condition. Unlike many existing approaches that either simply convert raw signals to symbols using different thresholds, or employ domain-agnostic signal processing methods to summarize sensor data, our technique combines medical knowledge-base with patient-specific personalization to derive symbolic motifs that are both readily communicative of

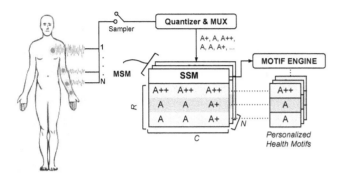

Figure 1: RASPRO framework for transforming the raw sensor data to a patient's health status in the form of Personalized Health Motifs (PHMs).

the patient health status as well as amenable to automated predictive analytics via machine/deep learning techniques. The major contributions as reported in this paper include:

- RASPRO: A personalized medical data summarization technique for converting raw sensor data to "motifs", based on medical domain knowledge.
- Comparative performance analysis (in terms of clinical effectiveness and bandwidth requirement) of RASPRO motifs against a widely accepted symbolic time-series representation technique called Symbolic Aggregate approXimation (SAX).
- Comparative performance analysis of RASPRO motifs against original raw sensor data.

As a concrete application for evaluating the RASPRO framework, we have selected a target disease condition called Acute Hypotensive Episode (AHE). Early detection and prediction of an AHE could greatly reduce the mortality rate.

Experimental results demonstrate the superior clinical accuracy of RASPRO in predicting AHE. In particular, the RASPRO motifs give a maximum F1-score of up to 0.83 as compared to the maximum F1-score of 0.61 given by SAX. Interestingly, RASPRO motifs outperform even the raw sensor data time-series suggesting that "less can be better". We also show that RASPRO motifs provide a much better trade-off between bandwidth cost and efficiency. Due to these advantages, RASPRO motifs could potentially be used to send emergency and critical health status updates to remote doctors even over an SMS without dependence on availability of high bandwidth data networks such as 3G/4G/LTE.

2   RELATED WORK

Data summarization techniques range from simple normal/abnormal threshold-based warning/alert systems such as [2] to more complex multi-sensor data fusion techniques [12] [15]. Machine/deep learning based methods have recently gained attention as potentially powerful frameworks for extracting diagnostic insights from historical data. The literature on this topic is rapidly expanding, but some representative works include [5] [8]. SAX [7] belongs to the class of techniques that convert data into simpler, dimensionally reduced symbolic representations. It is one of the most widely applied techniques for data reduction and has proven to provide very

high utility in various domains such as the ones discussed in [3] [9]. The applications of SAX, particularly for healthcare, have been discussed in [16] [6]. We observe that these and many other data reduction/transformation techniques [13] [1] are domain-agnostic. They do not leverage the medical value of the data and thereby potentially miss clinically relevant insights as we will see in the evaluation section (Section 4).

3   PERSONALIZED HEALTH STATUS MOTIFS

We begin this section by describing the RASPRO technique. Let us consider raw time-series data coming in from multiple (N) vital parameter sensors, $S_1, S_2, ..., S_N$, attached to a patient (see Figure 1). There are three major processing steps.

Step 1: The first step is converting the time-series of sampled raw sensor data into a time-series of patient-specific discrete (quantized) severity symbols such as 'A', '$A+$', '$A++$', '$A-$', '$A--$', etc., where the clinically defined normal range for a given sensor is assigned the symbol "A", while values which are above and below normal ranges are assigned increasing number of "$+$" and "$-$" suffixes according to the severity. Unlike typical systems with fixed severity thresholds for a sensor, in RASPRO the number of criticality levels L_{CRIT} and their mapping to corresponding sensor value ranges are customized according to the patient's condition as perceived by the doctor.

Medical knowledge driven decision-making 1: In the case of a patient who has been evaluated in the hospital and is suspected to have mild hypertension, but absolutely no risk for other cardiovascular morbidities, moderate thresholds would be assigned for $A+$, $A++$, etc., because some fluctuation in Blood Pressure (BP) would not be of concern. On the contrary, a patient with confirmed hypertension whose BP is not brought to target maintenance level, who also has additional cardiac risk factors such as, diabetes, obesity, or hypercholesterolemia, would be assigned more stringent thresholds. Moreover, based on their respective organ risks, a cardiologist, ophthalmologist, or nephrologist would assign different thresholds for the same BP parameter. This essentially makes the criticality range definitions highly personalized.

Step 2: In the next step of the RASPRO system, the time-series of these quantized severity symbols is passed through a multiplexer (MUX) that arranges it into a 2-dimensional single sensor matrix (SSM) of C columns and R rows. Here, each row represents a short continuous burst of observations and between the rows there may be a quiescent period. Multiple SSMs corresponding to different sensors are arranged to form a 3-dimensional Multi-Sensor Matrix (MSM).

Medical knowledge driven decision-making 2: If the doctor wants to monitor the BP of a patient every hour (the BP measurement being taken five times in an hour) for 24 hours, the SSM will have 24 rows with each row containing the five BP values corresponding to that hour. The exact number of columns and rows would be decided by the healthcare professional based upon the patients' condition, sensor type, and diagnostic relevance. The doctor may also decide to increase the sampling rate in case the patient is critical.

Step 3: In the third step of RASPRO, all the quantized severity symbols in a row are temporally summarized to one parameter, called the consensus symbol. A consensus symbol captures the dominant trend in the patient data. All the consensus symbols in an SSM are put together in a column fashion to arrive at a corresponding Personalized Health Motif (PHM) (see Figure 1).

Medical knowledge driven decision-making 3: For the specific purpose of predicting AHE using Mean Arterial blood Pressure (MAP) measurements, in this paper, we define consensus symbol as the most frequently occurring symbol in a row of SSM. If there are multiple candidates for a consensus symbol, the higher severity symbol is selected.

However, doctors might be interested in different kinds of summarization based on the sensor type, diagnostic interest, and patients' health condition. They might, for example, want to know the mean of values, frequency of peaks, value of highest peak, most frequent abnormality or other statistics. Accordingly, RASPRO provides a framework to define summarization differently for various clinical requirements.

In Figure 1, the first row of an SSM is summarized and the corresponding consensus symbol, "$A++$", is determined. A more formal approach to the definition of motifs and other ways of summarizing the data is discussed in one of our earlier works [10] which we do not reproduce here due to space limitation.

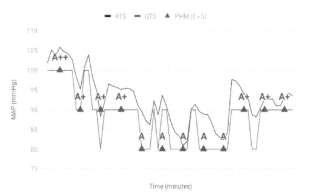

Figure 2: RTS, QTS and MTS of a patient's MAP values over 60 minutes with one MTS symbol every $C = 5$ minutes.

To obtain an intuitive idea of the RASPRO summarization process, we plot in Figure 2, the raw time-series data of a patient's MAP values over a period of 60 minutes (black solid line). We shall refer to this as the raw time-series (RTS). We also do an overlay plot of the corresponding quantized time-series (QTS) represented by the blue solid line. Finally, we also overlay the corresponding RASPRO PHM time-series (which we abbreviate as MTS for Motif time-series), represented by blue triangles together with severity symbols. In the figure, MTS symbols are determined once in every five minutes ($C = 5$).

Medical knowledge driven decision-making 4: Since our target application is episodes of acute hypotension, we consulted cardiologists to make the following criticality levels assignments to the corresponding MAP value ranges: "$A-$": 50-60 mmHg, "A": 60-90 mmHg, "$A+$": 90-100 mmHg, "$A++$": 100-120 mmHg. The also set $C = 5$ and $R = 12$ for a total of 60 minutes of data. These values are used to generate the plots in Figure 2.

In contrast to RASPRO's medical domain knowledge driven decision making process, domain-agnostic summarization techniques do not consider the clinical meaning of MAP values while quantizing. This could, for example, result in a value between 50-70

mmHg being quantized into a single value, hence losing the clinical significance of the data.

4 PERFORMANCE EVALUATION

We conduct three evaluations to analyze the performance of RASPRO: (a) we compare the RASPRO motifs against SAX (one of the most widely used methods for symbolic data summarization) in terms of AHE prediction accuracy, (b) we compare the AHE prediction accuracy of RASPRO against that of raw time-series data, and (c) we compare RASPRO and SAX in terms of their trade-offs between the bandwidth cost of summarization and corresponding predictive power.

4.1 Dataset

For performance evaluation we require vitals sensor data of patients that span a suitably long duration in order to predict the onset of a critical condition, e.g., data from patients who had acute hypotensive episodes (AHE). An AHE is characterized by prolonged decrease in MAP value of a patient below 60 mmHg for more than 90% of the time in a half-hour window. AHE is a potentially fatal condition and needs medication intervention. We obtained AHE patient and control group data from a widely used open source database, MIMIC II [14], which contains multi-parameter records such as MAP, SpO2, ECG, and Non-obtrusive BP. The curated dataset contains at least 60 minutes of MAP data for each subject before the onset of AHE. The dataset contains two groups: 27 patients termed as H-group, who had AHE and another with 15 patients, termed as C-group, who did not experience AHE during their stay in an ICU. Additionally, the dataset also includes the time of onset of an AHE event, marked as T_0. For all the predictive analysis tasks in this paper, we used MAP data that was 60 minutes prior to T_0.

4.2 Symbolic Aggregate Approximation (SAX)

SAX is a widely used technique for data reduction that uses a symbolic representation. In SAX, an arbitrary length of time-series data, n, is reduced to a string with a length smaller than n. This involves mainly two steps: (a) dimensionality reduction using Piecewise Aggregate Approximation (PAA) and (b) discretization using equiprobable symbols.

PAA: In this step, a given time-series data is first amplitude-normalized (by subtracting the global mean and dividing by the global standard deviation) and then partitioned into smaller subsets of size W time steps called frames. A mean value is determined for the data that lies within a specific frame. The frame is then replaced with the computed mean value as its equivalent low-dimensional representation. The above procedure, when repeated for each frame, generates a vector of corresponding mean values, which provides the data-reduced representation of the entire time-series.

SAX: The data-reduced representation obtained after implementing PAA is further discretized to produce symbols of equal probability. The SAX technique assumes that normalized time-series data follow a Gaussian distribution. To allot the symbols, first breakpoints are assigned to produce areas of equal size under the Gaussian curve. Each of these breakpoints is assigned a symbol. Thereafter, the PAA coefficients are mapped to the corresponding breakpoints to generate a symbolic SAX representation which is termed as a

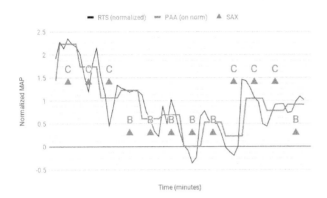

Figure 3: Amplitude-normalized MAP values of a patient over 60 minutes using RTS as well as the corresponding PAA and SAX representation for a frame size of $W = 5$ minutes.

word. We plot in Figure 3, the MAP values in the RTS as well as the corresponding PAA and SAX representations ($W = 5$ minutes). In contrast to MTS (see Figure 2) which incorporates medical domain knowledge, the SAX representation is domain-agnostic (see Figure 3).

4.3 Predictive Power: Comparison with SAX

We compare the performance of RASPRO's MTS against the time-series of SAX symbols on the task of predicting AHEs. For this purpose, 60 minutes of MAP data prior to the onset time T_0 was extracted and transformed to MTS and SAX series. Guided by medical knowledge, we used the following parameter choices to evaluate the performance of MTS: (a) $L_{CRIT} = 7, 9, 13$ levels and (b) $C = 5, 10, 15$ minutes, and the following parameter choices for SAX: (a) alphabet size = 7, 9, and 13 corresponding to values of L_{CRIT} in the RASPRO method and (b) frames of length $W = 5, 10, 15$ minutes corresponding to the values of C for MTS.

For ease of comparison, we use S to denote the alphabet size in SAX and the corresponding value of L_{CRIT} in RASPRO. We use W to denote both the frame length (in SAX) as well as the corresponding value of C (in RASPRO).

The MTS and SAX series were then vectorized[1] and fed into a Support Vector Machine (SVM) binary classifier, which is trained and tested using, respectively, 70% and 30% of the data. We used five fold cross validation and also tried two different kernels (rbf and linear). For each (S,W) pair, we report the best performance from among the two kernels. We chose SVM since it is a widely used classical classification technique which has moderate training and testing complexity and has proved to be highly effective in a number of applications. Other classifiers, e.g., based on neural networks, could potentially provide additional performance improvements.

We measure the predictive power of RASPRO and SAX via the F1-score, which is a statistical measure of binary classification that is the harmonic average of the precision and recall values. Table 1 summarizes the results of the SVM-based prediction task. We observe that RASPRO gives consistently higher F1-scores than

[1]Each symbol is assigned a numerical value corresponding to the *lower* end point of the numerical quantization range associated with it.

SAX across the range of S and W values. The relative F1-score improvements of RASPRO over SAX range from 20.9% for $S = 7, W = 5$ to 93.2% for $S = 13, W = 10$.

	F1-scores					
	$W = 5$ mins		$W = 10$ mins		$W = 15$ mins	
$S =$	RASPRO	SAX	RASPRO	SAX	RASPRO	SAX
7	0.52	0.43	0.61	0.43	0.76	0.47
9	0.77	0.45	0.77	0.47	0.69	0.47
13	0.83	0.61	0.83	0.43	0.83	0.47

Table 1: Comparison of F1-scores for the prediction of an AHE using SAX and RASPRO for different number of symbols S, and summarization time windows, W.

4.4 Comparison with RTS

Additionally, we also compare the F1-score of RASPRO motifs against that of RTS for the same AHE prediction task using SVM. RTS yielded a maximum F1-score of 0.70 compared to the maximum score of 0.83 ($S = 13$ and $W = 15$) for RASPRO motifs which uses only one-fifteenth of the RTS data and that too in quantized form. In fact, except for three (S, W) pairs in Table 1, RASPRO has an F1-score that is higher than 0.70. This clearly demonstrates that RASPRO summarization could be as effective, if not better than the raw time-series representation for many choices of S and W values.

4.5 Bandwidth cost

The trade-off between accuracy of data and bandwidth cost is an important aspect of study when it comes to summarization techniques. We define the bandwidth cost function f as:

$$f = \frac{\log_2 S}{W} \tag{1}$$

where, $\log_2 S$ is the number of bits needed to represent S symbols, and W the size of the summarization window. This cost function captures the data requirement for summarization given a pair of (S, W) values. Figure 4 summarizes our findings. Observe that the F1-score of SAX remains flat (between 0.43–0.47, close to the performance of random guessing) over most bandwidths and increases to 0.61 at $f = 0.74$. In contrast, the F1-score of RASPRO rises roughly monotonically from 0.61 to 0.83 as f increases. The relative improvement over SAX ranges from 20% for $f = 0.56$ bits/unit-time to a maximum of 90% for $f = 0.37$ bits/unit-time. This demonstrates that the medically-informed RASPRO motifs provide much greater clinical value per bit per minute than SAX.

5 DISCUSSION

The RASPRO technique has been designed with the dual objectives of summarization and enhanced interpretability to aid in better and faster clinical decision making. The PHMs present a succinct symbolic representation of a patient's health condition. We also see that these PHMs could be used as input to a machine learning algorithm for a classification task. It is interesting to note that domain-agnostic techniques such as SAX could lead to peculiar interpretations of data. For instance, in the PAA step of SAX it is

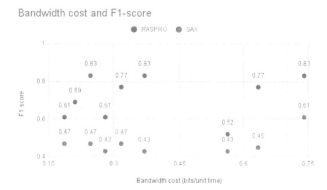

Figure 4: Comparison of bandwidth requirements for RASPRO and SAX using the cost function as defined in Equation (1) shows a clear advantage of RASPRO technique which provides a much higher predictive power for a given bandwidth cost incurred.

possible that multiple abnormal MAP values (say 59 mmHg) and few normal MAP values (say 65 mmHg) could be averaged and summarized to a normal value (above 60 mmgH), hence losing clinical meaning and value. From the experimental results presented in the paper, we observe that by quantizing the sensor data in a principled and clinically-aware way, the predictive power of the data is, in fact, enhanced. The RASPRO motifs showed a maximum F1-score of 0.83 compared to 0.61 for SAX. The performance of RASPRO motifs was also higher compared to the RTS, which gave an F1-score of 0.70. The comparison of bandwidth cost too shows that RASPRO motifs clearly outperform SAX by giving much higher predictive power for every bit used. The better-than-expected results could be attributed to using the medical domain knowledge in the two steps of RASPRO:

- The patient and disease specific quantizer removes irrelevant/redundant data, and represents it in a more clinically meaningful way.
- The motif summarization, when used judiciously with the optimum summarization window, effectively captures the normal and abnormal trends in the patient.

6 CONCLUSION AND FUTURE WORK

In this paper we have presented a novel summarization technique, called RASPRO, which can convert high-volume multi-sensor multi-parameter data from wearable sensors into a patient-specific severity description in the form of symbolic motifs (PHMs). While most of the existing algorithms use domain-agnostic summarization techniques, RASPRO adopts a medical-knowledge-driven approach. In comparison to one of the widely-used techniques for symbolic sequence generation called SAX, we have shown that RASPRO outperforms in improving the clinical effectiveness as represented by the predictive power. We also observed that the bandwidth requirement for sending large amount of sensor data could be reduced using RASPRO. We attribute the efficiency improvement to the use of patient and disease-specific summarization that RASPRO offers.

In the near future, we plan to translate the findings from this study to clinical experiments using the optimum parameters as discovered in our experiments. Additionally, we intend to experimentally validate the RASPRO framework for other disease conditions.

ACKNOWLEDGMENTS

The authors would like to thank Sri. Mata Amritanandamayi Devi, Chancellor, Amrita Vishwa Vidyapeetham for her guidance and support to conduct research that has direct societal impact. We also thank Dr. P Venkat Rangan for his valuable inputs for this paper.

REFERENCES

[1] Insaf Achour, Kaouther Nouira, and Abdelwahed Trabelsi. 2012. Reducing False Alarms in Intensive Care Units Based on Wavelets Technology. *International Journal of Bio-Science and Bio-Technology* 4, 2 (2012), 111–120.
[2] Mirza Mansoor Baig, Hamid GholamHosseini, Martin J. Connolly, and Ghodsi Kashfi. 2014. Real-time vital signs monitoring and interpretation system for early detection of multiple physical signs in older adults. In *Biomedical and Health Informatics (BHI), 2014 IEEE-EMBS International Conference on.* IEEE, 355–358.
[3] Petko Bakalov, Marios Hadjieleftheriou, and Vassilis J Tsotras. 2005. Time relaxed spatiotemporal trajectory joins. In *Proceedings of the 13th annual ACM international workshop on Geographic information systems.* ACM, 182–191.
[4] Jarod T Giger, Natalie D Pope, H Bruce Vogt, Cassity Gutierrez, Lisa A Newland, Jason Lemke, and Michael J Lawler. 2015. Remote patient monitoring acceptance trends among older adults residing in a frontier state. *Computers in Human Behavior* 44 (2015), 174–182.
[5] Eric M Green, Reinier van Mourik, Charles Wolfus, Stephen B Heitner, Onur Dur, and Marc J Semigran. 2017. Abstract 24031: Machine Learning Detection of Obstructive Hypertrophic Cardiomyopathy Using a Wearable Biosensor. *Circulation* 136, Suppl 1 (2017), A24031–A24031. arXiv:http://circ.ahajournals.org/content http://circ.ahajournals.org/content/136/Suppl_1/A24031
[6] Burcu Kulahcioglu, Serhan Ozdemir, and Bora Kumova. 2008. Application of symbolic Piecewise Aggregate Approximation (PAA) analysis to ECG signals. In *17th IASTED International Conference on Applied Simulation and Modelling.*
[7] Jessica Lin, Eamonn Keogh, Stefano Lonardi, and Bill Chiu. 2003. A symbolic representation of time series, with implications for streaming algorithms. In *Proceedings of the 8th ACM SIGMOD Workshop on Research Issues in Data Mining and Knowledge Discovery.* ACM, 2–11.
[8] Ivo C. Lopes, Binod Vaidya, and Joel J. P. C. Rodrigues. 2013. Towards an autonomous fall detection and alerting system on a mobile and pervasive environment. *Telecommunication Systems* (2013), 1–12.
[9] A McGovern, D Rosendahl, A Kruger, M Beaton, R Brown, and K Droegemeier. 2007. Understanding the formation of tornadoes through data mining. In *5th conference on artificial intelligence and its applications to environmental sciences at the American meteorological society.*
[10] R. K. Pathinarupothi and E. S. Rangan. 2017. Consensus motifs as adaptive and efficient predictors for acute hypotensive episodes. In *2017 39th Annual International Conference of the IEEE Engineering in Medicine and Biology Society (EMBC).* 1688–1691. https://doi.org/10.1109/EMBC.2017.8037166
[11] Rimma Pivovarov and Noémie Elhadad. 2015. Automated methods for the summarization of electronic health records. *Journal of the American Medical Informatics Association* 22, 5 (2015), 938–947.
[12] J Rajevenceltha, C Santhosh Kumar, and A Anand Kumar. 2016. Improving the performance of multi-parameter patient monitors using feature mapping and decision fusion. In *Region 10 Conference (TENCON), 2016 IEEE.* IEEE, 1515–1518.
[13] T. Rocha, S. Paredes, P. Carvalho, J. Henriques, and M. Harris. 2010. Wavelet based time series forecast with application to acute hypotensive episodes prediction. In *Engineering in Medicine and Biology (EMBC) society, 2010 annual international conference of the IEEE.* IEEE, 2403–2406.
[14] Mohammed Saeed, Mauricio Villarroel, Andrew T. Reisner, Gari Clifford, Li-Wei Lehman, George Moody, Thomas Heldt, Tin H. Kyaw, Benjamin Moody, and Roger G. Mark. 2011. Multiparameter Intelligent Monitoring in Intensive Care II (MIMIC-II): a public-access intensive care unit database. *Critical Care Medicine* 39, 5 (2011), 952. http://dx.doi.org/10.1097/CCM.0b013e31820a92c6.
[15] S. Sreejith, S. Rahul, and R. C. Jisha. 2016. A Real Time Patient Monitoring System for Heart Disease Prediction Using Random Forest Algorithm. In *Advances in Signal Processing and Intelligent Recognition Systems.* Springer International Publishing, 485–500.
[16] Hossein Tayebi, Shonali Krishnaswamy, Augustinus Borgy Waluyo, Abhijat Sinha, and Mohamed Medhat Gaber. 2011. Ra-sax: resource-aware symbolic aggregate approximation for mobile ECG analysis. In *Mobile Data Management (MDM), 2011 12th IEEE International Conference on*, Vol. 1. IEEE, 289–290.

Aspect-Based Sentiment Analysis of Drug Reviews Applying Cross-Domain and Cross-Data Learning

Felix Gräßer
Institut für Biomedizinische Technik
Technische Universität Dresden
felix.graesser@tu-dresden.de

Surya Kallumadi
Department of Computer Science
Kansas State University
surya@ksu.edu

Hagen Malberg
Institut für Biomedizinische Technik
Technische Universität Dresden
hagen.malberg@tu-dresden.de

Sebastian Zaunseder
Institut für Biomedizinische Technik
Technische Universität Dresden
sebastian.zaunseder@tu-dresden.de

ABSTRACT

Online review sites and opinion forums contain a wealth of information regarding user preferences and experiences over multiple product domains. This information can be leveraged to obtain valuable insights using data mining approaches such as sentiment analysis. In this work we examine online user reviews within the pharmaceutical field. Online user reviews in this domain contain information related to multiple aspects such as effectiveness of drugs and side effects, which make automatic analysis very interesting but also challenging. However, analyzing sentiments concerning the various aspects of drug reviews can provide valuable insights, help with decision making and improve monitoring public health by revealing collective experience.

In this preliminary work we perform multiple tasks over drug reviews with data obtained by crawling online pharmaceutical review sites. We first perform sentiment analysis to predict the sentiments concerning overall satisfaction, side effects and effectiveness of user reviews on specific drugs. To meet the challenge of lacking annotated data we further investigate the transferability of trained classification models among domains, i.e. conditions, and data sources. In this work we show that transfer learning approaches can be used to exploit similarities across domains and is a promising approach for cross-domain sentiment analysis.

KEYWORDS

Text classification; Sentiment Analysis; Clinical Decision Support System (CDSS); Health Recommender System

ACM Reference Format:
Felix Gräßer, Surya Kallumadi, Hagen Malberg, and Sebastian Zaunseder. 2018. Aspect-Based Sentiment Analysis of Drug Reviews Applying Cross-Domain and Cross-Data Learning. In *DH'18: 2018 International Digital Health Conference, April 23–26, 2018, Lyon, France*. ACM, New York, NY, USA, 5 pages. https://doi.org/10.1145/3194658.3194677

1 INTRODUCTION

Pharmaceutical product safety currently depends on clinical trials and specific test protocols. Such studies are typically done under standardized conditions in a limited number of test subjects within a limited time span. As a consequence, the discrepancies in patient selection and treatment conditions can have significant impact on the effectiveness and potential risks of adverse drug reactions (ADRs). Therefore, post-marketing drug surveillance, i.e. pharmacovigilance, plays a major role concerning drug safety once a drug has been released. Furthermore, clinical decision support systems (CDSS) which provide assistance with diagnosis and treatment decisions are expected to play an increasingly important role in healthcare. Approaches such as therapy recommender systems, which aim at helping to find an optimal personalized therapy option for a given patient and time, benefit from feedback on therapy outcome [8]. These systems, however, typically rely on structured data, i.e. data categorized into a number of classes on predefined scales. The amount of such data often is limited because it requires intense preparation which is not standard in clinical routine. Here, other sources, such as user reviews, offer great potential.

However, one major requirement for automatic processing and analysis of the information contained in large amounts of unstructured information is the transformation of inherent aspects into numerical ratings. One typical way of doing so, in the context of product ratings, is sentiment analysis, which is an extensively studied domain in processing free-text in web media analyses [11]. Many approaches to sentiment analysis are based on sentiment lexicons. These approaches recognize sentiment terms and patterns of sentiment expressions in natural language texts by matching textual units with opinion words in lexicons annotated for sentiment polarity. However, studies showed that sentiment analysis is often domain-dependent since the polarity of single terms can differ depending on the context they are used in [4, 6]. Furthermore, the language in online forums is highly informal and user-expressed medical concepts are often nontechnical, descriptive, and challenging to extract. Which is why typical lexicons are of limited use for drug review analyses. An alternative approach treats the task as classification problem. Here, machine learning is used to train classifiers on domain-specific data sets to detect the polarity at sentence or document level. Such approaches have the additional advantage to be capable of performing medical sentiment analysis over multiple facets, i.e. sentiments can be learned on specific aspects such as effectiveness and side effects.

Sentiment analysis of patient data in general and on drug experience in particular is a challenging research problem that is currently receiving considerable attention. One of the main issues, however, is the lack of annotated data, which is crucial for accurate sentiment classification. Especially, labeled data dealing with distinct aspects is rare. Moreover, the availability of labeled data is highly domain dependent. Patients suffering from certain conditions are more active in reporting experience on their treatment than others.

Consequently, this work studies (1) the possibility to apply sentiment analysis on drug reviews, and the identification of effectiveness of a drug as well as the type of side effect caused by a drug exploiting its reviews. Therefore, classification of side effects and effectiveness is treated as an aspect-based sentiment analysis problem. Furthermore, to address challenges related to the limited data availability, we investigate (2) the transferability of the trained models among domains, i.e. conditions, as well as (3) across data sources.

2 BACKGROUND AND RELATED WORK

Literature on drug reviews and pharmacovigilance can basically be divided into studies on identification of aspects such as automatic detection of ADRs or side effects and such works dealing with overall or aspect-based sentiment analysis.

Most approaches tackling ADR or side effect identification are lexicon-based and rely on mapping relevant terms and phrases from user data to specific vocabulary from various individual or combined lexicons [6, 10]. However, lexicon-based approaches suffer from phonetic and typographic misspellings. Therefore, recent works have also focused on machine learning techniques to overcome such limitations. Nikfarjam et al. applied association rule mining to find pattern, i.e. combinations in terms [14], or conditional random fields (CRFs), to extract mentions of ADRs [15]. Based on the underlying assumption that patients' posts about ADRs typically express negative sentiments, Korkontzelos et al. studied the effect of enriching a lexicon-based ADR identification method with sentiment analysis features [9]. Cavalcanti et al. demonstrate the extraction and classification of multiple aspects in drug reviews, e.g. adverse reactions, efficacy of a drug, symptoms and conditions, using a method based on syntactic dependency paths [2]. An extensive review on pharmacovigilance and ADR extraction techniques can be found in [16].

Works on drug review sentiment analysis can basically be divided into approaches applying lexicons with sentiment scores or such approaches learning sentiments employing supervised classification. In one of the earliest works on drug review sentiment analysis Xia et al. developed a topic classifier from patient data to eventually apply several polarity classifiers, one per topic [17]. Na et al. demonstrate a clause-level sentiment analysis algorithm considering multiple review aspects as overall satisfaction, effectiveness, side effects and condition. Here, a rule-based approach is employed that takes grammatical relations and semantic annotation into account and computes sentiment orientation of individual clauses based on a lexicon [13]. In [12], aspect-based sentiment analysis

of patient reviews is studied on oncological drugs. Here, opinion words are identified and overall sentiments derived utilizing a lexical resource. Gopalakrishnan et al. analyze patient drug satisfaction by using a supervised learning sentiment analysis approach. In this study three levels of polarity were classified comparing SVM with neural network based methods [7].

Many research studies have attempted to improve domain adaption or cross-domain sentiment classification, although not on drug review aspect-level but among various entities as products, movies or restaurants. In [1] a comprehensive systematic literature review on cross-domain sentiment analysis is presented.

3 DATASET

We used data from two independent webpages for retrieval of user reviews and ratings on drug experience. Drugs.com is, according to the provider, the largest and most widely visited pharmaceutical information website providing information for both, consumers and healthcare professionals. It provides user reviews on specific drugs along with related condition and a 10 star user rating reflecting overall user satisfaction. Similarly, Druglib.com is a resource on drug information for both, consumer and healthcare professionals. It comprises considerably fewer reviews but reviews and ratings are provided in a more structured way. Reviews are grouped into reports on the three aspects *benefits*, *side effects* and overall *comment*. Additionally, ratings are available concerning overall satisfaction analogously to Drugs.com as well as a 5 step side effect rating, ranging from *no side effects* to *extremely severe side effects* and a 5 step effectiveness rating ranging from *ineffective* to *very effective*.

We gathered user comments and ratings from both pages using an automatic web crawler. The data was scraped from raw HTML using the Beautiful Soup library in Python. Crawling these domains resulted in two data sets comprising 215063 reviews from Drugs.com and 3551 reviews from Druglib.com. Furthermore, we derived three level polarity labels for overall patient satisfaction and three level effectiveness and side effect scores using thresholds as specified in table 1. Both data sets were further split into training and test partitions according to a stratified random sampling scheme with the proportion of 75% and 25%, respectively. As shown in table 1, the total number of individual drugs in the Drugs.com data amounts to 6345 in comparison to the 541 drugs contained in the data derived from Druglib.com. However, the average number of reviews per drug is still considerably higher in the Drugs.com data (58.86) than in the Druglib.com data (7.66). The amount of unique conditions contained in the Druglib.com data, on the other hand, seems to exceed the number of the Drugs.com data. However, it is to be noted that conditions in the first platform are user created in contrast to Drugs.com where conditions are selected from a defined list, and thus standardized. Therefore, in case of Druglib.com, conditions are not normalized but comprise manifold variations in spelling, synonyms and combinations of conditions.

4 APPROACHES

In this section a description of the methods used in this work is detailed. The objective of this study was threefold:

Table 1: Data Description

Data	#Train	#Test	#conditions	#drugs	length	rating	label	%
Drugs.com								
Overall Rating	161297	53766	836	3654	458.32 (240.76)	$rating \leq 4$	-1	25
						$4 < rating < 7$	0	9
						$rating \geq 7$	1	66
Side Effects (Annotated)	-	400	141	243	500.385 (209.42)	No Side Effects	0	32
						Mild / Moderate Side Effects	1	28
						Severe / Extremely Severe Side Effects	2	40
Druglib.com								
Overall Rating	3107	1036	1808	541	277.57 (283.21)	$rating \leq 4$	-1	21
						$4 < rating < 7$	0	10
						$rating \geq 7$	1	69
Benefits (Effectiveness)	3107	1036	1808	541	212.87 (198.51)	Ineffective	0	8
						Marginally / Moderately Effective	1	19
						Considerably / Highly Effective	2	73
Side Effects	3107	1036	1808	541	177.36 (197.93)	No Side Effects	0	30
						Mild / Moderate Side Effects	1	53
						Severe / Extremely Severe Side Effects	2	17

(1) Prediction of the overall patients' satisfaction with applied medications and sentiments on side effects and effectiveness by employing classification-based sentiment analyses.

(2) Evaluating the transferability of models among medical domains, i.e conditions, by learning a model on data from one condition (source domain) to classify overall patient satisfaction in data from another condition (target domain).

(3) Evaluating the transferability of models across data sources, i.e Drugs.com and Druglib.com, by learning a model on reviews from one data source (source data) to classify overall patient satisfaction and sentiments on side effects in data from another source (target data).

Whereas for the first two tasks the ground truth is available for both data sets, distinct reviews covering the aspects side effect and effectiveness along with labels are only available for the Druglib.com data. To evaluate the transferability of side effect prediction models across data sets, 400 randomly picked samples from the Drugs.com data were manually labeled concerning side effects by two independent annotators. The inter-rater agreement measured with the Cohen's Kappa statistic [3] is 81.84% which is considered as very strong agreement. The annotators discussed all mismatching entities and agreed on a consensus.

Both approaches, sentiment analysis regarding overall patients' satisfaction and the aspect-based analysis of patients' sentiments on side effects and medication effectiveness were converted to classification problems. In case of overall patient satisfaction, the user ratings were converted to three disjoint classes representing the polarity of a patient's sentiment regarding the applied medication (negative, neutral, positive). In addition, also the severity of side effects and the level of effectiveness were transferred to three disjoint classes as described in table 1.

For all prediction tasks we apply a n-grams approach to represent the user reviews. That means both, single tokens, e.g. words, (unigrams) as well as two or more adjacent tokens (bigrams, trigrams), e.g. 2- or 3-word expressions, were used to derive features

for classification. Based on the total collection of occurring n-grams, i.e. the corpus, each review can be represented as a sparse vector of token counts.

Initially, all reviews were preprocessed according to a standard scheme: Alphabetic characters were transferred to lowercase and special characters, punctuation and numbers were removed. Subsequently, the preprocessed documents were tokenized on spaces to obtain the overall vocabulary and a feature space representation of each review. No stop words were removed from the texts. However, to reduce the feature space, terms that have a relative document frequency higher than a given threshold were discarded when building the vocabulary.

Using the extracted feature representations, logistic regression was employed for building sentiment models for the various prediction tasks. Model hyperparameters were tuned using a 5-fold cross validation grid search on the respective training data, targeting the best Cohens's Kappa score. Optimized hyperparameter include n-gram number of adjacent tokens, token document frequency threshold, and logistic regression regularization strength. As shown in table 1, besides the annotated subset from the Drugs.com data, labels are considerably unbalanced. To compensate for this disproportionate distribution, classification errors were penalized with a weight inversely proportional to the class frequency during training. All experiments were evaluated by computing confusion matrices and deriving both, accuracy and Cohens's Kappa scores.

5 EXPERIMENTS AND RESULTS

5.1 In-domain Sentiment Analysis

In an initial experiment, overall performance when applying sentiment analysis to drug reviews was studied. Therefore, one model for each data set (Drugs.com and Druglib.com), to classify overall patient satisfaction reviews, is trained and evaluated utilizing the corresponding training and test data. Additionally, as in case of the Druglib.com data the *comments* section might only contain

Table 2: In-domain Sentiment Analysis

Aspect	Source	Acc. / Kappa
Overall Rating	Drugs.com	92.24 / 83.99
Overall Rating	Druglib.com	69.88 / 28.45
Overall Rating (all)	Druglib.com	75.19 / 43.59
Benefits (Effectiveness)	Druglib.com	77.70 / 44.13
Side Effects	Druglib.com	76.93 / 60.13

supplementary remarks, a combination of all three reports (*benefits, side effects* and *comments*) of a patient on a respective drug were concatenated to represent the overall patient satisfaction review.

Furthermore, we studied the expression of sentiments on the two aspects *side effects* and *effectiveness* within patient generated texts. Therefore, two logistic regression models were optimized and trained on the *benefits* and *side effects* training data derived from Druglib.com, respectively. Both, predicted *effectiveness* and *side effect* labels were compared against the actual labels obtained from the user ratings.

As detailed in table 2, overall patient satisfaction can be mined from patient texts with very high accuracy and Cohen's Kappa score in case of the Drugs.com data. The significantly worse performance reported for the Druglib.com data is assumed to have two main reasons. First, the data set is considerably smaller, which hampers the modelling. Moreover, the *comments* section is mainly used for supplementary information on personal experience and drug application and not explicitly for comments on satisfaction. When combining all three aspects, i.e. patient reports, classification performance could be improved over the previous result. In both approaches concerning the Druglib.com data the largest error contribution results from neutral ratings classified as positive which cannot be improved by data combination. The performance improvement, however, results from the reduction of misclassified negative ratings.

Sentiment analysis related to the specific aspects *effectiveness* and *side effects* shows promising results. Especially the *side effects* comments seem to provide valuable features that facilitate mining sentiments on side effects. Here, errors are mainly due to misclassification of neighbouring classes, namely excessive missclassification as *mild / moderate side effects*. In case of *effectiveness* classification the largest error contribution stems from *marginally / moderately effective* reviews classified as *considerably / highly effective*, whereas *considerably / highly effective* labeled reviews can be classified correctly with 95% accuracy. However, it must be kept in mind that also comments on *benefits* not necessarily relate to effectiveness only but may also encompass other aspects.

5.2 Cross-domain Sentiment Analysis

In this experiment we studied the performance of models built on data from one condition, i.e. the source domain, and evaluated on data related to other conditions, i.e. the target domain. To do so, overall patient satisfaction models were trained on drug review subsets related to one selected condition only. These domain models were then evaluated on other condition related subsets. Domains, i.e. subsets of particular conditions, were selected by extracting five of the most frequent disorders present in the Druglib.com data set from

diverse medical fields. These are Contraception (38436), Depression (12164), Pain (8245), Anxiety (7812) and Diabetes, Type 2 (3362), with frequency in descending order. In-domain performances, i.e. training and testing of data from the same condition, are reported as averaged k-fold cross validation results (k=5).

The results summarized in table 3 demonstrate that the selected training domain has considerable impact on the classifier performance when applied to data from other domains. Especially, in-domain training and testing clearly outperforms all cross-domain setups. This finding clearly emphasizes the hypothesis of domain-specific vocabulary. For Contraception and Diabetes, even the overall rating classification using the entire data could be outperformed. However, the model trained on Depression data only seems to generalize better on the other domain data than e.g. a model trained on Diabetes data only. Furthermore, there are combinations showing better performances than others, e.g. Depression and Anxiety compared to Contraception and Anxiety, which is assumed to be due to underlying coherences of side effects or expressions and domain specific vocabulary used by patients. Moreover, the medical field dealing with Depression and Anxiety is closely related. From drugs concerning Depression (115) and Anxiety (81), 33 drugs are applied in both conditions whereas for Contraception (181) and Anxiety there is no overlap. Furthermore, the confusion matrices show that main classification errors occurred on neutrally labeled reviews for all domain combinations. Transferring the task to a binary classification problem without classification of neutral entities would result in substantially higher accuracy and Cohen's Kappa values.

5.3 Cross-data Sentiment Analysis

Finally, we study the transferability of the trained models among data sources. Overall patient satisfaction models were trained on both associated training data sets and evaluated on drug reviews from the other, independent data source test set. As discussed in 5.1, in case of the Druglib.com data a combination of all three reports (*benefits, side effects* and *comments*) were concatenated to represent the overall patient satisfaction review. Additionally, the performance of a classifier trained on *side effect* comments from the Druglib.com data is evaluated on the manually annotated data from Drugs.com.

Transferring a sentiment model trained on the significantly larger Drugs.com data to the Druglib.com data shows promising classification capabilities. Evaluating the model trained on the much smaller Druglib.com data with the Drugs.com data, however, doesn't perform satisfactorily. We assume such findings, on the one hand, to result from the limited training data size. On the other hand, differing data properties are likely to restrict the transferability. As stated previously, in contrast to the Druglib.com data Drugs.com reviews are highly unstructured covering multiple aspects in an entire review.

As summarized in table 4, applying the model trained on the *side effect* aspect to the Drugs.com reviews also performs poorly. The largest fraction of the classification error stems from reviews labeled as reporting *no* or *severe / extremely severe side effects* as *mild / moderate*. The features extracted from the Druglib.com data obviously don't contain sufficient discriminating power to classify the unstructured Drugs.com review which are not dealing with a

Table 3: Cross-domain Sentiment Analysis

		Train Data				
		Contraception	Depression	Pain	Anxiety	Diabetes, Type 2	avg. test
Test Data	Contraception	95.57 / 92.39	64.40 / 35.66	59.36 / 22.59	60.59 / 24.59	62.12 / 33.63	68.41 / 41.77
	Depression	62.05 / 31.51	90.13 / 78.07	75.21 / 40.69	77.07 / 43.95	66.98 / 33.93	74.29 / 45.63
	Pain	66.53 / 27.11	78.80 / 42.43	92.65 / 79.32	80.72 / 37.50	57.70 / 20.67	75.28 / 41.40
	Anxiety	64.35 / 28.14	82.64 / 51.22	79.74 / 43.43	92.37 / 78.41	67.51 / 30.64	77.32 / 46.37
	Diabetes, Type 2	69.90 / 44.50	71.83 / 43.37	68.17 / 32.32	69.48 / 34.18	94.74 / 89.84	74.82 / 48.84
	avg. train	71.68 / 44.73	77.56 / 50.15	75.03 / 43.67	76.05 / 43.73	69.81 / 41.74	

Table 4: Cross-data Sentiment Analysis

Aspect	Train Source	Test Source	Acc. / Kappa
Overall Rating	Drugs.com	Druglib.com	75.29 / 48.08
Overall Rating (all)	Druglib.com	Drugs.com	70.06 / 26.76
Side Effects	Druglib.com	Drugs.com	49.75 / 25.88

single aspects only. Utilizing a larger training data set, leading to less ambiguous features, might improve the results.

6 CONCLUSIONS

Within this preliminary work, we studied the application of machine learning based sentiment analysis of patient generated drug reviews. Logistic regression models were trained using simple lexical features such as unigrams, bigrams and trigrams extracted from the reviews. Besides patient satisfaction, sentiment aspects concerning effectiveness and experienced side effects were analyzed. Depending on aspect and data source, promising classification results could be obtained.

As labeled data sets for building classification models are rare or are only available in unstructured fashion, we investigated various approaches for model portability. Whereas in-domain (i.e. condition) training and evaluation shows very good classification results, the performance of models trained on one specific condition and tested on another condition, varies among domains. However, conditions which belong to similar medical fields and are partly treated with equal medications, also show higher potentials for model transferability. Cross-data evaluation, i.e. training and testing classifiers on data from different sources, was only unsatisfactorily possible with the applied classifier and features. Therefore, we believe that employing more sophisticated features and applying more powerful machine learning models, e.g. deep learning approaches as proposed in [5], can improve the achieved results. Furthermore, the results clearly indicate that especially aspect-based sentiment analysis requires more extensive data sets to extract features with sufficient generalization capabilities. However, we believe that this work contributes to open up future research directions, improves automatic extraction of aspect-related sentiments from patient drug reviews and promotes pharamcovigilance and development of CDSSs such as therapy recommender systems.

REFERENCES

[1] T. Al-Moslmi, N. Omar, S. Abdullah, and M. Albared. 2017. Approaches to Cross-Domain Sentiment Analysis: A Systematic Literature Review. *IEEE Access* 5 (2017), 16173–16192. https://doi.org/10.1109/ACCESS.2017.2690342

[2] Diana Cavalcanti and Ricardo Prudêncio. 2017. Aspect-Based Opinion Mining in Drug Reviews. In *Progress in Artificial Intelligence*, Eugénio Oliveira, João Gama, Zita Vale, and Henrique Lopes Cardoso (Eds.). Springer International Publishing, Cham, 815–827.

[3] Jacob Cohen. 1960. A Coefficient of Agreement for Nominal Scales. *Educational and Psychological Measurement* 20, 1 (1960), 37–46. https://doi.org/10.1177/001316446002000104

[4] Kerstin Denecke. 2015. *Sentiment Analysis from Medical Texts*. Springer International Publishing, Cham, 83–98. https://doi.org/10.1007/978-3-319-20582-3_10

[5] Xavier Glorot, Antoine Bordes, and Yoshua Bengio. 2011. Domain Adaptation for Large-scale Sentiment Classification: A Deep Learning Approach. In *Proceedings of the 28th International Conference on International Conference on Machine Learning (ICML'11)*. Omnipress, USA, 513–520.

[6] Lorraine Goeuriot, Jin-Cheon Na, Wai Yan Min Kyaing, Christopher Khoo, Yun-Ke Chang, Yin-Leng Theng, and Jung-Jae Kim. 2012. Sentiment Lexicons for Health-related Opinion Mining. In *Proceedings of the 2Nd ACM SIGHIT International Health Informatics Symposium (IHI '12)*. ACM, New York, NY, USA, 219–226. https://doi.org/10.1145/2110363.2110390

[7] Vinodhini Gopalakrishnan and Chandrasekaran Ramaswamy. 2017. Patient opinion mining to analyze drugs satisfaction using supervised learning. *Journal of Applied Research and Technology* 15, 4 (2017), 311 – 319. https://doi.org/10.1016/j.jart.2017.02.005

[8] Felix Gräßer, Stefanie Beckert, Denise Küster, Susanne Abraham, Hagen Malberg, Jochen Schmitt, and Sebastian Zaunseder. 2017. Neighborhood-based Collaborative Filtering for Therapy Decision Support. In *Proceedings of the 2nd International Workshop on Health Recommender Systems co-located with the 11th International Conference on Recommender Systems Italy, August 31, 2017*. 22–26.

[9] Ioannis Korkontzelos, Azadeh Nikfarjam, Matthew Shardlow, Abeed Sarker, Sophia Ananiadou, and Graciela H. Gonzalez. 2016. Analysis of the Effect of Sentiment Analysis on Extracting Adverse Drug Reactions from Tweets and Forum Posts. *J. of Biomedical Informatics* 62, C (Aug. 2016), 148–158. https://doi.org/10.1016/j.jbi.2016.06.007

[10] Robert Leaman, Laura Wojtulewicz, Ryan Sullivan, Annie Skariah, Jian Yang, and Graciela Gonzalez. 2010. Towards Internet-age Pharmacovigilance: Extracting Adverse Drug Reactions from User Posts to Health-related Social Networks. In *Proceedings of the 2010 Workshop on Biomedical Natural Language Processing (BioNLP '10)*. Association for Computational Linguistics, Stroudsburg, PA, USA, 117–125. http://dl.acm.org/citation.cfm?id=1869961.1869976

[11] Bing Liu. 2012. *Sentiment Analysis and Opinion Mining*. Morgan & Claypool Publishers.

[12] A. Mishra, A. Malviya, and S. Aggarwal. 2015. Towards Automatic Pharmacovigilance: Analysing Patient Reviews and Sentiment on Oncological Drugs. In *2015 IEEE International Conference on Data Mining Workshop (ICDMW)*. 1402–1409. https://doi.org/10.1109/ICDMW.2015.230

[13] Jin-Cheon Na and Wai Yan Min Kyaing. 2015. Sentiment Analysis of User-Generated Content on Drug Review. *Journal of Information Science Theory and Practice* 1, 1 (Mar 2015). https://doi.org/10.1633/JISTaP.2015.3.1.1

[14] Azadeh Nikfarjam and Graciela H. Gonzalez. 2011. Pattern mining for extraction of mentions of Adverse Drug Reactions from user comments. *AMIA Annual Symposium proceedings* 2011 (2011), 1019–1026.

[15] Azadeh Nikfarjam, Abeed Sarker, Karen O'Connor, Rachel E. Ginn, and Graciela Gonzalez. 2015. Pharmacovigilance from social media: mining adverse drug reaction mentions using sequence labeling with word embedding cluster features. In *JAMIA*.

[16] Abeed Sarker, Rachel Ginn, Azadeh Nikfarjam, Karen OÃ¢Ã¢ñâĎ¢Connor, Karen Smith, Swetha Jayaraman, Tejaswi Upadhaya, and Graciela Gonzalez. 2015. Utilizing social media data for pharmacovigilance: A review. *Journal of Biomedical Informatics* 54 (2015), 202 – 212. https://doi.org/10.1016/j.jbi.2015.02.004

[17] Lei Xia, Anna Lisa Gentile, James Munro, and José Iria. 2009. Improving Patient Opinion Mining Through Multi-step Classification. In *Proceedings of the 12th International Conference on Text, Speech and Dialogue (TSD '09)*. Springer-Verlag, Berlin, Heidelberg, 70–76. https://doi.org/10.1007/978-3-642-04208-9_13

A Multi Agent Approach to Facilitate the Identification of Interleaved Activities

Claire Orr
Ulster University, Jordanstown,
Northern Ireland

Chris Nugent
Ulster University, Jordanstown,
Northern Ireland

Haiying Wang
Ulster University, Jordanstown,
Northern Ireland

Huiru Zheng
Ulster University, Jordanstown,
Northern Ireland

ABSTRACT

This paper presents a Multi-agent approach to identifying interleaved activities in a smart environment. The use of binary contact sensors was explored to identify Activities of Daily Living with assistance from a system made up of agents. Activities were identified when an activity trigger event was detected. Upon detection, a time window would activate around the trigger event, prompting the activity agents to identify which of their events were present within the set time window, thus enabling them to calculate a percentage of likeliness that the activity was their own. As a result, the highest percentage of activity matches would be displayed as having occurred. To evaluate this approach, 36 interleaved activities were processed and compared with a single agent system in addition to 28 non-interleaved activities. As a benchmark, the results were compared to that of another study. Results presented a precision, recall and F-measure of 0.69, 0.81 and 0.74. This paper concluded that the Multi Agent System (MAS) is a promising approach for identifying interleaved activities when compared to methods that fail when presented with data that is not in a set order. However, several limitations are present which need to be overcome to make the results more accurate when compared to other approaches.

KEYWORDS

Multi Agent System; Ambient Assisted Living; Aging in Place

DH'18, April 23-26, 2018, Lyon, France.
© 2018 Association of Computing Machinery.
ACM ISBN 978-1-4503-6493-5/18/04...$15.00.
DOI: http://dx.doi.org/10.1145/3194658.3194684

ACM Reference format:
Claire Orr, Chris Nugent, Haiying Wang and Huiru Zheng. 2018. A Multi Agent Approach to Facilitate the Identification of Interleaved Activities. In *DH'18: 2018 International Digital Health Conference, April 23-26, 2018, Lyon, France.* ACM, NY, NY, USA, 6 pages.
DOI: http://dx.doi.org/10.1145/3194658.3194684

1 INTRODUCTION

As the use of pervasive computing is becoming more popular in healthcare it is beginning to bridge the gap between technology and the physical world [1]. With the growing ageing population and the need to reduce healthcare costs, encouraging the ageing to live independently for longer has placed more demand on the need for robust and scalable smart environments. As a result, it is now possible to perform automated human activity recognition and in return identify changes in activity patterns that may be linked to long term health issues [2]. Activity recognition can be used to identify activities of daily living (ADLs) performed by occupants of smart environments [3]. ADLs are recognized more easily when they are scripted, step by step in a set order, so ensuring a more realistic set of results would require using more complex scenarios such as interleaved activities [4]. This paper proposes a Multi Agent approach to the identification of interleaved ADLs within the context of a smart environment with the aim to provide monitoring of the elderly with cognitive declines such as dementia. Using binary contact sensors to monitor the opening or closing of doors or the movement of objects, and a Multi Agent System (MAS) activity recognition is carried out; with results being displayed according to the percentage of likeliness that agents, within the MAS, decide matches each ADL. This is achieved using a temporal algorithm, generating custom time windows based on the available sensor data. Time windows were triggered by an activation "trigger" sensor, with each ADL having their own unique 'trigger' assigned, generating a time window that will encompass the preceding N seconds of sensor data and the ensuing N seconds of sensor data. The use of a MAS facilitates these time windows to be considered simultaneously subsequently allowing for the detection of multiple activities at the same time. This paper presents the outcome of this approach and highlights the limitations found in comparison to a benchmarking method. The remainder of the paper is structured as follows. Related Work will highlight similar research within the areas of activity recognition, MAS and interleaved activities. The Methodology section presents an overview of the MAS and the algorithms used whilst highlighting each ADL and set of interleaved activities involved in the study. Experimental Results and Discussion present and discuss the findings from this study in comparison to a similar approach and highlights limitations. Finally, the Conclusion and Future Work section provides a critique of the findings and outlines the plans for future work.

2 RELATED WORK

Previous studies have investigated interleaved activities, activity recognition using agents and using multi-agent systems, however, none have combined these, especially using a MAS for the purpose of ambient assisted living. A study by Helaoui *et al.* looked at recognizing interleaved activities using a Markov logic method [5]. They took into consideration the start and end times of activities and evaluated it against activity recognition algorithms. The authors ensured the data they used included activities that were more complex such as overlapping and alternating events to provide a more realistic result. Nevertheless, their limitations made their work differ from this study. Firstly, they made assumptions about their activity recognition, where if an activity's start point is not detected then they did not consider this activity in their results. Therefore, if an activity was carried out as expected, with only the 'start point' missing, this activity was not acknowledged at all. Furthermore, they used wearable RFID tags to collect a proportion of their data, despite wearable technologies being a growing area in healthcare, it still produces many challenges. Wearable technology can be expensive to implement in addition to being difficult to gain trust with the elderly or persons intended for use [6]. Within their study the results of precision, recall and F-measure were 0.71, 0.99 and 0.82. Hamid *et al.* aimed to recognise ADLs from sets of events in a smart environment where 'One agent' activities were focused on and events were performed one at a time [7]. Strain gages were placed throughout their smart environment which collected data when walked over. They relied on the start and end event of activities to identify what the activity is and similar to the proposed method in this paper, activities were made up with local events, for example, if the fridge was opened then milk must be have been lifted out. They did not take in to consideration that some events may take longer than others and therefore did not test their approach with event duration in mind. A further study by Lu *et al.* [8] investigated interleaved activities using a location-aware activity recognition approach. They used RFID tags and a smart floor to collect data which they then used to identify activities based on the location of the participant. Limitations with this method again included costs of installation of a smart floor in addition to the complications that

came with requiring the participant to wear an RFID device [8]. This method was also quite complex in that multiple types of intrusive sensors were required, some such as cameras causing ethical issues mainly with privacy. Generally, limitations found included using an approach that did not take time in to consideration when carrying out activities and sensors that were pricey or intrusive to privacy having been used to collect data. The method presented in this paper did not possess any of these limitations; all events that took place were acknowledged as having taken place and all sensors used were contact sensors, so no major expense, trust or privacy issues had potential to arise.

3 METHODOLOGY

Nexa LMST-606 contact sensors [1] were placed around a smart environment, to detect actions which were then translated and identified as activities by set algorithms. 16 sensors were placed around the smart environment's bedroom (with en suite) and kitchen in specific areas to detect the opening and closing of doors, movement of appliances or to mimic the use of appliances and furniture such as the bed and kettle. Locations of each sensor are presented in Fig. 1, showing the overview of the smart environment with an 'x' marking the location of each Nexa sensor. Each sensor opening or closing represented an event, for example using the kettle or a cupboard opening or being closed.

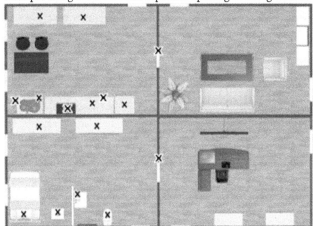

Figure 1: Image showing the layout of the smart environment where the approximate location of each of the 16 Nexa sensors have been marked with an 'X'.

Events were grouped together to form seven single activities and nine interleaved activities, all of which are listed in Table 1.

Table 1: List of activities in each Dataset

Activity	Dataset
Dressing	Non-Interleaved
Sleeping	Non-Interleaved
Toileting	Non-Interleaved
Preparing a Hot Drink	Non-Interleaved
Preparing a Cold Drink	Non-Interleaved
Preparing Food	Non-Interleaved
Cleaning	Non-Interleaved
Dressing & Sleeping	Interleaved
Dressing & Toileting	Interleaved
Sleeping & Toileting	Interleaved
Preparing a Hot Drink & Preparing Food	Interleaved
Preparing a Hot Drink & Preparing a Cold Drink	Interleaved
Preparing a Cold Drink & Preparing Food	Interleaved
Preparing a Hot Drink & Cleaning	Interleaved
Preparing a Cold Drink & Cleaning	Interleaved
Preparing Food & Cleaning	Interleaved

Interleaved activities were devised by pairing single activities together, with events within an interleaved activity carried out in a specific order to ensure that the activities would be properly interleaved within each other. As an example of this, Table 2 presents the order of events in the interleaved activity of Dressing & Sleeping, where their events are amalgamated.

Table 2: Table showing the formation of the interleaved activities of dressing and sleeping

Event Order	Event	Activity
1	Open bedroom door	Dressing & Sleeping
2	Open bedside drawer	Sleeping
3	Open Wardrobe	Dressing
4	Use the bed	Sleeping
5	Open Dresser	Dressing

To collect data, one researcher carried out each single activity and interleaved activity four times, creating two datasets: a non-interleaved (112 instances) and an interleaved (232 instances).

3.1 Multi Agent System (MAS)

The MAS used as part of this activity recognition system was created using Java. Each single activity had its own agent; there were seven activity agents in total: Dressing, Sleeping, Toileting, Hot Drink, Cold Drink, Food and Cleaning. Raw data was collected through sensor readings and stored within a database.

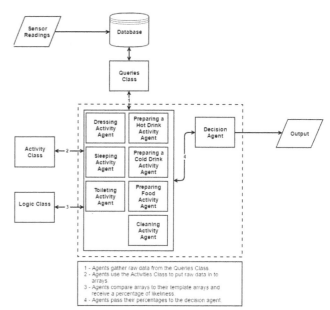

Figure 2: Image showing the relationship and communication flow between agents within the MAS.

The Queries Class accessed the data in the database so it could be used by the activity agents. Each agent looked for their assigned trigger event and set a time window around the trigger so that they would know what data was required from the Queries Class. Agents took the raw data and used the Activity Class to sort it in to arrays. Activity Agents used the Logic Class to compare and match the arrays to their own template arrays. By matching events, the agents worked out a percentage of likeliness of their activity being carried out and would inform the Decision Agent; who would then decide which percentages were the highest two, and display them as having taken place. Fig. 2 illustrates this process and shows the communication flow between these agents.

3.2 Time Windows

Activities were recognized when their events were carried out within a set time window. Time window parameters were set when a uniquely assigned event was found: these were known as Trigger Events, these are listed in Table 3.

Table 3: List of Trigger Events

Unique Trigger Event	Activity
Wardrobe	Dressing
Bed	Sleeping
Toilet	Toileting
Kettle	Preparing a Hot Drink
Crockery Cupboard	Preparing a Cold Drink
Microwave	Preparing Food
Cleaning Cupboard	Cleaning

Each time the MAS detected a Trigger Event, a set time would be set before and after the timing of the Trigger Event. Through ad hoc testing the optimal time window was found to be 120 seconds long, with 60 seconds preceding and proceeding the trigger event, and was applied for all activities. As an example, when the 'Kettle' Trigger Event was detected, the parameter was set around this and events within the time window set were noted: This is illustrated in Fig. 3.

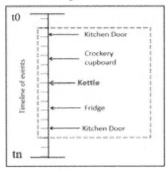

Figure 3: Image showing how a time window is set when the Trigger Event 'Kettle' is detected.

Once the events within the time window were noted, they were entered one by one in to an array. This array was then compared against set arrays within each activity agent in the MAS. The output consisted of how much (as a percentage) the activity found matched the activities in the MAS. For example, if 4 out of 5 of the events were found to match then this would be an 80% match. An example of pseudocode showing how percentages were calculated is presented in Fig. 4.

```
Algorithm  calculatePercentage(int[] template, int[] data, double
           totalPositives)
1.  Create result variable
2.  Create counter variable
3.  For
4.        Loop through template array
5.              for
6.                    Loop through data array (sensorIDs)
7.                          if data == template
8.                                Counter +1
9.                          End if
10.             End for
11. End for
12. Calculate percentage and assign to result
13. Return result
```

Figure 4: Example of pseudocode showing how percentages are calculated within the MAS.

3.3 Single Agent System

As a benchmark, a single agent system was created to compare with the MAS approach. This system was only able to read events in the order they occurred. The MAS differed from this as agents within it ran in parallel, looking for their own activities independently and working together to output their results. For example, when dressing and toileting were carried out, the single agent system identified the dressing events, until it recognized a toileting event in which case it decided that dressing must no longer be taking place and did not report a result.

4 EXPERIMENTAL RESULTS & DISCUSSION

This Section presents the results from this study, compares two different systems, a single agent system and the MAS, on their ability to identify interleaved activities, and states limitations

found. Accuracy was determined through measuring the precision, recall and F-Measure of results. Two experiments were carried out, one as a benchmark which was the single agent system, the second with the MAS. All agents in both the single and MAS implemented the same algorithm within the context of their individual activities. In each experiment, two sets of data were tested, the first being single activities carried out in order and repeated four times, the second being the interleaved dataset made up of nine pairs of activities, also repeated four times. In total, this resulted in 344 sensor events being recorded. For each experiment, the precision, recall and F-Measure were calculated at thresholds set in 20% increments. Each percentage increment represents the likeliness of the activity taking place, for example, if the system predicts that there is a 60% or higher chance that sleeping is taking place, this is marked as having happened. In the first experiment, the single agent system could detect all the activities as they were carried out in a precise order and all fell within the set time windows, results of this are presented in Fig. 5.

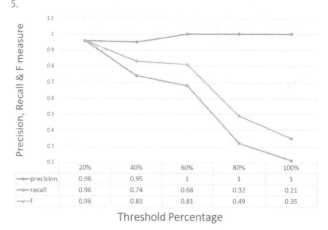

Threshold Percentage	20%	40%	60%	80%	100%
precision	0.96	0.95	1	1	1
recall	0.96	0.74	0.68	0.32	0.21
f	0.96	0.83	0.81	0.49	0.35

Figure 5: Line graph illustrating the thresholds in increments used to get the optimal Precision, Recall and F-Measure for identifying single activities in the single agent system.

When the interleaved dataset was tested with this system it was unable to identify any activities as no single activities were present in the interleaved dataset. Within the second experiment, the MAS identified the single activities, results of which can be seen in Fig. 6. Through ad hoc testing the optimal threshold was found to be 60% when identifying interleaved activities in the MAS; with a precision, recall and F-measure of 0.69, 0.81 and 0.74, respectively. Fig. 7 shows how the breakeven point of the results was at the threshold percentage of 80%, due to the recall and F-measure beginning to drop, as a result illustrating that 60% provided the most accurate results of thresholds tested.

As this MAS could identify the interleaved activities this was viewed as a success. A benefit of using a MAS was that agents all ran in parallel meaning if any changes or new implementations needed to take place it would have been easy to add in new agents or modify the specific agents as desired. The

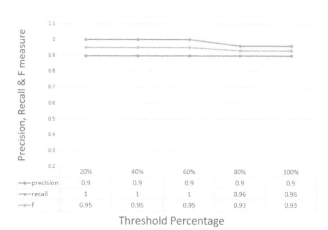

Figure 6: Line graph illustrating the thresholds in increments used to get the optimal Precision, Recall and F-Measure for identifying single activities in the MAS.

single agent system failed at identifying the interleaved activities as it read each event sequentially. With more agents, the MAS had the increased ability to assign each agent with their own roles, and thus provided them with the additional functionality to look for their own activities taking place, regardless of the order.

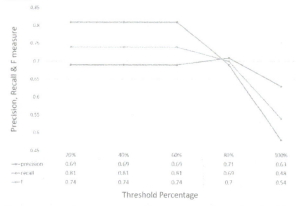

Figure 7: Line graph illustrating the thresholds in increments used to get the optimal Precision, Recall and F-Measure for identifying interleaved activities in the MAS.

By reading each activity in order the system would have been assuming that an activity had ended as soon as it detected an event from another activity, using the MAS removed this limitation.

5 CONCLUSION & FUTURE WORK

A Multi Agent approach has been used to develop an activity recognition method to identify interleaved activities in a smart environment. Time windows were used to allow agents to read events and decide upon a likelihood that their activity was being performed based on percentages estimated. This approach was tested and compared against a benchmark single agent system which could not identify if more than one activity was taking place at the same time. Thus, supporting that a MAS approach is successful at fulfilling the task of interleaved activity

identification due to its ability to run the agents in parallel, all looking for their own activities. When results were compared to that of the study by Helaoui *et al.* [5] it was found that the proposed methods' results were comparable to their study with a precision, recall and F-measure of 0.69, 0.81 & 0.74 as to their results of 0.71, 0.99 & 0.82. Their results were based around the assumptions that if the first sensor event is missed then the activity is not registered as happening. The study in this paper does not make any assumptions and performs almost as accurately. Limitations were however found within the proposed method. Within the MAS, each algorithm displayed a result every time the system was ran, therefore when an interleaved activity was carried out, the system identified most activities in that room as having taken place. To improve upon this a future study will be carried out to assign each ADL with a unique trigger id as before, only ensuring if this trigger is identified, only the percentage for that ADL will be displayed. As an example, when the activities of dressing and sleeping are carried out, results will only display results for these two activities and will not output the percentages of likeliness for all other activities. This would in turn result in a smaller false positive, thus producing more desirable precision, recall and F-measure results. In future, a larger dataset and/or a public dataset collected outside of this study could also be used to further benchmark against other data, this would be completed to gain a wider view into the accuracy and benefit of this method. Furthermore, future studies could also facilitate the identification of more than two activities occurring at once rather than limiting the system to a maximum of two.

REFERENCES

[1] R. Helaoui, M. Niepert, and H. Stuckenschmidt, "Recognizing Interleaved and Concurrent Activities: A Statistical-Relational Approach," Proc. 9th Annu. Int. Conf. Pervasive Comput. Commun., pp. 1–9, 2011.

[2] B. Kröse, T. Van Kasteren, C. Gibson, and T. Van Den Dool, "Care: context awareness in residences for elderly," Gerontechnology, vol. 7, no. 2, pp. 2–7, 2008.

[3] N. C. Krishnan and D. J. Cook, "Activity recognition on streaming sensor data," Pervasive Mob. Comput., vol. 10, pp. 138–154, 2014.

[4] L. Chen, C. Nugent, and G. Okeyo, "An ontology-based hybrid approach to activity modeling for smart homes," IEEE Trans. Human-Machine Syst., vol. 44, no. 1, pp. 92–105, 2014.

[5] R. Helaoui, M. Niepert, and H. Stuckenschmidt, "Recognizing interleaved and concurrent activities using qualitative and quantitative temporal relationships," Pervasive Mob. Comput., vol. 7, no. 6, pp. 660–670, 2011.

[6] N. Sultan, "International Journal of Information Management Reflective thoughts on the potential and challenges of wearable technology for healthcare provision and medical education," Int. J. Inf. Manage., vol. 35, pp. 521–526, 2015.

[7] R. Hamid, S. Maddi, A. Johnson, A. Bobick, I. Essa, and C. Isbell, "A novel sequence representation for unsupervised analysis of human activities," Artif. Intell., vol. 173, no. 14, pp. 1221–1244, 2009.

[8] C. Lu, Y. Ho, and L. Fu, "Creating Robust Activity Maps Using Wireless Sensor Network in a Smart Home," IEEE Int. Conf. Autom. Sci. Eng., pp. 741-746, 2007.

Machine Learning on Drawing Behavior for Dementia Screening

Kelvin KF Tsoi[2], Max WY Lam[1], Christopher TK Chu[2], Michael PF Wong[1,2], Helen ML Meng[1]

[1] Stanley Ho Big Data Decision Analytics Research Centre, The Chinese University of Hong Kong
[2] JC School of Public Health and Primary Care, The Chinese University of Hong Kong

Introduction[1]

Dementia is a public health problem which is affecting millions of elderly worldwide. Many screening tests are available for early detection on the symptoms of dementia, but most of them are in paper-and-pencil form. The guidance and judgment on test performance are heavily relied on healthcare professionals, but the subjective evaluation always incurs human bias. With advancement of technology, screening tests can be digitalized into computing format, and performed in any portable devices. Geometric drawing is one of the common questions among the screening tools, and digital screening platforms can real-time capture the drawing behavior which directly reflects the brain response during the screening. We had developed a platform to capture the drawing behavior and invited participants with different levels of dementia to be screened with this digital test.

ACM Reference format:
Kelvin KF Tsoi, Max WY Lam, Christopher TK Chu, Michael PF Wong, and Helen ML Meng. 2018. Machine Learning on Drawing Behavior for Dementia Screening. In *DH'18: 2018 International Digital Health Conference, April 23-26, 2018, Lyon, France.* ACM, NY, NY, USA, 2 pages.
DOI: https://doi.org/10.1145/3194658.3194659

Aim:

We applied machine learning to study the relationship of drawing behavioral data between participants with or without symptoms of dementia, and hypothesized that brain response time when drawing a simple figure can be digitalized for early detection of dementia.

Methods:

Patients diagnosed with moderate-to-severe stage of Alzheimer's disease (AD) were recruited from dementia clinics in Hong Kong. People without clinical symptoms of dementia were recruited from local community centers. Montreal Cognitive Assessment (MoCA) test was done in all subjects

before screening with the digital screening test. AD patients were classified with MoCA<22, and healthy subjects were with MoCA≥22 as suggested by Tan etal. [1] All participants had to draw two interlocking pentagons using their fingers on the touch screen in a tablet with reference to a sample figure. The drawing processes were modelled by Markov chains of order m, with n states of two continuous variables - drawing velocity and drawing direction. To transit from one state to another, for continuous variable we need a transition function instead of transition matrix. Gaussian processes were employed to specify the set of transition functions as distributions. This maintained a probabilistic tractability for Bayesian inference. Together the resultant combination of models is coined Gaussian process Markov Chains (GPMC). To maximizing specificity and sensitivity, we determined an optimal cut-off by plotting a Receiver Operating Characteristic (ROC) curve. The performance of the drawing platform was compared to the human judgement with reference to the scoring standard in the traditional screening test, the Mini-Mental State Examination (MMSE). Confidence intervals were calculated using Clopper-Pearson exact method.

Results:

A total of 798 participates was recruited, and 519 (65.0%) of them were classified with AD. The average age of AD patients was 80.3 years (SD=6.5), and average MoCA scores of 14.6 (SD=4.8). The median drawing time of the interlocking pentagons was 17.5 seconds. In the 279 healthy subjects, the average age was 75.5 years (SD=7.7), and with average MoCA scores of 24.9 (SD=2.1). The median drawing time on the pentagons was 12.7 seconds. The digital drawing platform shows a good diagnostic performance on the patients with AD with sensitivity of 74.1% and specificity of 72.3%. The comparison with the traditional scoring method in MMSE was shown in Table 1.

Conclusion:

Drawing behavior can be real-time captured with digital platform and further analyzed by machine learning methods for early detection of dementia. Other behavioral tests on memory, attention, and executive functions can be further developed as a digital platform for centralized cognitive screening. Big data on real-time behavioral features will be an emerging area in digital health research.

Table 1: Screening Performance of Different Screening Methods for Dementia

	MMSE's Scoring (95% CI)		Drawing platform (95% CI)	
Sensitivity	68.8%	(64.6%, 72.8%)	74.2%	(70.2%, 77.9%)
Specificity	52.5%	(45. 7%, 59.3%)	72.4%	(66.8%, 77.6%)
Positive predictive value	77.4%	(74.7%, 80.0%)	83.3%	(80.4%, 85.9%)
Negative predictive value	41.5%	(37.2%, 45.9%)	60.1%	(56.2%, 64.0%)

Abbreviation: CI: confidence interval

Reference

[1] Tan JP, Li N, Gao J, Wang LN, Zhao YM, Yu BC, et al. Optimal cutoff scores for dementia and mild cognitive impairment of the Montreal Cognitive Assessment among elderly and oldest-old Chinese population. Journal of Alzheimer's disease : JAD. 2015;43(4):1403-12.

Predicting Antimicrobial Drug Consumption using Web Search Data

Niels Dalum Hansen*
Statens Serum Institut, Denmark
nidh@ssi.dk

Kåre Mølbak
Statens Serum Institut, Denmark
krm@ssi.dk

Ingemar J. Cox†
University of Copenhagen, Denmark
ingemar.cox@di.ku.dk

Christina Lioma
University of Copenhagen, Denmark
c.lioma@di.ku.dk

ABSTRACT

Consumption of antimicrobial drugs, such as antibiotics, is linked with antimicrobial resistance. Surveillance of antimicrobial drug consumption is therefore an important element in dealing with antimicrobial resistance. Many countries lack sufficient surveillance systems. Usage of web mined data therefore has the potential to improve current surveillance methods. To this end, we study how well antimicrobial drug consumption can be predicted based on web search queries, compared to historical purchase data of antimicrobial drugs. We present two prediction models (linear Elastic Net, and non-linear Gaussian Processes), which we train and evaluate on almost 6 years of weekly antimicrobial drug consumption data from Denmark and web search data from Google Health Trends. We present a novel method of selecting web search queries by considering diseases and drugs linked to antimicrobials, as well as professional and layman descriptions of antimicrobial drugs, all of which we mine from the open web. We find that predictions based on web search data are marginally more erroneous but overall on a par with predictions based on purchases of antimicrobial drugs. This marginal difference corresponds to < 1% point mean absolute error in weekly usage. Best predictions are reported when combining both web search and purchase data.

This study contributes a novel alternative solution to the real-life problem of predicting (and hence monitoring) antimicrobial drug consumption, which is particularly valuable in countries/states lacking centralised and timely surveillance systems.

KEYWORDS

Web search query frequency, Prediction of antimicrobial drug use, Linear modelling, Gaussian Processes

ACM Reference Format:
Niels Dalum Hansen, Kåre Mølbak, Ingemar J. Cox, and Christina Lioma. 2018. Predicting Antimicrobial Drug Consumption using Web Search Data. In *DH'18: 2018 International Digital Health Conference, April 23–26, 2018, Lyon, France.* ACM, New York, NY, USA, 10 pages. https://doi.org/10.1145/3194658.3194667

---

*Work done while at IBM Denmark and University of Copenhagen, Denmark
†Also with Department of Computer Science, University College London, UK

---

1 INTRODUCTION

Surveillance of antimicrobial drug consumption, such as antibiotics, is an important element in dealing with antimicrobial resistance. Antimicrobial resistance is recognized as a major challenge, not only for the health care system, but also for economic growth and welfare [20]. Use of antimicrobials is one of the main factors responsible for the development, selection and spread of antimicrobial resistance [2]. This has become a serious threat to public health, notably because of the emergence and spread of highly resistant bacteria, and because there are very few novel antimicrobial agents in the research and development pipeline.

In the European Union the European Surveillance of Antimicrobial Consumption Network (ESAC-Net) [11] is collecting reference data from national antimicrobial drug consumption surveillance systems. The availability of national and EU-wide surveillance data has been a driving factor for the political commitment necessary for successful campaigns for responsible antimicrobial drug use [21]. The quality and granularity of the data varies widely even between European countries. Some countries, such as Denmark [28], have detailed surveillance systems that keep track of antimicrobial drug use both in primary care and hospitals with a coverage of approximately 97% of the total usage. While others, such as Germany [29], base their antimicrobial drug surveillance system on reimbursement data from insurance companies with a coverage of 85% the usage, but only for primary care. ESAC-Net is good example of the emerging focus on surveillance of antimicrobial drug use, and the importance of surveillance data. But many counties outside of the EU, such as the US, still lack nationwide surveillance systems, and many others have no monitoring at all. Hence, methods that can be implemented quickly and cost effectively are of great value.

Monitoring of antimicrobial drug consumption has several use cases in public health. Here we list two examples: 1) Knowing the consumption pattern of antimicrobials can be used as leverage in political discussions. Being able to document the problem and show measurable improvements can make a difference when discussing the allocation, or maintenance, of resources. 2) Identification of misuse is easier with access to detailed information about use patterns for antimicrobial drugs. An example could be if unusual quantities of macrolides, often used for mycoplasma pneumoniae, are being prescribed in periods with low mycoplasma pneumoniae incidence. This could indicate drug misuse, i.e. people are being treated for mycoplasma pneumoniae without being infected. In such a case it could be necessary to inform doctors on correct usage of macrolides.

To improve awareness and stimulate prudent use of antimicrobial drugs, monitoring is important. We hypothesize that antimicrobial drug consumption can be predicted, and hence monitored, from online behavior, such as the queries submitted to web search engines. This can benefit public health by: (i) Allowing countries without access to real-time data to forecast time trends and seasonal patterns of consumption; (ii) allowing all countries to analyze determinants of use, e.g. which types of web search queries are important as predictors of certain classes of antimicrobial drugs. This information can be used in communication efforts to stimulate antimicrobial stewardship; (iii) complementing syndromic surveillance, e.g. web searches that are predictive of drugs for respiratory infections can be used as an indicator of these diseases.

In this paper we study how well antimicrobial drug consumption can be predicted based on web search queries, and specifically the number of submitted queries to online search engines, e.g. how frequently people have searched for "fever" on Google in a specific time interval. To our knowledge such web search data has not been previously used to predict antimicrobial drug consumption. However, this type of web search data has been used previously to predict other health events, e.g. influenza like illness (ILI) [10] or vaccination uptake [6]. We compare web search based prediction to the more traditional method of predicting based on historical purchase data of antimicrobial drugs. We present two prediction models (a linear one, namely Elastic Net, and a non-linear one, namely Gaussian Processes), which we train and evaluate on almost 6 years of weekly antimicrobial drug consumption data from Denmark and web search data mined from Google Health Trends for the location of Denmark. We further present a novel method of selecting web search queries by considering diseases and drugs linked to antimicrobials, as well as professional and layman descriptions of antimicrobial drugs, all of which we mine from the open web. We find that the prediction error of swapping historical antimicrobial drug purchase data to web search queries is overall negligible, across different prediction offsets.

2 RELATED WORK

There is a large amount of work on using web search data to predict health events, though not antimicrobial drug consumption. Focusing on work related to public health, considerable effort has been used on estimating the incidence of various diseases based on web search query frequencies. Influenza like illness (ILI) prediction has been the subject of numerous papers [6, 10, 12, 17, 18, 23, 25], but other infectious diseases have also been predicted using web search data, e.g. dengue fever, gastrointestinal diseases, HIV/AIDS, scarlet fever, tuberculosis [3]. The domain is not restricted to infectious diseases: other papers have shown that web search data can be used for prediction of vaccination uptake [6, 13], hospital admissions [1] and dietary habits [30]. On an individual level, health events as diverse as pregnancy, allergy, eating disorder and post-traumatic stress disorder have also been identify based on web search query frequency analysis [32], illustrating the range and diversity of predictors available through web search frequency data.

We have not identified any studies on prediction of national drug consumption using web search frequency data. This does not mean that drugs have not been included in the previous studies. Inspecting the list of queries used in the prediction models for ILI reveals that brand names for cough medicine, such as Tessalon [5], Tylenol [17] or Robitussin [25], are included as predictors of ILI. This indicates that in the case of illness people query the web for information on the relevant medication [7], leading us to the hypothesis that drug consumption can be predicted based on web search query frequencies.

Prediction with web search query frequency data can be divided into two steps: (i) query selection and (ii) prediction using query frequency data. Query selection can for example be performed using hand picked seed words [10, 23], which are used to filter relevant from irrelevant searches, or using written descriptions of the event that is being predicted [6, 13]. Perhaps the most popular approach is to use the historical correlation between the query search frequency time series and the time series to be predicted [12, 18, 25]. When predicting using query frequency data, the most prevalent prediction models are linear models [12, 18, 25], but other non-linear models such as random forests [1, 6] or Gaussian Processes [16, 17] have also been used. While all these studies use web search data, other types of online data have also been used, e.g. social media data, such as Twitter messages [15, 22, 27]. In this work we use web search frequency data and make predictions using both a linear model and Gaussian Processes. We select queries based on a collection of written resources on antimicrobial drug consumption.

While there is, to our knowledge, no prior work on the prediction of antimicrobial drug consumption using web search data, there has been work in computational epidemiology regarding antibiotics on Twitter. In 2010 Scanfeld et al. [26] analyzed 1000 tweets mentioning antibiotics and categorized them into 11 categories. The top three categories were: "general use", "advice/information" and "side effects/negative reactions". Scanfeld et al. concluded that social media was used for sharing information about antibiotics and that the tweets could be used to identify potential misuse and misunderstandings regarding antibiotics. Later, in 2014, Dyar et al. [9] made a large scale analysis of worldwide Twitter activity mentioning antibiotics in the period September 2012 to 2013. They limited their analysis to four peaks in the twitter activity and examined the reason for those peaks. They concluded that the peaks were caused by institutional events, such as public announcements from the UK Chief Medical Officer regarding antibiotics. The peaks did not result in any sustained twitter activity, and activity was generally back to baseline level after two days. Kendra et al. [14] showed in 2015 that tweets regarding antibiotic usage could be categorized automatically using a neural network. Like Dyar et al. [9], they also observed that peaks in activity were correlated with public events such as a speech by the British prime minister and an executive order from the President of the US regarding antibiotic resistance. None of the studies address a potential relationship between Twitter activity related to antimicrobials and antimicrobial drug consumption. Since none of the studies collected data for more than one year, long term relationships between online activity and antimicrobial drug consumption have not been analyzed. In contrast, we use web search data spanning 5 years and 10 months.

Next we describe, the data collected for our analysis (Section 3), and then our prediction methods (Section 4).

3 DATA

We use three categories of data: (1) Sales of antimicrobials in Denmark collected by Danish health officials; (2) Web search query frequency data from Denmark; (3) Freely available online material related to antimicrobial drugs such as disease descriptions or information about antimicrobials. We describe these next.

3.1 Antimicrobial usage in Denmark

We use weekly data on purchases of antimicrobials for people in Denmark provided by the Danish Health Data Authority from the Register of Medicinal Product Statistics. This covers all purchases of

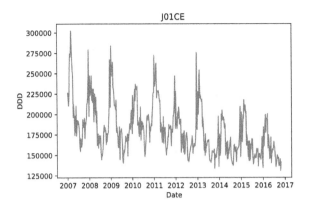

Figure 1: Weekly usage of antimicrobial J01CE in Denmark from 2007 to 2016. DDD denotes *defined daily doses.*

antimicrobials by people in Denmark, except for private hospitals and clinics (very few exist in Denmark), psychiatric hospitals, specialized non-acute care clinics, rehabilitation centers, and hospices. These exempted cases account for approximately 3% of the total antimicrobial drug consumption. The data spans the period 1 January 2007 – 23 October 2016, inclusive. Due to limitations on the web frequency data we only use data from 2011 onwards in the evaluation. The data is collected from pharmacies in Denmark and consists of sales data for several antimicrobial subgroups. Different subgroups are used for different diseases. We focus on the largest subgroup, namely *beta-lactamase sensitive penicillins*, with the Anatomical Therapeutic Chemical (ACT) classification system code J01CE. Usage is quantified as *defined daily doses* (DDD), meaning assumed average maintenance dose per day for adults for the condition the drug is registered for. Figure 1 shows the sales data of J01CE for the study period. We see that DDD tends to peak once or twice per year, and that from 2014 until 2016 the overall yearly range of DDD has decreased. There is a noticeable change in usage from 2014 onwards. This change is probably due to national campaigns aimed at reducing usage and change in usage to other antimicrobials. J01CE is often used for treatment of pneumonia and seasonal variations are therefore expected.

3.2 Web search query frequency

Our second category of data consists of web search queries and their frequencies. We retrieve them from the Google Health Trends API. This is an API maintained by Google and it is similar to Google Trends. Google Health Trends makes it possible to submit a query and receive aggregated weekly web search frequency data, i.e. a time series corresponding to how many times people have searched for that specific query each week. The Google Health Trends API is based on a uniform sample of 10%-15% of Google web searches. The results correspond to the probability of a short web search session matching the submitted query. It is possible to restrict the search both with respect to a time period and geographical region. We restrict our search to data from the period 2 January 2011 – 23 October 2016, inclusive, and for the geographical region Denmark. We only use data from 2011 and onwards because Google changed their geographical identification in 2011.

3.3 Online antimicrobial material

Our third category of data consists of freely available online information on antimicrobial drugs, and specifically on: (i) disease names, (ii) drug names, and (iii) descriptions of antimicrobials. For each of these, we extract data from the websites described below. We collect online data on antimicrobials to use them for selecting web search queries. We describe precisely how we do this in Section 4.1.

3.3.1. Disease names: Descriptions of diseases are downloaded from two online resources, both maintained by sundhed.dk (ENG: health.dk) a governmental web site functioning as a digital gateway for citizens to health services, e.g. electronic patient journals, hospital treatment records, etc. The two websites, Patienthåndbogen[1] (ENG: The Patient's Handbook) and Lægehåndbogen[2] (ENG: The Doctor's Handbook), are designed as encyclopedias of diseases. The target audience for The Patient's Handbook is laymen, and for The Doctor's Handbook health professionals.

3.3.2. Drug names: The organization Dansk Lægemiddel Information A/S (ENG: Danish Drug Information) maintains two websites, min.medicin[3] (ENG: My Medicine), and pro.medicin[4] (ENG: Pro Medicine), with descriptions of drugs available on the Danish drug market. The organization is funded by the medical industry and the Danish government. My Medicine targets laymen, while Pro Medicine targets health professionals.

3.3.3. Descriptions of antimicrobials: We choose descriptions from four websites describing to laymen what antimicrobials are and when to use them: www.ssi.dk, www.netdoctor.dk, www.sundhed.dk, and www.antibiotikaellerej.dk. The four websites are maintained by the following four groups: Danish Center for Disease Control, netdoctor.dk (a leading Danish health information website), sundhed.dk, and finally a collaboration of the Danish government, the pharmacist union, the doctors union, the society for general practitioners and the Danish Center for Disease Control. We consider all of the four groups to be authoritative and neutral.

4 PREDICTION OF ANTIMICROBIAL DRUG CONSUMPTION

The goal is to predict antimicrobial drug consumption using web search data. We do this in three steps: First, we select web search queries that are likely to indicate antimicrobial drug consumption (Section 4.1); then, for each query frequency time series we generate a number of lagged versions and decide which lags should be used for the prediction (Section 4.2); and finally we use appropriate prediction models to infer antimicrobial drug consumption (Section 4.3).

4.1 Query selection

For our analysis we use web search queries, and their frequencies, retrieved from Google Health Trends, as described in Section 3.2. We select these queries based on the online antimicrobials material described in Section 3.3 as follows.

We start with an empty set of queries and a set of seed words. Our seed words are the ATC code "J01CE", and the individual nouns of the

[1]https://www.sundhed.dk/borger/patienthaandbogen/
[2]https://www.sundhed.dk/sundhedsfaglig/laegehaandbogen/
[3]http://min.medicin.dk/
[4]http://pro.medicin.dk/

Query sets	#Queries
Disease names pro	47
Disease names lay	11
Drug names pro	7
Drug names lay	8
Descriptions lay	72
Descriptions lay frequent	18

Table 1: Number of queries in each query set.

antimicrobial name: "penicillin", "penicilliner" (plural form of penicillin) and "beta-lactamase". Using these seed words, we populate the set of queries in the following way:

Disease names (described in Section 3.3.1): A disease name is added to the set of queries if the treatment description for the disease mentions one of the seed words.

Drugs names (described in Section 3.3.2): A drug name is added to the set of queries if the description of the active substances mentions one of the seed words, or if the sub-heading of the drug description page contains one of the seed words.

Description of antimicrobials (described in Section 3.3.3): For each of the four descriptions (found in each of the four websites described in Section 3.3.3) we extract all unique words and remove stop words, that is commonly occurring words, such as "I", "and", etc. We use as stop word set the 100 most frequent words in CorpusDK [8], a corpus of text representing written Danish around year 2000. Based on these four sets of words, we select two partially overlapping sets of queries: (i) Words that occur in at least two descriptions of antimicrobials or antimicrobial usage targeting laymen, and (ii) words that occur in at least three descriptions of antimicrobials or antimicrobial usage targeting laymen.

The above process results in these six sets of queries:

(1) **Disease names pro:** Disease names used by health professionals.
(2) **Disease names lay:** Disease names used by laymen.
(3) **Drug names pro:** Drug names used by health professionals.
(4) **Drug names lay:** Drug names used by laymen.
(5) **Descriptions lay:** Words co-occurring in two descriptions of antimicrobials for laymen.
(6) **Descriptions lay frequent:** Words co-occurring in three descriptions of antimicrobials for laymen.

Table 1 shows the number of queries per query set. The highest number of queries is generated from *Descriptions lay frequent*, followed by *Disease names pro*. The queries generated from drug names (both *Drug names pro* and *Drug names lay*) are by far the fewest.

4.2 Time lag selection

Each query in the query sets described above has an associated time series (time stamps and search frequency). It is not unlikely that there exist lagged effects, for example increased search activity in one week might correspond to increased antimicrobial drug consumption two weeks after. To account for such effects we generate a number of lagged versions of each query frequency time series and include only a subset of them in our prediction models. We select these by fitting a linear model with the antimicrobial drug consumption data as target variable and lagged versions of the query frequencies as predictors:

$$y_t = \sum_{l=1}^{L}\sum_{i=1}^{N}\beta_{(l-1)N+i}Q_{t-l,i}, \tag{1}$$

where y_t denotes the antimicrobial drug consumption at time t, L is the number of lags, N the number of queries, $Q_{t,i}$ is the query frequency at time t for query i, and β is the model coefficient. Each model coefficient is related to a variable, i.e. a query and a time offset, and the size of the coefficient defines the importance of the variable in the prediction model. We use the size of the coefficients for selecting queries and corresponding lags, which is described below.

To fit the model, we use Elastic Net which combines L1 and L2 regularization. Two hyper-parameters, λ_1 and λ_2, control the L1 and L2 penalization for the Elastic Net regularization. Using matrix notation, the function being minimized can be written as:

$$\|y - \beta X\|^2 + \lambda_1\|\beta\|_1 + \lambda_2\|\beta\|_2^2 \tag{2}$$

where y is a vector with the target values, and X is a matrix with lagged query frequency time series. Elastic Net is well suited for problems where the number of variables is much larger than the number of training samples [33], which can be the case in our setups if many lags are used. In addition, Elastic Net groups correlated features and, either keeps them in the model, i.e. non-zero coefficient, or leaves them out [33]. This is a useful attribute for query selection, since we would like to select all correlated queries. To select queries, we sort the queries according to the absolute value of the coefficients, and pick the 100 with highest absolute value. While Elastic Net can be used for query selection without any threshold, i.e. by removing features with zero valued coefficients, there is no upper bound on the number of features. Due to problems with model fitting of the Gaussian processes, we enforce a hard threshold of 100 queries.

4.3 Prediction Models

Our goal is to predict antimicrobial drug consumption, i.e. the number of Defined Daily Doses (DDDs) of antimicrobials being consumed per week. To this end, we use two types of prediction models: (i) Linear models with Elastic Net regularization presented in Section 4.3.1. This is a common approach often used when predicting with web search data [12, 31]. (ii) Gaussian Processes, which are capable of capturing non-linearities in the data presented in Section 4.3.2. These models have successfully been applied to web search data to improve predictive performance [16, 17].

For both prediction models we use three setups for our predictions: (i) Using only web search data, (ii) using only historical antimicrobial drug consumption data, and (iii) combining historical antimicrobial drug consumption data and web search data.

We explain our prediction models next.

4.3.1 Linear models for antimicrobial drug consumption prediction. We use linear models because they are easy to fit and to interpret, allowing us to draw direct inferences between their output and the real life prediction problem at hand. Using only web search data, the prediction model is defined as:

$$y_{t+p} = \beta_0 + \sum_{i=1}^{N}\beta_i Q_{t,i} \tag{3}$$

where y_{t+p} is the antimicrobial drug consumption data at time t with a prediction offset of p, N is the number of queries, $Q_{t,i}$ is the query frequency at time t for query i, and the βs are the model coefficients.

When using only antimicrobial drug consumption data, we use a standard autoregressive model definition:

$$y_{t+p} = \alpha_0 + \sum_{j=1}^{M} \alpha_j y_{t-j} \qquad (4)$$

where M denotes the number of autoregressive terms, and the αs are the model coefficients. This is a similar model to the one used in [18].

To make predictions using both web search data and historic antimicrobial drug consumption data, we combine the two above models into a single model closely resembling the approach described in [31]. The model is as follows:

$$y_{t+p} = \theta_0 + \sum_{j=1}^{M} \theta_j y_{t-j} + \sum_{i=1}^{N} \theta_{i+M} Q_{t,i}, \qquad (5)$$

where the θs are the model coefficients, and the remaining notation is as defined above.

For all the linear models we use Elastic Net regularization for estimating the model coefficients, as described in Equation 2. The two hyper-parameters λ_1 and λ_2 are found using three fold cross-validation on the training data.

4.3.2 Gaussian Processes for antimicrobial drug consumption prediction. Gaussian Processes (GP) are probability distributions over functions, where any finite set of function values have a joint Gaussian distribution [24]. We focus on GP that learn functions that map from our input space of size m to a single valued output, i.e. $f : R^m \rightarrow R$. The size of the input space is defined by either the number of queries, autoregressive terms, or a combination of the two.

The functions drawn from a GP can be described by two functions: A mean function and a covariance function. The mean function is defined as:

$$E[f(x)] = \mu(x) \qquad (6)$$

where x is our input data, and μ denotes the mean of the function distribution at point x. The covariance function is defined as:

$$Cov[f(x), f(x')] = k(x, x') \qquad (7)$$

where x and x' are two input vectors, and k is a kernel function [24]. When working with GP it is customary to assume that the mean value is zero, and focus only on the covariance/kernel. The covariance function defines prior covariance between two input values and is typically controlled using two parameters: length scale and variance. For the Squared Exponential covariance function that we use, the variance defines the average distance from the mean, and the length scale defines how quickly the underlying signal changes, i.e. the antimicrobial drug consumption. Given the input data and the covariance function, it is possible to automatically infer the optimal parameters of the model given the data. A feature of GP is that covariance functions can be combined. This property can be used to create new covariance functions that can capture several aspects of the data. For example, combining covariance functions with different length scales could be used to model slow changes and quick changes. We use this property below.

We use two different setups, one for experiments involving web search data, and one when only historical antimicrobials data is used. The covariance function we use for web data is the Matern covariance function which allows for adapting to non-smooth changes by varying the parameter ν, and is defined as:

$$k_m^\nu(x, x') = \sigma^2 \frac{2^{1-\nu}}{\Gamma(\nu)} \left(\frac{\sqrt{2\nu} r}{l} \right)^\nu K_\nu \left(\frac{\sqrt{2\nu} r}{l} \right), \qquad (8)$$

where ν is a parameter that in our case is set to $3/2$ (a common choice), r is $|x - x'|$, l is the length scale, σ^2 is the variance, and K_ν is a modified Bessel function [24]. To model many different types of behaviour we use the additive properties of the covariance function and generate a new covariance function, k_{web}, for the web search data consisting of 10 Matern functions:

$$k_{web}(x, x') = \sum_{i=1}^{10} k_m^{\nu=3/2}(x, x'; \sigma_i, l_i) + N(\sigma_{11}), \qquad (9)$$

where $N(\sigma_{11})$ is Gaussian distributed noise.

When only working with historical antimicrobial drug consumption data, we use two other covariance functions: the linear and the squared exponential (SE). The linear covariance function can capture upwards or downwards trends in the data, and the SE function can capture short-term temporal variations in the data. The SE covariance function is defined as:

$$k_{SE}(x, x') = \sigma^2 exp\left(\frac{-(x - x')^2}{2l^2} \right), \qquad (10)$$

where l is the length scale, and σ^2 the variance. The linear covariance function is defined as:

$$k_{lin}(x, x') = \sigma^2 x^T x', \qquad (11)$$

with σ^2 as variance. Combing the two covariance functions we get a new covariance function that we use for the antimicrobial drug consumption data. We denote the covariance function $k_{antimicrobial}$ and define it as follows:

$$k_{antimicrobial}(x, x') = k_{SE}(x, x'; \sigma_1, l_1) + k_{lin}(x, x'; \sigma_2) + N(\sigma_3) \qquad (12)$$

Parameters for all models are found using gradient descent. Different covariance functions have been tested, and we report the results of the setup with the lowest error.

5 EXPERIMENTAL EVALUATION

5.1 Experimental setup

To simulate a real world prediction situation we test the models in a leave-one-out fashion, where we re-train the prediction model after each time step such that all available data is used. This is a common setup in health event prediction [6, 16, 31].

The number of autoregressive antimicrobial drug consumption terms varies between 4, 26 and 130 weeks, i.e. M in Equation 4 and 5. For the web search data we generate queries with a maximum lag of 4, 26 and 130 weeks, with the specific lags selected as described in Section 4.2. Four different prediction offsets are tested: 0, 4, 8, and 12 weeks. The prediction offset denotes how far into the future we are predicting. For example, an offset of 0 means that antimicrobial drug consumption in week t is predicted using web data and historical antimicrobial drug consumption data from weeks prior to t. For an offset of 4 the antimicrobial drug consumption in week $t+4$ is predicted using web data and historical antimicrobial drug consumption data from weeks prior to t.

The web search data covers 2 January 2011 – 23 October 2016, in total 304 weeks of data. Queries are selected using the first 104 weeks of data. Each experiment uses as a minimum 104 weeks of training

Offset	Data Source	GP	Elastic Net
	Web only	11011.0	11096.9
0 weeks	Antimicrobial only	11446.0	9980.9
	Web & antimicrobial	10644.3	**9970.8**
	Web only	11270.7	11398.1
4 weeks	Antimicrobial only	11498.2	9990.3
	Web & antimicrobial	10576.2	**9989.9**
	Web only	11026.1	11142.5
8 weeks	Antimicrobial only	11401.6	10301.0
	Web & antimicrobial	10564.4	**9781.0**
	Web only	10977.8	11189.1
12 weeks	Antimicrobial only	11231.0	10424.0
	Web & antimicrobial	10249.1	**9644.3**

Table 2: RMSE for best performing prediction (among all query sets) with the non-linear (GP) and linear (Elastic Net) prediction model, using web, antimicrobial purchase data, and their combination. Lowest error per offset is in bold.

Offset	Data Source	GP	Elastic Net
	Web only	8463.4	8507.7
0 weeks	Antimicrobial only	8571.0	7294.5
	Web & antimicrobial	8105.3	**7282.7**
	Web only	8938.2	9040.8
4 weeks	Antimicrobial only	9265.8	**7989.9**
	Web & antimicrobial	8440.0	8073.2
	Web only	8596.4	8579.8
8 weeks	Antimicrobial only	9053.2	8200.7
	Web & antimicrobial	8311.2	**7849.9**
	Web only	8258.8	8463.5
12 weeks	Antimicrobial only	8997.7	8257.6
	Web & antimicrobial	8056.7	**7750.0**

Table 3: MAE for best performing prediction (among all query sets) with the non-linear (GP) and linear (Elastic Net) prediction model, using web, antimicrobial purchase data, and their combination. Lowest error per offset is in bold.

data for model fitting. With the 12 weeks of prediction offset and up 130 weeks of autoregressive terms, we end up with an evaluation period of the 58 weeks leading up to 23 October 2016.

We evaluate predictions using the root mean squared error (RMSE) and mean absolute error (MAE). A feature of the RMSE is that large prediction errors receive a bigger penalty than small errors. This intuitively means that few large errors will result in a larger RMSE than many small errors. The MAE, on the other hand, assigns equal weight to all errors, and the final score is therefore easier to interpret. With respect to our data, a MAE of 10000 corresponds to the prediction on average being 10000 DDDs off on every weekly prediction. This corresponds to approximately 6% of the weekly average of DDDs.

The RMSE is calculated as:

$$RMSE = \sqrt{1/N \sum_{t=1}^{N} (y_t - \hat{y}_t)^2} \qquad (13)$$

where y_t is the true value at time t, $\hat{y}_t$ is the predicted value at time t, and N the number of predictions. The MAE is calculated as:

$$MAE = 1/N \sum_{t=1}^{N} |y_t - \hat{y}_t|. \qquad (14)$$

5.2 Experimental results

We start by presenting the results with respect to model selection and prediction offset. Subsequently in Section 5.2.1 we discuss the influence of query set and time lag selection.

Tables 2 & 3 show the RMSE and MAE when predicting antimicrobial drug consumption using (i) only web search data, (ii) only historical antimicrobial purchase data, and (iii) both web search and antimicrobial purchase data. Only the best performance (lowest error) is reported per data source, prediction model, and offset.

We see that predictions based on a combination of web and antimicrobial purchase data give almost always the lowest error. With Gaussian Processes as the prediction model, predictions based only on web data outperform those based on antimicrobial purchase data; with Elastic Net, the situation is reversed: predictions based on antimicrobial purchase data outperform those based on web data. Comparing the two prediction models (Gaussian Processes and Elastic

Offset	Data Source	GP	Elastic Net
	Web only	5.4%	5.4%
0 weeks	Antimicrobial only	5.4%	**4.6%**
	Web & antimicrobial	5.1%	**4.6%**
	Web only	5.7%	5.7%
4 weeks	Antimicrobial only	5.9%	**5.1%**
	Web & antimicrobial	5.4%	**5.1%**
	Web only	5.5%	5.5%
8 weeks	Antimicrobial only	5.8%	5.2%
	Web & antimicrobial	5.3%	**5.0%**
	Web only	5.2%	5.4%
12 weeks	Antimicrobial only	5.7%	5.2%
	Web & antimicrobial	5.1%	**4.9%**

Table 4: MAE as a percentage of the average weekly antimicrobial usage for the 58 week evaluation period.

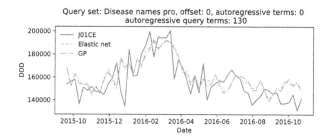

Figure 2: Prediction using only web search data.

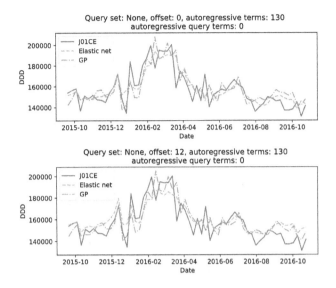

Figure 3: Prediction using only historic antimicrobial purchase data.

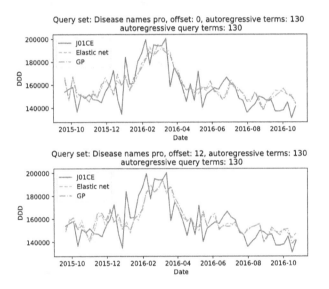

Figure 4: Prediction using both web and antimicrobial purchase data.

Net), we only observe minor differences, generally favouring the linear models. These results fit well with the general prevalence of linear models for prediction using web search data, though it is curious why Gaussian Processes in other work outperform Elastic Net on similar tasks [16, 17]. One explanation could be that the feature selection described in Section 4.2 uses Elastic Net, which means that we are selecting features that have a linear relationship with the target variable, i.e. antimicrobial drug consumption. In other words, we have a priori selected features that are well suited for the Elastic Net model.

Overall, the fluctuations in error (both RMSE and MAE) across different prediction models, data sources, and offsets are generally

small. This is also illustrated in Table 4, which shows the MAE scores of Table 3 as the % of average weekly consumption in the evaluation period. We see that our predictions are, in the best case, off by 4.6% of the average weekly consumption, and in the worst case by 5.9%.

We also observe in Tables 2 – 4 that error remains generally stable independent of offset. Looking back at Figure 1 we observe two things which might explain this: (i) The antimicrobial drug consumption is strongly seasonal, therefore models that capture the latent seasonality will perform well even with a large offset. (ii) As will be described next, many of the queries with highest model coefficients have approximately 1 year lag. Combined with the fact that the consumption patterns in the last three years of the time series are very similar, we should expect to be able to predict the antimicrobial drug consumption relatively accurately one year into the future.

In Figures 2 – 3 we further plot the predictions by the two models (GP and Elastic Net) using only web or only antimicrobial purchase data against actual antimicrobial purchase data (J01CE). The precise settings of these four runs are stated in the figure titles. We see that, when using web data only, seasonal variations are generally captured; however, a drop in antimicrobial drug consumption in January 2016 is not captured. Visually, the difference between a 0 week offset and a 12 week offset is hard to spot. When using only antimicrobial purchase data, on the other hand, the GP model captures the drop in consumption in January 2016, both with a 0 week offset and a 12 week offset. Again differences between 0 week offset and 12 week offset are negligible. Finally, Figure 4 shows the combination of the two data sources. Here neither model captures the drop in January 2016. Differences between 0 week offset and 12 week offset are, as before, minor.

Overall, we find that the use of web data only gives predictions that are slightly more erroneous, but generally not that far off, from those made when using only historical antimicrobial purchase data. For both types of data we find that long term variations are consistently captured, while precise short term predictions, e.g. drop in consumption in January 2016 Figure 3, are better captured using historic antimicrobial data. As a tool for maintaining political focus and analyzing general usage patterns, short term precision is likely of less importance. The fact that the difference between the data sources is so small is valuable for countries lacking timely access to centralised antimicrobial purchase data, because it means that we can approximate predictions that are roughly less than 1% point erroneous compared to those using antimicrobial purchase data (for the same offset – cf. Table 4). This performance appears generally stable across different prediction offsets and linear (Elastic Net) vs non-linear (GP) prediction models.

Next we analyse the impact of web search query selection to prediction performance.

5.2.1 Web search query analysis. Depending on the amount of maximum number of lags used, different queries are selected from the six query sets displayed in Table 1. We vary the maximum number of lags between 4, 26 and 130 weeks. Table 5 shows the top 10 queries from each query set when using 4 weeks of historical antimicrobial data. The queries are selected using the method described in Section 4.2. We see that most of the queries listed in Table 5 are diseases curable with antimicrobials, such as Scarlet Fever and pneumonia. We also see diseases such as psoriasis, which itself is not treatable with antimicrobials, but which increases the risk of skin infections. It is interesting to note that even rare diseases, such as anthrax (typically a non-lethal skin infection) and syphilis, are in the top 10; this occurs because both of these diseases have antimicrobials as primary

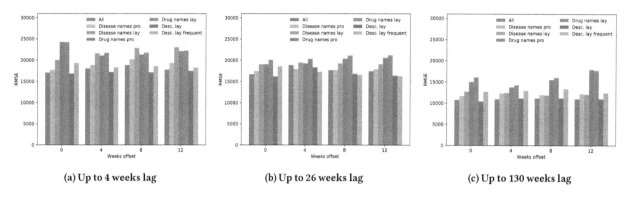

(a) Up to 4 weeks lag

(b) Up to 26 weeks lag

(c) Up to 130 weeks lag

Figure 5: Prediction based on web search data with different query sets and lags, using Gaussian Processes.

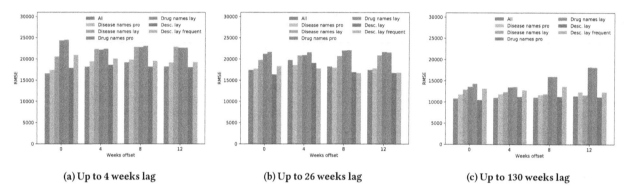

(a) Up to 4 weeks lag

(b) Up to 26 weeks lag

(c) Up to 130 weeks lag

Figure 6: Prediction based on web search data with different query sets and lags, using Elastic Net.

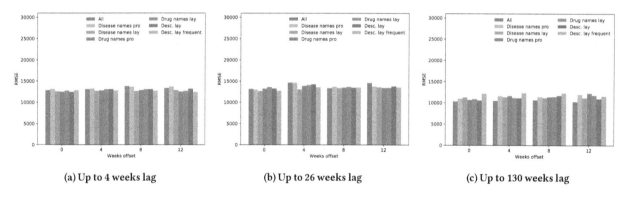

(a) Up to 4 weeks lag

(b) Up to 26 weeks lag

(c) Up to 130 weeks lag

Figure 7: Prediction based on both web data and antimicrobial purchase data (130 autoregressive terms), with different query sets and lags, using Gaussian Processes.

treatment. For the queries derived from the laymen descriptions of antimicrobials, there is a number of spurious correlations, e.g. words such as "one", "effect", etc. While these queries are apparently well correlated to antimicrobial drug consumption, they are semantically unrelated to antimicrobial usage, meaning that their generalisable discriminative strength is limited.

Table 6 further shows the top 10 queries for a lag of up to 130 weeks. In this case we clearly begin to see the effect of seasonality (seen in Figure 1), because several of the diseases have lags of approximately one year, i.e. 52 weeks. In the top 10 for *Disease names*

pro are two chronic diseases: type-2 diabetes and COPD. For both of these the lag does not correspond to a yearly seasonality. This likely indicates that, it is not these precise diseases that are treated by antimicrobials; rather, patients of these diseases are likely to develop weaker immune systems, indicating that after one or two years they are more prone to complications needing antimicrobial treatment.

Similarly to Table 5, we also observe in Table 6, that *Descriptions lay* and *Description lay frequent* yield words unrelated to antimicrobials as queries. Inspecting the lag of the unrelated words, e.g. 94 weeks for "growth", we observe that they are spurious correlations,

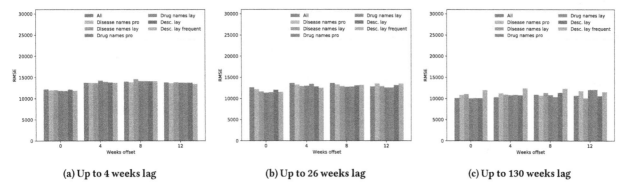

(a) Up to 4 weeks lag   (b) Up to 26 weeks lag   (c) Up to 130 weeks lag

Figure 8: Prediction based on both web data and antimicrobial purchase data (130 autoregressive terms), with different query sets and lags, using Elastic Net.

Query set	Top 10 queries
Disease names pro	psoriasis$_{t-2}$, skarlagensfeber$_{t-3}$ (*Scarlet Fever*), skarlagensfeber$_{t-2}$, lungebetændelse$_{t-4}$ (*pneumonia*), prostatitis$_{t-4}$, diabetes - type 2$_{t-3}$, psoriasis$_{t-3}$, blindtarmsbetændelse$_{t-3}$ (*appendicitis*), lungebetændelse$_{t-3}$, blyforgiftning$_{t-4}$ (*lead poisoning*)
Disease names lay	skarlagensfeber$_{t-2}$, skarlagensfeber$_{t-3}$, skarlagensfeber$_{t-1}$, endokardit$_{t-2}$ (*endocarditis*), endokardit$_{t-1}$, endokardit$_{t-3}$, endokardit$_{t-4}$, brystbetændelse$_{t-1}$ (*mastitis*), syfilis$_{t-3}$ (*syphilis*), miltbrand$_{t-2}$ (*anthrax*)
Descriptions lay	lungebetændelse$_{t-3}$, én$_{t-2}$ (*one*), lungebetændelse$_{t-2}$, én$_{t-4}$, virkning$_{t-3}$ (*effect*), én$_{t-1}$, lungebetændelse$_{t-4}$, halsbetændelse$_{t-1}$ (*sore throat*), stoffer$_{t-1}$ (*drugs*), én$_{t-3}$

Table 5: Top 10 queries for each query set generated with a maximum lag of 4 weeks and a 0 week prediction offset. The subscript denotes the offset from the current prediction point. *Drug names lay, drug names pro* and *descriptions lay frequent* have zero valued coefficients and are therefore omitted from the Table. English translations in brackets.

Query set	Top 10 queries
Disease names pro	blindtarmsbetændelse$_{t-6}$ (*appendicitis*), caries$_{t-1}$, skarlagensfeber$_{t-52}$ (*Scarlet Fever*), diabetes - type 2$_{t-121}$, kol$_{t-83}$ (*COPD*), gasgangræn$_{t-38}$ (*gas gangrene*), kol$_{t-3}$, caries$_{t-125}$, diabetisk neuropati$_{t-112}$, kol$_{t-82}$
Disease names lay	skarlagensfeber$_{t-52}$, skarlagensfeber$_{t-53}$, skarlagensfeber$_{t-51}$, skarlagensfeber$_{t-50}$, skarlagensfeber$_{t-55}$, skarlagensfeber$_{t-54}$, gasgangræn$_{t-100}$, skarlagensfeber$_{t-3}$, gasgangræn$_{t-38}$, skarlagensfeber$_{t-103}$
Drug names pro	novu$_{t-59}$, novu$_{t-111}$, novu$_{t-116}$, novu$_{t-30}$, novu$_{t-9}$, novu$_{t-62}$, novu$_{t-32}$, novu$_{t-7}$, novu$_{t-127}$, novu$_{t-82}$
Drug names lay	novu$_{t-59}$, novu$_{t-111}$, novu$_{t-62}$, novu$_{t-9}$, novu$_{t-30}$, novu$_{t-66}$, novu$_{t-7}$, novu$_{t-116}$, novu$_{t-33}$, novu$_{t-32}$
Descriptions lay	skyldes$_{t-107}$ (*due*), vækst$_{t-94}$ (*growth*), udvikle$_{t-123}$ (*develop*), immunforsvar$_{t-83}$ (*immune system*), resistens$_{t-4}$ (*resistance*), allergi$_{t-92}$ (*allergy*), bivirkninger$_{t-9}$ (*side-effect*), dræbe$_{t-99}$ (*kill*), behandlingen$_{t-85}$ (*treatment*), skyldes$_{t-104}$
Descriptions lay frequent	infektion$_{t-51}$ (*infection*), vækst$_{t-55}$, vækst$_{t-94}$, infektion$_{t-78}$, medicin$_{t-4}$ (*medicine*), virus$_{t-102}$, bakterier$_{t-83}$ (*bacteria*), vækst$_{t-42}$, behandling$_{t-62}$, bakterierne$_{t-117}$

Table 6: Top 10 queries for each query set with a maximum lag of 130 and a 0 week prediction offset. The subscript denotes the offset from the current prediction point. English translations in brackets.

but not seasonal, as has been previously observed for the prediction of influenza like illnesses [5, 18]. Such spurious correlations cannot be expected to reliably model rapid changes in antimicrobial drug consumption, as discussed above.

Figures 5 & 6 show the prediction error when only using web search data from the different query sets and for different lags, for Gaussian Processes and Elastic Net, respectively. While we previously saw in Tables 5 & 6, that *Drug names pro* and *Drug names lay* were the data sources with the most semantically relevant queries, we now see that *Descriptions lay* generally is the best performing query set. We previously observed that *Descriptions lay* contained spurious correlations, so it seems strange that this query set performs

best. Similar observations have been made with respect to ILI prediction, where the semantically relevant query set was outperformed by a less relevant one [5]. This likely happens for two reasons: (i) spurious correlations can model the expected seasonality well, (ii) lack of evaluation data can make correlations due to chance more likely [19].

We also see in Figures 5 & 6 that there is a noticeable reduction in prediction error, for all query sets, when moving from a maximum lag of 26 weeks to 130 weeks. This is likely due to the modeling of seasonal variations that we noticed in Table 6. Even when predicting 12 weeks into the future, the prediction error is still relatively stable. As we saw in Table 6, there are long term effects of antimicrobial drug usage, either seasonal changes or long term predictors such as type-2 diabetes, and these are likely some of the reasons why prediction into the future works well.

The impact of query selection upon prediction performance significantly diminishes when prediction is based on a combination of web data and historical antimicrobial purchase data, i.e. when high quality time series data is available. We see that in Figures 7 & 8.

Finally, as we noted previously, the consistent prediction performance across a prediction offset of 0 weeks and 12 weeks strong. Figure 1 shows that the three last years of our antimicrobial consumption time series are very similar. This is likely one of the reasons for the consistent performance independent of the prediction offset. It is not unlikely that the prediction models will perform significantly worse in case of a sudden change, as was observed with Google Flu during the 2009 swine flu [4]. In such a scenario we would expect the semantically relevant queries to remain correlated with the consumption, while the search pattern for the irrelevant queries should remain unchanged given changes in antimicrobial consumption. Given such a change in consumption, it is likely that the difference between the *Disease names pro* query set and *Descriptions lay* query set would become apparent.

6 CONCLUSION

We studied the extent to which consumption of antimicrobial drugs, such as antibiotics, can be predicted from web search data. We compared this to predictions based on more traditional historical purchase data of antimicrobial drugs. We experimented with different prediction models (Elastic Net and Gaussian Processes), and a novel method of selecting web search queries indicative of antimicrobial drug consumption by mining antimicrobial related information from publicly available descriptions of diseases and drugs linked to antimicrobials. Experiments with more than 9 years of weekly antimicrobial drug consumption data from Denmark showed that prediction using web search data are overall comparable and marginally more erroneous than predictions using antimicrobial drug sales data. The difference in error between the two is equivalent to 1% point mean absolute error in weekly consumption. This performance was found to be relatively stable across variations in prediction offsets, prediction models, and query selection methods.

Competing interests. The authors have declared that no competing interests exist.

REFERENCES

[1] Vibhu Agarwal, Liangliang Zhang, Josh Zhu, Shiyuan Fang, Tim Cheng, Chloe Hong, and Nigam H Shah. 2016. Impact of predicting health care utilization via web search behavior: a data-driven analysis. *Journal of medical Internet research* 18, 9 (2016).
[2] EFS Authority et al. 2015. ECDC/EFSA/EMA first joint report on the integrated analysis of the consumption of antimicrobial agents and occurrence of antimicrobial resistance in bacteria from humans and food-producing animals. *EFSA Journal* 13, 1 (2015).
[3] Theresa Marie Bernardo, Andrijana Rajic, Ian Young, Katie Robiadek, Mai T Pham, and Julie A Funk. 2013. Scoping review on search queries and social media for disease surveillance: a chronology of innovation. *Journal of medical Internet research* 15, 7 (2013).
[4] Samantha Cook, Corrie Conrad, Ashley L Fowlkes, and Matthew H Mohebbi. 2011. Assessing Google flu trends performance in the United States during the 2009 influenza virus A (H1N1) pandemic. *PloS one* 6, 8 (2011), e23610.
[5] Niels Dalum Hansen, Kåre Mølbak, Ingemar J Cox, and Christina Lioma. 2017. Seasonal Web Search Query Selection for Influenza-Like Illness (ILI) Estimation. In *Proceedings of the 40th International ACM SIGIR Conference on Research and Development in Information Retrieval*. ACM, 1197–1200.
[6] Niels Dalum Hansen, Kåre Mølbak, Ingemar J Cox, and Christina Lioma. 2017. Time-Series Adaptive Estimation of Vaccination Uptake Using Web Search Queries. In *Proceedings of the 26th International Conference on World Wide Web*. 773–774.

[7] Radu Dragusin, Paula Petcu, Christina Lioma, Birger Larsen, Henrik Jørgensen, Ingemar J. Cox, Lars Kai Hansen, Peter Ingwersen, and Ole Winther. 2013. FindZebra: A search engine for rare diseases. *I. J. Medical Informatics* 82, 6 (2013), 528–538.
[8] DSL. 2002. Korpus2000. (2002). http://ordnet.dk/korpusdk/
[9] Oliver J. Dyar, Enrique Castro-Sánchez, and Alison H. Holmes. 2014. What makes people talk about antibiotics on social media? A retrospective analysis of Twitter use. *Journal of Antimicrobial Chemotherapy* 69, 9 (2014), 2568–2572.
[10] Gunther Eysenbach. 2006. Infodemiology: tracking flu-related searches on the web for syndromic surveillance. In *AMIA Annual Symposium Proceedings*, Vol. 2006. American Medical Informatics Association, 244. https://doi.org/PMC1839505
[11] European Center for Disease Prevention and Control. 2018. European Surveillance of Antimicrobial Consumption Network (ESAC-Net). https://ecdc.europa.eu/en/about-us/partnerships-and-networks/disease-and-laboratory-networks/esac-net. (2018). Accessed on 21-01-2018.
[12] Jeremy Ginsberg, Matthew H Mohebbi, Rajan S Patel, Lynnette Brammer, Mark S Smolinski, and Larry Brilliant. 2009. Detecting influenza epidemics using search engine query data. *Nature* 457, 7232 (2009), 1012–1014.
[13] Niels Dalum Hansen, Kåre Mølbak, and Christina Lioma. 2016. Ensemble Learned Vaccination Uptake Prediction Using Web Search Queries. In *Proceedings of the 25th ACM International on Conference on Information and Knowledge Management*, Vol. 24-28-Octo. ACM, New York, NY, USA, 1953–1956.
[14] Rachel Lynn Kendra, Suman Karki, Jesse Lee Eickholt, Lisa Gandy, Jesse Lee Eickholt, and Pearce Hall. 2015. Characterizing the Discussion of Antibiotics in the Twittersphere: What is the Bigger Picture? 17 (2015), 1–12.
[15] Vasileios Lampos, Tijl De Bie, and Nello Cristianini. 2010. Flu detector - Tracking epidemics on Twitter. *Machine Learning and Knowledge Discovery in Databases* (2010), 599–602.
[16] Vasileios Lampos, Andrew C Miller, Steve Crossan, and Christian Stefansen. 2015. Advances in nowcasting influenza-like illness rates using search query logs. *Scientific reports* 5 (2015).
[17] Vasileios Lampos, Bin Zou, and Ingemar Johansson Cox. 2017. Enhancing Feature Selection Using Word Embeddings: The Case of Flu Surveillance. In *Proceedings of the 26th International Conference on World Wide Web*.
[18] David Lazer, Ryan Kennedy, Gary King, and Alessandro Vespignani. 2014. The parable of Google Flu: traps in big data analysis. *Science* 343, 14 March (2014).
[19] Christina Lioma and Niels Dalum Hansen. 2017. A study of metrics of distance and correlation between ranked lists for compositionality detection. *Cognitive Systems Research* 44 (2017), 40–49.
[20] Jim O'Neill. 2016. *Tackling drug-resistant infections globally: Final report and reccomendations*. Technical Report. HM Government and Welcome Trust: UK.
[21] World Health Organization. 2018. Surveillance of Antimicrobial Use. http://www.who.int/medicines/areas/rational_use/AMU_Surveillance/en/. (2018). Accessed on 21-01-2018.
[22] Michael J Paul, Mark Dredze, and David Broniatowski. 2014. Twitter improves influenza forecasting. *PLoS currents* 6 (2014).
[23] Philip M Polgreen, Yiling Chen, David M Pennock, Forrest D Nelson, and Robert A Weinstein. 2008. Using internet searches for influenza surveillance. *Clinical infectious diseases* 47, 11 (2008), 1443–1448.
[24] Carl E. Rasmussen and Christopher K. I. Williams. 2004. *Gaussian processes for machine learning*. Vol. 14. 69–106 pages.
[25] Mauricio Santillana, D Wendong Zhang, Benjamin M Althouse, and John W Ayers. 2014. What can digital disease detection learn from (an external revision to) Google Flu Trends? *American journal of preventive medicine* 47, 3 (2014), 341–347.
[26] Daniel Scanfeld, Vanessa Scanfeld, and Elaine L Larson. 2010. Dissemination of health information through social networks: Twitter and antibiotics. *American journal of infection control* 38, 3 (2010), 182–188.
[27] Alessio Signorini, Alberto Maria Segre, and Philip M Polgreen. 2011. The use of Twitter to track levels of disease activity and public concern in the US during the influenza A H1N1 pandemic. *PloS one* 6, 5 (2011), e19467.
[28] Statens Serum Institut; National Veterinary Institute, Technical University of Denmark; National Food Institute, Technical University of Denmark. 2016. *DANMAP 2015 - Use of antimicrobial agents and occurrence of antimicrobial resistance in bacteria from food animals, food and humans in Denmark*. Technical Report.
[29] Klaus Weist, Arno Muller, Dominique Monnet, and Ole Heuer. 2014. *Surveillance of antimicrobial consumption in Europe 2012*. Technical Report. European Centre for Disease Prevention and Control.
[30] Robert West, Ryen W White, and Eric Horvitz. 2013. From cookies to cooks: Insights on dietary patterns via analysis of web usage logs. In *Proceedings of the 22nd international conference on World Wide Web*. ACM, 1399–1410.
[31] Shihao Yang, Mauricio Santillana, and S C Kou. 2015. Accurate estimation of influenza epidemics using Google search data via ARGO. *Proceedings of the National Academy of Sciences* 112, 47 (2015), 14473–14478.
[32] Elad Yom-Tov, Diana Borsa, Andrew C Hayward, Rachel A McKendry, and Ingemar J Cox. 2015. Automatic identification of Web-based risk markers for health events. *Journal of medical Internet research* 17, 1 (2015).
[33] Hui Zou and Trevor Hastie. 2005. Regularization and variable selection via the elastic net. *Journal of the Royal Statistical Society: Series B (Statistical Methodology)* 67, 2 (2005), 301–320.

Learning Image-based Representations for Heart Sound Classification

Zhao Ren
ZD.B Chair of Embedded Intelligence
for Health Care and Wellbeing,
University of Augsburg, Germany
zhao.ren@informatik.uni-augsburg.
de

Nicholas Cummins
ZD.B Chair of Embedded Intelligence
for Health Care and Wellbeing,
University of Augsburg, Germany
nicholas.cummins@ieee.org

Vedhas Pandit
ZD.B Chair of Embedded Intelligence
for Health Care and Wellbeing,
University of Augsburg, Germany
vedhas.pandit@informatik.
uni-augsburg.de

Jing Han
ZD.B Chair of Embedded Intelligence
for Health Care and Wellbeing,
University of Augsburg, Germany
jing.han@informatik.uni-augsburg.
de

Kun Qian
Machine theIntelligence and Signal
Processing Group, Technische
Universität München, Germany
andykun.qian@tum.de

Björn Schuller*
GLAM – Group on Language, Audio
& Music, Imperial College London,
UK
schuller@ieee.org

ABSTRACT

Machine learning based heart sound classification represents an efficient technology that can help reduce the burden of manual auscultation through the automatic detection of abnormal heart sounds. In this regard, we investigate the efficacy of using the pre-trained Convolutional Neural Networks (CNNs) from large-scale image data for the classification of Phonocardiogram (PCG) signals by learning deep PCG representations. First, the PCG files are segmented into chunks of equal length. Then, we extract a scalogram image from each chunk using a wavelet transformation. Next, the scalogram images are fed into either a pre-trained CNN, or the same network fine-tuned on heart sound data. Deep representations are then extracted from a fully connected layer of each network and classification is achieved by a static classifier. Alternatively, the scalogram images are fed into an end-to-end CNN formed by adapting a pre-trained network via transfer learning. Key results indicate that our deep PCG representations extracted from a fine-tuned CNN perform the strongest, 56.2 % mean accuracy, on our heart sound classification task. When compared to a baseline accuracy of 46.9 %, gained using conventional audio processing features and a support vector machine, this is a significant relative improvement of 19.8 % ($p < .001$ by one-tailed z-test).

*Björn Schuller is also with the ZD.B Chair of Embedded Intelligence for Health Care and Wellbeing, University of Augsburg, Germany.

CCS CONCEPTS

• **Computing methodologies → Supervised learning by classification**; • **Applied computing → Health care information systems**; **Health informatics**;

KEYWORDS

Heart Sound Classification, Phonocardiogram, Convolutional Neural Networks, Scalogram, Transfer Learning.

ACM Reference Format:
Zhao Ren, Nicholas Cummins, Vedhas Pandit, Jing Han, Kun Qian, and Björn Schuller. 2018. Learning Image-based Representations for Heart Sound Classification. In *DH'18: 2018 International Digital Health Conference, April 23–26, 2018, Lyon, France*. ACM, New York, NY, USA, 5 pages. https://doi.org/10.1145/3194658.3194671

1 INTRODUCTION

Heart disease continues to be a leading worldwide health burden [16]. Phonocardiograph is a method of recording the sounds and murmurs made by heart beats, as well as the associated turbulent blood flow with a stethoscope, over various locations in the chest cavity [11]. *Phonocardiogram* (PCG), as the product of phonocardiograph, is widely employed in the diagnosis of heart disease. Enhancing conventional heart diseases diagnostic methods using the state-of-the-art automated classification techniques based on PCG recordings, is a rapidly growing field of machine learning research [13]. In this regard, the recent PhysioNet/ *Computing in Cardiology* (CinC) Challenge in 2016 [3], has encouraged the development of heart sound classification algorithms, by collecting multiple PCG datasets from different groups to construct a large, more than 20 hours of recordings, heart sound database. The two-class classification of normal/ abnormal heart sound was the core task of the PhysioNet/ CinC Challenge 2016.

In recent years, *Convolutional Neural Networks* (CNNs) have proven to be effective for a range of different signals and image classification tasks [7, 9]. In particular, large-scale CNNs have revolutionised visual recognition tasks as evidenced by their performances in the ImageNet Large Scale Visual Recognition Competition (ILSVRC) [23]. On the back of the challenge, a large number of pre-trained CNNs have been made publicly available, such as AlexNet [10] and VGG [30]. Similarly, CNNs have also been successfully used for the detection of abnormal heart sounds [14].

Herein, we utilise the *Image Classification CNN* (ImageNet) to process *scalogram images* of PCG recordings for abnormal heart sound detection. Scalogram images are constructed using wavelet transformations [22]. Wavelets are arguably the predominate feature representation used for heart sound classification [8], and have successfully been applied in other acoustic classification tasks [19–21]. Moreover, instead of training CNNs from scratch, which can be a time-consuming task due in part to the large hyperparameter space associated with CNNs, we explore the benefits of using the aforementioned pre-trained ImageNet to construct robust heart sound classification models. Such an approach has been employed in other acoustic classification paradigms [1, 4], but to the best of the authors' knowledge it has not been verified for PCG based heart sound classification. Further, we also explore if transfer-learning based adaptation and updating of the ImageNet parameters can further improve the accuracy of classification.

The remainder of this paper is structured as follows: first, we describe our proposed approach in Section 2; the database description, experimental set up, evaluation method and results are then presented in Section 3; finally, our conclusions and future work plans are given in Section 4.

2 METHODOLOGY

In this section, we describe the classification paradigms we test for abnormal heartbeat detection. This consists of: (i) a conventional audio-based baseline system; (ii) two deep PCG representation systems combined with a *Support Vector Machine* (SVM) classifier; (iii) two end-to-end CNN based systems.

2.1 Baseline Classification System

As a baseline, we use a system based on the INTERSPEECH COMPUTATIONAL PARALINGUISTICS CHALLENGE (COMPARE) audio feature set [29], and SVM classification. The combination of COMPARE features and SVM have been used in a range of similar acoustic classification tasks such as snore sound classification [28]. The COMPARE feature set is a 6373 dimensional representation of an audio instance and is extracted using the openSMILE toolkit [5]; full details of the audio features presented in COMPARE can be found in [5].

2.2 Scalogram Representation

In this study, to transform the PCG samples into images which can be processed by an ImageNet, the scalogram images are generated using the *morse* wavelet transformation [17] with 2 kHz sampling frequency. We have previously successfully used these scalogram images for acoustic scene classification [21]. When creating the images, we represent frequency, in *kHz*, on the vertical axis, and time, in *s*, on the horizontal axis. We use the *viridis* colour map, which varies from blue (low range) to green (mid range) to red (upper range), to colour the wavelet coefficient values. Further, the axes and margins marking are removed to ensure only the necessary information is fed into the ImageNet. Finally, the scalogram

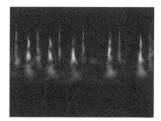
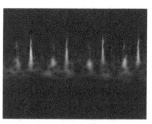

(a) Normal (*a0007.wav*)   (b) Abnormal (*a0001.wav*)

Figure 1: The scalogram images are extracted from the first 4 s segments of normal/ abnormal heart sounds using the *viridis* colour map. The samples from which these scalogram images have been extracted are described in parentheses.

images are scaled to 224 × 224 for compatibility with the VGG16 ImageNet [30], which will be introduced in Section 2.3.

The scalogram images of a normal and an abnormal heartbeat are given in Figure 1. It can even be observed by human eyes that, there are some clear distinctions between the two classes in these (exemplar) images.

2.3 Convolutional Neural Networks

We use an ImageNet to process the scalogram images for heart sound classification. The VGG16 ImageNet is chosen due to its successful application in the ILSVRC Challenge[1]. VGG16 is constructed from 13 ([2, 2, 3, 3, 3]) convolutional layers, five maxpooling layers, three fully connected layers {*fc6, fc7, fc*} and a soft-max layer for 1000 labels according to the image classification task in the ImageNet Challenge. The receptive field size of 3 × 3 is used in all of the convolutional layers. The full details of VGG16, including the training procedure, are described in [30]. The structure and parameters of VGG16 are obtained from Pytorch[2]. Further, we use VGG16 for either *feature extraction* or *classification* by transfer learning, both of which are described in the following sub-sections.

2.4 Deep PCG Feature Representations

ImageNet has gathered considerable research interest as a feature extractor for a task of interest, e. g., [1]. In this regard, this subsection presents two methodologies for unsupervised PCG feature extraction using VGG16.

2.4.1 PCG Feature Extraction from ImageNet. The activations of the first fully connected layer *fc6* of VGG16 are employed as our feature representations. These features have previously proven to be effective in the task of acoustic scene classification [21]. Essentially, we feed the scalogram images into VGG16 and then the deep PCG feature representations of 4096 attributes are extracted as the activations of all neurons in the first fully connected layer *fc6*.

2.4.2 PCG Feature Extraction from adapted ImageNet. As VGG16 is normally employed for image classification tasks on a very different data from that required for heart sound classification, the

---

[1]http://www.image-net.org/challenges/LSVRC/
[2]http://pytorch.org/

feature extraction method described in the previous sub-section may yields a sub-optimal feature representation. We therefore also employ a transfer learning methodology (see Section 2.5.2) to adapt the parameters of VGG16 to better suit the task of abnormal heart sound detection. After the adaptation according to Section 2.5.2, the scalogram images are fed into the updated CNN model and a new set of deep representations (also with 4096 attributes) are extracted from the first fully connected layer fc6.

2.4.3 Classification Methodology. We perform classification of the heart sound samples into one of two classes: normal and abnormal. The process is achieved for the deep PCG feature representations via a linear SVM; the robustness of SVM for such a classification task is well-known in the literature [6]. Herein, our two deep feature representations are denoted as *pre-trained VGG+SVM* for the set-up described in Section 2.4.1 and *learnt VGG+SVM* for the set-up described in Section 2.4.2.

2.5 End-to-end ImageNet based Classification

With the aim of constructing a robust end-to-end heart sound CNN classifier, we adapt the parameters of VGG16 on the heart sound data by transfer learning. To achieve this, we use two different approaches, both of which are described below.

2.5.1 Learning Classifier of ImageNet. Noting that there are three fully connected layers in VGG16, we create our ImageNet classifier, herein denoted as *learning Classifier of VGG16*, by freezing the parameters of the convolutional layers and *fc6*, and updating (using scalogram images of heart sound data) the parameters of the final two fully connected layers and the soft-max layer for classification.

2.5.2 Learning ImageNet. In this method, herein denoted as *learning VGG*, we replace the last fully connected layer with a new one which has 2 neurons and a soft-max layer in order to achieve the 2-class classification task. We then update the *entire* network (again, using scalogram images of heart sound data) so that *all* VGG16 parameters are adapted to the heart sound data. This method represents a faster way to achieve a full CNN based classification than training an entire CNN from scratch with random initialisation of parameters.

2.6 Late-fusion Strategy

As the PCG recordings in the PhysioNet/ CinC Challenge are of varying lengths (cf. Section 3.1), we segment the recordings into non-overlapping chunks of 4 seconds. We therefore employ a late-fusion strategy to produce a single label (normal/ abnormal) per recoding. Our strategy is based on the probabilities of predictions, $p_i, i = 1, ...n$ of each i-th segment of a PCG sample, as outputted by the SVM or the soft-max layer; we choose the label of a PCG sample according to the highest probability max $\{p_i\}$ gained from each chunk.

3 EXPERIMENTS

3.1 Database

Our proposed approaches are evaluated on the database of PhysioNet/ CinC Challenge 2016 [12]. This dataset is focused on classification of normal and abnormal heart sound recordings. As the test

set labels for this data are not publicly available, we use the training set of the database and split it into a new training/ development/ test set. There are totally 3240 heart sound recordings collected from 947 pathological patients and healthy individuals. The dataset consists of six sub-databases from different research groups:

(1) **MIT heart sounds database:** *The Massachusetts Institute of Technology heart sounds database* (MIT) [31, 32] comprises 409 PCG and ECG recordings sampled at 44.1 kHz with 16 bit quantisation from 121 subjects, in which there are 117 recordings from 38 healthy adults and 134 recordings from 37 patients. The recording duration varies from 9 s to 37 s with a 32 s average length.

(2) **AAD heart sounds database:** *Aalborg University heart sounds database* (AAD) [25–27] is recorded at a 4 kHz sample rate and 16 bit quantisation. It contains 544 recordings from 121 healthy adults and 151 recordings from 30 patients. The recording length varies from 5 s to 8 s with an 8 s average length.

(3) **AUTH heart sounds database:** *The Aristotle University of Thessaloniki heart sounds database* (AUTH) [18] includes 45 recordings in total from 11 healthy adults and 34 patients. Each healthy adult/ patient gives one recording and the recording length varies from 10 s to 122 s with a 49 s average length. The sampling rate is 4 kHz with 16 bit quantisation.

(4) **UHA heart sounds database:** *The University of Haute Alsace heart sounds database* (UHA) [15] is sampled at 8 kHz with a 16 bit quantisation. It contains 39 recordings from 25 healthy adults and 40 recordings from 30 patients. The recording length varies from 6 s to 49 s with a 15 s average length.

(5) **DLUT heart sounds database:** *The Dalian University of Technology heart sounds database* (DLUT) [33] includes 338 recordings from 174 healthy adults and 335 recordings from 335 patients. The recording length varies from 8 s to 101 s with a 23 s average length. The sampling rate is 8 kHz with 16 bit quantisation.

(6) **SUA heart sounds database:** *The Shiraz University adult heart sounds database* (SUA) [24] is constructed from 81 recordings from 79 healthy adults and 33 recordings from 33 patients. Except for three recordings sampled at 44.1 kHz and one at 384 kHz, the sampling rate is 8 kHz with 16 bit quantisation. The recording duration varies from 30 s to 60 s with a 33 s average length.

A detailed overview of database is described in Table 1. In this work, we split the dataset into a training set (including MIT, AUTH, UHA, and DLUT) and a test set (including AAD and SUA). Further, we carry out a three-fold cross validation by excluding the databases MIT, AUTH, or UHA (in their entirety) for fold 1, fold 2, or fold 3 (c. f., Table 2) respectively for validation, noting that due to its large size, DLUT is always used in system training.

3.2 Setup

We generate scalogram images using the Matlab-2017 wavelet toolbox[3]. During training/ adaptation of VGG16, both for last two layers of VGG16 (cf. Section 2.5.1), and the entire network (cf. Section 2.5.2), the *learning rate* is 0.001, the *batch size* is 64, and the *epoch* is set as 50. The *cross entropy* is applied as the loss function and *stochastic gradient descent* is used as the optimiser. The deep representations (cf. Section 2.4), with a dimensionality of 4096, are extracted from *fc6* of VGG16.

---

[3]https://de.mathworks.com/products/wavelet.html

Table 1: An overview of the training and test partitions used in this work. The training set is structured by four sub-sets from four different databases of the PhysioNet/ CinC dataset, and the test set is by two. The PCG recordings in this dataset are annotated by the two-class labels (normal/ abnormal).

Dataset	Database	Recordings	Normal	Abnormal	Durations (s)			
					Total	Min	Max	Average
Training	MIT	409	117	292	13328.08	9.27	36.50	32.59
	AUTH	31	7	24	1532.49	9.65	122.00	49.44
	UHA	55	27	28	833.14	6.61	48.54	15.15
	DLUT	2141	1958	183	49397.15	8.06	101.67	23.07
Total		2636	2109	527	65090.86			
Test	AAD	490	386	104	3910.20	5.31	8.00	7.98
	SUA	114	80	34	3775.45	29.38	59.62	33.12
Total		604	466	138	7685.65			

Table 2: Performances comparison of the proposed approaches with baseline. The methods are evaluated on the 3-fold development set and the test set. The experimental results are evaluated by *Sensitivity* (*Se*), *Specificity* (*Sp*), and the *Mean Accuracy* (*MAcc*).

	Development set												Test set		
	fold 1			fold 2			fold 3			mean					
performance [%]	Se	Sp	MAcc	Se	Sp	MAcc	Se	Sp	MAcc	Se	Sp	MAcc	Se	Sp	MAcc
COMPARE+SVM (baseline)	23.6	93.2	58.4	58.3	100.0	79.2	00.0	100.0	50.0	27.3	97.7	62.5	76.8	17.0	46.9
pre-trained VGG+SVM	57.2	70.9	64.1	41.7	85.7	63.7	17.9	81.5	49.7	38.9	79.4	59.1	24.6	87.1	55.9
learnt VGG+SVM	58.6	57.3	57.9	83.3	57.1	70.2	32.1	70.4	51.3	58.0	61.6	59.8	24.6	87.8	**56.2**
learning Classifier of VGG	68.2	51.3	59.7	79.2	14.3	46.7	35.7	40.7	38.2	61.0	35.4	48.2	33.3	63.7	48.5
learning VGG	83.6	40.2	61.9	95.8	28.6	62.2	53.6	44.4	49.0	77.7	37.7	57.7	12.3	95.7	54.0

When classifying by SVM, we use the LIBSVM library [2] with a linear kernel and optimise the SVM complexity parameter $C \in [10^{-5}; 10^{+1}]$ on the development partition. We present the best results from this optimisation as the final result.

3.3 Evaluation Method

According to the official scoring mechanism of the PhysioNet/ CinC Challenge 2016 [12], our predictions are evaluated by both *Sensitivity* (*Se*) and *Specificity* (*Sp*). For two-class classification, *Se* and *Sp* are defined as:

$$Se = \frac{TP}{TP + FN}, \quad (1)$$

$$Sp = \frac{TN}{TN + FP}, \quad (2)$$

where TP denotes the number of true positive abnormal samples, FN denotes the number of false negative abnormal samples, TN denotes the number of true negative normal samples, and FP denotes the number of false positive normal samples.

Finally, the *Mean Accuracy* (*MAcc*) is given as the overall score of the predictions, which is defined as:

$$MAcc = (Se + Sp)/2. \quad (3)$$

3.4 Results

The experimental results of the baseline and proposed methods are shown in Table 2. All CNN-based approaches achieve improvements in *MAcc* over the baseline on test set. Although this consistency is not seen on the development set, the *MAcc*s achieved on the test set indicate that the deep representation features extracted from scalogram images perform stronger and more robustly than conventional audio features when performing heart sound classification.

When comparing the methods 'learning Classifier of VGG' and 'learning VGG', it is clear from the results that adapting the entire CNNs is definitely more effective than only updating the last two fully connected layers. Moreover, an in-general trend of the SVM classification of features extracted from either the pre-trained or the learnt VGG topologies performing stronger than the CNN classifiers can be observed. This could be due in part to the SVM classifiers being better to suit to the relatively smaller amounts of training data available in the PhysioNet/ CinC dataset than the soft-max classifiers.

Finally, the strongest performance, 56.2 % *MAcc*, is obtained on the test set using the method 'learnt VGG+SVM'. This *MAcc* offers a significant relative improvement of 19.8 % on our baseline classifier ($p < .001$ by one-tailed z-test), COMPARE features and a SVM. Therefore, our learnt CNN model is shown to extract more salient deep representation features for abnormal heart sound detection when compared with features gained from the pre-trained VGG16 model.

4 CONCLUSIONS

We proposed to apply and adapt pre-trained *Image Classification Convolutional Neural Networks* (ImageNet) on scalogram images of *Phonocardiogram* (PCG) for the task of normal/ abnormal heart sound classification. Deep PCG representations extracted from a task-adapted version of the popular ImageNet VGG16 were shown to be more robust for this task than the widely used CoMParE audio feature set. The combination of learnt VGG features and a *Support Vector Machine* (SVM) significantly ($p < .001$ by one-tailed z-test) outperformed the CoMParE based baseline system. We speculate this success is due to the autonomous nature of the feature extraction associated with the 'learnt VGG' topology; the representations are adapted to the dataset and therefore are more robust than a 'fixed' conventional feature set.

In future work, data augmentation will be investigated for heart sound classification to compensate for the unbalanced nature of the dataset. Further, a new ImageNet topology based on the scalogram images will be developed and validated on a variety of heart sound datasets, e. g., AudioSet[4], to build a robust ImageNet for heart sound classification.

ACKNOWLEDGMENTS

 This work was partially supported by the German national BMBF IKT2020-Grant under grant agreement No. 16SV7213 (EmotAsS), the EU Horizon 2020 Innovation Action Automatic Sentiment Estimation in the Wild under grant agreement No. 645094 (SEWA), and the EU H2020/ EFPIA Innovative Medicines Initiative under grant agreement No. 115902 (RADAR-CNS).

REFERENCES

[1] Shahin Amiriparian, Maurice Gerczuk, Sandra Ottl, Nicholas Cummins, Michael Freitag, Sergey Pugachevskiy, Alice Baird, and Björn Schuller. 2017. Snore sound classification using image-based deep spectrum features. In *Proc. INTERSPEECH*. Stockholm, Sweden, 3512–3516.
[2] Chih-Chung Chang and Chih-Jen Lin. 2011. LIBSVM: A library for support vector machines. *ACM Transactions on Intelligent Systems and Technology* 2, 3 (Apr. 2011), 1–27.
[3] Gari D. Clifford, Chengyu Liu, Benjamin Moody, David Springer, Ikaro Silva, Qiao Li, and Roger G. Mark. 2016. Classification of normal/abnormal heart sound recordings: The PhysioNet/Computing in Cardiology Challenge 2016. In *Proc. Computing in Cardiology Conference (CinC)*. Vancouver, Canada, 609–612.
[4] Jun Deng, Nicholas Cummins, Jing Han, Xinzhou Xu, Zhao Ren, Vedhas Pandit, Zixing Zhang, and Björn Schuller. 2016. The University of Passau open emotion recognition system for the multimodal emotion challenge. In *Proc. CCPR*. Chengdu, China, 652–666.
[5] Florian Eyben, Felix Weninger, Florian Groß, and Björn Schuller. 2013. Recent Developments in openSMILE, the Munich open-source multimedia feature extractor. In *Proc. ACM Multimedia*. Barcelona, Spain, 835–838.
[6] Steve R. Gunn. 1998. Support vector machines for classification and regression. *ISIS technical report* 14, 1 (May 1998), 5–16.
[7] Andrej Karpathy, George Toderici, Sanketh Shetty, Thomas Leung, Rahul Sukthankar, and Li Fei-Fei. 2014. Large-scale video classification with convolutional neural networks. In *Proc. CVPR*. Columbus, OH, 1725–1732.
[8] Edmund Kay and Anurag Agarwal. 2016. DropConnected neural network trained with diverse features for classifying heart sounds. In *Proc. Computing in Cardiology Conference (CinC)*. Vancouver, Canada, 617–620.
[9] Yoon Kim. 2014. Convolutional neural networks for sentence classification. *arXiv preprint arXiv:1408.5882* (2014).

[10] Alex Krizhevsky, Ilya Sutskever, and Geoffrey E. Hinton. 2012. Imagenet classification with deep convolutional neural networks. In *Proc. NIPS*. Lake Tahoe, NV, 1097–1105.
[11] Aubrey Leatham. 1952. Phonocardiography. *British Medical Bulletin* 8, 4 (1952), 333–342.
[12] Chengyu Liu et al. 2016. An open access database for the evaluation of heart sound algorithms. *Physiological Measurement* 37, 12 (Nov. 2016), 2181–2213.
[13] Ilias Maglogiannis, Euripidis Loukis, Elias Zafiropoulos, and Antonis Stasis. 2009. Support vectors machine-based identification of heart valve diseases using heart sounds. *Computer Methods and Programs in Biomedicine* 95, 1 (July 2009), 47–61.
[14] Vykintas Maknickas and Algirdas Maknickas. 2017. Recognition of normal-abnormal phonocardiographic signals using deep convolutional neural networks and mel-frequency spectral coefficients. *Physiological Measurement* 38, 8 (July 2017), 1671–1679.
[15] Ali Moukadem, Alain Dieterlen, Nicolas Hueber, and Christian Brandt. 2013. A robust heart sounds segmentation module based on S-transform. *Biomedical Signal Processing and Control* 8, 3 (May 2013), 273–281.
[16] Dariush Mozaffarian et al. 2016. Heart disease and stroke statistics–2016 update: A report from the American Heart Association. *Circulation* 133, 4 (Jan. 2016), e38–e360.
[17] Sofia C. Olhede and Andrew T. Walden. 2002. Generalized morse wavelets. *IEEE Transactions on Signal Processing* 50, 11 (Nov. 2002), 2661–2670.
[18] Chrysa D. Papadaniil and Leontios J. Hadjileontiadis. 2014. Efficient heart sound segmentation and extraction using ensemble empirical mode decomposition and kurtosis features. *IEEE Journal of Biomedical and Health Informatics* 18, 4 (July 2014), 1138–1152.
[19] Kun Qian, Christoph Janott, Vedhas Pandit, Zixing Zhang, Clemens Heiser, Winfried Hohenhorst, Michael Herzog, Werner Hemmert, and Björn Schuller. 2017. Classification of the excitation location of snore sounds in the upper airway by acoustic multifeature analysis. *IEEE Transactions on Biomedical Engineering* 64, 8 (Aug. 2017), 1731–1741.
[20] Kun Qian, Christoph Janott, Zixing Zhang, Clemens Heiser, and Björn Schuller. 2016. Wavelet features for classification of vote snore sounds. In *Proc. ICASSP*. Shanghai, China, 221–225.
[21] Zhao Ren, Vedhas Pandit, Kun Qian, Zijiang Yang, Zixing Zhang, and Björn Schuller. 2017. Deep sequential image features on acoustic scene classification. In *Proc. DCASE Workshop*. Munich, Germany, 113–117.
[22] Olivier Rioul and Martin Vetterli. 1991. Wavelets and signal processing. *IEEE Signal Processing Magazine* 8, 4 (Oct. 1991), 14–38.
[23] Olga Russakovsky, Jia Deng, Hao Su, Jonathan Krause, Sanjeev Satheesh, Sean Ma, Zhiheng Huang, Andrej Karpathy, Aditya Khosla, Michael Bernstein, Alexander C. Berg, and Li Fei-Fei. 2015. Imagenet large scale visual recognition challenge. *International Journal of Computer Vision* 115, 3 (Dec. 2015), 211–252.
[24] Maryam Samieinasab and Reza Sameni. 2015. Fetal phonocardiogram extraction using single channel blind source separation. In *Proc. ICEE*. Tehran, Iran, 78–83.
[25] Samuel E. Schmidt, Claus Holst-Hansen, Claus Graff, Egon Toft, and Johannes J. Struijk. 2010. Segmentation of heart sound recordings by a duration-dependent hidden Markov model. *Physiological Measurement* 31, 4 (Mar. 2010), 513–529.
[26] Samuel E. Schmidt, Claus Holst-Hansen, John Hansen, Egon Toft, and Johannes J. Struijk. 2015. Acoustic features for the identification of coronary artery disease. *IEEE Transactions on Biomedical Engineering* 62, 11 (Nov. 2015), 2611–2619.
[27] Samuel E. Schmidt, Egon Toft, Claus Holst-Hansen, and Johannes J. Struijk. 2010. Noise and the detection of coronary artery disease with an electronic stethoscope. In *Proc. CIBEC*. Cairo, Egypt, 53–56.
[28] Björn Schuller, Stefan Steidl, Anton Batliner, Elika Bergelson, Jarek Krajewski, Christoph Janott, Andrei Amatuni, Marisa Casillas, Amdanda Seidl, Melanie Soderstrom, Anne Ss Warlaumont, Guillermo Hidalgo, Sebastian Schnieder, Clemens Heiser, Winfried Hohenhorst, Michael Herzog, Maximilian Schmitt, Kun Qian, Yue Zhang, George Trigeorgis, Panagiotis Tzirakis, and Stefanos Zafeiriou. 2017. The INTERSPEECH 2017 computational paralinguistics challenge: Addressee, cold & snoring. In *Proc. INTERSPEECH*. Stockholm, Sweden, 3442–3446.
[29] Björn Schuller, Stefan Steidl, Anton Batliner, Alessandro Vinciarelli, Klaus Scherer, Fabien Ringeval, Mohamed Chetouani, Felix Weninger, Florian Eyben, Erik Marchi, Marcello Mortillaro, Hugues Salamin, Anna Polychroniou, Fabio Valente, and Samuel Kim. 2013. The INTERSPEECH 2013 computational paralinguistics challenge: Social signals, conflict, emotion, autism. In *Proc. INTERSPEECH*. Lyon, France, 148–152.
[30] Karen Simonyan and Andrew Zisserman. 2015. Very deep convolutional networks for large-scale image recognition. In *Proc. ICLR*. San Diego, CA, no pagination.
[31] Zeeshan Syed, Daniel Leeds, Dorothy Curtis, Francesca Nesta, Robert A. Levine, and John Guttag. 2007. A framework for the analysis of acoustical cardiac signals. *IEEE Transactions on Biomedical Engineering* 54, 4 (Apr. 2007), 651–662.
[32] Zeeshan Hassan Syed. 2003. *MIT automated auscultation system*. Ph.D. Dissertation. Massachusetts Institute of Technology.
[33] Hong Tang, Ting Li, Tianshuang Qiu, and Yongwan Park. 2012. Segmentation of heart sounds based on dynamic clustering. *Biomedical Signal Processing and Control* 7, 5 (Sep. 2012), 509–516.

---

[4]https://research.google.com/audioset/dataset/heart_sounds_heartbeat.html

Simulation and Sensitivity Analysis of Sensors Network for Cardiac Monitoring

Yaël Kolasa
Cybernano
Villers-lès-Nancy, France
ykolasa@cybernano.eu

Thierry Bastogne
U. Lorraine, CNRS, CRAN, UMR 7039
INRIA BIGS
Vandœuvre-lès-Nancy, France

Jean-Philippe Georges
U. Lorraine, CNRS, CRAN, UMR 7039
Vandœuvre-lès-Nancy, France

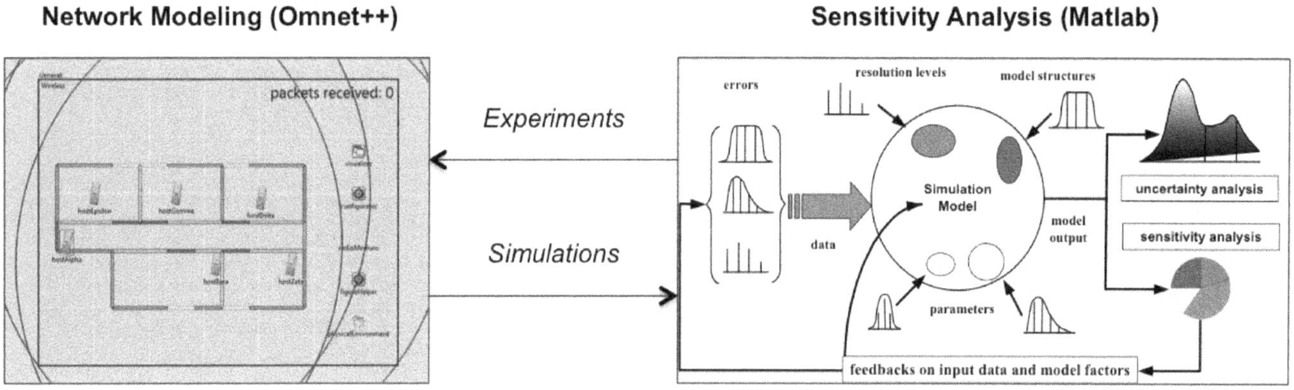

Figure 1. Design of numerical experiments for the robustness analysis of sensors networks

Abstract

This study's aim was to create a modelisation, and a simulation of a wireless sensor network in conjunction with the use of sensitivity analysis, robust analysis, and multicriteria optimization. The idea behind this is to use this technology in the medical scope of home cardiac monitoring. After an initial phase of research to find the right network simulator, the definition of the simulation parameters has started the robust analysis and sensitivity analysis using HDMR method. Next stage was to implement this method into Matlab, and to define a communication protocol between Matlab and the simulator, so they can exchange parameters and results. At last, gathered data analysis will help to define a product with optimized characteristics.

CCS Concepts • **Computer systems organization** → **Simulation**; *Sensors*; • **Networks** → Network reliability; Security; • **Statistics** → **Robustness Analysis**;

DH'18, April 23–26, 2018, Lyon, France

ACM ISBN 978-1-4503-6493-5/18/04.
https://doi.org/10.1145/3194658.3194686

Keywords Internet of Things; Simulation; Sensitivity Analysis; Cardiac Monitoring

ACM Reference Format:
Yaël Kolasa, Thierry Bastogne, and Jean-Philippe Georges. 2018. Simulation and Sensitivity Analysis of Sensors Network for Cardiac Monitoring. In *DH'18: 2018 International Digital Health Conference, April 23–26, 2018, Lyon, France.* ACM, New York, NY, USA, 2 pages. https://doi.org/10.1145/3194658.3194686

1 Introduction

This study comes from a double context, the high throughput analysis in pharmaceuticals and the growing use of smart or connected objects to monitor patients' health. In both cases, the goal is to transmit cardiac signals for remote processing. These past few years, the improvement of measuring systems in pharmaceutical laboratories allowed to gather more accurate and numerous data during preclinical analysis. This increase in data size has two direct consequences : problem of storage, and sharing over internet [1, 3, 5]. Furthermore, some of those can contain sensitive data for which confidentiality must be ensured. In parallel, more and more smart objects are available and allow to monitor daily cardiorespiratory activity over long period of time, longer than traditional ECG (10s) or Hölter ECG (24h). Those huge generated files beget transfer problems to which are added network connectivity constraints. Both times, files' size can cause long transfer times, files' corruption, and a poor users' experience quality. In order to ensure a reliable, safe transfer of quality (both in QoS and QoE meaning), it is necessary to estimate all parameters and their effect on the transfer. So we decided to combine network simulation, robust and sensitivity analysis, to help define products according to particular specifications.

2 Network Modeling

2.1 A Study Case

The study case was to simulate a network of five sensors. One of them was moving, and was the only emitter of messages. Another one was the sink of the network, the only target, which was able to acknowledge received messages. The other three were retransmitters, used to forward the messages if they received them. The emitter moves through a modeled flat with different materials, such as wood, cement, glass, etc and ensuing different perturbations.

2.2 Omnet++ Implementation

This case was implemented in Omnet++ with the library INET, which provides realistic elements to build a simulation with. It integrates widely used TCP and UDP protocols, sensor networks, energy management, interferences, etc.

2.3 Model & Simulation Parameters

The parameters chosen to vary in our different runs of simulation are the following, based on a relatively simple sensor network : the message length, the send interval, radio types and associated parameters, battery power, mac type, the use (or not) of acknowledge receipt of a packet, carrier frequency, energy detection and associated parameters, bit rate, max queue size, header bit length, path loss type and antenna type. They were selected to have a wide range of action on the sensors' capacity to interact with their environment.

3 Sensitivity Analysis

Sensitivity analysis is the study of how uncertainty in the output of a model can be apportioned to different sources of uncertainty in the model input [4]. It was split into two phases. The first one aims at screening the most active parameters through a minimal number of simulations while in a second step a global sensitivity analysis was carried out to rank the total effects of the parameters selected after the screening study.

3.1 Screening of Parameters

A Plackett-Burman design of experiments was used to implement the preliminary selection of active parameters [2].

3.2 HDMR-ANOVA

Once the most active simulation factors have been identified, a Sobol' sequence was implemented to generate the simulated data we need to estimate the sensitivity indices by an Analysis of Variance approach based on a High Dimensional Model Representation (HDMR-ANOVA) [4].

3.3 Matlab Implementation

Matlab was used to generate a Sobol' sequence of experiments and Omnet++ was launched via a batch file created to run each simulation of the experimental design. Afterwards, the sensitivity indices were estimated according to the algorithm proposed in [4].

4 Results

Two outputs were studied during the simulations. The first one was the number of packets received by the sink at the end of each simulation. The second output is the reception cache hit percentage. For the first response variable, two critical parameters were identified: the message length and the bit rate. For the second output variable, the first two most critical factors were the background noise power and the energy detection of the radio receiver.

5 Conclusion

A prototype sensitivity analysis of a sensors network guided by simulations has been proposed. Preliminary results have demonstrated its practical feasibility by combining two simulation environments: Omnet++ and Matlab. A two-step statistical approach was proposed to speed up the analysis given the large number of simulation parameters to be tested. Such a technique allows to quickly identify the most critical parameters impacting the whole quality of service of the network. In short term perspective, parameters of the medical application, such as oxygen level monitoring, flow rate and remaining quantity during transfusion, will be added to assess the robustness of the remote cardiac monitoring.

References

[1] Mohammed Aledhari and Fahad Saeed. 2015. Design and Implementation of Network Transfer Protocol for Big Genomic Data. In *2015 IEEE INTERNATIONAL CONGRESS ON BIG DATA - BIGDATA CONGRESS 2015 (IEEE International Congress on Big Data)*, Barbara, C and Khan, L (Ed.). IEEE; IEEE Comp Soc; Serv Comp; Serv Soc; Comp Cloud; Serv Comp; BIG Data; Hp; IBM; ERICSSON; SAP; IBM Res; HUAWEI; OMG Object Management Grp; IEEE Cloud Comp; Business Proc Integrat & Management; IT Profess; Intl Journal Web Serv Res; Comp Now Access Discover Engage; IEEE Transact Serv Comp, 281–288. https://doi.org/{10.1109/BigDataCongress.2015.47} IEEE International Congress on Big Data, New York, NY, JUN 27-JUL 02, 2015.

[2] G. A. Lewis, D. Mathieu, and R. Phan-Tan-Luu. 2005. *Pharmaceutical Experimental Design*. Marcel Dekker.

[3] V. Marx. 2013. The Big Challenges of Big Data. *Nature* 498 (2013), 255–260.

[4] A. Saltelli, M. Ratto, T. Andres, F. Campolongo, J. Cariboni, D. Gatelli, M. Saisana, and S. Tarantola. 2008. *Global Sensitivity Analysis - The Primer*. Wiley.

[5] Brian Tierney, Ezra Kissel, Martin Swany, and Eric Pouyoul. 2012. Efficient Data Transfer Protocols for Big Data. In *2012 IEEE 8TH INTERNATIONAL CONFERENCE ON E-SCIENCE (E-SCIENCE) (Proceeding IEEE International Conference on e-Science (e-Science))*. IEEE; IEEE Comp Soc. IEEE 8th International Conference on E-Science (e-Science), Chicago, IL, OCT 08-12, 2012.

Specification, Use and Impact of the Persuasive Serious Game S'TIM in a Rehabilitation Process for Patients with Dysexecutive Syndrome

Julie Golliot*
Clinique RGDS Provence-Bourbonne
and IMSIC, Université de Toulon
julie.golliot@ensc.fr

Michèle Timsit
Clinique RGDS Provence-Bourbonne
m.timsit@ramsaygds.fr

Cathy Herrera
Clinique RGDS Provence-Bourbonne
c.herrera@ramsaygds.fr

Elodie Fontugne
Clinique RGDS Provence-Bourbonne

Alexandre Abellard
IMSIC, Université de Toulon
alexandre.abellard@univ-tln.fr

Michel Durampart
IMSIC, Université de Toulon
michel.durampart@univ-tln.fr

ABSTRACT

The aim of this multidisciplinary study is to specify and develop a Serious-Game (SG) to immerge patients with a dysexecutive syndrome in a virtual word. With an elaborate scenario and various challenges, the SG we named *S'TIM* is used on a robotised and easy-to-use touch table. The high stakes for patients are firstly to break anosognosia and intrinsically motivate patients to implicate them in their rehabilitation; Secondly to enable them to reach a sufficient metacognition level to develop their own strategy and select the most relevant in each context. Finally, to facilitate these strategies transfer in daily-life. Changes in organisations will also be observed.

CCS CONCEPTS

• **Social and professional topics** → **Assistive technologies**; **People with disabilities**; • **Applied computing** → **Computer-assisted instruction**;

KEYWORDS

Serious-Game,Rehabilitation,Dysexecutive Syndrome,Tactile Table,Cognitive Impact,Organisational Change

ACM Reference Format:

Julie Golliot, Michèle Timsit, Cathy Herrera, Elodie Fontugne, Alexandre Abellard, and Michel Durampart. 2018. Specification, Use and Impact of the Persuasive Serious Game S'TIM in a Rehabilitation Process for Patients with Dysexecutive Syndrome. In *DH'18: 2018 International Digital Health Conference, April 23–26, 2018, Lyon, France.* ACM, New York, NY, USA, 2 pages. https://doi.org/10.1145/3194658.3194687

1 INTRODUCTION

New technologies are more and more developed and used by people of all ages. In a context of cognitive rehabilitation, most of

*Corresponding author

the tools are traditional with activities on papers or table games. Improvements are observed but the transfer in daily-life is very limited and patients don't recover their autonomy. The ecological validity of conventional tests (with only one task mostly initiated by therapists) seems to be an issue, since they don't take care of the patients' environment. This artificial situation doesn't reproduce complexity of daily life activities and patients don't use their executive functions in order to elaborate strategies and adapt their behaviour. Ecological practices have been elaborated but they are hard to use (lack of therapists, legislation). Therefore, rehabilitation specialists are looking for a new tool to help the patients to recover their capacities and daily-life.

2 CONTEXT

In this PhD Project (preparation stage), we focus on patients with dysexecutive syndrome which can be observed after a cerebrovascular accident, a head injury with frontal lobe damage or degenerative diseases, amongst other things. Executive functions are implicated in cognitive processing requiring coordination of several sub-processes to achieve a particular goal [1] when reflex actions are insufficient. Executive troubles impair capacities of planning, strategies elaboration, updating, shifting, inhibition and attention. There are cognitive, emotional and behavioural consequences. Patients lose their autonomy and are unable to recognize their disorders (anosognosia) which limits their implication in rehabilitation.

3 MATERIAL AND METHOD

The aim of this research program is to specify and develop a persuasive serious-game to immerge patients in a virtual world with an elaborate scenario with various challenges.

We base our research on the self-determination theory highlight three basic needs: competence, relatedness and mostly autonomy [2]. According to this psychological theory, patient intrinsic motivation is a central element to facilitate socio-cognitive and socio-affective changes, since motivation is higher when people do not act for rewards.

The device has to be designed in order to make the most of serious-games characteristics. Interactivity, feedbacks, playful challenges, based on rules and with a clear goal [3]. As it uses persuasive communication according to Teresa de la Hera Conde-Pumpido

Figure 1: Screenshot of S'TIM.

model, it contains signs (haptic, sound, visual and linguistic persuasion), systems (cinematic, procedural and narrative persuasion) and context (social, affective, tactical and sensorial persuasion).

Three levels are used with persuasive serious game to bring about behaviour, socio-affective and socio-cognitive changes [4]. First narration, simulation, individual adaptation and feedbacks increase patient motivation. Second, social learning by modelling and role-taking further socio-affective change. Finally, flow increases competence feelings and motivation.

In order to modify behaviours, therapists have to support patient autonomy. This engaging communication enables a self-determinate motivation. Moreover, interaction between therapists and patients around the device is crucial to favour metacognitive knowledge. Observations in a rehabilitation centre, interviews and meetings have been done for heighten months. It enabled a coordination between rehabilitation doctors, occupational therapists, neuro-psychologists, engineers and information and communication scientists. This work allowed pertinent and extensive specification of the serious-game before development on Unity 3D and clinical trials.

4 RESULTS

The chosen device is a robotised touch table of 46 inches which allows all degrees of movements (low-high, horizontal-vertical or any another degree). It is easy-to-use by people of all age, with or without wheelchair, sight troubles, and so on. Other applications are already used on the device and therapists haven't noticed difficulties with any patients.

Each detail of the serious-game and its use was discussed with all the experts listed above to take into account the various needs. Furthermore, this device is designed for patients and therapists ; thus, their implication since the beginning of the process reduces objections and rejections. With therapists' care, patients should be implicated, acquire pertinent strategies, be intrinsically motivated (self-determination theory), improve their self-respect, their self-efficiency and be more empathic. Collected data will enable qualitative and quantitative analyses. The serious-game development is made on Unity3D, a game development platform.

A first prototype using the main decided mechanisms has been developped. Patients and therapists' feedbacks give tools to improve the future version (Fig. 1). With therapists' care, S'TIM will transfer patients at the heart of their rehabilitation.

5 LIMITS AND PERSPECTIVES

This technology presents some limits. Patients could reject it or have worse results than expected if they have mental difficulties. Moreover, only some therapists were implicated in the development, so others could reject the device if the accompanying is insufficient. For patients, three stakes are expected and analyzed in clinical studies. First, to break the anosognosia and intrinsically motivate patients to implicate them in their rehabilitation. Second, to enable them to reach a sufficient metacognition level to develop their own strategy and select the most relevant in each context. Finally, to facilitate these strategies transfer in daily-life.

Standardized psychometric tests will be conducted before the study, after the two-months rehabilitation training and three months later in order to validate the serious-game pertinence (GREFEX set for cognitive evaluation, HAD scale for thymic criterion and IDSC scale for the behavior).

Therapists will keep their fundamental role. They will not have to give some background but to contextualize knowledge to favour transfer (didactic action). Patients should be more implicated, intrinsically motivated, participate more [5] and be less dependent. Standardized situations with the SG will allow the study of quantitative data and to objective changes.

Finally, articulation between goals, actor system and technic dimension will create organisational change [6]. The introduction of this technology has to be guided to avoid a situation with more disorders than solutions and optimize the device use.

6 CONCLUSION

This new, innovating and multidisciplinary study presents high stakes for the future of patients with dysexecutive syndrome. Theories of information and communication sciences, educational sciences, cognitive sciences, psychology and neuropsychology are implicated in the design and the use of this new technology by rehabilitation centers already established. With therapists' implication, S'TIM will increase patient autonomy and transfer them at the heart of their rehabilitation and give them a chance to go back to their daily life.

REFERENCES

[1] Olivier Godefroy and coll. 2004. Syndromes frontaux et dysexécutifs. *Rev Neurol* 160, 10 (October 2004), 899-909. https://doi.org/10.1016/S0035-3787(04)71071-1
[2] Richard M. Ryan and Edward L. Deci. 2002. Overview of self-determination theory: An organismic dialectal perspective. In *Handbook of self-determination research*. University of Rochester Press, Rochester, NY, 3-33.
[3] Julian Alvarez and Djamel Djaouti. 2012. *Introduction au Serious Game* (2nd. ed.). Questions Théoriques, Paris.
[4] Didier Courbet and Marie-Pierre Fourquet-Courbet. 2015. Les serious games, dispositifs de communication persuasive: quels processus socio-cognitifs et socio-affectifs dans les usages? Quels effets sur les joueurs? Etat des recherches et nouvelles perspectives. *Réseaux* 33, 194, 199-228.
[5] Carole Groleau and Anne Mayère. 2007. L'articulation technologies – organisations: des pistes pour une approche communicationnelle. *Commun. Organ.* 31 (July 2007), 140-163.
[6] Willy Barroy, Michel Durampart, and Philippe Bonfils. 2016. Les dispositifs numériques de formation: un enjeu de changements organisationnels. *Proceedings of MTO*, Presse des Mines, Paris.

Socially Shared Health Information

Kjeld S. Hansen[1,2,3]

[1]Centre for Business Data Analytics
Copenhagen Business School
Frederiksberg, Denmark
kh.digi@cbs.dk

[2]Mobile Technologies Lab
Westerdals Oslo ACT
Oslo, Norway

[3]CopenRehab
University of Copenhagen
Copenhagen, Denmark

ABSTRACT

In this PhD project, I am investigating how health organizations are sharing health information on social media. My PhD project is divided into two parts, but in this paper, I will only focus on the first part: To understand current practices of how health organizations engage with health information and users on social media (empirical studies 1,2,3) and to develop a theoretical model for how it is done efficiently and effectively. I have currently conducted and published on two empirical studies (1,2). I am in the process of collecting data for a revised version of empirical study (2) and for empirical study (3).

Author Keywords

Health Information; Big Data Analytics; Social Media; Digital Health; Digital Sharing; Social Influence.

ACM Reference Format:

Kjeld S. Hansen. 2018. Socially Shared Health Information. In DH'18: 2018 International Digital Health Conference, April 23–26, 2018, Lyon, France. ACM, NY, NY, USA, 2 pages.
https://doi.org/10.1145/3194658.3194688

1. INTRODUCTION

Some of the most serious global health issues today are chronic diseases such as diabetes and obesity [1,2]. Some important risk factors for these diseases are peoples' behaviors such as physical inactivity and inadequate diets. Generally, most people know what is considered healthy and unhealthy behavior. Despite knowing this, many people continue to make questionable health choices and do venture into destructive or risky behaviors. Health organizations have tried to influence peoples' behaviors through health campaigns on traditional media, but generally they have not been efficient and effective. From social sciences studies and studies of social influence [3], I believe there are good indications that people might change their behaviors, if they experience social influence.

Social Media harness the dynamics of social networks and social influence in an online setting. Facebook is arguably an integrated part of many peoples' social lives with more than 2 billion active monthly users [4]. Hence, Facebook arguably knows more about what people think, feel and do than any other organization on Earth. It might therefore be important to understand how health organizations and users interact with health information on Facebook.

I term health information shared on social media platforms as "Socially Shared Health Information" (SSHI) [5]. Each research question (RQ1-4) is designed to address a central aspect of the phenomenon, which I have termed SSHI. The first two research questions are:

- RQ1: What are the goals and critical success factors for organizations engaging in SSHI?
- RQ2: What are the structural, temporal, social, linguistic, and computational aspects of the artifacts resulting from SSHI?

My PhD project focus on how health organizations (, which are grouped into six domain specific health areas: General health, lung health, heart health, diabetes, cancer and physical activity) in Denmark, Norway, United Kingdom and United States, interact with health information and users on Facebook.

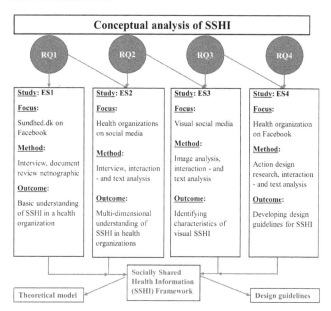

Figure 1. The research design of the PhD project on Socially Shared Health Information (SSHI)

2. RESEARCH DESIGN

The research design is a multiphase, multi-project study, where each study informs the next study. Apart from the conceptual analysis, the PhD project contains of 4 empirical studies that informs the framework for understanding SSHI (see Figure 1).

Summary of Methods for Empirical Study 1 & 2 (ES 1&2)

In ES1, I conducted a mixed-method case study of the national Danish health portal, Sundhed.dk. I used interviews, netnographic analysis, document reviews and relevant statistical methods [5]. In ES2, I conducted an analysis of 153 public health organizations Facebook walls. I used netnographic analysis to identify the organizations and relevant statistical methods to analyze the results of the data [6]. Both articles are based on historic data sets collected from Facebook using the Social Data Analytics Tool (SODATO) [7].

3. PRELIMINARY RESULTS OF ES 1&2

In ES1, the study showed that Sundhed.dk's social media strategy was very well aligned with their organizational strategy, but that they were challenged to move beyond the generic social media metrics to define good indications for successful SSHI. Sundhed.dk needed domain-specific indicators in new public health to measure the effectiveness of their social media strategy, tactics, and operations [5].

In ES2, the study shows a rise in engagements on the Facebook walls from 2014, which suggest an increasing interest from users. Facebook posts containing a photo, or a link represent the most engaged with posts compared to other information sharing techniques. Health organizations might therefore want the photo to inform the textual content of their posts. They might need enhanced knowledge of how visual content about health information can form part of their health communication and campaigns [6].

4. DISCUSSION

The overall goal of my PhD project is to form a framework for understanding SSHI. In the first part of my PhD project, which is described in this paper, I have focused on understanding the phenomenon of SSHI and developing a theoretical model for how SSHI is done efficiently and effectively. The theoretical model is based on the conceptual analysis and the findings of ES1-3. In the second part of my PhD project, I will focus on testing the findings of the first part by applying action design research techniques in health organizations in Denmark and Norway. My goal is to use the results of the second part to define design guidelines for how health organizations observe the rules of the theoretical model in their practical design of SSHI. The findings of the two parts will help define my overall framework for SSHI, which is the kappa of my PhD dissertation.

5. FUTURE RESEARCH

I intend to analyze the visual data from ES2 and present the findings in ES3. I am preparing an action design research study (ES4) in two public health organizations for testing my findings from ES1-3. The findings will inform the development of my design guidelines for SSHI.

ACKNOWLEDGMENTS

I would like to thank my three supervisors: Prof. Tor-Morten Grønli (Westerdals Oslo ACT), Prof. Henning Langberg (University of Copenhagen) and Prof. Ravi Vatrapu (Copenhagen Business School) for their excellent guidance.

REFERENCES

1. Zimmet, P. (2000), Globalization, coca-colonization and the chronic disease epidemic: can the Doomsday scenario be averted?. Journal of Internal Medicine, 247: 301–310. doi:10.1046/j.1365-2796.2000.00625.xACM.

2. Hoffman, C., Rice, D., and Sung, H.Y. Persons with chronic conditions. Their prevalence and costs. JAMA: The Journal of the American Medical Association 276, 18 (1996), 1473-1479.

3. Christakis NA and Fowler JH. Connected: the surprising power of our social networks and how they shape our lives. New York: Little, Brown and Co., 2009.

4. Constine, J., 2017. Facebook now has 2 billion monthly users... and responsibility. Link. (27 June 2017.). Retrieved January 7. 2018 from https://techcrunch.com/2017/06/27/facebook-2-billion-users/

5. Hansen, Kjeld, Raghava Rao Mukkamala; Abid Hussain; Tor-Morten Grønli; Henning Langberg; Ravi Vatrapu. Big Social Data in Public Health : A Mixed-Methods Case Study of Sundhed.dk's Facebook Strategy, Engagement, and Performance. The 6th International Conference on Current and Future Trends of Information and Communication Technologies in Healthcare (ICTH-2016). ed. /Ansar-Ul-Haque Yasar; Nik Bessis. Amsterdam: Elsevier Science 2016, p. 298-307 (Procedia Computer Science, Vol. 98)

6. Straton, Nadiya, Kjeld Hansen; Raghava Rao Mukkamala; Abid Hussain; Tor-Morten Grønli; Henning Langberg; Ravi Vatrapu / Big Social Data Analytics for Public Health: Facebook Engagement and Performance. 2016 IEEE 18th International Conference on e-Health Networking, Applications and Services (Healthcom). ed. /Alois Paulin. Los Alamitos, CA : IEEE 2016, p. 442-447

7. Hussain, A., Vatrapu, R., Hardt, D., & Jaffari, Z. (2014). Social Data Analytics Tool: A Demonstrative Case Study of Methodology and Software. In M. Cantijoch, R. Gibson, & S. Ward (Eds.), *Analyzing Social Media Data and Web Networks* (pp. 99-118): Palgrave Macmillan.

Design and Implementation of a Web-based Application to Assess Cognitive Impairment in Affective Disorder

Pegah Hafiz
Copenhagen Center for Health Technology, Technical
University of Denmark
Lyngby, Denmark
pegh@dtu.dk

Kamilla W. Miskowiak
Psychiatric Center Copenhagen, University Hospital of
Copenhagen
Copenhagen, Denmark
kamilla.woznica.miskowiak@regionh.dk

Lars V. Kessing
Psychiatric Center Copenhagen, University Hospital of
Copenhagen
Copenhagen, Denmark
lars.vedel.kessing@regionh.dk

Jakob E. Bardram
Copenhagen Center for Health Technology, Technical
University of Denmark
Lyngby, Denmark
jakba@dtu.dk

CCS CONCEPTS

• **Software and its engineering** → *Software design engineering*;

KEYWORDS

Design; Implementation; Cognitive Assessment

ACM Reference format:
Pegah Hafiz, Kamilla W. Miskowiak, Lars V. Kessing, and Jakob E. Bardram.
2018. Design and Implementation of a Web-based Application to Assess
Cognitive Impairment in Affective Disorder. In *Proceedings of 2018 International Digital Health Conference, Lyon, France, April 23–26, 2018 (DH'18)*,
2 pages.
https://doi.org/10.1145/3194658.3194691

1 INTRODUCTION

Affective disorder causes mood disturbance and includes depression and bipolar disorder. Cognitive impairment is one of the determinants of poor functioning in patients suffering from an affective disorder. For example, memory impairment in bipolar patients brings about confusion in their daily life. Other cognitive domains include attention, executive function, and psychomotor speed. Cognitive function of these patients are assessed by means of neuropsychological tests such as California Verbal Learning Test (CVLT) and Trail Making Test (TMT) that are used to examine verbal memory and psychomotor speed, respectively.

The "Screen for Cognitive Impairment in Psychiatry" (SCIP) is a simple and brief screening tool for psychotic disorders including bipolar disorder and depression. It examines cognitive skills namely verbal learning, working memory, verbal fluency, and psychomotor speed [2]. SCIP is a paper-based test battery and is used in clinical setting, in which the examiner explains the instructions and read several words and letter-number sequences to the patient.

However, current computerized test batteries require direct supervision of clinicians in a clinical setting. To our knowledge, none of the computerized test batteries for affective disorders have implemented SCIP in a form of a patient-administered assessment tool.

In this project we are developing a web-based cognitive assessment tool called "Internet-based Cognitive Assessment Tool" (ICAT) for bipolar and depressive patients. This application is a computerized and web-based version of SCIP, in which the third part of SCIP – the verbal fluency task – is replaced with Wechsler Adult Intelligence Scale (WAIS) letter-number sequencing task. In total, ICAT then consists of five sequential tasks, which are explained in section 3.

The aim of this project is to design and implement ICAT as a web-based cognitive assessment tool and examine its validity by running a clinical trial, which compares ICAT with the paper-based SCIP test as the golden standard.

2 RECENT WORKS

Computerized applications for cognitive assessment are currently limited. The Cambridge Neuropsychological Test Automated Battery (CANTAB) [5] is one of the validated test batteries implemented for a wide range of mental disorders. However, CANTAB has inadequate tests to cover affective disorder. The NIH EXAMINER (Executive Abilities: Measures and Instruments for Neurobehavioral Evaluation and Research) [3] is a computerized test battery which measures several cognitive domains. Although this application has multiple tests, a clinician should read a set of words to the patients when assessing verbal memory, which points to the direct supervision of clinicians. THINC-it [4] is a computerized cognitive assessment tool developed for Major Depressive Disorder (MDD) patients. It uses cognitive tasks like Digit Symbol Substitution Test and TMT (part B). However, this system doesn't support cognitive assessment of bipolar patients.

3 ICAT SYSTEM

3.1 Design Methods

The ICAT system is being developed in a user-centered design process involving neuro-psychologists, psychologists, computer

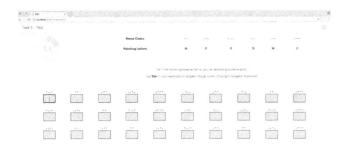

Figure 1: Task 5 uses a table of Morse codes and their matching letters to assess psycho-motor speed.

scientists, and front-end developers. Once the first prototype of ICAT is implemented, it is been planned to test it with some affective disorder patients.

3.2 ICAT Cognitive Tasks

ICAT includes five tasks which are described below:

- *List Learning*: A list including 10 words are read to the patient using a sound file. The patient should recall as many words as possible. This task is repeated 2 more times with the same set of words. It measures declarative memory and the score ranges from 0 to 30.
- *Consonant Repetition*: It has three letters, a starting number, and a delay (in seconds) for each of the 8 items. The patient counts backwards from the starting number. Then, after a delay, the patient should recall three letters. It measures working memory and the score ranges from 0 to 24.
- *WAIS Letter-Number Sequencing*: It has 7 sets, each set includes 3 letter-number sequences. For each sequence, the numbers should be sorted in ascending order and the letters in alphabetical order. The patient can proceed to the next set only if at least one of the sequences in the current set is reproduced correctly. It measures working memory and the score ranges from 0 to 21.
- *Delayed List Learning*: The word list in task 1 is not played and the patient is asked to recall the earlier words. It measures declarative memory and the score ranges from 0 to 10.
- *Visuo-motor Tracking*: A table including 6 letters and their matching Morse codes are shown to the patient. In 30 seconds, the patient should type the matching letters for 30 Morse codes. It measures executive skills and the score ranges from 0 to 30.(See Figure 1)

3.3 Feedback

Scores of all tasks are displayed to the patients at the end of the assessment. Later during a face-to-face visit, the examiner can interpret the results for the patient and compare his or her performance to a healthy reference group.

3.4 Implementation

The front-end of ICAT system is built using React v16.2.0. We are using the Open m-Health platform [1] as the data back-end. For this purpose, we are designing a Open m-Health JSON schema for cognitive functions, which will be used to store patient's cognitive profile. This profile includes cognitive skills such as memory and executive function.

In the original paper-based version of the SCIP method, the examiner reads the instructions, words, and letter-number sequences aloud to each participant. The main challenge in the implementation of this system is to convert the role of an examiner from in-person to a digitized format. For this reason, we are examining the use of Google speech recognition web API. It is developed for over 110 languages and will enable us to store each word that patients recall in text format for task 1 and 4.

3.5 Clinical Verification

ICAT will be subject to usability tests focusing on the ability for test subject to understand and perform the cognitive assessment tasks. Once ICAT has been improved based on the usability testing, a clinical verification trial is planned. The goal is to verify and compare the computerized ICAT system against the manual SCIP method as the golden standard.

4 CONCLUSION

We are creating a set of simple and short tasks similar to SCIP in a web application. The use of speech recognition module is supposed to maintain the short duration of the tasks. It has been estimated that 10,000 affective disorder patients in Denmark will use ICAT along with the progress of this PhD project.

5 ACKNOWLEDGMENTS

This project is under development during the early stage of PH's PhD. PH is an early stage researcher of Technology Enabled Mental Health (TEAM) for Young People. TEAM has received funding from the European Union's Horizon 2020 research and innovation programme under the Marie Skłodowska-Curie grant agreement No. 722561.

REFERENCES

[1] D. Estrin and I. Sim. Open mhealth architecture: an engine for health care innovation. *Science*, 330(6005):759–760, 2010.

[2] J. Gómez-Benito, G. Guilera, Ó. Pino, E. Rojo, R. Tabarés-Seisdedos, G. Safont, A. Martínez-Arán, M. Franco, M. J. Cuesta, B. Crespo-Facorro, et al. The screen for cognitive impairment in psychiatry: diagnostic-specific standardization in psychiatric ill patients. *BMC psychiatry*, 13(1):127, 2013.

[3] J. H. Kramer, D. Mungas, K. L. Possin, K. P. Rankin, A. L. Boxer, H. J. Rosen, A. Bostrom, L. Sinha, A. Berhel, and M. Widmeyer. Nih examiner: conceptualization and development of an executive function battery. *Journal of the international neuropsychological society*, 20(1):11–19, 2014.

[4] R. S. McIntyre, M. W. Best, C. R. Bowie, N. E. Carmona, D. S. Cha, Y. Lee, M. Subramaniapillai, R. B. Mansur, H. Barry, B. T. Baune, et al. The thinc-integrated tool (thinc-it) screening assessment for cognitive dysfunction: Validation in patients with major depressive disorder. *The Journal of clinical psychiatry*, 78(7):873–881, 2017.

[5] T. W. Robbins, M. James, A. M. Owen, B. J. Sahakian, L. McInnes, and P. Rabbitt. Cambridge neuropsychological test automated battery (cantab): a factor analytic study of a large sample of normal elderly volunteers. *Dementia and Geriatric Cognitive Disorders*, 5(5):266–281, 1994.

Robust Laughter Detection for Wearable Wellbeing Sensing

Gerhard Hagerer
Chair of Embedded Intelligence for Health Care and
Wellbeing, University of Augsburg
Augsburg, Germany
gerhard.hagerer@informatik.uni-augsburg.de

Nicholas Cummins
Chair of Embedded Intelligence for Health Care and
Wellbeing, University of Augsburg
Augsburg, Germany
nicholas.cummins@ieee.org

Florian Eyben
audEERING GmbH
Gilching, Germany
fe@audeering.com

Björn Schuller
Imperial College
London, United Kingdom
bjoern.schuller@imperial.ac.uk

ABSTRACT

To build a noise-robust online-capable laughter detector for be-havioural monitoring on wearables, we incorporate context-sensitive Long Short-Term Memory Deep Neural Networks. We show our solution's improvements over a laughter detection baseline by inte-grating intelligent noise-robust voice activity detection (VAD) into the same model. To this end, we add extensive artificially mixed VAD data without any laughter targets to a small laughter train-ing set. The resulting laughter detection enhancements are stable even when frames are dropped, which happen in low resource en-vironments such as wearables. Thus, the outlined model generation potentially improves the detection of vocal cues when the amount of training data is small and robustness and efficiency are required.

CCS CONCEPTS

• **Computer systems organization** → **Neural networks**; • **Human-centered computing** → *Mobile devices*; • **Applied computing** → *Health informatics*;

KEYWORDS

Health Monitoring, Laughter Detection, Recurrent Neural Networks

ACM Reference Format:
Gerhard Hagerer, Nicholas Cummins, Florian Eyben, and Björn Schuller. 2018. Robust Laughter Detection for Wearable Wellbeing Sensing. In *DH'18: 2018 International Digital Health Conference, April 23–26, 2018, Lyon, France.* ACM, April 23-26, 2018, Lyon, France, 2 pages. https://doi.org/10.1145/3194658.3194693

1 INTRODUCTION

Over the last years, the market of mobile health software on wear-ables shows a constant and strong growth with respect to sales numbers of tracking apps analysing the behaviour and habits of customers in terms of health and wellbeing monitoring [1, 2]. A

relevant use case therefore is laughter tracking on wearables as laughing affects health and wellbeing in a positive way [4, 5].

In terms of audio processing, automated laughter detection re-search so far has its primary focus on offline analysis of speech, e. g., [3, 6, 9]. However, for in-the-wild real-time monitoring tasks, there – to our best knowledge – appears to be no research consid-ering robustness, e. g., frame drops and several noise types. Thus, we propose a data-driven method to improve laughter detection Recurrent Neural Networks (RNNs) on sparse laughter training targets while making it robust to difficult real-life scenarios.

In Section 2, we explain our modelling technique and data prepa-ration. Section 3 describes the experimental design and results. These are concluded by Section 4.

2 LAUGHTER DATA & MODELLING

Our laughter detection system is based on the Long Short-Term Memory (LSTM) RNN methodology presented in [7, 8] with the main difference of containing a laughter detection output in addi-tion to a voice activity detection (VAD) output.

Multitask Learning. For the present work, Multitask Learning is utilised, since the laughter data at hand is lacking many condi-tions which are relevant for our target use case scenario of laughter tracking on wearables. Some of the relevant factors are robustness to stationary and non-stationary background noises, signal loss, microphone types, and environmental impulse responses. By train-ing a robust VAD [8] on a correspondingly prepared corpus, we explore the effects on integrated laughter detection when this data is combined with sparse laughter targets.

Laughter Corpus. As a basis to train our presented laughter detec-tion models, we utilise the labelled laughter data from the SSPNet Vocalization Corpus (SVC) from the 2013 Interspeech Computa-tional Paralinguistics Challenge Social Signals subtask [9].

VAD Corpus. The training data created for VAD is described in [8]. We mixed conversational and emotional speech with multiple background and convolutive noises to ensure robustness to difficult acoustic conditions. This corpus is called the *noisy VAD corpus*, the one without background noises is called *VAD corpus.*

Combined Laughter and VAD data. Since there is no laughter data in the VAD corpus, the annotated laughter recordings from the SVC dataset are added to the VAD training and development set. On this combination, both the VAD and laughter output of the net are trained. The sparse laughter annotations from the VAD

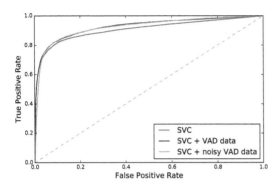

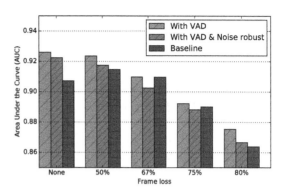

Figure 1: Receiver operator characteristics of frame-wise laughter detection. The proposed models trained on SVC and our VAD data improved the SVC-only baseline.

Figure 2: Area Under the Curve (AUC) measures decline the more frames are dropped. The combined VAD+SVC models outperform the baseline in most cases.

data are suppressed. As compensation, the SVC laughter targets are weighted during backpropagation by a factor of 10.

3 EXPERIMENTS & RESULTS

Experiments. Three laughter detection models are compared to each other; differing on the data they were trained on:

SVC: Only SSPNet Vocalization Corpus (SVC) with laughter targets. This is referred to as the *baseline model* or *dataset*.

SVC + VAD: This is the combination of SVC laughter *and* VAD data *without* background noise. The VAD targets on SVC are set to undefined. On the VAD set, the laughter targets are suppressed.

SVC + noisy VAD: Same as SVC + VAD, except of background noise being added to the VAD audio data, but not on SVC.

The assumption is that the laughter detection RNN improves when VAD is included in the model. Thus, the network distinguishes not only between laughter and non-laughter, but also between laughing, general, and absence of speech. We speculate this improves the laughter detection, since it has a more accurate understanding of what is *not* laughter, i. e., general speech activity and background noise. The influence of the latter is considered separately in our experiments by the SVC + noisy VAD train data.

Results. Regarding performance, we evaluate our models only on the laughter targets of the SVC test set. Figure 1 gives an impression in terms of receiver operator characteristics (ROC); the blue and green curves, coming from the two SVC + VAD models outperform the SVC only baseline. This is also reflected by greater *area under the curve* values – see [7]. From this it is apparent that training with the additional VAD data is beneficial for laughter detection.

As we found out when running our laughter detection system under real-life conditions [7], the runtime environment of wearables is randomly dropping audio samples and feature frames respectively due to processing overload. However, from Figure 2 it is apparent that our models consistently perform better than the baseline even when frames are dropped as we did it in our experiments. Moreover, a comparison with laughter detectors from related work given in [7] indicates that our approach performs comparable to key studies performed on the same dataset.

4 CONCLUSION

This paper shows an easily extensible way to increase accuracy, generalisation, and robustness of a vocal cue detector exemplified for laughter detection by adding an according output to a VAD neural network and respective vocal cue data to a VAD training corpus. Furthermore, we showed that these advantages hold even when frames are dropped, as we experienced it on smartwatches. Thus, our approach can be used for in-the-wild use cases, where real-time processing, efficiency, and robustness to signal loss or noise are required. In the future, we plan on training and evaluating integrated models for the detection of a variety of vocal cues.

5 ACKNOWLEDGEMENTS

 This work was supported by the EU's 7th Framework and Horizon 2020 Programmes under grant agreements No. 338164 (ERC StG iHEARu) and No. 688835 (RIA DE-ENIGMA).

REFERENCES

[1] 2015. *mHealth App Developer Economics 2015.* research2guidance. 5th annual study on mHealth app publishing based on 5,000 plus respondents.
[2] 2016. *mHealth App Developer Economics 2016.* research2guidance. 6th annual study on mHealth app publishing based on 2,600 plus respondents.
[3] Raymond Brueckner and Bjorn Schuller. 2014. Social signal classification using deep BLSTM recurrent neural networks. In *Acoustics, Speech and Signal Processing (ICASSP), 2014 IEEE International Conference on.* IEEE, 4823–4827.
[4] Adam Clark, Alexander Seidler, and Michael Miller. 2001. Inverse association between sense of humor and coronary heart disease. *International journal of cardiology* 80, 1 (2001), 87–88.
[5] Lee S. Berk et al. 1989. Neuroendocrine and stress hormone changes during mirthful laughter. *The American journal of the medical sciences* 298, 6 (1989).
[6] Rahul Gupta, Kartik Audhkhasi, Sungbok Lee, and Shrikanth Narayanan. 2016. Detecting paralinguistic events in audio stream using context in features and probabilistic decisions. *Computer Speech & Language* 36 (2016), 72–92.
[7] Gerhard Hagerer, Nicholas Cummins, Florian Eyben, and Björn Schuller. 2017. "Did you laugh enough today?"–Deep neural networks for mobile and wearable laughter trackers. *Proc. Interspeech 2017* (2017), 2044–2045.
[8] Gerhard Hagerer, Vedhas Pandit, Florian Eyben, and Björn Schuller. 2017. Enhancing LSTM RNN-based Speech Overlap Detection by Artificially Mixed Data. In *Audio Engineering Society Conference: 48nd International Conference: Semantic Audio.* Audio Engineering Society.
[9] Björn Schuller, Stefan Steidl, Anton Batliner, Alessandro Vinciarelli, Klaus Scherer, Fabien Ringeval, Mohamed Chetouani, Felix Weninger, Florian Eyben, Erik Marchi, et al. 2013. The INTERSPEECH 2013 computational paralinguistics challenge: social signals, conflict, emotion, autism. (2013).

MAVIE-Lab Sports: a mHealth for Injury Prevention and Risk Management in Sport

PhD Student Track

Madelyn Yiseth Rojas Castro*
Univ. Bordeaux, INSERM U1219 IETO
Bordeaux CEDEX, France
madelyn-iseth.rojas-castro@
u-bordeaux.fr

Marina Travanca
Univ. Bordeaux, INSERM U1219 IETO
Bordeaux CEDEX, France
marina.travanca@u-bordeaux.fr

Marta Avalos Fernandez
Univ. Bordeaux, INSERM U1219
SISTM, INRIA
Bordeaux CEDEX, France
marta.avalos-fernandez@
u-bordeaux.fr

David Valentin Conesa
Univ. de València
Burjassot, Spain
David.V.Conesa@uv.es

Ludivine Orriols
Univ. Bordeaux, INSERM U1219 IETO
Bordeaux CEDEX, France
ludivine.orriols@u-bordeaux.fr

Emmanuel Lagarde[†]
Univ. Bordeaux, INSERM U1219 IETO
Bordeaux CEDEX, France
emmanuel.lagarde@u-bordeaux.fr

ABSTRACT

Smart-phones technology and the development of mHealth (*Mobile Health*) applications offer an opportunity to design intervention tools to influence health behavior changes. The MAVIE-Lab is a mHealth application including a DSS (*Desicion Support System*) to assist in the personalized evaluation of HLIs (*Home, Leisure and Sport Injuries*) risk and to promote the adoption of prevention measures. *MAVIE-Lab Sports* will be the first module of the mobile application.

The purpose of this PhD project is to improve a particular module of MAVIE-Lab, devoted to sports (MAVIE-Lab Sports), in different aspects: statistical modeling, design and ergonomics. It also aims to evaluate system usability, acceptability, safety and efficacy. The development structure proposed and executed in this thesis will be replicated for the development of future modules for different types of HLIs.

This document develops the argument, objectives and advances in the development of the MAVIE-Lab Sports and the future work.

CCS CONCEPTS

• **Mathematics of computing → Bayesian networks**; • **Human-centered computing → Personal digital assistants**;

KEYWORDS

App; eHealth; Injury; HLIs; Prediction

---

*PhD Student Public Health - Epidemiology (early stage)
†Thesis director

ACM Reference Format:
Madelyn Yiseth Rojas Castro, Marina Travanca, Marta Avalos Fernandez, David Valentin Conesa, Ludivine Orriols, and Emmanuel Lagarde. 2018. MAVIE-Lab Sports: a mHealth for Injury Prevention and Risk Management in Sport: PhD Student Track. In *DH'18: 2018 International Digital Health Conference, April 23–26, 2018, Lyon, France.* ACM, New York, NY, USA, 2 pages. https://doi.org/10.1145/3194658.3194694

1 INTRODUCTION

Injuries are a main concern in Public Health, leading cause of mortality, leaving further major consequences on the quality of life of the population. Each year in France, HLIs cause more than 11 million victims and 20,000 deaths [5]. In Horizon 2020 call for Research and Innovation actions, the European Commission promoted the development of DSSs to empower individuals to self-management their health condition[4].

This context offers a novel opportunity to develop the MAVIE-Lab, an innovative mHealth for primary prevention of HLIs.

The MAVIE-Lab has been developed under the MAVIE project framework (http://www.observatoire-mavie.com/), a large web-based cohort study with the objective of prospectively collecting data related to HLIs in France. Currently, over three years of recruitment, 27 000 volunteers have already been enrolled in the cohort.

A first version of MAVIE-Lab Sport is based on this available MAVIE volunteers information. This prototype is available online, and includes: running, hiking, road cycling, downhill skiing and basketball (https://ssl3.isped.u-bordeaux2.fr/MAVIE-OBS/Appli/#/). However, the statistical models currently included in the App are non-optimal model predicting personal risk. Besides, it did not achieve a design, structure and popularity for a potential success as intervention tool.

This thesis aims to maximize the potential of MAVIE-Lab Sports. The first objective is to select and to implement an appropriate methodology to develop a *personalized prediction risk model* using MAVIE cohort data together with experts information. In addition, the thesis also aims to improve the App scientific value, design and ergonomics and to evaluate it among MAVIE volunteers.

DSSs are intended to induce beneficial behavior changes, specifically, the use of a DSS with the possibility of virtually experiencing solutions is hypothesized to enhance perceived susceptibility, perceived vulnerability, perceived behavioral control of self-efficacy [2, 7]. Our assumptions are that good personalized advice will call the attention of the users. The exposition to this DSS could induce change in risk behaviors and the adoption of safety tools.

2 METHODOLOGICAL PROPOSAL

2.1 MAVIE-Lab Sports Development

2.1.1 Data Sources. The MAVIE cohort is composed of approximately 6,000 practitioners over 15 years old who have authorized the use of their data. MAVIE survey includes detailed information: demographic, life-style, health data, environment and sport practice. In addition, there are specific variables about training, coaching, protective clothing, equipment, among others. Moreover, there are HLIs injuries follow-up, together with information about their causes, consequences and severity.

2.1.2 Modeling. We suggest implementing *Bayesian Networks models* (BN) using re-sampling techniques [6]. BN combine quantitative and qualitative modeling, probabilistic conditional dependencies and causal diagrams reasoning DAGs (*Directed acyclic Graph*). It allows us to combine previous qualitative causal relationships between variables (risk and protection injury factors), quantitative previous knowledge and MAVIE data evidence.

2.1.3 Design and software. The BN model relations and risk predictions will be used to build a DSS to produce adequate personal prevention advice. This DSS system will allow the user to virtually experiment the impact of a range of preventive decisions. The functions that have been designed for this objective are:

(1) A graphical overview of each risk as compared to the average level of risk between different sports.
(2) An estimation of the personal injury risk.
(3) Experience potential risk change for a set of proposed behavioral changes, protective devices, equipment or sport practice environments.

Graphic design, software programming and use of technologies for the development of Apps is carried out as an interdisciplinary work in the IETO (*Injury Epidemiology, Transport, Occupation*) team following the practices proposed by HAS (*The French National Authority for Health*) to mHeath development [3].

2.1.4 Evaluation. The evaluation will be carried out among the volunteers of the MAVIE cohort. It will include the following components:

(1) *Safety.* Experts will evaluate if the advice and recommendations given by the App are suitable for users health.
(2) *Acceptability.* A questionary will be integrated into the application asking about user perception.
(3) *Usability.* Tracking statistics of *Google Analytics* which are being taken for the current version of MAVIE-Lab.
(4) *Efficacy.* Change in prevention behaviors and reduction of injury rates will be evaluated comparing MAVIE-Lab users and non-users, before and after MAVIE-Lab implementation.

3 RESULTS AND ONGOING WORK

The most important work done so far relates to the development of the first version of MAVIE-Lab Sports. Nevertheless, the main thesis progress has been the statistical methodological proposal for the improvement of prediction models in the App.

BN elicitation requires a complete review of scientific literature, results of similar studies and expert information to correctly quantify the different degrees of knowledge of risk and protection factors and their relationships in terms of probability. Currently, we are working in DAGs structures using literature information. On the other hand, we are working on an *elicitation protocol* adapted to risk injury evaluation according to recommendations of previous experts elicitation applications [1].

4 CONCLUSION

MAVIE-Lab is a novel idea for safety promotion and HLIs prevention. The key expected result is to achieve a validated and functional version of the MAVIE-Lab Sports that would motivate users to change their behavior regarding injury prevention. The research aims to evaluating whether the exposition to a DSS displaying personalized risk could generate behavioral changes leading to the reduction of the effective number of victims, which remains a major public health problem.

5 COMPETING INTEREST

The authors have declared that no competing interests exist.

6 ETHICAL CONSIDERATIONS

The MAVIE project has already received the approval of the CNIL *Commission Nationale Informatique & Libertés* (France), which will be updated to take into account the specificity of the MAVIE-Lab, in particular on the issue of the provision of personalized advice without the possibility of human intervention. MAVIE volunteers signed online the informed consent to participate in the research.

REFERENCES

[1] Knol Anne, Slottje Pauline, van der Sluijs Jeroen P, and Lebret Erik. 2010. The use of expert elicitation in environmental health impact assessment: a seven step procedure. *Environmental Health* 9 (April 2010), 19. https://doi.org/10.1186/1476-069X-9-19
[2] Sleet David and Carlson Gielen Andrea. 2003. Application of Behavior-Change Theories and Methods to Injury Prevention. *Epidemiologic Reviews* 25 (Feb. 2003), 65–76. https://doi.org/10.1093/epirev/mxg004
[3] Haute Autorité de Santé. 2013. Good Practice Guidelines on Health Apps and Smart Devices. (2013).
[4] European Commission Decision. 2015. Horizon 2020 Work Programme 2014 2015. (April 2015). Retrieved January 31, 2018 from http://ec.europa.eu/programmes/horizon2020/en/official-documents
[5] Richard Jean-Baptiste, Bertrand, Thélot, and Beck François. 2012. Les accidents en France: évolution et factores associés. *Revue d'Épidémiologie et santé publique* 61 (Jan. 2012), 205–212. https://doi.org/10.1016/j.respe.2012.10.007
[6] Mujalli Randa, Lopez Griselda, and Garach Laura. 2016. Bayes classifiers for imbalanced traffic accidents datasets. *Accident Analysis and Prevention* 88 (April 2016), 37–51. https://doi.org/10.1016/j.aap.2015.12.003
[7] Chou Wen ying Sylvia, Prestin Abby, and Lyons Claire. 2013. Web 2.0 for Health Promotion: Reviewing the Current Evidence. *American Journal of Public Health* 103, 1 (Jan. 2013), e9–e18. https://doi.org/10.2105/AJPH.2012.301071

Author Index